HOMECOMING

An Autobiography

HOMECOMING

An

Autobiography

by

FLOYD DELL

KENNIKAT PRESS
Port Washington, N. Y./London

HOMECOMING

Copyright 1933, © 1961 by Floyd Dell
Reissued in 1969 by Kennikat Press by arrangement with
Holt, Rinehart and Winston, Inc.
Library of Congress Catalog Card No: 75-93061
SBN 8046-0674-9

Manufactured by Taylor Publishing Company   Dallas, Texas

To

B. MARIE GAGE

Not only that I love you—that in you
I find old dreams incredibly come true,
And you in every dream, world without end,
Goddess and girl-child, lover and guest and friend . . .

CONTENTS

PREFACE

THE REASON I have the courage to write the story of my life is that it is to some extent the story of the lives of many other people. Once upon a time I supposed that I was different from other people. But I wrote a book—a novel called 'Moon-Calf'—about the odd sort of child and boy and youth that I had been; and I was surprised to hear from many people who wrote me, saying: 'You have told the story of my life.' One of them was in prison, another was a clergyman, another a successful business man, another a pioneer adventurer in Alaska. Some of them sent me snapshots of scenes and persons in their lives, identifying them with the scenes and characters of my novel. This was startling; then it seemed to show that beneath varying circumstances we are all human beings who go through much the same course of emotional adventure in growing up. But some of us are more and some less conventional; the story of the growth, triumphs and follies of the more conventional kind of youth had often been written; I had written, with some candor, the story of the growth, triumphs and follies of the less conventional kind of youth, whom I called 'Felix Fay'.

That novel was based upon a selection of memories, with a very few bits of invention to piece it out. Subsequently some very early and deep-buried childhood memories came to light, which put the whole story into a new perspective, and made the book, as a psychological study, seem sentimental at some points and false at others. In the meanwhile, the 'Felix Fay' about whom it was written had grown up, at the time of its writing, to be me. And I was very much interested in the way 'Felix Fay' had become me. I had originally intended to write the whole story; but it was too long, and so I left 'Felix' about to go to Chicago. The rest of the story would have told, in some fashion, of the ten stormy and baffled years that followed—an early marriage, ending in divorce, and a life in Greenwich Village. All through these ten years 'Felix Fay' had had two quite definite wishes—to achieve continuity and stability in his work, and the same in his love life. He was tired of writing short things—

short stories, novelettes, poems, one-act plays, articles, criticisms; and tired of little love-affairs, however beautiful, and whether giving three long days or three short years of happiness. He wanted to finish the long novel which told the story of his own childhood and youth, a novel worked on at intervals for several years in an effort at self-understanding; and he wanted to stay in love with a girl and be married to her for the rest of his life. He had become convinced that his difficulties in achieving stability in love and work were internal and not external. It would seem that he was right. For, having gained some self-insight through psychoanalytic therapeusis, he did fall in love and get married, with the conviction, never held before, that it was for life; and early in this marriage, he finished the long novel upon which he had been at work, the story of his own childhood and youth, 'Moon-Calf'.

These events, in their inward meaning and outward color, seemed to me to deserve to be told. I was interested in the psychological revolution which had made it possible for a young Moon-Calf to enjoy the responsibilities of marriage and presently of parenthood. My acquaintance with the new science of psychoanalysis had made me aware that I was not alone in having psychological difficulties in growing up. But for various reasons the rest of the story was not told with any degree of literalness, and was scattered about among various books.

Now, for what seem to me good reasons, I wish to put together the scattered true things I have written about 'Felix Fay's' life, with such corrections as are necessary, and such additions as may be required. But the fictional convenience of calling myself 'Felix Fay' will have to be dispensed with; I shall have to use my own name, and confine myself as strictly as possible to the truth. It should be unnecessary for me to add that in telling the truth about myself I do not propose to tell other people's secrets. But this book, though about my life with no fictional pretenses, is substantially identical with the autobiographical novel which I once intended to write. It is the study of a certain kind of person, who happens to be myself.

So I hope it will be understood that I do not write my autobiography in the spirit of one who has lived a life so remarkable that it needs to have a book written about it, at least any more so than the next person's; my most remarkable feat is supporting a family, which lots of other people—somewhat to my amazement—have done. From my point of view, the remarkable thing about Floyd Dell is that he actually *could* do, and finally did do, most of the things that other people do. This will be the story of, first, how he got into that fix of not getting the ordinary satisfactions out of life—getting instead some valuable artistic and intellectual satisfactions; and then the story of how he triumphantly got most of the commonplace everyday satisfactions, without surrendering all the others—though some of them had to go by the board in the process.

I believe that, in taking so long to learn some of the simple values of life, I know them better than other people who merely took them for granted; but that may be just my egotism. But I think that my way of growing up does dramatize sharply some of the things that happen to a great many people in growing up. If I thought I were vastly different from others, I should keep still about it.

I have written a few good novels, some amusing plays, some intelligent criticisms, some very serious books, and nearly got put in prison once—all of which I am quite proud of; but that is not what this book is about.

I was a child; I had a father and a mother to love and escape from; I grew up in a confused and difficult world with the help of certain modern intellectual ideas; I learned at last to make a living; I had beautiful friendships; I was afraid of love, and fell into it, and learned its joys and its griefs; I took a long time finding out what I was like, what I wanted out of life, and how to get it; I was poor, lucky, despairing, happy; I hated and loved the world I lived in; I had joy in my work, and in my thoughts; and life became more interesting, larger, and deeper, with every year that passed; out of all this it seemed to me that I had learned something. That is the life I intend to write about—the life of the one human being that I know best.

HOMECOMING

An Autobiography

CHAPTER I

FOOL'S PARADISE

1

MY FATHER's people, the Dells, were of Pennsylvania-Dutch stock—that is, presumably of German origin. My mother's people, the Crones, were Protestant Irish, some of whom had first gone to live in the South. The Dells and the Crones were early settlers in Illinois, and at some date moved to Pike County, which lies along the Mississippi river, midway down the State, the nearest good-sized town being Hannibal, Missouri. St. Louis is not far south, and beyond are Memphis, New Orleans and the Gulf. But, though vaguely permeated by Southern influences—a touch of laziness, quite a lot of mud, and, like the scent of honeysuckle, a whiff of the romantic attitude toward life—Pike County nevertheless feels itself to be a part of that great Middle West which centers in Chicago. From Pike County the way to Chicago is by steamboat up to Quincy, Illinois—a trip which my family made when I was twelve; then by steamboat again up to Davenport, Iowa—where we went when I was sixteen; and then by rail across the corner of Illinois to Chicago —where I went when I was twenty-one. The trip can be made in a shorter time by one who knows where he is going; but I did not know.

Anthony Dell, my father, was born on his father's farm, downstate in Madison County. He was called 'Banty' as a youth—he was a 'bantam', small and pugnacious. When the Civil War broke out, he was twenty-two years old; he enlisted in Company K, Second Illinois Cavalry, fought in many battles, and was at last wounded and left for dead on the field. There he was captured, and sent to a Southern prison-camp, from which he was released at the war's end. Going back to Pike County, where the family had moved, he went into the butcher business in the small town of Barry, with a partner. At the age of thirty-one, he married a young school-teacher, Kate Crone, who was twenty-four years of age, slender, dark-haired, shy, energetic, and a lover of poetry—to some extent a writer of it. They had two sons and a daughter; and then, after a long interval, I was born, on June 28th, 1887. My father was then forty-eight, and my mother forty-one; while my older brothers were about fifteen and thirteen years old.

It is here that my story begins. It begins with some memories of incidents occurring very early in my life—from three to seven. In order, however, to give these early memories their due meaning, I shall have to put them in a frame of narrative facts not known to me as a child.

2

Seventeen years had passed since my father's and mother's marriage. There is a photograph of my father which dates back to the time of his marriage, or thereabouts. The young daredevil cavalryman has become rather portly, and very dignified. In the photograph he is seated in the midst of his farmer brothers, who stand behind him; they look like the personified four humours of Hippocrates, sanguine, phlegmatic, melancholic, choleric. He, it would seem, is the important one of the group—a prosperous business man. And those later years following the war were years of prosperity. Railroads were being built everywhere; all kinds of industries were thriving; success was in the air. And presently Grant was in the White House. Anthony Dell, in 1872, was one of Barry's thriving young business men. He could look forward to building himself a fine house; and Kate Dell, with her first son in her arms, could look forward to sending him to college to become a lawyer or doctor. They were securely, as it seemed, members of the class which was, in Pike County, and perhaps all through America, called 'respectable'. 'Respectability', in Pike County, meant the appearance and presumption of belonging to the class of those who lived by their superior brains, preferably upon profits, interest or rent, rather than unambitiously and stupidly by manual labor. There was an elaborate code of dress and of manners which connoted 'respectability'.

Then came the panic of 1873. . . . I do not know when the butcher-shop of Dell & Preston ceased its struggle to exist. But by the time I was born it had been long a thing of the past, which served only to give the family in its own estimation the needed status of middle-class 'respectability'. I can remember, when I was first able to walk so far, being taken down to a butcher-shop where my father was employed—that was when we still had a hired girl, and before my brother's pigeons were sold. Later, my father was a foreman in the woolen mills; I remember, when he came home, rushing to have the proud privilege of pulling off his felt boots—being Papa's boot-jack. One winter one of my big brothers worked in the woolen mills, too, and the other went to Quincy to look for work. Both of them had dropped out of school, because they didn't like to wear patched clothes.

The family was, in fact, losing its hold upon the golden ladder. But all the more it clung to its 'respectable' status. The condition of being a workingman was one which a recently prosperous business man must not admit, except as a temporary piece of bad luck. My father's age, of course, was against him; in his fifties now, he stood no chance of getting back—not much chance, even, of competing with younger men for available jobs.

The older children were adjusting themselves to the situation as well as they could. They got jobs, any jobs they could get, and held them until they were fired. The first jobs from which they were not fired, furnished them their trades for the rest of their lives. That was the method of vocational choice by which one of my big brothers, a sensitive artist, with a love of drawing, became a harnessmaker; and the other, who was good at figures, a sash-and-door factory employee, running a saw which presently took off a thumb.

But here was a new baby, myself. A mother in her forties, seeing her hopes for the older children blasted by harsh circumstances, would center new fond hopes upon this golden-haired blue-eyed boy. And, early in childhood, there were ways, perhaps not as infallible as those now in vogue, of recognizing the intelligence of children. Quickness in understanding, quickness in learning, memory, vocabulary, these and other things were noted; and they spelled to an Irish mother a future 'scholar,' from whom wonderful things might be expected.

She was a nice Irish mother, small and slender and physically frail, sweet and gentle, patient and lovable. She had given her little son many beautiful gifts—love, and tenderness, and devotion, lullaby music and poetry, stories about real and imaginary people and places. The beauty of flowers and skies was first shown to me by her pointing finger. She taught me to understand words, and to speak them, and no little bit of childish progress was too small for her to notice and reward with praise. Queen of the mysterious universe in which I was a helpless stranger, she did not laugh at my clumsy blunders; she took me by the hand and led me into the universe to be its prince. For me there always would be, in almost every region of beauty and knowledge, the sweet ghostly presence of my mother, who first guided me in those realms, kindling my eyes to see and my ears to hear, blessing my infant understanding with smiling looks of approval. And from her too I had the mysterious knowledge of Right and Wrong; she gave me a Conscience to govern my most imperious impulses, a phantom of herself to be with me always, closer than blood and breath. She was the Lawgiver. I learned from her the sense of *ought*. If I followed obscure unruly impulses, if I were selfish, greedy, lazy, quarrelsome, afraid, unwilling, then I was afflicted with her sorrowful eyes, not to be endured. My shame was a worse punishment than any outward one that could be inflicted. I *had* to be all that she expected of me.

I was—and all this is up to the winter after my sixth birthday—an arrogant, eager, friendly, confident, innocently bumptious little boy. I had been trained in the manual of arms by my father, and I had a soldierly bearing. But I was vastly talkative, and profoundly impressed by the Fourth of July speeches I had heard in the Square. I was going to be a lawyer. My mother had heard that Ann Arbor was the best college to study law in, and so I was going there. When I got to be a lawyer, I was going to make Fourth of July speeches from the band-stand in the Square. And then I was going to be President of the United States. I had asked my mother if I could be, and she had said that I could if I worked hard and studied and got the most votes. I was going to be a Republican President, of course. All this was clear and certain in my mind. My mother was encouraging to my ambitions, though not so definitely set on the Presidency as I was. She said, "You're going to be Somebody, all right." My Presidential ambition was somehow mixed up with my admiration for my father, whose political discourses I had listened to with profound respect, and with whom I had been privileged to go to hear patriotic orations in the Square.

One morning, as I was looking at a story-book, I discovered that I could read. The words of the story, of course, I knew by heart; but I found now that I knew each word separately, and the realization of it almost took my breath away. It was true! In my excitement, I screamed, "Mamma! Mamma!" and she came running from the kitchen, her arms white with flour. "I can read!" I cried. Hardly less excited than I, she sat down with me, and I demonstrated this new magical power. She kissed me fondly and said, "You shall go to school this fall!" I was not yet five, but I would be in June.

It may have been some time that summer, when I was being taken for a walk in my white starched kilts by my big sister, that some ladies stopped and said to her, "What beautiful curls your brother has." My mother was proud of them; she should have been, for she made them herself, by twisting my hair around her finger and stiffening it with the white of an egg. I was proud of them, too. So when one of the inquiring ladies went on to ask, "Does his hair curl that way naturally?" I spoke up for myself. "Yes'm," I said, "and my mother fixes it with white-of-egg." From their smiles, and my sister's scornful jerk on my arm, I knew that I had said the wrong thing, and felt ashamed. . . . In the respectable world into which I was growing up, there were all sorts of things that must not be said even though they were true, and other things that must be said whether they were true or not; but it takes a little boy time to learn that code.

At school the first day, I was so bumptious as to be a nuisance. I corrected the teacher, told her she must say 'Fire!' and not 'Shoot!' when putting us through our military drill. I made moustaches on my face, which pleased everybody but the teacher; and when told to wash my face, I clumsily spilled the water from the wash-basin on to the floor. Sent to the janitor for a mop, it took me an hour to find him, but at last I came back triumphantly with the mop over my shoulder. When everybody laughed, the teacher said, "Floyd, you have caused us a great deal of trouble today." That grieved me, for

I felt toward my teacher the same emotions of loyalty and obedience that I felt toward my mother. I wanted to be a good little boy.

At recesses, I began to be tormented by a big bully who would snatch my cap and run away with it, and then offer it to me, but throw it away, and get it before I could. I was in misery, for at that time my cap was a part of me, which I had to follow about and try to rescue. My sister once slapped the big boy's face and got my cap for me, but she could not be watching over her baby brother all the time. I endured these torments for weeks, and then, one morning, coming upon the boy around the corner of the building, I sprang at him in a fit of rage and tears, hitting and kicking. I knocked out one of his front teeth, and he ran away, spitting blood, with me after him, not yet glutted with revenge. After that I was never afraid to fight, and did not hesitate to attack bigger boys, though I always got licked. If I knocked my opponent down, I would chivalrously wait till he got up; but if he got me down, he would sit on my chest and pound my head against the sidewalk.

But fighting was something I did only in rage or pride, never for fun; dare-base and other games where swiftness counted more than strength were my favorites. It was in the schoolroom, however, that I felt that I was cock-of-the-walk. And my teacher, when she found that I wasn't trying to be obstreperous, but just didn't know any better, gave me her approval. I learned everything easily, and had a prodigious memory, my only fault being absent-mindedness.

It was not considered necessary to tell me anything about the financial status of the family. I was not able to make comparative observations in school, because I was sent there immaculately dressed. And I knew that my mother regarded some of the children in the neighborhood as not nice enough for me to play with. I thought we were just a little bit more 'respectable' than other people. I did not realize that in the currency of 'respectability' a father who used to have a butcher shop was not quite on a par with a father who was cashier of the bank. My father spoke familiarly of the Mayor and other city dignitaries. And, as I understood it, his membership in the G. A. R. made him one of what I felt to be the aristocracy of the nation—certainly on Decoration Day he was treated as such. So I had no idea that we were not the very flower of Barry 'respectability'. There undoubtedly were plenty of things that might have enlightened me about our financial condition. But there was a deceptive parental softening and evasion of harsh facts for my benefit. A child, in their opinion, should be protected from unpleasant things. And the parental gloss marvelously protected me from the facts that were before my eyes. . . .

So, next year, I didn't know there was a Panic. The shutting down of the Barry woolen mills was in my young mind, as in my father's talk, a political and not an economic tragedy. Grover Cleveland was to blame for it all. He was a Democratic President, and that was why he did it. Governor Altgeld was a Democrat, too—that was why he pardoned the Haymarket Anarchists. I wondered why Democrats were allowed to exist.

3

(Memories of childhood are strange things. The obscurity of the past opens upon a little lighted space—a scene, unconnected with anything else. One must figure out when it happened. There may be anomalies in the scene, which need explanation. Sometimes the scenes are tiny fragments only. Again they are long dramas. Having once been remembered, they can be lived through again in every moment, with a detailed experiencing of movement and sensation and thought. One can start the scene in one's mind and see it all through again. Exactly so it was—clearer in memory than something that happened yesterday, though it was forty years ago. And, oddly enough, if there is some detail skipped over, lost out of the memory picture, no repetition of the remembering process will supply it—the gap is always there.)

That fall, before it was discovered that the soles of both my shoes were worn clear through, I still went to Sunday school. And one time the Sunday-school superintendent made a speech to all the classes. He said that these were hard times, and that many poor children weren't getting enough to eat. It was the first that I had heard about it. He asked everybody to bring some food for the poor children next Sunday. I felt very sorry for the poor children.

Also, little envelopes were distributed to all the classes. Each little boy and girl was to bring money for the poor, next Sunday. The pretty Sunday-school teacher explained that we were to write our names, or have our parents write them, up in the left-hand corner of the little envelopes. . . . I told my mother all about it when I came home. And my mother gave me, the next Sunday, a small bag of potatoes to carry to Sunday school. I supposed the poor children's mothers would make potato soup out of them. . . . Potato soup was good. My father, who was quite a joker, would always say, as if he were surprised, "Ah! I see we have some nourishing potato soup today!" It was so good that we had it every day. My father was at home all day long and every day, now; and I liked that, even if he was grumpy as he sat reading Grant's 'Memoirs'. I had my parents all to myself, too; the others were away. My oldest brother was in Quincy, and memory does not reveal where the others were: perhaps with relatives in the country.

Taking my small bag of potatoes to Sunday school, I looked around for the poor children; I was disappoinetd not to see them. I had heard about poor children in stories. But I was told just to put my contribution with the others on the big table in the side room.

I had brought with me the little yellow envelope, with some money in it for the poor children. My mother had put the money in it and sealed it up. She wouldn't tell me how much money she had put in it, but it felt like several dimes. Only she wouldn't let me write my name on the envelope. I had learned to write my name, and I was proud of being able to do it. But my mother said firmly, *no,* I must *not* write my name on the envelope; she didn't tell me why. On the way to Sunday school I had pressed the envelope against the coins until I could tell what they were; they weren't dimes but pennies.

When I handed in my envelope, my Sunday-school teacher noticed that my name wasn't on it, and she gave me a pencil; I could write my own name, she said. So I did. But I was confused because my mother had said not to; and when I came home, I confessed what I had done. She looked distressed. "I told you not to!" she said. But she didn't explain why. . . .

I didn't go back to school that fall. My mother said it was because I was sick. I did have a cold the week that school opened; I had been playing in the gutters and had got my feet wet, because there were holes in my shoes. My father cut insoles out of cardboard, and

I wore those in my shoes. As long as I had to stay in the house anyway, they were all right.

I stayed cooped up in the house, without any companionship. We didn't take a Sunday paper any more, but the Barry Adage came every week in the mails; and though I did not read small print, I could see the Santa Clauses and holly wreaths in the advertisements.

There was a calendar in the kitchen. The red days were Sundays and holidays; and that red 25 was Christmas. (It was on a Monday, and the two red figures would come right together in 1893; but this represents research in the World Almanac, not memory.) I knew when Sunday was, because I could look out of the window and see the neighbor's children, all dressed up, going to Sunday school. I knew just when Christmas was going to be.

But there was something queer! My father and mother didn't say a word about Christmas. And once, when I spoke of it, there was a strange, embarrassed silence; so I didn't say anything more about it. But I wondered, and was troubled. Why didn't they say anything about it? Was what I had said I wanted (memory refuses to supply that detail) too expensive?

I wasn't arrogant and talkative now. I was silent and frightened. What was the matter? Why didn't my father and mother say anything about Christmas? As the day approached, my chest grew tighter with anxiety.

Now it was the day before Christmas. I couldn't be mistaken. But not a word about it from my father and mother. I waited in painful bewilderment all day. I had supper with them, and was allowed to sit up for an hour. I was waiting for them to say something. "It's time for you to go to bed," my mother said gently. I *had* to say something.

"This is Christmas Eve, isn't it?" I asked, as if I didn't know.

My father and mother looked at one another. Then my mother looked away. Her face was pale and stony. My father cleared his throat, and his face took on a joking look. He pretended he hadn't known it was Christmas Eve, because he hadn't been reading the papers. He said he would go downtown and find out.

My mother got up and walked out of the room. I didn't want my father to have to keep on being funny about it, so I got up and went to bed. I went by myself without having a light. I undressed in the dark and crawled into bed.

I was numb. As if I had been hit by something. It was hard to breathe. I ached all through. I was stunned—with finding out the truth.

My body knew before my mind quite did. In a minute, when I could think, my mind would know. And as the pain in my body ebbed, the pain in my mind began. I *knew*. I couldn't put it into words yet. But I knew why I had taken only a little bag of potatoes to Sunday school that fall. I knew why there had been only pennies in my little yellow envelope. I knew why I hadn't gone to school that fall—why I hadn't any new shoes—why we had been living on potato soup all winter. All these things, and others, many others, fitted themselves together in my mind, and meant something.

Then the words came into my mind and I whispered them into the darkness:

"We're poor!"

That was it. I was one of those poor children I had been sorry for, when I heard about them in Sunday school. My mother hadn't told me. My father was out of work, and we hadn't any money. That was why there wasn't going to be any Christmas at our house.

Then I remembered something that made me squirm with shame —a boast. (Memory will not yield this up. Had I said to some Nice little boy, "I'm going to be President of the United States"? Or to a Nice little girl: "I'll marry you when I grow up."? It was some boast as horribly shameful to remember.)

"We're poor." There in bed in the dark, I whispered it over and over to myself. I was making myself get used to it. (Or—just torturing myself, as one presses the tongue against a sore tooth? No, memory says not like that—but to keep myself from ever being such a fool again: suffering now, to keep this awful thing from ever happening again. Memory is clear on that; it was more like pulling the tooth, to get it over with—never mind the pain, this will be the end!)

It wasn't so bad, now that I knew. I just *hadn't known!* I had thought all sorts of foolish things: that I was going to Ann Arbor—

going to be a lawyer—going to make speeches in the Square, going to be President. Now I knew better.

I had wanted (something) for Christmas. I didn't want it, now. I didn't want anything.

I lay there in the dark, feeling the cold emotion of renunciation. (The tendrils of desire unfold their clasp on the outer world of objects, withdraw, shrivel up. Wishes shrivel up, turn black, die. It is like that.)

It hurt. But nothing would ever hurt again. I would never let myself want anything again.

I lay there stretched out straight and stiff in the dark, my fists clenched hard upon Nothing. . . .

In the morning it had been like a nightmare that is not clearly remembered—that one wishes to forget. Though I hadn't hung up any stocking, there was one hanging at the foot of my bed. A bag of popcorn, and a lead pencil, for me. They had done the best they could, now they realized that I knew about Christmas. But they needn't have thought they had to. I didn't want anything.

CHAPTER II

CHILD STOIC

1

IT WAS, I think, right after this Christmas-Eve renunciation of all the good things of life that I fell sick, with a long and severe and wretched sickness centering in my stomach.* Memory brings back a bedquilt world, with the vast squares of the coverlet stretching endlessly before me. Yellow lamplight, shapes of people going to and fro. Whispers. Medicine bottles on a chair at the head of my bed. The flower-pattern in the wall-paper. Cracks in the ceiling, and stains that made grotesque pictures. Nausea. 'Try to keep something down, darling.' Dreams of geometrical Space that widened out towards infinity, and myself in the middle, smaller and smaller —waking in fright just before I became Nothing. . . .

From this I emerged to play quietly around the house, sitting preferably with my toys and picture books.

My father, as I remember, had a job hauling dirt for a road which the county was building. In the spring we moved to a cheaper house, on the edge of a gully. It was only part of a house; the people that owned it liv 1 in the other part.

I cannot remember very much about that house, nor the life we lived there for a year and a half. It is covered with a kind of darkness, through which there are only a few peep-holes. I see my father sitting in the big arm chair by the window, reading Grant's

---

*It would be interesting to know if there is any usual connection between the emotion of renunciation and stomach trouble. That celebrated Stoic, Marcus Aurelius, is said to have died of 'a chronic stomachic disease.' Curiously enough, there is a possible, though apparently only accidental, relation of 'Stoic' and 'stomach' in Greek. At any rate, the stomach remained for me the organ devastatingly affected by severe self-denial. And I have been startled and amused to discover the philosophic identity in detail of the principles and theories of Epictetus with my own most cherished intellectual ideas throughout life.

14

'Memoirs'. I see my brother—the one who is still at home—coming
back to my mother after he has given her his pay-envelope, and
asking to 'borrow' another quarter this week; and the way she is
torn between her wanting to give him money to spend and her
knowledge of the unpaid grocery bill. And the attic—I remember
something about that, though that is all mixed up with dreams and
fantasy.

It was remarked that my sickness had changed me, as sicknesses
often do change children. I was quieter, more polite, more even-
tempered. And I never teased for pennies to spend. I was a
window-shopper.

The center of interest in the town through which I passed on my
way to and from school was the grassy Square and the streets on
each side with their row of shops and stores. I would loiter on the
way home and look at everything. In the Square itself the boys
played marbles and spun tops, and in the noon hour groups of idlers
stood about talking and telling stories, with a fringe of boys for an
audience. The bandstand in the Square had an upper story, with
no steps or ladder reaching up there; but somehow, as I knew, big
boys got up there and lay reading 'dime novels', which really
cost a nickel, and were forbidden literature. This escape from the
world of people fascinated me, and may have had something to
do with my attic fantasies, which presently began. I walked slowly
about the Square, making a side trip around the corner to stand
at the door of the blacksmith shop, and watch the red-hot horse-
shoes being dropped sizzling into a bucket of water, and smell the
pungent odor of seared hoofs and hear the music of hammer on
anvil. Back on the Square, I would loiter in front of the stationery
store window, studying its changing display of 'Diamond Dick' and
'Nick Carter' and 'Frank Merriwell' novels, on the covers of which
some new and exciting episode was displayed in picture every week.
There was nothing wrong in looking at these novels; it was only
wrong to read them, which I had no wish to do. Then I would press
my nose against the glass of other shop-windows, looking at knives,
tops, marbles, kites, toys. My fingers, however, did not itch to play
with these things; I was content to look at them. I was particularly
fascinated by the display of tools of all sorts in the windows of the
hardware store; but so far was I from wishing to use any of these

tools that when, much later, at the age of twelve, I first held the familiar tools of carpentry in my hands at school, I hardly knew how to handle them. When I was taken into a store full of exciting things, the little-boy tendency to reach out and touch—or grab—was not operative in me. I didn't even pick flowers, when I was out in the woods; I only looked at them. Sight aroused no motor impulses. And this made me seem very well-behaved indeed. But I enjoyed thoroughly the sight of things which, if I had ever wanted to buy them, might have been a painful reminder that I was poor. So long as I didn't want to own or use them, I had a fine time just looking at them. When one is in a Museum, if one is well bred, one does not think of carrying off its treasures. Perhaps it may be regarded as the proper grown-up attitude. But I had it at seven, and never quite got over it. Always there was an invisible plate-glass window separating me from the things I looked at. My hands hung at my sides, and I touched things only with my gaze. Before I found the library, I had begun to take note of the shapes of things, and to draw pictures like those that one of my big brothers drew.

It was the sign, 'Free Public Library', that attracted me. I went up the stairs and into a room with a counter in front of serried bookshelves, guarded by a grey-haired woman. Against the front windows was a long table covered with magazines. I watched, and people picked them up carelessly and looked through them. That was permitted, then. I sat down and read. For some reason what seems to have interested me most in that first day's reading was a long controversial article in the back of one of these magazines, with diagrams, on the flush-bowl toilet. I had never seen one.

Afterward, I found that books could be taken away. The greyhaired librarian took pains to keep young readers going in the same series, if possible. She started me off with the Elsie books; apparently I was going to have to read them all before I got anything else to read. But luck was with me, and I switched to 'Frank on a Gunboat' before my budding literary enthusiasm was blighted. I liked Frank. He carried me into the war my father had fought in. "Damn the torpedoes!" cried Farragut, and in a rain of shot and shell we swept past the rebel batteries to victory. . . . Then there was the bound volumes of 'St. Nicholas'. And, intermixed with these, were more 'grown-up' books. My father usually had plenty of time to read now, too. When one would finish a book the other would begin it. I remember that when I was ten we both read, and were impressed but puzzled by, a book which opened most promisingly with the words: " 'Dead for a ducat, dead!' cried Dick" . . . a book which turned out not to be an adventure story but a description of Utopia. My father read, and I tried hard to read, Dickens and Thackeray; I could not go them—an incapacity which has been permanent. But we both read and enjoyed deeply Defoe's 'Captain Jacques', and a book which I was to read over and over at intervals for many years, Hugo's 'Les Miserables'.—Not at seven years old, but soon afterward; years pass quickly in public libraries, and one may grow as old as Rip Van Winkle in that enchanted cave, while remaining a child in the outside world.

I spent all the time I could at the public library, preferring its peace rather than the environment of a home where there was always some painful reminder of our poverty.

In school, where there was always time left over after the studying of lessons, but where outside books were forbidden, drawing was a solace. To the general rule of my not asking for money to buy anything, there was one exception—drawing and writing materials, a modest want which it did not strain our family poverty to supply. Picture-making, like writing, was an intermittent and never abandoned pleasure. If I had chanced to become a painter, I should, looking back, have thought pictorial art my obviously destined career, for I should have been able to trace from my earliest imitations of my big brother's pictures a fairly continuous practice of drawing. But, as I sat on the couch with a drawing-board on my lap, I had no intention or wish or hope to become an artist. I was just being an artist, without thinking of anything except the picture I was drawing. And so it was with writing.

A curtain was drifting down, fold upon fold, in my mind, shutting out the past. I did not remember what I was like when I was a little boy, except that I had been sick a good deal. And there were some pigeons—my brother's pigeons (I had called them 'doves')—sold before I had half seen enough of them. And there had been Corbett the cat. And a hired girl named Sack Sheets. . . .

Somewhere in the oblivion of childhood was hidden an ambition. I had now no notion of what it had been. I had no plans of going to any college, or of practicing any profession when I grew up. I had no plans for the future at all. I never thought about the future.

There were some children to play with, in our new neighborhood, in spite of my mother being so particular about my playing with nice children. There was a little boy whose father worked in the bank; I liked him until he asked me distastefully, "Why do you smell the way you do?" I answered, "I guess it's because I eat potato soup so often"—and after that I avoided him. There was a nice little girl, with whom I walked to school every day for a week or so—a dark-eyed, quiet little girl. But when I was gently teased about my 'little sweetheart', I stopped. Having a sweetheart meant, I knew, buying candy for her; and I had no money to buy candy with.

There was a little boy that year who bought some candy and shared it with me as we were walking to school; a few days later, he asked me when I was going to 'treat back'. I went to my mother in shame, hating to ask her for money, and resolved never to get into that trap again. With her nickel I bought some candy, gave the other boy half, and grimly ate my own half. Next time I would know better.

I had no real friends, no chums, no one I trusted or let myself care for.

2

We sometimes went out into the country to visit our relatives, my mother and I, in the summer. I think it was on an earlier visit that I asked why the milk didn't taste like milk, and was shushed; they had a separator, and all the cream went to the city. It was this time, I think, that I asked my uncle, upon arrival, "Have you got a library?" He replied judiciously, "A moderate one." The moderate library consisted of a Bible and a scrap-book. Into the scrap-book, years before, some growing girl who would never escape from the farm had pasted every scrap of poetry that ever was printed in the local weekly paper. They had also, turned up by the plough in many years, a large collection of Indian arrow-heads and battle-axes. I pored over them lovingly, neglecting the conch-shells which came from Heaven knows where. I wanted some of those Indian arrow-heads as I had never wanted knives, tops, kites or marbles.

One whose heart is steeled against all the things money can buy, which indeed exist only to coax money out of the pockets of little boy's fathers, may fall a stricken quivering victim to the wish for something which has no market value. I would have been eternally grateful for the smallest, crookedest, brokenest arrow-head; but my heart ached for one of those arrow-heads in vain.

I don't know why I should have looked up from some reverie over these arrow-heads—I, a great big boy who should have known better—and asked my mother, right there in front of everybody, "Mamma, where do babies come from?" She was embarrassed, and said we would talk about it later. She was probably ashamed of me not only for my bad manners, but because I had already been told all about babies. She had always told me very clearly and truthfully anything I asked on that subject; and now that I could read, I had free access to the pages and diagrams of a quite instructive Family Doctor Book. I knew, at that age, all the 'facts of life', and was better informed upon all these subjects in a bookish or scientific way than any of my playmates ever were. But since my sickness I had become increasingly shrinking and prudish about these matters. I was now 'modest' about any exposure of my person in dressing or taking a bath, and about underclothes in general, to an extent that caused me to be mildly laughed at by my family; and jokes which quite respectable women and girls among our neighbors thought not too improper to laugh at, brought a blush to my cheeks. I did not think such things were funny, and I shut my ears to them when I could. And it may be that I had succeeded in forgetting what I knew about the origin of babies.

After I went back home, that summer, I was invited to join the secret sessions in the woods of several boys and two little girls— one of the little girls of a poor family of 'foreign' parentage and manners, and not regarded as respectable, ('those gipsies', they were called); the other of a family which was highly respectable;—and would have, I was told, a chance to 'see what little girls looked like' —something I had already accidentally learned from a little girl's tumble in the schoolyard. From the accounts I was given—which I listened to with interest, though I had no intention of accepting the invitation, and evaded it in a frightened way—they undressed and compared themselves and told all the dirty stories they knew.

The knowledge that not only little 'gipsy' girls but apparently nice little girls behaved in that way was very perturbing.

3

There was not any easy and open sociability of boys and girls. At school, the girls' playgrounds were separate from the boys', though there was a large neutral space. And groups of boys in ordinary summer play never included any girls; the girls played by themselves. At a certain age, boys commenced to spend money on girls; there must have been picnics together in the upper age-groups. But unless an accidental propinquity made it easy, a boy might go all through childhood without touching a girl. Yet somehow, out of books and not out of life, I formed an ideal of a jolly and exciting companionship with a girl. In books, a boy and a girl *did* play and talk together; perhaps they reflected the manners of some civilized part of the world where such companionships existed; or perhaps the authors made it up out of their own heads. In Barry, whatever might go on in the woods, boys were either shy in the presence of girls, or rough to conceal their shyness. In school, at our double desks, boys sat with boys and girls with girls. But sometimes, when a class was large, a boy and a girl would have to sit together for a day, until another desk was installed. That fall, I think it was, under those circumstances, I was told to share my seat with a girl. I accepted the arrangement without any embarrassment; but the girl blushed and giggled until the teacher had to lecture her on 'false modesty'. Books, if not life, would have made me enjoy having a girl seat-mate whom I liked.

In the house where we lived, which was not made to be a double house, the partitions were sufficiently thin so that at night I could hear the old man and the girl who lived there saying their prayers and then calling good-night to one another. The girl was his granddaughter, I think, fourteen or fifteen years old, a tall, dark, quiet girl. She took no notice of me, who was now eight.

In the ceiling of the room in which I slept was a trapdoor. I moved the furniture and climbed up there, into an unused, dusty attic. There was some way of entering it from the other side of the house, but no one came there. And I made it mine that winter. It was a place away from people, a place to day-dream in.·

What else I day-dreamed I do not know, but I day-dreamed of the tall, quiet, dark girl who lived in the other side of the house. I day-dreamed of a companionship with her.

And then—did the girl come up in the attic one day? Or was that part of my day-dream only? It was so long-cherished a day-dream, so beautiful a day-dream, that it came to have the same vividness in my memory as if it were real—and yet I know that most of it wasn't true. Was any of it ever true? There is in that dream-story, as I remember it, an atmosphere of guilty innocence, of a sweet companionship that is in danger of being discovered, that is discovered and cruelly broken up. . . . Upon some slight fragment of timid, secret companionship of an older girl and a young boy up there in the attic, the whole dream-story might have been built up. But was there ever a fragment of reality to build it on? I do not know.

CHAPTER III

YELLOW CURLS

1

I STILL WORE my long yellow curls. The sight of me coming home
from the public library, my head with its cluster of yellow curls bent
over a book which I read as I walked, and another book tightly
clasped under my arm, was commented upon. My mother loved
those curls, and would *not* have them cut.

Mothers do things like that to their pet little boys. But little
boys do not have to stand for it. There are always scissors around
a house. Three or four snips, and the curls are gone. Why, I have
to ask myself, did I let my mother make a Little Lord Fauntleroy
of me?

The reason was that I did not care what anyone else thought
about those curls that my mother wanted me to wear. I had no
admired boy chums whose opinions I could have respected or whose
appearance I could wish to imitate. My brothers were young men
of voting age and older; they were like uncles. The one who was
at home did protest about my curls; and so did my father. But my
mother liked them, and I preferred to please her. Curls are, for
that matter, pretty—as on mediaeval page-boy in a picture or play.
They may be inconvenient, but I did not find them so. I fought my
fist-fights in them without feeling any incongruity. The importance
of a hair-cut is wholly a symbolic one. There was in me at that time
no identification with the masculine world such as would make me
wish to look 'like a boy'.

And for such a boy one would be inclined to predict trouble. The
question would arise, how is he going to become masculine enough
in his attitudes, to hold a job, or accept a responsible relationship to
the other sex? The whole problem of ultimate success in love and
work comes up.

That is a considerably more important question for this boy than the question of whether he will ever become a writer or not. So let us pursue it.

2

But first, how has it happened that a child stoic has turned into Little Lord Fauntleroy? A stoic is one who no longer expects anything good. But in whom has he placed his naive and boundless trust? In whom can a child place his trust, but in his all-powerful, heroic, wonderful, beneficent father? And when he finds that he is not a prince but a pauper, he is cruelly disillusioned in his father. He has, in fact, lost the god-like, all-powerful father of his childhood, as if by death; this jobless workingman who sits around the house trying to maintain authority over growing children who are supporting the family, is no such personage as the father that the boy lost one Christmas Eve. Who he is, and what the boy can do about him, remains to be seen. But evidently he can be, at present, no model, no hero, no masculine influence in his son's boyhood, no guide along the pathway of life, no evoker of ambition.

There remains the Mother. A little, bent, ailing, tireless woman, she is yet, within her own realm, an all-powerful Goddess. And her own realm is not just the kitchen where she bends over the hot cook-stove, or the table, where she sits anxiously on the edge of her chair so as to be ready to jump up and serve her husband and children. Her realm, for her youngest son certainly, is the Ideal Universe. . . . Before I could see very much of the wide world myself, it was already there in my mind, a far-flung world taken on trust from her teaching lips, a world that extended in Time as well as in mere Space. It grew in my mind, that Ideal Universe, until it was infinitely vaster than the small world which my young body inhabited, the small world of which I could learn something for myself by my five senses. The Picture of the World in my mind stretched out further than my swift little legs could ever run, on and on past the furthest hills that my young eyes could see—out, out beyond the familiar house and yard, the half-explored neighborhood, the partly-glimpsed small town, out past Pike County itself, into America, an America come to by my pioneer ancestors as a free country, a country to be proud of, with Washington and Lincoln to reverence, a flag to cherish as a soldier's son; out, out to a world beyond that, the older world from which Columbus came, with knights and heroes in it, Greece and Rome to remember, China and Africa to civilize and explore. This firm clear sketch that my mother drew for me, after being gradually disentangled from the other pretend-world of giants and fairies and dragons, was presently being filled in at school by women like my mother, beautiful and wise and good and firm and kind—at least, some of them were. And always, before I came to anything as I went further and further into the world, before I could hear it, see it, smell it, touch it, taste it, I had it already in my mind, in its place among other things, explained and understood in advance. Books were taking up the work; the Ideal Universe grew every day larger, brighter, more orderly, more understandable, more complete.

And all this Ideal Universe, her gift to me, was filled with a sense of *ought* and *must*—her laws, which I must obey. Whom should I trust, if not her? Whose opinion or taste or authority could I rank above hers? Not my father's, not my brothers' or sister's, not the neighbors'. If she wanted me to wear curls, that was surely little enough to do for her. There was no possibility of my being anything else but a 'mamma's boy'.

So that was how the fiercely cold child-stoic that crept into my mind upon Christmas Eve had turned me into Little Lord Fauntleroy. He had given me the strength never to want anything that a father could give, lest I be disappointed. But he had no power to shield me from the inexorable radiance of a mother's love.

And the question is: who can supply other influences which will keep a good mother's love from turning her helpless son into a perfect sissy?

'He ought to have boys of his own age to play with.' Well, I did; and in their company I escaped for moments from my mother's world of *ought* and *must*. It was a relief, too. In the play world of my own age-group, in activities that were real and imaginary both at once, I experienced the joys of being rather than the joys of understanding. This world of play was not orderly; it had none of the qualities that reigned in my Ideal Universe. Yet it was not real freedom; for the play world was subject to criticism and punishment from my Ideal Universe; the delicious green apples of the play world gave (not always, but sometimes) the bellyaches which righteously belonged to them in my Ideal Universe, my Moral Universe; the water in the pond, so cool and exciting to splash around in naked, did (as I had been told it would) drown one of my school-mates. I myself could never be one who habitually and recklessly lived in this small world of joyous experience; but sometimes I did make, then and later, brief excursions into its anarchic freedom, knowing that it would serve me right if I got my neck broken in forbidden climbs, my hands blown off by gunpowder experiments, my good name irretrievably lost in some small-boy gang-theft, marvelously ingenious, of apples or candy—and, at the time, being quite indifferent to any price I might have to pay for my anarchic self indulgence. Afterward it always seemed a miracle that I had come off scot-free. And, though the universe of actuality had not punished me, I did not go unpunished. The Ideal Universe in my mind had power to punish me, even if mere reality had been so disorderly and lacking in justice as to neglect to do it. I could vividly imagine all the things that *might* have happened, that *should* have happened, and suffer from those.

Though I never quite lost touch with this realm of lawless fact, I was much more at home in the Ideal Universe; and from its inexorable *oughts* and *musts* I found a safer refuge in that permitted realm of imaginary experience, the reading of stories. These, too, gave a kind of freedom from *ought* and *must;* they had the wild charm of lawlessness, yet incurred no blame: unless they were in paper covers with colored pictures on them.

Playmates were not the answer to the problem which I did not know existed: how to gain some moral freedom from the overwhelming domination of a good mother's love. But there was at least the possibility of an inch of freedom being gained, through the intervention of that Ideal Universe which she had built up in my mind. By the just laws which eternally reigned there and judged all things, she must herself be judged.

She was, as I have said, always particular about whom I played with, and I sought to understand her discriminations. Politeness, neatness and lack of profanity seemed to be the chief points in her social decisions. But one Sunday I found a nice little colored boy out in front of the house, who was very polite, and quite neat, and used no bad words: moreover, he had a pocket full of colored chalks with which pictures could be drawn on the sidewalk. Nevertheless, my mother called me back into the house. I could not understand why, and demanded fretfully, "He's a nice boy, isn't he Mamma?" My mother looked embarrassed and ashamed, and did not reply.

This ashamed silence of hers somehow threatened the moral fabric of my universe. From the window I could see the little colored boy, after waiting a while, gather up his chalks, turn his back on the house, and slowly walk away. "Why, Mamma? Why can't I play with him?" No answer. At least, she had the grace to be ashamed.

She did not know that at school I had kept the laws of her Ideal Universe which she was playing fast and loose with. There, at a double desk, I had sat with a little colored boy, whom the other boys didn't want to sit with. . . . How did my teacher know that I did not regard girls or Negro boys as my inferiors? Anyway, she was right. I took seriously the story about my father having fought and suffered in the war to set free the slaves.

It is horribly painful for a child to judge a parent; but it has to be done. Once the trial is over, the reluctant verdict is forgotten, a free pardon wipes it off the records. One seems not to know, but one acts as if one did know. I did know something, scarcely to be put in words. It was the only way in which my mother ever did fail to be entirely consistent with the just and beautiful ideals which she taught me—in this one thing, of timidly and ashamedly attaching importance to 'what people might think'; she tried to keep up all the pretenses of prosperous respectability, that a little boy couldn't help knowing were false. And when a loving son found her out, he could only become an unwilling conspirator in her pretenses. She was, in part, human; not absolutely perfect. It was an inch of freedom gained for a little boy fast tied to her apron strings.

My father grew sick of the sight of those girlish curls on his son, and took me over to the barber shop. The curls were snipped off. My father said with satisfaction that I looked like a boy at last. He put the curls in his pocket. When I came home and showed my shorn head to my mother, she cried. My father took the curls from his pocket and gave them to her. She put them away in a little tin box with the baby dresses of her dead child.

CHAPTER IV

EGOTISM

1

SOME TIME THAT winter, I think it was, we moved to another house, not far away. But it was a house which we would live in by ourselves. There was a good deal of ground, and we could have a garden, raise our own vegetables and potatoes, and cut down the grocery bills. There was a barn, and we must have got a little ahead, for we bought a cow, and were presently selling some milk to a more prosperous neighbor. We could raise chickens, again, too, and have eggs to eat and sell, and an occasional chicken dinner on Sundays. My father got a job picking apples. We were going to be at least comfortably poor, not miserably poor, as we had been.

I lived in this house to the age of twelve. Here I remember that we had a sheet-iron stove—an 'improved Franklin', it was called, though it bore no resemblance to the real Franklin stove which I later used and loved; but it had a cap on the front which could be taken off, letting the firelight out to flicker among the shadows of the living-room at twilight, exactly as if it were a fireplace; and, lying on the floor in front of it, I could gaze into the red embers and see pictures in them to set me musing and dreaming. I do not remember if it was then or later that I began to read Washington Irving's 'Tales of the Alhambra', and fell in love with the 'Arabian Nights'. On the one hand, a taste for literary realism was formed in those early years by Defoe and Charles Reade, so that I still found it impossible to read the clever but unreal books of Dickens and Thackeray; at least I could learn something about the world I lived in from Defoe and Reade. It was meritorious in those days to admire Dickens and Thackeray, and it was with some pain that I gave up the exceptional merit which being a juvenile admirer of their books would have given me; and I dared not say right out how silly I thought these two celebrated writers were. But, on the other hand, I had a taste for true romantic literature, like the 'Arabian Nights', and the Lang series of Yellow, Blue and other-colored books of fairy tales. At twelve, I think it was, I read Mark Twain's books, and his 'Connecticut Yankee in King Arthur's Court' gave me a permanent democratic contempt for medieval glories; and his 'Innocents Abroad' fixed in my mind with equal permanence an attitude of democratic scorn for all that was still medieval-aristocratic in modern Europe; his 'Prince and Pauper' also affected me deeply, and made it all the easier for me to become a Socialist in my adolescence. In poetry, my first love was for poems that could be recited aloud, like 'Sheridan's Ride' and 'Barbara Frietchie'; and Macaulay's poem about Horatius at the bridge was so fixed in my mind that I could recite it now—I still think it a noble and beautiful poem. Better, I think, even than the stories in the bound volumes of St. Nicholas at the library, I liked the tricks explained and illustrated at the back of the magazine, which showed how to make shadow pictures on the wall with one's hands, how to fold paper into curious pretty boxes and boats, and how to do fantastic and improbable things with a piece of string. 'Alice in Wonderland' I did not care for; it is, I think, a story for grown-ups, not children. To me as a child it was a strange, ugly and painful nightmare, with no excuse for existence. Jules Verne's scientific fantasies about submarine-boats and trips to the moon I adored, and in time they would lead me on to the early H. G. Wells and a worship of the Future.

2

What my mother had cried about, I think, when my curls were shorn, was that she couldn't keep me any longer in the haven of childhood. I was growing up. I would have to go to work some-time—though she was fiercely determined that I should at least have a high-school education.

In my mind the eventual obligation of going to work was connected with only one thing—the proper support of my mother. Our family poverty was, by me, felt rather than thought of as the failure of her menfolk to support her in a better way. I day-dreamed vaguely of doing something grand for her when I grew up—but I didn't know what, and these day-dreams were deep, incoherent, unrememberable. I wanted her to sit in the parlor, and not be bending over a hot stove. I regarded the wages which my brother brought home as *her* money; he had, in my opinion, no right to spend money on himself. Especially he had no right to spend a penny of it in a pool-room or saloon.

Somebody was sending us through the mails a weekly 'temperance paper', which I read regularly; and from it I derived an explanation of our family poverty. My father 'drank'! It was true that he liked to stop at the saloon for an occasional glass of beer, when he had done an odd job for somebody and had money in his pocket; and it also was true that he kept in the cupboard a bottle of whisky from which he sometimes took a bed-time nip; that was all. But I had darkly come to feel that it must have been the Saloon which brought us into our poverty. I read stories in the 'temperance paper' about little boys and girls who reformed their fathers—after which there were new clothes for everybody, plenty to eat, and money in the bank. I began to fantasy myself in that savior rôle. And so I wrote my first poem—a moral, propaganda poem.

It was addressed to one of my brothers; for I was afraid of my father, and so began indirectly. The poem was an appeal to my brother to stop drinking, and not break his mother's heart. It was in eight or ten stanzas, quite a long poem; it came out easily, rhymes and all, under the force of my emotion. I had not known I could write poetry! I slipped the poem into my brother's pocket, and imagined him finding it there one evening in a saloon; he would read it, dash his drink to the floor, and come home—he would get my father to 'take the pledge' with him; then we would be prosperous and happy, my father would get a good job and save up money and go back into the butcher business, we would all have new clothes— and I would be recognized as the one who had saved the family.

I waited. But nothing happened; my brother never referred to the poem in any way; I realized that I had only made a little fool of myself. I was glad that my father didn't know anything about it.

3

It was then, I think, when I was ten years old, that I laid public claim to my birthplace, and was officially rebuked for my presumption in doing so.

I had had pointed out to me, as the house in which I was born, the great brown-painted frame building now known as Blair's Boarding-House. I was not quite pleased with it as a birthplace. Perhaps I felt that I should have been born in a log-cabin, like Lincoln. There was only one log-cabin in Barry, and I went to look at it several times and stared curiously at the old Irishwoman who lived there.

Blair's Boarding-House was on my way to and from school. And one morning not long before I left Barry, I wrote my name all along the side of the house in large letters with a piece of chalk.

And that afternoon it happened that the principal of the school, a tall, rubber-heeled man who liked to catch somebody doing something wrong and make an example of him, visited the room. The writing exercise was going on. I had finished it long since, and sat dreaming—perhaps of future greatness. And as I dreamed, I unconsciously wrote on my tablet, 'Floyd Dell' and the date of my birth.

The principal was softly making the rounds of the room. I had not seen him enter, and was not aware of his presence until I saw the tall shape leaning over my shoulder, looking at my tablet. I was proud of my handwriting, and I pushed the writing exercise over for the principal to see. But the principal kept looking at my name on the tablet.

"Are you Floyd Dell?" he asked.

"Yes, sir."

"Did you write your name on the side of Blair's Boarding-House?"

The question came like an earthquake. I had forgotten all about that.

"Yes, sir." I said faintly.

"What did you do that for?" the principal asked sternly.

At that moment I became conscious of the tell-tale words written on the paper in front of me. I blushed all over. These words seemed to me a naked revelation of all my secret thoughts. I wanted to destroy the paper, but I could not make a movement.

"I don't know," I said dully.

"You don't know?" repeated my torturer. "You must be very proud of your name." He took up the tablet on which the name was written, and read what else was written there.

I shrank in my clothes, while the principal read it over carefully to himself. Then he turned to me.

"I want you," he said bitingly, "to show the room what you have been doing instead of writing your lesson.—Write that on the board three times."

My teacher flushed angrily, and made a protesting gesture.

Like one under sentence of death, pale, but rigid to conceal my trembling, I walked slowly to the blackboard, faced the whole room with its hundred staring eyes, and summoned the pride not to care what they thought. Then I turned to the blackboard and wrote the offending words slowly in large defiant letters.

Then I broke the chalk between my fingers, let it drop to the floor, and walked back to my seat.

There was a hush all over the room. Nobody knew what it all meant. My bearing was so little that of a culprit that it did not seem that they were intended to laugh at my discomfiture. The principal was embarrassed.

"That," he said, "is what is known as egotism," and went out.

The teacher hastily called the arithmetic class, and herself erased from the blackboard the words I had written. I left the room, took my cap, and hurried to Blair's Boarding-House, trembling with rage and shame. Ignoring the people about, I commenced to rub out my name with my handkerchief, my cap, my coat-sleeve, my bare hands. The letters seemed to have grown gigantic, overtopping my height. A crowd began to gather. I stopped suddenly, and ran home.

That night I tossed in bed in sleepless torment. But a kindly rain came and washed the offending letters from the wall. They were not there to reproach me with my egotism when I went to school the next day.

4

That summer there was a fire at our house; and afterward the story was all over town that one of the Cedarwall boys had saved Floyd's life, when Floyd rushed back into the smoke and flames 'to save his beloved books'!

That foolish story disgusted me, and I denied it indignantly. I owned no book I would have lifted a finger to save; I wouldn't have gone into that burning house to save a whole Barry public library full of books.

However, something important did happen at that fire. I discovered the smoke, and told my father. I rushed to get the hatchet at his bidding, while he improvised a ladder by which to reach the low kitchen roof. He hacked away the blazing shingles, while I pumped water and carried it to him to throw on the flames. We worked together, father and son. The out-of-work father, with nothing to do but sit around the house, was a hero now, saving our home—and I was helping him. We fought the fire together until the fire department arrived. Then I pumped water for my father until the pump-handle flew off and hit me on the nose, and I was relieved at my station by a neighbor. Happy with the bruised nose which was a token of my participation in that gallant engagement, I retired to enjoy the spectacle. Now, I didn't really care much whether the house burned down or not! I had been my father's helper.

And it was right after this, in the heat of the political campaign of 1896, that I began to adopt with immense enthusiasm my father's Republican political opinions. He had a violent grudge against Democrats in general—he said they were as bad as rebels, and deserved to be hanged; against Governor Altgeld, who in 1893 had pardoned the surviving Haymarket 'Anarchists'—which my father said, showed that Democrats were just the same as Anarchists and bomb-throwers; and against President Cleveland—who, he said, 'literally tore from the statute-books the laws protecting American industry.'

I took over all these opinions. I could not realize that their bitter extravagance was the direct result of the closing down of the woolen mills in Barry, and the panic of 1893—the time when he lost forever his precarious hold upon middle-class respectability, and slid down into joblessness and penury—when he ceased to be able to support his children or secure them an education, when he became one of a miserable proletariat in harsh fact if never in proud self-esteem. Of course he could not blame the panic of '93 upon President Grant, his great Civil-war General and hero, under whose amiable administration the financiers had built up to the highest skies those towering structures of speculation which overwhelmed America, and the Barry woolen mills, and my father, in their gigantic crash. He had to blame it all on the Democrats.

I believed every word of it. I made a nuisance of myself at a Democratic meeting in the Square, calling out opprobrious remarks to the speaker, until my face was smashed by some Democratic boys, and I was dragged out by the scruff of the collar from the mêlée by my big brother. But my black eye and bloody nose were wounds in the glorious Republican cause.

I also engaged in a violently argumentative political correspondence with a Populist girl cousin in Missouri, in which I denounced Grover Cleveland (not that a Populist girl would have minded what I said against him—Bryan was her hero). I used my father's words: 'He literally tore from the statute-books—' "Did he do it literally, Pa?" I knew the difference between *literally* and *figuratively,* but I wouldn't know about administrative procedure, and my father would. "Yes, siree, *literally*—that's just what he did!" So *literally* was what I wrote to my girl-cousin. . . .

Then I found out that Presidents didn't tear statutes out of statute-books—not literally. There must have been other disillusionments in the course of that campaign, experiences to teach me that my father was not a fountain of perfect political wisdom, but this was the one thing my memory selected to retain as a warning illustration of the fact that I could not *literally* believe everything my father said.

And so, though our side won, and the country was saved from Bryan and the demagogues and bomb-throwers, I could not feel in the triumph of McKinley a triumph for my father such as would restore him to the position of authority he must have in my mind if he were to be a father.

CHAPTER V

Elsie and Inza

1

I HAD NOW much companionship with boys of my own age, but still no acquaintance at all with girls. The girl problem, however, from which I endeavored to escape into books, pressed upon me from the outside world. It was something which I earnestly and uncomfortably tried not to think about. During the period from five to twelve, I somehow managed not even to know what the almost universal auto-erotic pleasure-habit of childhood was—I took the constant references to it to be a silly and meaningless joke. But the world in which I lived was full of disquieting hints and rumors about sex; not restricted by any means to adult behavior.

I walked to school one day with a boy younger than myself, whom I did not know very well, but who confided to me, with very convincing details, what he and a little girl who lived near by had been doing together, of which he was very proud, taking for granted that it proved in my eyes, as in those of all his peers, that he was graduated satisfactorily from being a child. He asked me if his hips showed it—he insisted that it made the hips larger.

Now this was not the first time I had heard stories of such a kind. Its importance lay in the fact that this boy was one who in clothes, language and manners was one whom my mother would have picked out as a nice boy, a wholly desirable friend and playmate for me; and the little girl who had been his partner in these exploits was shown by some of the details of his story to be one whom his mother approved of—a nice little girl.

A good boy who belongs to a poor family knows what to think when stories like this are told by boys whose language is rough and whose manners are tough. The invitations which I, if my ears had

34

not deceived me, had received from time to time to come along and take part in these exploits, were easy to decline—or rather, casually evade, since tough little boys were sensitive to any airs of moral superiority on the part of others, and it was best to pass off with a laugh these appeals for companionship.

But the case was different when it was a well-dressed boy with refined manners and good language who, with all the satisfaction of a young scholar who had successfully passed his examination in arithmetic, recounted such achievements as these—and not with the washerwoman's little girl, either. It was difficult to import any ready-made moral attitudes into the consideration of the misbehavior of perfectly respectable little boys and girls among themselves.

But, after all, it did not concern me, their behavior; they might have their own laws, and I still abide by mine. I need not judge them; and what I did was to build another moral universe, beside my own. I stayed in mine; and that little boy and girl could stay in theirs.

It sprang up overnight, this new moral universe, like a palace built by a genie in the Arabian Nights, pieced together out of scraps of things seen and heard, out of jokes and observations, out of a thousand bits of truth which did not fit into a maternally-constructed moral universe. There it stood, for all to dwell in who chose, secure from maternal judgment. That was its purpose, to make it unnecessary for me as a good little boy to think evil of those who lived by different laws—particularly nice little girls, whom it pained me to judge harshly. Their freedom did not concern me otherwise; though I pressed my nose against the glass sides of that new universe of moral freedom, and contemplated its treasures thoughtfully, I was a window-shopper only—I was not going inside, I did not want anything that was there for myself, I would just look and then go on about my business.

Meanwhile, that little girl whom the well-dressed boy had told me about—she went to this school, was one of the little girls who romped on the little girls' playground. I didn't know, would never know, which one she was; she might be *any* of these little girls! A good little boy couldn't help but wonder. . . .

During all this time there was an inward feeling that girls and boys ought to be playing together, enjoying each other's company, as they did for example in most of the Louisa M. Alcott stories. Perhaps what I wanted was to be one of a large family of boys and girls, among whom the spending of money by boys on girls was not an alarming requirement, and between whom no sweethearting was expected. Those, precisely, were my terms for companionship with girls; and so far as I knew, they were terms which the world of real girls did not care to meet and which had to be fulfilled for me only in day-dreams. That earlier day-dream of attic companionship with a girl friend had been revived, revised to suit my age, which was now more nearly upon an equality with the girl's age at that earlier time, and expanded to new dimensions, until what then had been (if there was anything) real at its core was covered deep with iridescent films of fantasy.

2

Grown-up young women, who were maternally kind to a boy and yet wonderfully beautiful and charming, with all the sweetness of their sex and none of its dangerousness, were much more approachable than small girls. One of my teachers was my first love; for her sake I endured the agony of learning to 'tip my hat'. I hung about her desk, happy to serve her in any way. Once, when she had to stay after school, she gave me a note to her sister in the candy-store. Her sister was not there, and chivalry debated with common sense as to whether to open and read the note; chivalry won, and I carried the note to her sister's house; but I had passed her sister on the way, and so back to the candy store; the note asked merely for some candy, which I now took back to the school; but all this going to and fró had taken a long time—the janitor told me the teacher had gone home; back to her home once more, to be thanked graciously, and offered a piece of candy, which did not keep me from feeling like a fool. It was my first experience of the fact that when in love no fellow has all his wits about him. But grown-up girls would be kinder than young ones to a silly little boy. They would not laugh at my ridiculous behavior.

3

When I was eleven years old, the battleship Maine was blown up in Havana Harbor; when war was declared against Spain, my eldest brother enlisted, getting as far as Florida. All this was very exciting, and it set me to playing military games again.

In my war-games I combined my picture-making enthusiasms with my military ones. I was in fancy a war-correspondent, and my idea of a war-correspondent was one who took photographs. With a wooden sword in my right hand and a cigar-box camera in my left, I cried "Come on, men!" and charged into the gooseberry bushes. Snap-snap, went the camera; slash! went the sword.

That war created, among several heroes of more evanescent fame, the Rough Rider whom my father called 'Teddy Rosenfelt' and devoutedly admired from that time on. And it also created in the public mind the romantic figure of the war-correspondent. It romanticized the Reporter. And, if it had not been too daring a thought, I should have then formed the ambition of sometime becoming a Newspaper Man. No other career ever showed itself to my young gaze in which a fellow could actually make a living and have a good time.

4

But even playing at war-games was not a complete refuge from the girl question. A boy at school had uttered some words which threatened my happily arranged dual universe. He put in definite words something which had been implicit in many jokes and remarks of the boy-world, but could be ignored until put forward as an assertion of a general truth. He said that girls were afraid, later, because something might happen if they did such things then; now was the time, and they wanted to be asked. In his further remarks his tone cast intense moral scorn upon those boys who were afraid to ask. And again the consideration of fleeting time was evoked; now was the golden hour, it was made clear.

As one of those who were letting their golden hours go to waste in the sands of book-learning, I had kept silent. The idea that I might have a duty in this matter was considered for a moment only, and then rejected. I was going to stay in a moral universe where I was at home, and not go blundering about in the strange paths of freedom. But I had a sinking feeling that what he said about little girls might be true—that they might really wish to be asked. I felt sure that more boys than I had thought—not just 'bad' boys—

were asking them; they probably expected it. I discerned a kind of mockery in their attitude toward me, a good little boy. And any flirtatious glance became a possible challenge against which I had to steel myself to indifference.

5

The war over, my eldest brother came home from the army camp crippled with rheumatism, to sit about the house, a fretful invalid, and read five-cent novels. This kind of reading matter was not approved at our house, but these were exceptional circumstances; and for the first time, I read some of this forbidden literature. I was greatly disappointed in Diamond Dick and Nick Carter. As thrillers, these could not hold a candle to some of my library books, such as 'Les Miserables' and 'The Count of Monte Cristo'. Nevertheless, since another boy at school was writting a thriller, I wrote one myself. It was all about a cave full of jewels, as I remember, and there was a good deal of fighting in it. My sister said she would try to get it printed, and I thought that was fine, but nothing happened. I made up another story about a lost city on top of an Arizona mesa, and pored much over the map in the geography, but did not ever finish writing the story.

My brother settled down for the winter to a pursuit of the collegiate fortunes of Frank Merriwell; and so did I. In the first 'novel' I read, there was Frank between two girls—Elsie, a blonde, and Inza, a brunette. Frank was sweet on Inza, who was (as any reader with half an eye could see) plotting against the success of the football team. But Frank, poor fool, believed that Elsie was the villainess; whereas it was Elsie who really loved him and Yale. Hoping to get this thing straightened out, I hastened to read the next one in the series. Good! Frank had found Inza out, and all was well between him and Elsie—but, what was this? Could it be that we had misjudged these girls? For it now looked awfully much as though it were Elsie who was plotting against Frank, and that it was poor broken-hearted Inza who really loved him! Anxious to have justice done, I read the next number. Inza was restored to Frank's favor, as justice required; but just when I had begun to get used to that idea, it suddenly appeared as though we had been right the first time in thinking that Inza was a villainess. It would cost my brother another nickel to find out. . . . I never did make sure—though I thought it was Elsie, the blonde, who was Frank's friend. But this was too much like life; I went back to public library fiction by reputable authors, who take the reader into their confidence and tell him what is what about the girls to whom he is introduced in their pages. A girl in a public library novel is either a good girl or a bad girl, and there are no two ways about it.

The dubiousness attaching to the characters of Elsie and Inza was a reflection in a trivial glass of a problem of profound importance which was besetting my mind. It was one that I scarcely dared think about. The thoughts which I might have had to think, had I ever faced the question, were too appalling.

6

My eldest brother was well enough the next spring to go back to Quincy to his job. The family, what was left of it, with all three of the elder children gone to Quincy, moved into one corner of a big house lived in by an old lady and her crippled nephew. I would write letters at the old lady's dictation to her daughter in Chicago: "If I ever needed you, now is the time I need you most," was the burden of them all.

In this new neighborhood I found a new friend, one with whom I could discuss the girl problem in a philosophic spirit. The time had now come for both of us when the golden age of safe amours was over; and he, like me, had passed his youth in scholarly and monkish virtue. Like two elderly gentlemen in stories that I have since read, we sighed a little over the lost opportunities that we could clearly recall, now it was too late.

We were both much relieved that it was too late; very glad indeed that these performances would no longer be expected of us by any girl schoolmates. But our feeling of security in having passed the dangerous age of safety was, it soon appeared, premature; for not long afterward, from a cigarette-smoking youth who came to hang paper on the walls, I heard that there were easily available ways and means by which these pleasures were made perfectly safe for adolescent youth. The news was rather terrifying.

But I forgot these new alarms in poring over a book the old lady had given me—a great book called 'Hill's Manual', which told how to meet all, at least of the respectable, emergencies of life, legal, social and literary. It told how to write a constitution; it contained a rhyming dictionary; and it set forth all the rules of etiquette. I began to study the writing of constitutions, when I should have been memorizing the rules of etiquette.

I was sitting on the doorstep, reading this valuable book, when I happened to look up and out at the chickens in the yard. We had practically always had chickens, and I would have supposed that there was not one single trait in that silly fowl's behavior which I did not know in every absurd detail, and at all ages, from the time the yellow bill first chips through the shell to its ending in the pot; and yet my surprised eyes now saw for the first time the comic behavior of a hen and a rooster in their rudimentary amours. I was convulsed with laughter.

7

It was decided that my mother and father and I were to go to Quincy before school opened in the fall; we would join my two brothers and my sister, who all had jobs there, and the family would have a home together.

While I waited to go, an old day-dream took possession of my mind—the girl-companion of the attic.

Many years later, when I was writing my more-or-less autobiographical novel, 'Moon-Calf', and when I showed the manuscript of the first chapters to a woman friend, she begged me to put a girl into the story before going further with it. A girl? I hadn't known any girls at that age. And then I remembered the attic and my dream-companion. It made no difference in a novel, so I wrote it as if it were all real. It seems as vivid as reality to me as I read it. Their night in the woods. . . .

'The bonfire blazed and roared, the coffee bubbled, and the bread and meat tasted as never did bread and meat before. It is true, the potatoes refused to roast, but who cared? It grew dark, and a few stars came out. They laughed and sang in the exhilaration of their escape. Rose put on his hat, rakishly, and he stuck behind his ear a flower which she had worn. A cool breeze came up, and they crept close together for warmth, and wrapped themselves in the heavy shawl she had brought. Hours had passed. It must be dreadfully late. They were silent, regretting that all this must presently come to an end.

' "I don't want to go home," said Rose in a muffled tone, her head on his shoulder.'

And she recited poetry to me.

That was what I wanted. I had to dream it.

CHAPTER VI

CHOICES

1

GOING to Quincy was an important event in my life—if only because it was a new town. Barry seemed to me the scene of innumerable pains and humiliations. I felt that I was leaving behind me my childhood, with all its awkwardness and ignorance. I wanted to forget it all. And presently a curtain fell softly behind me, fold upon fold, cutting off the past.

Quincy was a river town of some thirty thousand inhabitants, the largest in the surrounding region. The older boys and my sister all had factory jobs, and my father hoped to get one. The new house in which our family was reunited was one half of a double house on the edge of a cheap residence district, flanked by a gully and a ragged bluff, upon which I would lie at sunset looking across the ugly railway tracks and factories, at the rolling Mississippi. The house held with difficulty the household goods collected by the Dells in thirty years—old wooden bedsteads, moth-eaten couches, battered bureaus, rickety chairs with cane seats repaired with heavy twine, ancient stoves, an extension table with many 'leaves', the family portraits 'enlarged' in crayon, a trunkful of books, including the Family Dispensary and all the school books ever used by the children, and a vast quantity of rags, which my mother intended to make into a carpet. And finally, there was the 'what-not'—a series of little triangular shelves tied together with string and made to hang in a corner of the parlor; its front decorated with stiff brown paper, folded like the scales of a lizard, and painted over with a shiny black. It was loaded with family photographs, colored fans, ornamental cups and saucers, china shepherdesses, curiously shaped flasks which had once contained perfume and were still preserved as objects of art; all kinds of pathetic trinkets accumulated by my mother for parlor decoration in the odd moments of a lifetime spent in the kitchen; once accepted and admired by all the family, it now was valued by no one except her. Gradually it had become a sort of filing cabinet for grocery bills, rent receipts, letters from relatives, and old copies of the Barry 'Adage'. With these accustomed articles of furniture disposed about the five rooms, upstairs and down, the house began to look like all the houses we had ever lived in.

The house was only a few blocks from Franklin School, where I resumed my education. There were new studies, that I had no grounding in, such as music and manual training, in which I felt helpless and hopeless; and the school, with its small cinder yard after the generous grassy and tree-strewn expanse of the schoolyard in Barry, and with the radiator pipes running around the schoolrooms with a disconcerting suggestion of being prison-bars, did not seem as though it would ever be a happy place. But I forgot these outward circumstances when the first lines of 'The Merchant of Venice' were shown to fall into a pattern of light and heavy accents —iambic metre, it was called. And there were other patterns of sound in verse:

> 'Trochee trips from long to short;
> From long to long in solemn sort
> Slow Spondee stalks—strong foot! yet ill able
> Ever to keep with the Dactyl trisyllable.
> Iambics march from short to long;
> With a leap and a bound the gay Anapests throng.' . . .

—Why, this was the secret of poetry!

2

After school there was the library, a grey stone building on the corner of the Square, with young women behind the counter instead of an old lady. And, though it was against the rules, I was allowed by these sympathetic guardians of the books to go behind the counter, direct to the shelves; two others in town enjoyed that privilege, one a robust clergyman who rode a bicycle and wore knickerbockers, and the other the deep-bosomed maternal-looking secretary of a woman's club.

A book which enchanted me was a pseudo-scientific work by Ignatius Donnelly, purporting to prove the reality of Plato's Atlantis, and the origin of human culture there. I believed it all; and when I found that the 'proofs' were false, I could bear the author no grudge, for the Atlantis myth remained a beautiful theme for imaginative reverie. And the book led me into the gorgeous realms of archaeology and anthropology. I saw Schliemann's spade uncover Troy. I was with Champollion when with the key of the Rosetta Stone he deciphered the Egyptian hieroglyphics. I wandered through Yucatan with Stephens and Catherwood. I looked on breathlessly while Tylor traced the laws of the primitive mind. I watched the canny, poetic finger of Andrew Lang poking into the rubble heap of myth and custom. Much have I traveled in those realms of gold since then, and many goodly states and kingdoms seen, but then was I like Cortez upon a peak of Darien. Too soon the public library had yielded up the last of its treasures, and the subject was pursued in the periodical files of the Quincy Academy of Sciences, which sometimes amid all their quartz-dust yielded up a grain of gold.

For all in me that was student this was pure happiness, and if fortune had offered me my dearest wish it would have been only the choice of setting out to Mesopotamia with a pick and shovel or starting for Yucatan with a camera obscura.

It might have been the simplest solution for all the problems of my life. At least, if those competent observers Jules Verne and Conan Doyle have reported truly the personalities of the romantic and adventurous explorers in the name of science, they are all infantile; in Mesopotamia or Yucatan it makes no difference, I believe. I collected railway folders showing the best routes to Yucatan. But fortune did not smile on me, the hussy! I had to stay in civilization and do my best to grow up and learn to make what is called an honest living.

But I didn't have to think about that—yet. I wandered about Quincy with pencil and paper, drawing pictures. There was a Moorish castle in Quincy—somebody's idea of a home; I approved his taste, and drew pictures of it from all angles. The owner had been to France; he admired the French—I heard him tell the young assistant public librarian that. She had heard that they treated their cab-horses cruelly. He replied stiffly that he did not judge a great people like the French by the way they treated their cab-horses. I envied anyone who could travel. But I would not have gone to France, I would have gone to Yucatan—or Mesopotamia.

3

I was interested in no girl who was before my eyes in Quincy, but I began in absence to remember some of the beautiful girls left behind in Barry. One in particular haunted my memory; she would hardly have known who I was, and I do not remember that I ever actually spoke to her—a girl two or three grades above mine in school, about fourteen or fifteen years old when I last saw her: Belle Day, a romping girl-goddess, sturdy and yet everywhere soft to look at, with golden hair, a peaches-and-cream complexion, blue eyes, and sweet red laughing lips. I had feasted my gaze upon her until I had the picture of her to keep with me always, and deep in my mind I could hear the sound of her golden laughter, as she came romping home from school.

For ten cents I bought a book and started a library. The book, soon flanked on one side by Emerson's Essays at the same price and on the other by Carlyle's 'Past and Present', was Ik Marvel's 'Reveries of a Bachelor'. It was an innocent and charming version, Victorian-American in spirit, of that perennial theme, the memoirs of a lost youth and its loves. Nothing could have been more inoffensive to the severest moral censorship than these sweet little romances, memories and fantasies which the middle-aged bachelor evoked from the coals of his dying fire as he sat before it smoking his cigar at midnight. But, however pure the sentiments, there were a lot of girls; and he didn't marry any of them! It was the first book I had ever read which suggested that love does not necessarily and solely exist in order to bring about the wedding of two hearts forever. Love exists for its own sake, said this subtly immoral book. Love affairs are pleasant to remember, it urged. And how infinitely agreeable, in middle-age, to be able to call to mind, one after another, the images of all the beautiful girls whom one has loved! Love does not have to be eternal; it does not have to lead to marriage; it is beautiful all the same—and the more girls one can remember, the more beautiful it is: such was the lesson taught in Ik Marvel's gentle reveries.

It set for my imagination a possible goal, and one infinitely easier for me to contemplate than the one held up by ordinary romance, in which the boy made good and the girl married him. It also said in a sufficiently refined and idealistic way what all the perturbing jokes and insinuations about girls had said; in another key, sentimental instead of crudely physical, it said they were not angels—just girls, but awfully nice as such. It was a very beautiful and comforting book. I could think of myself as an old bachelor, looking back upon beautiful girls whom I had loved and lost.

Certainly that was easier than to think of myself as ever a married man with a family.

What had once been a favorite day-dream about the girl in the attic became now transformed into an actual dream, which recurred from time to time—only in the night-dream it was a bare, empty hayloft (a barn-attic as I thought of it in my dream), which was the scene of our companionship. Always my dream-companion read poetry to me. When I woke up, I remembered the dream vividly, but the girl herself I never could recall clearly. This curious dream-companionship lasted for twenty years.

4

One September day, when we had been in Quincy a year, a nice lady came to our house canvassing for a set of books. I forget exactly what they were, but I think they were historical, and I know that they were to me very fascinating. My mother ought not to have listened to the lady canvasser's serpent-tongue; but the poor are reckless, and my mother loved her bookish son, and she saw how much I wanted that set of books, and she would have signed on the dotted line if I had not suddenly remembered the public library, and blurted out something about it which awoke my mother from the seductive spell.

Then the nice lady canvasser suggested a way for me to get the books for nothing and make a lot of money besides.

"Your son, Mrs. Dell—I've been admiring his interest in books, and the way he can talk about them," she said. "There are few boys of his age who know that much, or can speak up for themselves that way. Now, as you know, Mrs. Dell, fluency of language is the most important part of salesmanship—and salesmanship is what makes money in these days. Your son has presence, too—he is so tall and manly and self-assured! How old is he? Only thirteen? Really? I wouldn't have believed it. He looks like a young man of sixteen. Is he going to college? —Of course you *hope* so; but that isn't enough—you should make sure of it. Perhaps you don't realize it —I don't suppose you've ever thought about it—but he could get the money to take him through college very easily, by canvassing for this set of books."

(Ah, you Irish wretch! Talk like that to another Irishwoman, will you, about her white-headed boy—choose the words that will magically transform him before her eyes from an awkward spindling lout into all that a mother's heart could desire him to be—hold out to her anxious mind the hope of a college education for her book-worm son, who had ignominiously quit his vacation job because it was too hard—wheedle some of her tiny hoard from under the paper of the bottom bureau drawer! But you, Lady Canvasser, maybe *you* had a son to support? And was this the only way our civilization gave you a chance to feed that boy, clothe him, send him to college? Then my curses on that lying, cheating, swindling, thieves' civiliza-tion, instead of on you; and may it come to its end soon!)

It only cost ten dollars for the district rights as a canvasser, includ-ing the folder showing the binding, sample pages, and illustrations, and the instructions, all of which she would leave right here with me. But she saw by our faces that ten dollars was too much. So she made it eight dollars, as a favor to us. She pointed out that the agent kept so-much out of the first payment on every set of books sold; also that he could sell agency rights to others, and keep so much of that. And with Floyd's ability—she was calling me Floyd, now— that investment would be turned into a fund for a college education in no time at all, just by canvassing for an hour or so in my spare time after school and on Saturdays. Eight dollars wasn't much, was it, to pay for a college education?

The nice lady canvasser got my mother's eight dollars, and de-parted.

With her golden eloquence still ringing in our ears, my mother and I looked at each other with a wild surmise of a happy future for me—a way of making money for which I was really fitted by my gift of gab, that would see me through college.

My mother said: "I don't think I'll tell Pa and the others about this—just yet."

Something in her tone struck me. "Ma," I said, "you didn't use the Rent Money?"

Rent Money was sacred—not to be touched.

"Well," she confessed, "I didn't have quite enough. I used two dollars of the Rent Money."

Two dollars—I could replace that out of my first sale. So that was nothing to worry about.

The next morning, all dressed up in my best serge suit, with shoes carefully shined, hair slicked down, and a manly necktie tied by my mother's hands, rather scared but very brave, with the prospectus under my arm and the sales-arguments in my capacious and retentive memory, I went out to canvass.

That morning I did not get my foot inside of a single door; but I remembered that I was not to be discouraged by a few preliminary failures. It was all good practice. There were no results in the afternoon, either. But I kept it up. There were no results all the rest of the week.

Then school opened, and I had only my spare time afternoons and on Saturdays. It wasn't as easy as I had thought it was going to be. My self-confidence was evaporating. A doubt crept into my mind. Did I really have salesmanship? Was I learning how to sell things, and preparing to earn the money with which to go to college? Or was I just wasting my time in a ridiculous and unpleasant way?

But—if I didn't have salesmanship, then what did I have? Nothing; and there would be no choice but for me to go on working in a factory when I finished high school. The grime of such work was for me mixed with the sweat of anxiety, humiliation, and fear. I was trying to escape from that into some kind of serenity and leisure.

"No, we don't want any books."

"But Madam, if you will just allow me to show you——"

"I haven't got any time."

"It will only take a minute, and there is no obligation on your part. I would just like to——"

"I said No!" Bang.

And even when I got in, and said everything there was to say, I couldn't 'clinch the sale.'

Two weeks passed. Three weeks.

Something in me whispered that it was no use, that I couldn't make the grade, that I didn't have the stuff in me to make a salesman. But I wouldn't listen. I kept up an artificial courage. It was getting harder and harder to go in through the gate, up to the door, and knock. I didn't like the looks of some houses, I had premonitions of defeat, I wanted to pass by—but I forced myself through the rigmarole. And so on to the next. Oh, if I could only tell my mother when I got home that I had sold a set of books!

It was late in September now. One afternoon I sat down on a curbstone to rest. And suddenly I saw, grimly, that the woman had played a dirty trick on my mother. Just for money. We had been played for suckers. Fooled. Cheated. Bamboozled. That about my going to college—it was just a part of the trick.

So far as I was concerned, it meant that I would have to be a factory-hand. But then, that was what I had always supposed I would have to be. That was no news. But my mother had taken two dollars out of the Rent Money. Only the drunkenness of a foolish hope could have made her do it. I thought of the hunted look there was sometimes in her eyes as rent-day approached. Nothing worse would happen than her having to tell Pa and the others, and being made to look ridiculous—if I didn't replace that two dollars. But I didn't want them to know our foolish dreams. I *had* to get my mother's money back for her—and it was nearly the first of October. I *had* to sell some books. There were only a few days left.

If there had been anyone to kill and rob, to pay my mother back, I would cheerfully have contemplated that.

In my discouragement, I gave up trying to make any sales in those hateful houses with green lawns in front; and so, by accident, on the way home, I began trying again in a district where poor people lived —people who can't afford to buy expensive sets of books, but do. And I found a very old Irishwoman, smoking a clay pipe, who listened with interest to my eloquence—including, of course, my story of how I was earning money to go to college this way. She was interested because she had a grandson, Pat I think his name was, who was a bright lad and fond of books; he had quit school this year and gone to work, she said. I went on with my palaver about this set of books being a cultural necessity in any home where intellectual matters were cherished. I knew I had the old lady going, but I could scarcely believe it when she caved in and signed on the dotted line, and dug up the five dollars from a cupboard. Oh, God! My mother would have her money back, anyway. Then in came her grandson Pat, the one she had been telling me about. He was a year or two older than I—a pale, freckled, gawky youth. "Tell him," said the old lady encouragingly, "about your earning the money for college with your book-canvassin'. Maybe he would like to do the same."

The boy looked at his grandmother anxiously. "You didn't spend any of the Rent Money, did you, Granny?" he asked quickly.

Then I knew that a good salesman would have sold Pat a district agency. A slick talker could do it; and I had the gift of gab. But I was ashamed of what I had already done, and went away. The youth looked after me with hatred. I had cheated him out of a week's earnings, maybe. But that kind of cheating was all right in our civilization; that kind of cheating *was* our civilization, from top to bottom. So he didn't knock me down and take back his money— that would have been violence and robbery; he looked hate at me and let me go.

I went home feeling pretty sick. I didn't want to cheat him. But my own mother came first, didn't she? And I had got the rent money back for her.

But I canvassed no more. I burned up the prospectus. The whole thing became a sore memory, until I succeeded in forgetting it. And that was the end of my career as a business man.

5

At this time I first saw a Socialist paper, handed to one of my brothers by a shopmate and brought home in his pocket; it was called The Appeal to Reason, and after reading it all through I gravely announced that it should be called The Appeal to Treason. It was obviously an unpatriotic and inflammatory sheet. My father, who had been visiting relatives in Pike County, brought back with him and left unread a book urged upon him by an old Socialist farmer, Jimmy Houseweart; I read it—Gronlund's 'Co-operative Commonwealth', a sketch of a kind of Governmental Super-Trust, which was obviously a more orderly system than the one I vaguely knew existed in the outside world; but the book did not disturb my Republicanism much. I repeated familiar Republican arguments to the Bryanite father of a schoolmate, and heard from that big grimy iron-moulder savage denunciations of Mark Hanna and Wall Street, without having my political aplomb disturbed at all.

I was going to the Presbyterian Sunday School, in sociable accompaniment of a boy who lived in the neighborhood. And in the spring, when the whole Sunday School class joined the church, I joined too, like a good fellow.

But while we waited for the ceremonial of which we were to be the center, one of the boys in the class nudged me, and nodded toward a group of blue-clad inmates of the Quincy Soldiers' Home filing into a reserved pew. "Look at the blue-bellies," he said, and in his voice there was humor and contempt.

I was shocked. To me that blue Soldiers' Home uniform was sacred, made holy by the blood shed in battles whose names were like a roll of trumpets and thunder of drums, Vicksburg, Chickamauga, Missionary Ridge, Shiloh, Corinth, Antietam, Gettysburg, Spotsylvania. . . . My father, if his rheumatism got any worse, was going to stay in this Soldiers' Home for a while. These were men like my father. And to this well-dressed young son of a prosperous Quincy business man, my father would be a 'bluebelly'. I suffered from a tormented filial rage all through the ceremonial. And perhaps that was one reason why I never set foot in that church again.

I caught cold, and was out of school for several weeks. I can't remember whether the minister came to see his young convert, or whether it was in some other way that 'Nelson on Infidelity'—a volume of sermon-essays defending the Bible against the infidels— came into my hands. I read it, and was much impressed, re-read it, and spotted the disreputable reasoning; read it a third time, with mocking marginal annotations, and declared myself an Atheist. The book attacked Ingersoll, so I read Ingersoll; and his eloquent writings became a new gospel to me. It was a gospel of human self-reliance. 'To plow is to pray; to plant is to prophesy; and the harvest answers and fulfills.'

My mother was at first perturbed by my Atheism; but, as it did not keep me from making good progress in my studies in school, and did not lead me into any low companionships, she soon did not mind it.

As an Atheist, I was for the first time really religious; a disorderly and meaningless Jehovah had been removed from the universe, and Law put there to rule instead. The Law was, I felt, good, just and wise. I had to reconcile myself to the thought of Death presently; I could see that unless people died, the planet would be too crowded to live on—or else, if there were no Birth either, I should never have been here at all; and if old things died, new things could be different and better. But the thought that really reconciled me to Death was that my atoms would become part of the flowers. I wanted to be cremated, and my ashes strewn at the foot of some rose-bush, thus accepting and co-operating with Nature's wise, just and beautiful laws.

CHAPTER VII

MONEY VS. HEROISM

1

My MOTHER went the next summer to visit relatives back in Pike County; and being proud of her tall son, she took me along to show me off.

Out in the country, at the house of my uncle and aunt where we spent the first week in July, there was a pretty girl-cousin, Lela, about my age or a little older. On the Fourth, we were all loaded into the surrey and taken to the county-seat, I think it was, to enjoy the celebration. My mother took me aside beforehand and gave me a quarter. "Treat your cousin Lela to some ice-cream," she said.

Black misery descended upon me. A thing like that might seem easy, but it wasn't. I had had no practice in that sort of thing. I had never had any money. I had never learned how to treat.

The life of a stoic does not fit one to meet an emergency like this. But for my mother's sake I would have to do this thing. I tried to figure it out. You had to say something to the girl, first. I knew the sort of thing that was said, and I tried over several verbal formulas in my mind. 'Shall we have some ice-cream?' But I didn't think I could say that. 'Come on, let's get some ice-cream'—that was better. But it had to be said naturally. I knew that any other boy would be able to say it naturally. But I was afraid I couldn't. My tongue became paralyzed at the very thought of saying it. Perhaps I could lead up to it in some roundabout way. . . . But all the things I thought of saying seemed to lead away from ice-cream, not toward it.

Meanwhile I wasn't saying anything. I was sitting there in the surrey beside my pretty cousin Lela, silent and helpless and scared. My mother was expecting me to behave like the manly little boy

53

that I seemed. She had given me her fond approval as a little boy who never spent any money; but now, when she wanted to show me off, I was supposed to act as if I were accustomed to carrying quarters in my pocket and spending them on girls!

We arrived at the Square in town, and the others began to climb down from the surrey. Now was the time to say something to Lela about ice-cream. But I couldn't speak. I sat there, white and helpless. Lela got down. Everybody got down, except me. I couldn't move.

I am told that at this point I impressed people with my cool, self-sufficient airs. Nobody knew I was a helpless child. Nobody gave me a shove and told me what to do. "Don't you want to see the races?" asked my uncle. I said "No," evidently in a way that settled the matter. They all went away, leaving me alone.

But they would come back. And then what would I do? Nothing. I couldn't do anything. The battle was lost. I despised myself. I hated the quarter in my pocket. I wished—and wished truly, and for the only time in my life—that I could die.

I should have liked to die trying to stop a runaway horse, and saving Lela's life. I could be a hero if I had a chance. (And I haven't the slightest doubt I would have jumped at the chance.) But any kind of death—any kind at all—would be better than this.

It went on all day.

I had time, again and again, to say those words, 'Let's have some ice-cream.' But I couldn't.

I just sat there, stonily, in frozen despair.

The icy child-stoic that had crept into my brain that Christmas Eve was stronger than anything else in me. And it seemed that nothing outside myself could shake his power. I was in his grip.

When we got back to the farm late that afternoon, the hateful quarter was still in my pocket. I gave it back to my mother. "Here!" I said bitterly, and put it into her hand.

2

Now it happened that out in the country I met the Socialist farmer who had given my father that book on the Co-operative Commonwealth. He was a gentle and intellectual man with a white beard. He was respected in Pike County for having found natural gas on his farm and lighted his barns and henhouses with it; though at the same time, as a Socialist, he was regarded by solid Republican farmers (with their farms mortgaged up to the hilt) as an impractical visionary. I talked with him about the book he had lent my father; he was pleased that I had read it, and he listened without condescension to my Republican criticisms and answered them thoughtfully, which was very flattering. In the course of our discussion he remarked that Socialism was not a matter of economics only, but of a different kind of life, based upon service for the common good and not on money. "It is the kind of world a poet would want to live in," he said, looking at me. "Or a hero," he added. I had no reason to think of myself as a poet, and would have blushed at being caught thinking of myself as a hero. But his words impressed me. And when I went home I re-read the book and thought better of it. At the same time I became aware of Markham's poem, 'The Man with the Hoe', which had made a great stir in America the year before. I soon knew the lines by heart: *'Plundered, profaned, and disinherited'* . . .

This is not especially the story of my political opinions or of my intellectual development, but rather of my quest for life, liberty and happiness. It seems to me that I was engaged at this time in a desperate search for grounds of emotional reconciliation with my father. I was certainly badly in need of some inward strength to save me from another such frightful experience as I had just had in my helplessness. The connection of Socialism with these needs is not apparent, I know. But it happened to answer these needs in certain ways, and that is why I tell about it.

When we had moved to Quincy, the first thing that one of my new schoolmates said to me was, "My father is a doctor—what's yours?" I evaded answering, and told my mother about it. She said: "Tell them that your father is a retired butcher." I couldn't tell them that. I wanted to tell them to go to hell.

That next fall, in school, suddenly and with little outward reason, I wrote a poem—the second I had ever written. Again the lines poured out easily, rhymes and all. It was on the subject of Lincoln, the martyr President. But, underneath that (I am quite sure), I was praising and excusing my father. Heroism was enough; the hero did not have to be a good business man. What if my father had not supported his family in respectable style? I could be proud of him! That, certainly, was how I suddenly felt. American respectability had taken my father away from me. Socialism was giving me a chance to get him back.

And I had him back, not only in a poem, but, already that summer, in fact. In a rather silly but very satisfying way, it happened. As my father sat reading his Sunday paper, I began—strange behavior in so dignified a boy—to tickle his ear with a broomstraw. He thought it was a fly, and brushed at it. I kept it up until he turned and saw me. Even then I did not stop, but persisted in this silly trick until— "You seem to want a spanking," he said, "so I'll give it to you!"— and he did. I burst out laughing. I was happy.

He seemed to understand, for he invited me to go fishing with him. I dug the worms, and we started. On the way to the creek we passed the 'Last Chance' saloon, and my father went in for a glass of beer, telling me that I might come in and have a glass of soda-pop if I liked.

But I was embarrassed, and stood waiting for him outside.

At that moment when I decided to stay outside, I was my mother's little boy.

But some new self within me made me feel ashamed. I wished I had gone in with him.

And after our fishing was done, on the way back, when we stopped there again, I marched in proudly and happily at his side. And when my soda-pop was served me in a bottle with a straw, I insisted on having it in a glass. I shyly pushed the glass along the bar till it touched my father's, and then drank deep.

3

In a moment I will tell what kind of father it was that I got back. But first I must say a little more about my Socialism, and what it had to do with my feelings about my father.

In search of further information, I tried to read a small digest of the Marxian theory, which I found at the public library, but it was too algebraic for my comprehension. However, I proceeded to read several books, beginning with Kennan's, and including something of Kropotkin's, on the Nihilist movement in Russia, and I became happily at home in those scenes of heroic conspiratorial effort on behalf of human liberty. Also I read an interesting Populist novel by Ignatius Donnelly, the author of the 'Atlantis' book, giving an imaginative account of an American revolution, one not accomplished by votes but by a violent and bloody uprising against a ruthless Napoleonic dictator. From these it is possible that I got a more realistic notion of revolution than I would have had from current Socialist Party propaganda, which was at that time very peacefully Parliamentarian. At all events, this revolutionary literature provided for me an imaginative world in which considerations of respectability and manners did not count, and in which heroism was conceived as being directed to the creation of a better world rather than to setting the wedding bells to ringing. What this Nihilist literature did for me was to put an end to any hold of respectability upon my conscience. And at the same time it lifted from my shoulders a frightful burden of obligation which I owed to my mother—the obligation of doing or being something by which she should be enabled to sit on a cushion in the parlor. The rest of the burden of my obligation to her was at least more bearable. And by lifting this burden from myself, I kept it lifted, in my own mind, from my father—who was thus no longer, by any relapse into an earlier attitude, to be regarded as morally culpable in having failed to maintain her and us in respectable comfort. I had no right to expect my father to be anything but what he was.

Now about my father. I listened to his war-stories again for the first time since my very earliest childhood. One story which I now enjoyed immensely (and still do), was the one about how, as a staff orderly attached to the hospital at camp, he thought he was going to be left behind when his company was being shipped to the front. He appealed to the General, whom he found seated behind a mahogany desk in an office building. The General told Private Dell that he would have to obey orders, and Private Dell disgustedly spat tobacco juice on the General's carpet. The outraged General fined him a month's pay, and Private Dell, as he related the story, said: "You might as well make it a million dollars, General—I'll never pay it!" And he galloped his horse to the boat, and, while Company K cheered, rode on board just as the gangplank was lifted. And he didn't pay that fine, either, for, when he was reported dead, the fine was crossed from the rolls; "otherwise," he said, "I'd have sued the government!" Among his war memories was the remark of Colonel Clodd, whose orderly he was: "Banty, you'll either be shot for general insubordination, or promoted for extraordinary and use-less daring, and I don't care which!" Around Vicksburg (if his son remembers rightly) he had the chance to earn a commission by enlisting a company of Negroes; he enlisted them at the point of a carbine, very successfully; but then, while he awaited his commission, he was put in charge of them while they built a road for the artillery in the marshy ground along the river; he got tired of that, told the colonel he'd be damned if he'd be a nigger overseer, and was sent back to the company. After the war, released from the rebel prison, he swam half way across the Mississippi, but then got to thinking about the alligators, and climbed into the rowboat that was following along.

And this belligerent and adventurous father of mine was happier now, I think, when he was out of his home town, in a strange city, where he did not have to uphold his respectability as a formerly prosperous business man. He was in his sixties, now; he dyed his hair and moustache, and demanded a job—and sometimes got one.

The fact that he could not get work as a butcher never ceased to puzzle him, for he knew himself to be a better butcher than any of the young snips he saw behind the marble counters in Quincy. He did get a job as a bartender, but he had to hold it by stealth, for the fraternal insurance society to which he belonged virtuously forbade such employment, and he dared not lose the insurance upon which he had kept up his payments for so long. That job was ended by a dispute with the bartender. He was reduced for the most part to washing dishes at home.

He was less aldermanic now in appearance than he had once been —much less imposing than I remembered him as being in my child-hood. He had something of jauntiness in his manner, and carried his small plump body with the vestiges of a military pride. His tongue was sharp, and his eyes bright; his cheeks were jolly, his jaw stubborn. He was now amusingly militant in his economic ad-ventures; if he was an unwanted old man who always got fired, he managed to get some fun out of it, and not merely humiliation, as before.

One of his job-losing stories in Quincy, much enjoyed by our whole family at the supper table, was about the glucose factory. He had managed to get a job there nailing up boxes packed with cans of corn-syrup. He had held it a week and a half when the superintendent happened to stroll through the packing-room. The superintendent was young and English; it is possible that my father may have been misled by a Ha'va'd accent, but the superintendent was English in his story. The superintendent had stopped to watch my father nail up a box, and then had said: "You'll have to work faster than that, my man!" My father, in telling the story, reproduced the broad English *a* in 'faster,' and emphasized the preposterous phrase, 'my man'; and anyone who heard it understood why we had fought two wars with England. Of course my father had ignored him and had gone on working. And then the young fool actually kicked him!—or at least touched my father's kneeling body with the toe of his shoe. "Do you heah me?" he had asked.

My father, who had in his time defied a General, rose. In front of him was a container marked in large letters, 'Sulphuric Acid.' My father stooped, ladled out a dipperful of the liquid, and turned to the superintendent.

"Do you know what this is?" he demanded fiercely.

"Why, it's sulphuric acid!" said the superintendent, looking frightened.

"Then get down on your knees, you dog," said my father, "or I'll throw this right in your damned insolent face. And be quick about it!"

"And," my father would say, telling the story at the supper table, "he got down on his knees. And then—everybody in the room was looking, and didn't know what to make of it—then I put the dipper up to my mouth and drank it down. It was nothing but drinking water. And damn if that Englishman didn't just crawl out on his hands and knees."

He was a perfectly grand father for a boy to have.

CHAPTER VIII

WORK AND PLAY

1

MY OWN economic career was becoming as varied as my father's. I worked during the summer vacations; and in the course of four summer vacations in Quincy I was to have experience as a bundle boy for a department store, an elevator boy in the same, a helper in a harness factory, an assistant shipping clerk in the same, a solicitor of subscriptions for newspapers, a book-canvasser, and a worker in a candy factory. That figures out to about five weeks per job. And the lesson was to be plain enough in the end: I was the sort of boy who could always get a job, if there were jobs to give; a bright-looking boy. But, although a great success socially, that is conversationally and argumentatively and as a promoter of high spirits and good humor in my older fellow-workmen, it was to be gravely concluded by the responsible heads of one after another of Quincy's business concerns that I had no future in their particular lines; nor was I to feel that they were far wrong in thinking so.

2

At school there was not the same objection as in factories to my turning the institution into an open forum and vaudeville theatre, in which everybody could have a good time. I organized, with the approval of the principal, the Franklin School Literary and Athletic Society, and was its first president; since I was more interested in literature than in athletics, we had debates, read essays, and ran a school paper. Then I engineered the starting of a school library. And at the general graduation exercises in June I was one of two representing Franklin School on the platform. I delivered an oration upon 'The Influence of Oratory Upon History.'

Here I can see my most youthful self, the six-year-old would-be lawyer, orator and President, cropping out unexpectedly. It seems to me that my emotional reconciliation with my father had something to do with this, as also with the social energies newly liberated from a rather shy, seclusive and stoical nature. But the instrumentality of Socialist ideas was not merely accidental. Even behind the temporary recrudescence of a lost childhood ambition, there was a Socialist book—a book by Laurence Gronlund, on the French Revolution, with Danton as its hero. Strangely enough, it was always to be at the touch of revolutionary enthusiasms that the most self-confident and energetic of my selves waked to life.

The whole family came to hear me deliver my graduation oration. In honor of the occasion I had a new suit, with long trousers. My eldest brother, always the dandy of the family, anxious that I should not appear in public in my usual slovenly aspect, superintended my dressing for the occasion. The celluloid collar which I ordinarily wore, because it could be cleaned with one rub of a damp cloth, was discarded for a high linen one, and my eldest brother lent me a fancy stickpin for the occasion.

The oration itself was disappointing to me when I delivered it, though not, I think, to anyone else. After all, they were not expecting me to be a combination of Demosthenes and Danton; I was the only one who was trying the actualities of the performance by some supernal standard, born of a childhood ambition, the result of hearing the Fourth of July oratory in the Barry Square of 'Maj.' Klein, or was it Mr. Retallic? The audience expected only to see and hear a fourteen-year-old boy deliver a graduation oration, and they probably thought he did it very well. Some of the oration was printed in the paper, along with my photograph, and my mother fondly clipped these out and put them away with her treasures. My other brother kissed me and gave me a five-dollar gold piece and told me I would be a great credit to the family. Only I myself was dissatisfied; for in the midst of my oration, I had seen myself, standing stiffly on the platform, a thin pale figure in a stiff blue suit, uttering my oration toward the vaulted roof, and heard my voice, which was changing, break into shrillness. This vision was disillusioning.

3

At some time during those four summers, I wrote two plays. Both were upon more or less military subjects. The first was upon Benedict Arnold, showing how a gallant soldier becomes corrupted by domestic emotions—by his love for an extravagant Loyalist wife —into a traitor. The second play was about John Brown of Osawatomie, and showed him taking his sons with him into conspiracy, insurrection and death on behalf of a great cause. The plays, though in prose, were based upon the familiar model of the plays of Shakespeare, having short scenes which shifted from place to place. The ideas were gained whole from reading, and there was no attempt at originality in point of view or treatment; it was simply that the history-book statements, summarized above, about two careers, interested me so much that I had to state them at length in dramatic form, letting Benedict Arnold and John Brown speak for themselves. I did not know that the two plays had any connection with each other, or with my own life. I did not realize that until this moment, when I set down what the plays were about. Having done so, it seems to me pretty clear that they were rejections of the obligation of being a good ordinary citizen who got a job and did his duty by his family. What else could they mean? Benedict Arnold did his duty by his wife according to respectable standards, and lost his soldier's honor. John Brown failed in every respectable obligation as the father of a family: and *his soul goes marching on.*

4

Since I had no contact with any Socialist organization, my interest in that subject soon became merely a certain bent in reading, which exhausted all too soon, in its Nihilist phase, the resources of the Quincy public library. And Nihilism had, so far as I was aware, nothing to do with America, nothing to do with me or my future. I did not recall those Haymarket 'Anarchists' whom Governor Altgeld had pardoned, nor know a whit more about that whole side of American history than I had known at the age of six. The history of America which I studied in school judiciously concealed from me, as a future citizen, all knowledge of any disturbing truths of any kind. This history preserved President Grant as a noble image for

me to respect, while Governor Altgeld of Illinois was left discreetly
unmentioned, along with the Haymarket 'Anarchists'. Nihilism
was for me located in a kind of Slavic Forest of Arden, or Sherwood
Forest, where Robin Hood and Maid Marian robbed and killed the
rich and helped the poor. My father sat on one side of the dining-
room table of evenings and I sat on the other, and when I had
finished a Nihilist book he began it; the devil only knows what an
old Civil War veteran made of these books; perhaps bomb-throwing
was right and proper in Russia, if not in America.

The sense of youthful justice and the craving for high adventure
were well satisfied by these books; and in this Nihilist realm, too,
the Girl Question was very satisfactorily settled.

In the first place—and what a contrast to American life and fiction!
life for the Nihilists did not center in personal romance or achievement. It was a combination of student life and military life; the
goal of effort was freedom—freedom from superstition, from hypocrisy and from tyranny; students and soldiers, they studied, conspired, taught, killed, and endured their punishment, not as individuals but as comrades in a cause greater than themselves—and in this
work there were always men and women together. Together—again
how vast a difference from American life and fiction, where men and
women were only supposed to *play* together; and where, if a girl did
work in the company of men, it was only until some man fell in love
with her and married her and took her out of the factory or store or
office into his private home, where she henceforth had her own kind
of work to do as a 'home-maker'—whether that meant doing the
family cooking and washing, or sitting in the parlor in graceful idleness awaiting the homecoming of her husband so as to cheer his
tiredness with her smiling looks. In America, men worked, and
made the money by which women were supported in the home. In
this Nihilist realm, they studied, worked and fought side by side.

It did not occur to me to wonder where they got the money to
live on, any more than I would wonder where an army got the
money to live on; perhaps they lived on the country, like Sherman's
army, or Robin Hood's men; and if the poor gave them the money
or if they robbed the rich to get it, would have made no difference to
me. A young Stoic is temperamentally akin to soldiers and revolu-
tionaries, as also to early Christians and beggar-monks and scholar-

gypsies and wandering minstrels, according to his tastes, between all of whom he can choose, in finding imaginative objects of admiration and emulation.

In this Nihilist companionship of men and women, there was much gaiety as well as much seriousness. Here was an atmosphere of happy comradeship between girls and men, such as did not exist for me in any American reality I had ever known. A girl student revolutionary might share her room with a man comrade for the night for any reason of convenience or safety; her invitation was not sexual or romantic, and he was not a ridiculous figure like Joseph in the Bible story, if he did not make love with her. What a relief to a boy's imagination into which a thousand anecdotes, jokes and innuendoes had been poured, the purport of which was that women were not human beings but females merely!

While I was working at one of my vacation jobs, in a harness-factory, I came across a little red-covered pamphlet. It was a Socialist pamphlet. Of all possible introductions to Socialism, it was the strangest—but to me the most alluring one that could have been devised. It said not a word about economics. It told about Greek ideals of beauty in art and life; and it was illustrated with photographs of two Greek statues, the Venus of Melos and the Discus Thrower, which were interpreted in the text as examples of the gloriously alive and happy nature of Greek manhood and womanhood.

To desire to live like that—to want a world in which such life was possible—to be willing to put aside any institutions and ideas and beliefs that stood in the way of such glorious life—that was to be a Socialist, the pamphlet said.

5

There was a first year of high school, in which I doubtless studied my lessons and recited them. But I made no new friends there, and I seem in memory to have dispensed with old ones. There was a very good friend that I had made in Franklin school during my first year there, from whom I was now estranged. He had a ferocious and piratical temper, and I was used to it and did not mind; but one day as we sat playing some children's gambling game on the floor, and he swore fiercely at me, which was no new thing, I walked out of his house and never went back. The real reason, which never occurred to me until just now, referred back a few days to an exchange of Christmas presents, in which I had given him something which cost less than the present he gave me, and I felt that he thought me stingy; some old childish nerve of sensitiveness about my poverty had been touched, perhaps merely by a surprised glance or ironic tone in his thanks; or perhaps I made it all up out of a mind too sensitive upon the question of money and my lack of it; at any rate, I behaved as though I had found myself in a situation in which something more might be expected of me in the way of money-spending than I could manage; and so I gave up my only real friend, quietly. I did not know why I was doing it; I just walked out of the house when I was sworn at (while we were playing the game I had given him); and I couldn't go back. My ruthlessly self-protective stoicism made it possible for me to give up my closest and only real friendship without a word, without mentioning the matter to anybody, or behaving as though it were anything of importance. He was angry at my behavior, and when we went back to school he wouldn't speak to me; but I spoke to him. That was the time of the organization of the school library and a new election; and for some reason I manipulated the slate so that he got elected librarian and I assistant librarian. When he discovered these results, he said in chagrin, "Damn you, I thought I was running against you!" We managed the library efficiently together for the rest of the school year, but the friendship was never renewed. . . . My undue sensitiveness worked out into an odd pattern of behavior; but it seems less egregious than that of my father, who, as I later learned, having had his feelings hurt (over a question of money, too), would not speak to one of his brothers for all the rest of his life. That seemed to me sad and absurd when I heard about it. My father, however (who was going to sue the Government for that month's pay the General had fined him, if it hadn't been stricken from the rolls) wanted money; and I wanted, for much the same reason, a world without money.

6

By the principal of Franklin high school, Mr. Hinton, who remained my very kind friend, I was asked, the next year, to organize a club of boys of about my own age, fifteen, but all of whom were at work on jobs of some kind, as I remember. The club was to meet in a place which seems to me now like a social settlement house without residents—a place with a gymnasium, reading-rooms, rooms for checker-playing and chess, and rooms for club meetings: we called it 'The Orphans' Home' as a joke, until my friend the principal earnestly said we must not do so. The meetings of the club occupied one or perhaps two evenings a week, during my second year of high school. We had essays and debates, and it seems to me we must all have enjoyed ourselves heartily, for I remember the plaintive plea of my friend the Principal when he dropped in on us: '*Please* moderate your voices, boys!' When we could not think of any other way to interrupt somebody in a headlong argument, he would be adjured by us in the Principal's plaintive tones to please moderate his voice. It was a good, noisy club. Afterward we might adjourn to somebody's steps next to a store where there were a lot of apples inside near the window, and a small hole broken in the upper part of the window, so that with a long pointed stick and some acrobatic skill refreshments could be procured for all. I was pretty good at it.

After a devout admiration of Poe, I suddenly that year became a story-writer. A long and highly stylized tale, laid in Poe-land, was published in two parts in the high-school magazine. I had never been especially interested in grammar or punctuation before, for both my plays and my oration were thought of as the spoken word, and poetry was to me something to be recited aloud; this was my first definitely literary effort, intended to be read with the eyes, and the placing of commas was an important part of the silent rhythm of the sentences. And though I had only indifferently succeeded in learning or remembering the names of the parts of speech, the structural value of all these parts became a matter of intense interest to me when I built those long beautiful sentences.

Toward the end of the year I fell awkwardly and rather helplessly in love with the caretaker's young sister at the place where my club had its meetings. She was a sweet laughing dimpled girl of my own age, not one whom I could hope to interest by my ideas or anything except my humor and high spirits, and it was these that I felt myself losing as I came under the spell of her presence. She came down from upstairs and turned on the gaslights and lit them, and then turned them off again, with a long contraption on a pole; and one could assist her and talk with her about nothing in particular, if one came early or stayed late. I was not the only member of our club who did both.

At last—and this, I think, was a real triumph over my childish attitude about girls—I bought her some candy. I didn't know how to give it to her, and so I sort of left it on the piano for her to find. The other early-comers of our club found it first, the dogs; and from their remarks about whatever fool had brought it, I gathered that it wasn't the right kind of candy to bring to a girl. If I had paid more attention in Barry to learning the very elaborate code of respectable manners, I should have known what Hill's Manual in its pages on etiquette failed to teach me, that a gentleman should bring a lady chocolates. I had brought her gumdrops.

If the girl knew I loved her, it was only because I hung around her early and late. The other boys in the club knew it because I walked past the place whenever I went from any part of the town to any other part of the town. But I didn't say anything to her about it. What was there to say? And I was too much in awe of her to think of laying hands on her. There was for me still that invisible plate-glass window between me and all the beautiful things in the world. I still walked with my arms at my sides, and there didn't need to be for me any sign saying 'Do Not Touch the Flowers.' I was sufficiently intoxicated by her presence, and the touch of our glances was an overwhelming intimacy.

I look at the memory picture I have of her, and I see this girl of fifteen as a full-blown young woman. I look at the memory picture of myself and my friends of the club—I see some young men, a few incongruously dressed in short pants; even these are not what I see when I look at boys of thirteen and fourteen today, who are mere children to my paternal eye. No, we were young men, capable of being as upset over a pretty girl as any voter. When it comes to that, twenty-four is only fourteen in long pants. But I was fifteen, and a serious thinker; I knew no good could come of this, and I had better stay away. So I did. But at least I did bring her gumdrops.

CHAPTER IX

Ideas, Friendship and Love

1

QUINCY is not far from Nauvoo, where there had once been a Mormon colony; there must have been a group of Mormon sympathizers in Quincy, for in a bonfire of old magazines I saw and pulled out from the burning some Mormon 'literature'; this led me to read the Mormon bible, which I found very trashy indeed; and the Koran, which seemed only less so; and then such parts of a great set of the Sacred Books of the East in the public library as were at all readable by patient and imaginative effort; and if this put the final seal of my contempt upon the intellectual claims of all the Great Religions of the World, it increased enormously my admiration for the Old Testament as great literature. After all, I had not gone to Sunday School enough to have it spoiled for me.

There had been nothing militant about my Atheism. It had been first an intellectual recognition of the falsity of the claims made in behalf of the Bible as a true record. There was in my school histories the story of the Spanish Inquisition and other churchly tyrannies. It required only the slightest use of the mind to perceive that all religions were superstitious and tyrannical. Indeed, every Sunday School boy knew *that* about all other religions than the one in which he was being brought up. What hindered the operations of simple logic was 'belonging' to the family and social group which held by this particular religion; that 'belonging' exempted it from logic. But my family had been only vaguely Christian, not church-goers as far back as I could remember. Since it is usually women who keep up a family's church-going habits, my mother's non-attendance was presumably the result of not having clothes good enough to show off at church. Church was a place to demonstrate,

68

among other things, one's prosperity; and absence was the tribute her pride paid to that felicity. But I was always encouraged to go to Sunday School; membership in a church congregation has great potential value to a poor boy, in encouragement, advice, material help. In America it was not difficult for a 'bright' and well-behaved poor boy to get from more prosperous townsmen and women the encouragement, advice and help he may need in going to college; and the church is of great use in this respect. If my mental gifts had been demonstrated within the sympathetic range of a church congregation to which I belonged, if my youthful organizing, argumentative and high-spirited social talents had been let loose within the field of church activities, I would have been a valued possession of the congregation, and would have been sent to college and assisted into some respectable career; there is little doubt of that in my mind. It was that Christmas Eve which changed my destiny. Specific encouragement to achieve a respectable career was not given me, because no one knew that I supposed a respectable career impossible for me; a boy who worked with such intensity and success was presumed to have an aim and a goal, and he was respected rather than encouraged. Advice I never sought from anybody, at that or any other time; it simply never occurred to me to seek counsel from anybody, for if a father is not wise enough to guide a child aright, the belief in authoritative wisdom shrivels up and dies; wisdom there was in books for me, but I was the judge of whether it was wisdom; and so I made all my decisions by myself, announced them, and carried them out. As for help of a material sort in my career, in order to get that I should have had to accept a respectable point of view from which my father was a person of whom I would have to be ashamed. And it was at the first sight of the finger of respectability pointed at my father in mockery, the day I joined the church, that I cut myself off from it forever. It was an old grudge that I had against Respectabiliy—an old wound, dealt me by it when I was a child; and if it seemed to be healed over, and I complacently adjusted to the struggle for respectable success, it needed only for that scar to be painfully touched to make me suddenly feel myself an enemy alien in whatever respectable spot I stood. It was this emotional alienation which made possible that simple logical operation which led me to Atheism. It was revealed as not *my* church, but the church of the respectable; and as such I could put it where it logically belonged, in the same category which included the savage superstitions and rites that I had been studying in Anthropology.

Toward the end of my second year in high school, when I was all but sixteen years old, I found a fellow-Atheist and hence a friend. His name was Harry, and he was a year older than I, in the class above me in high school. One evening at the public library we discovered that we had a common enthusiasm for Haeckel's 'History of Creation'. It was so almost incredible to each of us that there could really be another in the Quincy high school who held heretical views, that our preliminary conversation was shy and cautious. But it was true that we were kindred spirits; and a friendship blazed into existence like a star in the void.

Harry was a tall, rather quiet youth, whose clothes—and his house when I subsequently visited him there one Sunday—showed him to belong to a well-to-do family. I had no means of making accurate distinctions between the rich and the merely comfortable middle-class, then or for a long time afterward. But I knew what workingmen's homes looked like, and, what with boiled cabbage and codfish and the clothes-boiler, smelled like; I knew how workingmen's children were dressed, and the best achievements of maternal neatness in cleaning and patching an old blue serge suit that was shiny on the seat and too short in the sleeves could be instantly distinguished from an expensive cheviot suit however baggy and carelessly worn. Homes where there was space, and an atmosphere of serenity and leisure, however old the furniture (for that in a workingman's home might be shiny new, just bought on the instalment plan from the department store), homes in which Mother, however motherly and homey, did not come in with a red face from the kitchen stove, but had a maid to do the cooking; homes in the back of which there wasn't a kitchen garden carefully cultivated to save the grocery bills, but a spacious lawn in front that the man of the house enjoyed cutting for exercise when he came home from his work, and flower-beds that the lady of the house had time to stoop over and watch and tend:—to me such places as these were all indistinguishably the homes of the upper class, of a kind of Aristocracy. My friend Harry had such a background, and I was uneasy in it, not knowing at table what some of the cutlery beside my plate was for, and conscious that the manners very carefully taught me by my mother were not quite the same as those which casually reigned in this dining-room and parlor.

It was requisite that I should invite my new friend in return to my house. I did not want to. I knew that a boy should not be ashamed of his home and family. But I did not wish to expose to the gaze of anyone of the 'upper-class' a home that was in such painful contrast to the one to which he had so casually invited me. And my mother, a bent old woman, worn out in household drudgeries, weak in strength and health and all but spirit; eager to serve, sitting at table next to the kitchen door on the very edge of a tilted chair, so that she could rise and wait on the family; without even the dignity of age, for a pair of crooked brass-rimmed spectacles which she habitually wore (saving her gold ones, like her best dress, for grand occasions which never came) gave her thin face a sadly comic aspect: how could anyone else see in her the eager girl, the indomitable spirit, the angel with the flaming sword, that a son knows in his mother?

I think I did invite my friend; I have a vague impression of much uneasy suffering on my part, and of his behaving with perfect courtesy and ease, as though my house were like anybody else's house and my family like anybody else's family. But I cannot bring back the scene; and we were in one another's houses no more, but met in the perfect equality of the public library.

From that rendezvous we would wander, walking and talking. Sometimes we would stroll through the Square, where on Saturday evenings the band played and a crowd gathered, full of pretty girls. Our companionship was not wholly intellectual; we tacitly recognized each other as being in the same plight, of youthful existence in a world full of pretty girls, whom we could not take on any of the terms upon which they were apparently to be had; he was a window-shopper, too. We were both virtuous youths, and could not be otherwise until we had forged some philosophy and found some circumstances which would content our consciences. Meanwhile, we could express intellectually pagan views, hate the church for the preposterous morality which it had inflicted upon the world, and enjoy, in the dusk of evening, while the band played in the Square, the bright eyes and silver giggles of passing girls, the *frou-*

frou of their skirts (they really did make that delectable swishy noise then, girl's skirts and petticoats), and the romantic aroma of cigar smoke in the air.

When we had endured enough of this poignant beauty (oh, God, those girls were so lovely!) we would go to Tracey's ice-cream parlor, and order champagne ice. We had agreed that it was probably made with an inferior brand of champagne; but there was a magic for us in the word 'champagne'. It was a symbol—mutually understood without explanation—of our pagan attitude toward life. The flavor that melted softly between tongue and teeth was the flavor of freedom and joy. The icy particles tingled with a splendid rebellion against the God in Whose name our youth was restrained from the joys that were rightfully ours. The band in the Square would play 'In the Good Old Summer Time'. Two girls might eye us in a friendly way from the next table, and one of them provocatively hum,

> 'Strolling down a shady lane
> With your Baby Mine,
> She holds your hand and you hold hers——'

But life was not so simple as that for us. And what the Church, despite all its efforts to frighten us with hell fire, could not do for us, in the way of taking our youthful minds off the subject of girls' eyes, lips and breasts, we did for ourselves, by hating the Church. We merged our wrongs in all those which humanity had suffered through the ages from that spiritual tyranny; and so we ceased to see the pretty girls who were bobbing their breasts at us, breasts the like of which we had never yet touched. Talking of Ingersoll, who had freed our minds from that ghostly tyranny, we left the ice-cream parlor, to wander along moonlit streets. Once we sat down on the steps of a church, driving away by our talkative presence a youth and girl who had been holding each other tightly in the shadow of the great doorway. We looked at the church, and saw it as if it were covered with gargoyles, summing up the hateful hypocrisy and terrorism of Christendom—the Inquisition, witchcraft, infant damnation. We remembered Luther at Wittenberg, his theses nailed to the door of the church. We thought of doing the same to this church, drawing up a statement of our Atheist rejection of all churchly creeds, and nailing it to this door. I took out pencil and paper and began to write it. But then it occurred to us that it ought to be signed by a committee; and we didn't know any other Atheists in Quincy. As we walked away in discouragement, another youth and girl slipped into the shadow of the great door.

2

Even if my friend was, by his Atheist views, a comrade, his family was highly respectable; and the touch of respectability, which set an old wound to aching, aroused me to further self-defense. Atheism was not enough. Frank Norris's novel 'The Octopus' stirred my mind. And that spring, down in a small park near my home, I heard a man make a Socialist speech to a small and indifferent crowd. Afterward I talked to him; he was a street-sweeper. I believe William Morris has a street-sweeper Socialist in 'News from Nowhere'; but this is not a literary echo, this Socialist street-sweeper in Quincy —he was real. And my long-slumbering Socialism woke up. Of course I was a Socialist! I went to a meeting of the Socialist local, a group of only seven or eight who met in the back room of, if I remember rightly, a jewelry store. And between that and the next meeting I converted my friend—conversion is a task which friendship makes extraordinarily easy—and brought him in triumph to the back room. We both joined the local and paid our dues; this was irregular, because eighteen was the lowest age for membership in the Party, and I was just barely sixteen now, and my friend but a year older. However, members we were. And now it seemed to me as if I had always been a Socialist. I remembered old Jimmy Houseweart, the Socialist farmer with the white beard, and the book he had lent my father; I remembered the Socialist book I had read on Danton and the French Revolution; I remembered Kennan, and Kropotkin, and the Nihilists. My life seemed now to have some meaning, to be a whole. Atheism was a natural part of Socialism. And I was an enemy of the established order, Church and State both, out to destroy it. I was one of the working-class. I need not pretend to belong to the respectable world, nor try to struggle for a place in it. I could accept my destiny as a workingman with a good grace, for it was by my class that this whole sham civilization would be destroyed, and a new one erected all over the world.

3

My way of getting a summer job was to walk into the first place where a sign said 'Boy Wanted'. This now took me into a candy store, and thence to the candy factory overhead. I was hired and told to report Monday. I did so, and was set to work turning the crank of a caramel cutter. This was at one end of a long table, on both sides of which were seated the girls who wrapped the caramels, with deft movements and incredible swiftness, in little squares of oiled paper. I felt very shy in the presence of six girls, and attended strictly to my duties, scarcely noticing their existence. My duties were somewhat varied, but cutting caramels was the chief of them. The girls got used to my silent presence, and talked and behaved as if I were not there. I was hardly there. This mechanical work could not hold my mind's attention, it could be done without thinking, and my mind was free to cultivate its own interests in fields far from this candy factory. Though I took pride in being a workingman, I could not take pride in the work I was doing—turning a crank, so that schoolgirls should spoil their teeth and ruin their digestion, and somebody put his profits on the transaction into the bank.

There was little work in candy-making in summer, and the force in the small factory was reduced to the foreman, who actually made all the candy, a fourteen-year-old 'starch-monkey' who was his helper, the six girls, and me. The foreman seldom came into our end of the factory; when he did, the buzz of talk stopped and the fingers flew faster; then he went away, and the place was our own again.

Among the six girls there was one younger, handsomer and more full of wit and character than all the rest. She was a girl of seventeen, with imperious dark eyes, beautiful smooth arms bare to the shoulder, and a graceful body. There was a variety of charm in her lively manner—sometimes girlish and sometimes boyish, sometimes kittenish and sometimes maternal, and always delightful. I had come out of my protective trance and now took part in the girls' talk and arguments. I rather ruthlessly won all the arguments. When they found that I was human after all, they liked me. And I was entranced with Margaret.

I had persisted in wearing into the hottest days of July the 'sleeve-protectors' my mother had made for me. Ridicule left me unmoved. Bare-armed Margaret said it made her hot just to look at those 'sleeve-protectors'. In the noon hour after one of those jesting discussions, I felt her hand on my arm, and turned in perturbation to face her. I was not used to a girl's touch, or even to such dazzling nearness. "Stand still," she said, "I'm going to fix you up." I submitted, and she took off the 'sleeve-protectors' and rolled up my sleeves. Her head was close to mine, and her hair dizzied me. When she had finished, she smiled into my eyes. And my knees suddenly became weak. I walked away unsteadily, wondering what was the matter with me. At first I thought it was perhaps the heat. Then I wondered if this strange physical weakness could have anything to do with love.

That afternoon, as sometimes happened, the girls sang. Margaret had a clear, sweet voice. When the song ended, our eyes met, and clung. I forgot everything else. How long it lasted, I did not know. But one of the other girls suddenly laughed and cried out: "See them! See them!"

The laughter and mockery jostled between us, and we looked down. "Never mind," said the fat girl cheerfully, "we all knew it anyway!"

To conceal the trembling of my body, I walked out of the room. When I came back the foreman was there and everybody was silent. He went, and still nobody spoke. I thought I could tell that Margaret had been crying.

One of the girls looked up and said, "We need some more boxes." Margaret rose. "I'll get them," she said. "Floyd, you come along with me. Let's give them a chance to talk about us." She drew my arm into hers. Together we went upstairs to the stock-room, a dark emptyish place under the rafters. Margaret knocked the dust from a packing-case with her apron and sat down, leaving room for me beside her. I hesitated, then sat down silently. "Floyd," she said softly, "we mustn't mind what they say." I made no attempt to reply. She smiled at me. "We can't help it that we're such sillies, can we?" "No," I replied helplessly. We groped for each other's hands. There was vast comfort in the touch. After a while she rose, drew her hands softly away, and whispered, "Now let's get the boxes." I took them from the shelf, and we proceeded soberly downstairs. Laughing glances met us, but our haughty demeanor did not encourage anyone to say anything aloud.

It takes time before thought is possible about something like this. It reverberated through my mind; I didn't think.

I was seeing my friend of evenings. I had told him something about 'the girl at the factory'. Perhaps he didn't think there could be in a factory a girl like the one I described; he seemed to be un-sympathetic. But I didn't tell him about this last event. We talked of Ingersoll's birthday, which would be tomorrow, August the eleventh. In honor of the day, we were each going to wear a red carnation. If anybody asked us about the carnations, we were going to tell why we were wearing them. It was a form of propaganda as well as of piety.

There was a florist's shop on the way to the factory, just opening up as I went to work. I bought a red carnation and put it into my buttonhole. In the factory, Margaret looked at me quizzically. "Why the posey?" she asked. "I'm celebrating," I said. "Celebrating what? The fact that we're all likely to be laid off this week?" "Somebody's birthday," I said. "Whose?" she asked. "Guess," I said.

She puckered her brows, then laughed, clapped her hands, and cried: "Why, Bob Ingersoll's, of course! I had forgotten! But it *is* today, isn't it?"

It was a miraculous world in which such things could happen.

But she said: "Why, I was brought up on Bob Ingersoll. My father is a Socialist and freethinker." "And you never told me?" "Why should I tell you? You never asked me. But I always knew you were a Socialist, too, by the way you argued."

Visions opened before me of a Socialist girl friend. We would go to the local together.

The next day the impending lay-off was confirmed by the starch-monkey. "I don't care," he said to me. "I'm coming back in the fall. I've taken an interest in things, and the foreman likes me. I'm going to be a candy-maker. You could get to be one, too, if you had any sense. But you're too much interested in girls." He went on to give me his views of girls, and how to keep them off one's mind. Not being in complete possession of all my faculties, I replied indignantly, and was so indiscreet as to give away the fact that I was quite inexperienced in sexual exploits. At first he was incredulous, then scornful. "Why, even my little brother—" he said, and measured off the height of the small boy who was already initiated into these manly experiences.

But that week I learned at home that we were going to move to Davenport just before school opened. This had been in prospect, but I hadn't thought about it. I wouldn't be able to keep up this wonderful friendship with Margaret. Just when begun, it was to end! I was bewildered and sad. It does not seem to have occurred to me to meet Margaret outside, or to go to see her at her house. I enjoyed each moment of her presence, but was incapable of making any claim upon more of it than came to me without any effort.

Saturday was the last day at the factory—and the last day we would all be together. The girls would scatter to other factories. And this sense of finality made the day a special one for all of us. We came early, and the girls all looked their prettiest, with fresh dresses and ribbons in their hair. It reminded me somehow of Graduation Day at school.

The foreman came in, paused at the table, and said, "We're going to have to lay you off for the season. You can quit at noon."

We made cocoanut cakes, toasted them in a gas-oven, and packed them. Margaret, looking like a charming housewife in her apron, fed the brownest of the cakes to me. It was a domestic scene, and as we stood there at the stove together, I was enjoying in fantasy the thought that we were married; I thought she was, too.

Finished with the cakes, we went back to caramels, and sang all the songs we knew. The last caramel was wrapped on the stroke of noon. The girls put on their things, wrapped their factory clothes in bundles, and bade each other good-bye. Margaret and I lingered a moment after the others. We looked shyly at each other. She held out her hand. I took it. "Good-bye, Floyd," she said. "Good-bye, Margaret." I wanted to kiss her, but didn't know how. In another moment she was gone.

I got a job soliciting newspaper subscriptions during our remaining two or three weeks in Quincy. I knew where Margaret lived —whether she told me, or whether I looked it up in the directory, I do not know—and I walked past her house several times, but did not go to her door until the morning just before we sailed on the steamboat for Davenport.

A kindly-looking woman opened the door, her mother, no doubt. I asked for Margaret. "She isn't in." "Oh!" I backed away, and the door closed. At the gate I turned and looked back at the house. For a fleeting instant I saw, or thought I saw, Margaret's face at the window—two black, startled eyes gazing at me. I went on home, joined the family, and we boarded the steamer Bald Eagle.

CHAPTER X

Being a Poet

1

THE PERIOD of adolescence is so sentient a time and yet so helpless a one that it would not be strange if all boys and girls became poets then. To be grown up in capacity to wish, to love, to suffer, and yet a child in power to deal with the world, is more than the heart can bear, unless there is some magic by which our wishes can be fulfilled—if not in actualty, then in some seeming, true to the heart, assuaging grief and pain. As the steamer Bald Eagle carried me away from Margaret, I became a poet. I created her image in magic words. *Those wayward locks that ripple down*—these words gave me her hair. Her eyes, her lips—all I dared possess of her in a lover's dream, was mine, made mine by words. Not ordinary words in any ordinary sentences such as are used to convey practical information— but magical words, arranged in a powerful spell. If one speaks the right words in the right order, one can have power over Nature—that is Magic. But the words must be the only words possible, and they must be chanted. So the locks of time and space are broken, far becomes near, the heart's impossible wish is granted; and if it is only an illusion, at least the illusion comforts the sick heart. As a lover in absence holds tenderly a piece of pasteboard, looks at it as if it were truly his beloved, although it is only a picture of her—so the lover become poet repeats over and over again the rhythmic incantation which has might to grant him the wish to see her, to hold her in his arms.

It is only, perhaps, for him that these words have such magical power—to some other they may be only silly rhyming lines. If he is so mighty a magician that he can make other people's wishes come true for them, then there is, to be sure, a 'career' for him in the

making of incantations, for which he will be less adequately rewarded than if he made caramels, or even merely turned a wheel
and cut them. I, as a useful worker in a civilization which set a
proper value upon caramels, had been making more money in that
factory than most of the world's poets had made by their poetry, than
any poet was likely to make by his poetry; certainly I did far better
financially by caramel-cutting than Wordsworth ever did by poetry-
making—he didn't make enough to pay for his shoe-strings, he said,
while I paid for my summer's keep. By caramel-cutting or some
such really useful labor a youth can hope to be at least self-support-
ing; but Wordsworth, and how many other poets, not born to proper-
tied security, lived on the bounty of others all their grown-up lives.
It is a rash thing for a boy or girl to write poetry, for sooner or later
the question must arise: 'is this a gift of so much value to youths and
girls still unborn and to be born in generation after generation that
I must cherish and cultivate it in despite of the kicks and jeers which
will be the only likely payment now from a world which prefers
caramels?' A terrible question for a boy or girl to have to answer.
But it did not trouble the boy on the Bald Eagle; he was making
magic for his heart's comfort. The steamer rounded the bend, the
wind took his hat playfully and flung it into the river; he looked up,
bewildered—the spell was broken, he and Margaret were not in some
Elysium together, but she was back there, and he was here, making
his entrance hatless into Davenport.

2

We lived in one side of a double house on West Sixth street. Davenport was one of three towns which altogether had a population of
about a hundred thousand people. Across the river, with Rock Island and its Government Arsenal in between, was the city of Rock
Island, and beside it Moline with its great plow-factories. One of
my brothers had a harnessmaker's job at the Arsenal; my other
brother and sister less distinguished jobs—but still, jobs; and my
father had hopes.

Davenport had a large German population, some of it with the
traditions of the exiles of '49; and a considerable Jewish population;
both of these facts were to be of some importance as affecting my
happiness. The town had the bravado of an old Mississippi river-

port, and the liberal 'cosmopolitan' atmosphere of a place that is in touch with European influences. It had its nose not too closely pressed against the grindstone of 'practical' fact. It had an intelligentsia, who knew books and ideas. It had even some live authors, a famous one, and some who might one day be famous. Supposing, as a young person is prone to do, that all really famous people have been dead a long time, I naturally took for granted that 'Octave Thanet' was so, and was greatly astonished and rather incredulous when told she was actually alive. However, at that time the only American authors who existed for me were Frank Norris and Mark Twain; and Frank Norris had died last year, while Mark Twain was only a boyhood memory. Fiction did not interest me much.

But I retained from Frank Norris's 'Octopus' a picture of a girl that was to haunt me always—a sturdy, earth-strong girl, with hair as yellow as the ripe wheat, serene, calm-browed, happy-hearted. I was in love with her image in my mind.

And now I was reading poetry. Back in Quincy a footnote in Prescott's 'Conquest of Peru' had sent me to Southey's 'Thalaba'; I had read all of Southey, and admired it all. But Byron now swept Southey out of existence. Keats came next, a never-to-be-forgotten delight. I read, in a five-and-ten-cent store, standing on one foot and then the other, the 'Rubaiyat', and carried home in dazed wonder that casket of enchantments. Browning's poems became mine at the same price; my library was growing. I was reading English and some other poetry at the rate of one great poet a week; I read and knew vastly by heart Wordsworth, Shelley, Walt Whitman, Kipling, Wilde, the Rossettis, Tennyson, Wilfred Scawen Blunt, Herrick, Milton, Heine, Swinburne, John Donne, Marvell, Drayton, Shakespeare's Sonnets; some Persian and Chinese poetry of which I made my own rhymed versions; among living Americans I was enthusiastic about Bliss Carman and William Vaughn Moody; then came a magnificent discovery that for a long time no one in Davenport would share—A. E. Housman's 'Shropshire Lad', bought with a dollar that was being saved to buy shoes with; and with an appetite geared to that pitch, the world has seemed, ever since, in this respect, a poor barren starveling place, which cannot produce more than two or three great poets in a century.

In the intervals of reading poetry, I made poetry. I didn't especially intend to make it, and I certainly never knew what it was going to be about in advance. I could feel a poem coming on; and I was able to sympathize with the behavior of a cat who feels that she is going to have kittens and searches restlessly about for a good place to have them. I knew just how the cat felt; and I probably had the same glazed look in my eye as I wandered off into the night to have a poem. Night and solitude were best; interruption in the process was frightfully painful. So, late at night, I walked across the bridge that crossed from Davenport to the Government Island. Policemen would pass at intervals, swinging their clubs, pairs of late lovers would emerge slowly from the darkness into the glare of an arc-light. I went past them, walking rapidly, head bent down. Where the bridge came to an end, a stone walk began that skirted the Island toward Moline, where at intervals the darkness was suddenly burst open by the crimson flare of a blasting furnace. I paused at the parapet, looking at the lights reflected in the river. Lines would begin to emerge entire from my mind. I would say them over, holding on to them with my memory, listening to the rhythm. *I dare not look into your eyes—For fear I should see there—The naked soul behind the guise—That earth-born spirits wear.* I turned homeward. *Lest gazing on immortal love—I should go mad, like him—Who saw Her bathing in a grove—The Huntress white and slim.* I whispered the lines over and over, walking faster, overtaking the policeman. The late lovers stepped from my path impatiently. Behind me the furnace flares lighted the sky at lurid intervals. My solitary tramp sounded noisily on the bridge. I emerged from the fantastic shadowy tangle of girders upon the streets of Davenport. Bathed in an enchantment of beauty, I walked swiftly along the homeward streets, whispering aloud the words that eased my heart.

At home, the light was burning. I hoped that my mother had had sense enough to go to bed. But no, there she was, coming downstairs wrapped in her old brown shawl, to make sure that her boy was safe. "Mother, you haven't been waiting up for me?" "No, I just wasn't sleepy." While she hovered about, I would get the poem written down on paper. And then, awakened from my trance, I looked at it, and wondered: 'But what the devil is this poem about?' My mother, lingering, asked, "Have you written something new?" "Oh, just a poem." Its literal meaning was not obscure, but to whom was it addressed? Not to Margaret. Not to any girl I knew. Yet it had meant something to me. "Will you read it to me?" Mothers are like that. They want to be proud of their sons; they want to believe in them; and so—if it gives her any satisfaction—

> I dare not look into your eyes,
> For fear I should see there
> The naked soul, behind the guise
> That earth-born spirits wear.
>
> Lest, gazing on immortal love,
> I should go mad, like him
> Who found Her bathing in a grove,
> The Huntress white and slim.

"That's all. It's a short poem. The Huntress is Diana, of course." "I think it's very pretty," my mother replied. She looked about, saw nothing to do, and went back up the stairs. And I, looking at the lines, reflected: 'It doesn't make any difference what a poem is about, anyway, if it sounds all right.'

3

I liked Davenport. It was, or so it seemed to me, different from its sister towns across the river, Rock Island and Moline. Rock Island was merely commonplace and uninteresting. Moline seemed like a nightmare—the inconceivably hideous product of unrestricted commercial enterprise; its center was occupied by the vast, bare, smoke-begrimed structures of the greatest plow-factory on earth; a little fringe of desultory shops, insulted and apparently pushed aside by incessantly switching trains of freight-cars, gave way to a drab and monotonous area of cheap and hastily-constructed workingmen's dwellings, each house exactly like the next, street after street and mile after mile—while afar, set almost inaccessibly upon the hills like the castles of robber barons, could be discerned the houses of Moline's leisure class. The town of Davenport was like neither of these towns. It had a kindlier aspect. Its long tree-shaded streets, its great parks, its public buildings, even its shops and homes, seemed to have a kind of dignity and serenity, as though it were understood that in this town life was meant to be enjoyed.

I had heard that there were many Socialists in Davenport, and that

they had their meetings in Turner Hall. So, one afternoon, not long
after we came to town, I had tried to find them. I went to Turner
Hall in quest of information. It was an imposing building, with
four entrances, one of them the lobby of the German Theatre. The
man in the box-office knew the price of seats for the German play to
be given there that evening, but he didn't know anything about where
the Socialists met. So I tried the next entrance, and found myself
suddenly in a gymnasium, where a bloomered class of young frauleins
were at that moment engaged in turning handsprings. The director
plainly regarded me as a rash intruder, and refused to give me any
information about anything. So I backed out, apologizing. The
third entrance revealed a flight of steps. I went up. At the first
landing I came upon someone who seemed to be the janitor; but he
did not understand English very well, so I explored for myself.
There were many lodge-halls at the top of the first flight of stairs,
with no sign to indicate that any of them was a Socialist meeting-
place. I went on from door to door, entering and looking about. I
did not know exactly what I was looking for—perhaps a red banner;
but I found nothing distinctively Socialist in any of the little rooms.
Nevertheless, I continued to look, and having exhausted the possibilities of that floor, I went on to the next. On the top floor, I broke
in upon an assembly of German matrons. They seemed angry and
suspicious, and I went downstairs in great embarrassment. But I
had not given up. There was still another entrance. It opened upon
a saloon. The busy bartender admitted that he had heard of the
Socialists, and in a reflective interval in the serving of drinks he
seemed to remember that they met on Fridays—in just which hall
he couldn't say.

So on the next Friday evening I stood again in front of the building. Flocks of people came and went, in and out. There was something discouragingly commonplace about these people, something
which made it difficult for me to imagine them as Socialists. But I
followed some of them up the winding stairway, and watched them
enter one or another of the little halls. I thought of knocking and
inquiring at each doorway in turn. The number of doors, however
large, was still finite, and in time I should come to the right one.
But the appearance of the people that I saw within the rooms discouraged me. I could not face their stolid, unimaginative stares forty

times. I went slowly downstairs, and again took up my position by the door. I was too hopeless now to ask anyone for information; I waited, as if I were expecting someone to come up and hail me. Perhaps my inward feeling was that the Socialists should recognize me as one of them. But no one came up and greeted me.

At last I went home. But the next Friday evening I went again, this time without much confidence, and hung about the doorway, till the crowd thinned and ceased and the street was deserted.

The next summer, having in the meantime not succeeded in discovering any Socialists in Davenport, I saw in the paper a notice of a Socialist lecture to be given at a church a few blocks from my home, and I went there. It was a Negro church. The congregation was there, and the pastor, and ice-cream and cake were in readiness for a sociable aftermath. But Michael Kennedy, the Socialist candidate for something, did not show up to deliver his lecture. Everybody waited and waited. I had taken my place in one of the front pews. I was the only white person there. Finally the pastor came to me and asked me if I were a Socialist. "Why, yes," I said. "It doesn't look as if Mr. Kennedy was going to get here," said the pastor; "and I was wondering if you would give us a little speech on Socialism." "Well, all right," I said. "Will you just tell me your name, sir, and I'll introduce you." So I went up into the pulpit, and delivered a lecture upon the materialist conception of history, the class-struggle, and the program of Socialism. My lecture was very enthusiastically applauded, and afterward I joined the congregation in eating ice-cream and cake.

One evening, at the public library, I saw a man I would have liked to know. He was talking to somebody, and he had a beautiful voice, and a keenly intelligent mind; he was, though indefinitely older than I, young-looking, with a slender figure, and a sensitive, dark, foreign-looking face. I thought of him as a poet, someone it would be delightful to know. I stared at him intently, and then became embarrassed. I went out of the library, and paused on the steps. The man came out, smiled at me in which seemed a faintly satiric way, sniffed eagerly at the evening breeze, and spoke to me. He said: "What a beautiful night!" And I, who had been wishing I could talk to this man, said nothing whatever in reply. I wanted his friendship too much to believe that it was possible for me to have it. The man added, with a gesture: "See—the moon!" And as if that gesture, or the words, or the singularly beautiful tune of the man's voice, had called it into being, I became aware of the great white moon over the roofs—aware too of the breeze with its odors of cool dampness—aware of the poignant wonder of night. I was ashamed at the thought that I might have revealed this rush of feeling to what might be hostile eyes. The man made a little signal of farewell, and started to walk away. Then I was sorry I hadn't talked to him. I wanted to rush after him; but I couldn't. And upon some evening afterward, a poem came into my mind:

> As each one passed I scanned his face,
> And each, methought, scanned mine;
> Each looked on each a little space,
> Then passed, and made no sign.
>
> And every cold glance answered Nay!
> Would no one understand?
> None brush the cobweb bars away,
> Stand forth and clasp my hand?
>
> But as into each face I peered,
> My glance was cold as theirs,
> That they whose scornful laugh I feared
> Might pass me unawares.

4

As a poet, I was happy with a strange happiness that was made out of pain. Night, the moon, the shadows of the trees, the wind with its strange scents, all the beauty that tortured me, became strangely comforting when they turned into words in my mind. Through streets that were not the streets I knew by day, down light-and-shadow-enchanted ways, I wandered by night, making my poems. I entered for a long golden hour an enchanted land where there was neither desire nor fear, only the solace of magic words. I grew indifferent to the outer world. It seemed less real to me than this realm of dreams into which I was transported in an instant.

And I was not lonely in that realm, for I was companioned by a shadow, soft and vague—a mere hint or whisper, so unobtrusive it was, of a being almost without sex as it was almost without existence, yet faintly breathing the perfume of girlhood—a delicate and perfect comradeship.

> Midway of that enchanted ground
> There is a lazy well-sweep found,
> And dreaming waters, at whose brink
> On summer noons we stop to drink.
> Out underneath the listless boughs,
> Down in the grass the shadows drowse,
> And all the indolent slow hours,
> No breezes come to wake the flowers,
> Or cast a ripple in the lake,
> To writhe, a ghostly water-snake.
> And there for you and me is peace,
> Where passions fade, ambitions cease;
> For all the loves and hates that toss
> The helpless soul, come out across
> The far-off purple hills that lie
> Aswoon beneath that sapphire sky.

But meanwhile, there was the world of reality that I had to live in. I felt that I ought to be at work earning money to help the family. My destiny was to be a factory hand. I had no illusions of being able to rise from the ranks. I would remain a factory-hand, and an ill-paid one. I saw myself falling in love with some girl at a factory; getting married some day, having children, and living in a little house that was like all the others up and down the block. Some workingmen had gardens in their back yards; my brother Harry had a nice little garden within the narrow confines of our back yard here. If I had a garden, it would be the worst garden on the block where I lived. It would be the worst, because I would be thinking about poetry, instead of about potatoes. And if I thought about poetry at my factory job, I would get fired. It wasn't a cheerful prospect.

I was walking through the streets as I thought of these things one day, and I stopped in front of a window to look at the crimson and gold wings of a dead butterfly pinned to a card, with the words, 'We can't all be butterflies'. No, I reflected, not even butterflies can! For those wings, which people thought merely pretty, were part of the serious business of life to that butterfly. He must wing his way to the nectar-cup for his dinner, and seek his mate with them; and when that is finished, he cannot drink any more nectar, for his thorax contracts (or so I had read). Life is through with him, and he dies.

> They know thee not, who deem thy hues
> The splendid appanage of pride,
> As on some idle pleasure-cruise
> Thou seemest royally to guide
> With summer's soft and languorous tide
> Down crimson-bannered avenues. . . .

I walked away, framing the words into rhythmic sequence.

> Yet is that fancy dear to me!
> It is not good to look around
> And see no single creature free
> From these chains wherewith I am bound.
> I still believe that thou hast found
> Release from laws men think to be
> Relentless, from the dreary round
> Of . . .

Of what? The phrase eluded me. I looked at the workingmen's houses about me, thinking of the life lived within them. That was the fate of others, why should it not be my fate, too? Why should I ask something better—something like the fancied life of the butterfly? Yet I did. . . .

> And if in bitterness and scorn
> I walk the ways my fathers trod,
> Thou, flashing through the perfumed morn,
> Shalt be my plea to God!

Someone talked to me about going to business college. I thought it over, and decided that I would rather end in the poorhouse than go to business college and work in an office.

5

At school, I had gained the reputation of being 'a shark' at my studies. Always I had been clumsy in mathematics; but one day my algebra teacher made a mistake while demonstrating a problem on the blackboard; and in my eagerness to set her right, I went up to her, took the chalk from her fingers, and worked out the problem swiftly and correctly; and after that, I had no excuse for thinking myself stupid about algebra. My Socialist reading gave me a clue to history which made me remember and understand my history lessons. I did not think of myself as a good student, and I am not sure that I was; but that was what I was supposed to be. I did not study much, and spent most of my study hours in school revising my poems.

One day the teacher in charge of the study-hour, Mr. Myers, my history teacher, caught my eye and beckoned me to his desk. At the same time he made a gesture which indicated that I was to bring along what I was writing. A long-forgotten memory of that cruel and stupid principal at Barry flashed into my mind, and for a moment I was overcome with sick, childish fear. But my history teacher was a genial and friendly soul. "A poem?" he asked. "Yes, sir," I said. "May I see it?" I handed it over. "Very good, I should say," my teacher remarked, after reading it; and he asked: "May I keep it till tomorrow?" He added that he wanted to show it to the English teacher. I went back to my seat wondering.

The next day I found out. The history teacher asked me to stay a moment after the class period, and explained to me that the school was sending a volume, representative of the school work, to the World's Fair at St. Louis. He had heard that I wrote poetry. He had shown my poem to the English teacher, who was his room-mate, and they had both thought that it would be an excellent idea if I would write a poem for the volume. Of course, the poem ought if possible to have some relation to the work of the school; and he himself thought it would be fine if I would write a historical poem.

I went away from that interview in a most agreeably fluttered state. I had never dreamed of any of my poems being important to anyone besides myself; not important, exactly, but useful—think of that!— and a credit to the school. As for a historical poem, I had never thought of writing such a thing; but if my history teacher thought I could, why, he must not be disappointed.

That afternoon I hurried to the library and read hastily and excitedly a volume on the Moors in Spain. That, I had decided, was to be the subject of my historical poem. Then, with my head full of pictures of the marble courts that were to be splashed with blood, the flower-beds that were to be trampled, the busy looms that were to be smashed to bits by savage Christian hatred, the scrolls that were to be flung into bonfires, all the pagan beauty and joy and wisdom that were to be destroyed, I composed, as I walked the streets, a bitterly ironical 'Ballad of the Moors' Expulsion.' It was, indeed, beneath all its historical guise, a poem about myself—though I was unaware of it—a poem about my having to go to work in a factory— the triumph of reality over my dreams. The paradise destroyed by Christian hate was my own paradise of poetry.

> Where fountains toss their flashing spray,
> And roses glow serene,
> Where lute and viol charm the day,
> And minstrels chant unseen,
> Vultures shall quarrel o'er their prey—
> Ravens and beasts unclean.

I enjoyed the praise of my history teacher, and I had a private view of the World's Fair Book, an imposing volume in green tooled leather, containing an array of maps, drawings of flowers and birds, and pages of Greek, among all of which my own neatly lettered poem still seemed to have an air of distinction of its own.

6

Miss Freeman, the librarian of the public library, I had seen from afar—as she came and went about the library with a light step, disappearing all too quickly into that secluded and sacred region, her private office. I knew her name and her official position; but to me she was not so much the librarian as the spirit, half familiar and half divine, which haunted this place of books. She might have been evoked by my imagination, even as were the shining spirits of wood and stream in an earlier day. She had, like these books of which she was the guardian, a spirit above the rush and stress of common life. Something in her light step, her serene glance, personified for me the spirit of these literary treasures; she was their spirit, made visible in radiant cool flesh. More lately I had noted her quick smile, and heard her impetuous soft speech. But I had never thought of her as quite belonging to the world of reality. And now suddenly she appeared to me among the bookstacks, holding out her hand, saying, "You are Floyd Dell, aren't you? I am Marilla Freeman."

Marilla Freeman was an extraordinarily beautiful young woman, tall and slender, wide-browed, with soft dark hair, grey-blue eyes, a tender whimsical mouth, and a lovely voice—an idealist, and also a practical person, who immediately took charge of my destinies. I fell in love with her deeply, and became from the first moment of our friendship involved in a battle of wills with her—a battle not mitigated by the great affection we had for one another. From her point of view, the situation was a simple one: here was a young poet, who, besides encouragement, needed to learn conscious control of his art; and who needed friends among those who were interested in writers and writing. This very wise program was rebelled against by me, violently protested at every point, but on every point yielded to and carried out. The fact was that for the first time I had met a person capable of bossing me; and though the bossing was done with angelic sweetness and patience, it was implacable. I resented it bitterly that a goddess should stoop to these practical matters. I wished to remain in the enchanted circle of her affection; I wanted her to be a kind of mother-goddess. And she, with all the powers thus given her, was very gently and very firmly and very wisely pushing me out into the world of reality.

I had already accepted the fact that I must live in the world of reality; but I always thought of that as earning a living in a factory. Writing was a part of an ideal world—it had nothing to do with making a living. My intention was to get a factory job and then write for my own pleasure. But, as this program of mine was never stated, it could not be discussed. Nor was Marilla's program ever stated—she took it for granted that a writer must want to make a living by his writing; it was unnecessary, she thought, to argue about that—it was only necessary to suggest ways and means. We were at cross-purposes. And the cross-purposes were further complicated by the fact that the only kind of writing I was doing was poetry—which I did not ever for a moment believe I could make a living with, and which I would rather be allowed to practise without any thought of ever selling it. This attitude appealed to Marilla as an idealist, but it seemed to imply an unworldly dedication of myself to poetry as an art—the rôle of 'genius', in fact, which I definitely rejected. I obeyed her commands—she did not know they were commands, since they were only friendly suggestions, offers and questions; but I obeyed these commands chiefly because they were difficult and painful, and because I had adopted as a maxim for my guidance a sentence from

Emerson to the effect that whatever one was afraid to do was the thing for him to do.

As to learning conscious control of my art, that was something against which I had at first all the indignant and mournful rebellion of the amateur who produces works of art by a mysterious unconscious process which he does not understand. But in an elderly and sweet poet-journalist, Charles Eugene Banks,—tall, Windsor-tied, with hair that dripped over his eyes,—I found a critical intelligence which I could respect, and, with his permission, exploited it ruthlessly; he taught me patiently how to criticise my own work, and how to revise it—a lesson of more use to me later in prose than then in poetry, and one for which I came to be even more grateful than I had been at the time.

As for learning how to make a living by my art, which I did not believe possible, my experience in peddling poems to magazines only confirmed me in my disbelief, in spite of the fact that some of the poems did presently sell to several of the great literary magazines. What is usually taken by young poets as a sign of arrival and a prognosis of success was by me regarded as a conclusive proof of the uselessness of such efforts. The mills of the magazines ground too slowly to make me think otherwise. A poem written at eighteen did not sell until I was nineteen, if I remember the dates rightly, and was not printed until I was twenty-one. Nor did I believe that an editor's judgment counted for anything in the world. I read the poetry printed in the great American magazines, and the prospect of admission to that gallery did not flutter my heart. But, since that was a practical test—a test of something, of my enterprise, if not of my poetic worth—I was willing to meet it. Magazine publication would at least expose my poems to the eyes of strangers, a healthy thing for poems; it would be nice to see my name in print again; and it would please my mother.

Finally, as for extending my acquaintance among people interested in writers and writing, I resented and resisted that, too, even while I conscientiously submitted myself to the process, and even when I found the results, as I did, gratifying. It was in the 'upperclass' world that such acquaintance must be extended, a world into which I could go only with reluctance, and whose benefits I could receive only with some suspicion. It was very hard for me to receive kindnesses. But Davenport seemed determined to be kind to me—all the more so when, the next fall, it appeared that I was working in a factory instead of taking my last year in high school.

Since such a decision is ordinarily not made except under extreme pressure of necessity, it would ordinarily be presumed, if my family were at all interested in my future, that the situation had been very seriously talked over in a family council. Nothing of the kind had occurred. I had made up my mind, and then had stopped thinking about it; I had not said anything to my mother, because I did not want her to feel bad about it in prospect; I had not said anything to anybody else, because I did not wish to be argued with about it. Late in August, I announced at home that I was going to keep on working in the factory; and I announced it with such a casual decisiveness that nobody said anything, except my mother, who said softly, "I'm sorry."

The poet part of me was sorry, too; I had made, by my Socialist philosophy, self-respecting terms upon which I could become a workingman. But the poet part of me never accepted that point of view, nor regarded having to go to work in a factory as anything but a frightful doom and a loathsome degradation. It was thus necessary for me to cut my life in two in order to be both a poet and a workingman. But it was hard to confine the poet in me to proper evening hours; sometimes poetry-making intruded its trance-like state into the day's work, with humiliating results. The poet needed to be curbed; and the foreman, manager, and all the stockholders of the factory couldn't do it; the only one who could curb the poet in me was the Socialist in me. As a Socialist, while planning the destruction of capitalism, I was interested in machinery, got along well with my older fellow-workmen, and learned not only my work but to take pride in my ability to endure whatever pain there was (and, partly because of my youth and clumsiness, and partly because of the nature of the work, there was a good deal of physical pain to be endured).

Whatever might have been the attitude of the church crowd back in Quincy toward a talented youngster—if he had not suddenly turned Atheist—the attitude of my new friends in Davenport was unmistakable. There was a plan, of which I did not hear until several years later, to see me through college. A man known for his generous assistance in helping young people of promise in that way was invited to dinner to meet me. I did not know what was afoot, but I remember the evening very well. The subject of a college education in general was brought up, and I was asked what I thought about it. I, from my Socialist ramparts, blasted college education with a withering fire of criticism. My tactful hostess asked me if I did not think colleges were of value if one were going to be a writer. I demolished the pretensions of colleges in that respect also, pointing out that the actualities of life were the only school in which one could learn to write. The talk then turned to something else.

CHAPTER XI

SPIRITS FROM THE VASTY DEEP

1

ALL OF MY poetic prowling about the streets of Davenport at night, after the public library closed, was not confined to lonely streets. I saw all there was to see in Davenport, and thought about it, and absorbed it in some fashion. And one of the strangest parts of Davenport, of which I had a sufficient view from the outside, was the 'red-light district'—some streets down by the river, with houses of prostitution, in which plump women in flaming kimonos could be seen at the open windows, out of which came the sounds of laughter and piano-music, and into the doors of which well-dressed young men, talking gaily, entered. At the corner of one of these streets was a dance hall—Nick Bingo's dance hall, I will call it here, since the proprietor has probably become a respectable bootlegger by now. A view of the crowded interior of this dance hall could be had in a quick glance by a boy passing by upon his poetic and philosophic business. The girls were dancing and drinking, and many of them were young and pretty—one, a fluffy-haired little blonde, looked barely eighteen. I asked no questions of anybody about this place, for it was not generally understood that Nick Bingo's was a theme for poetic and philosophic consideration; I had to figure it all out for myself.

I knew, from neighborhood observation, something of what I took to be the early career of those girls—the factory-work at incredibly low wages, far from enough for a girl to live on, not enough for her to pay for her keep in her own home and leave her anything for herself, only 'pin-money' wages—two dollars or so for a whole week's work; and the parents wanted it to help pay the grocery bill and the girl wanted it for clothes; the girl wanted to 'have a good time,' and her parents wanted her to turn in her pay and stay home of evenings; and when she stayed home there was nothing but maternal reproaches and warnings, until she flounced out of the house; and finally the time when she got home late and was locked out of the house, and maybe she got the policeman or the priest to argue with her father and let her in or maybe she didn't. Then, from another angle, I knew the attitude of the young men who went hunting for girls at parks and amusement places, and boasted that a girl could be had for a glass of beer; the contemptuous degradation of girls in men's minds to a single physical function, and the degradation of that to a convenience for what the men regarded in themselves as a vulgar male necessity; the fundamental sexual contempt which underlay the men's admiration, their easy gallantries, their kidding of the girls who were to be induced to serve their temporary masculine needs—the implicit attitude of the lords of the earth toward a slave class, or, sometimes, of a hungry tramp toward an apple-tree loaded with ripe fruit; if they did not feel this way about girls, why should they talk this way about them?—for this was the way they did talk about them; 'that was a good apple,' they said, with the air of one who has just tossed the core away. Girls were *things*. And this was an old rôle for girls; church and state joined in denying them rights as individuals, and employers kept them in a position of helplessness by cheap wages; when all these had done their work, Nick Bingo gave them a good time in his dance-hall, and so they were gathered into the houses of prostitution down the street —well trained by then to accept their destiny of being used for pleasure and profit, with no say-so of their own.

That was what it looked like until one saw the girls. They didn't think they had no say-so about their lives! Incredible, amazing romanticists, at every stage of their helpless victimization, they cherished the illusion of free will. They wanted a good time, and by God they were having it! Here in Nick Bingo's dance-hall, the pretty little girl on her way to the whorehouse was having a good time; and the pretty little whore already there was having a good time, too. They couldn't believe they were being used; they were as loyal to Nick and the Madam as they were to Church and State; they accepted their sexual inferiority as if it were a natural condition of their being, and inside of that they did whatever they damn pleased;

and even when they had reached the stage of Villon's Fair Helmet-maker Grown Old they didn't know the truth. . . . Or—did they have some truth of their own? Did they illustrate some magnificent rightness, cruelly twisted awry?

The poet in me ignored these thoughts at first, and produced one evening the following sonnet:

> I watched last night; and watching there with me
> There stood two joyless shades, the ghost of mirth
> And the grey ghost of laughter; so we three
> Watched till the dawn lighted the shuddering earth,
> And all the music and the dancing ceased.
> And, as I went, I wondered: not, to find
> Each sorry forehead chartered to the beast—
> But still I wondered, seeing you so blind;
> Who make strange sounds and deem that it is laughter,
> Who weary hour by hour and call it joy,
> Who flee so fast before what follows after,
> You are not man and woman, girl and boy,
> But strange, sad creatures, dreary and dull-eyed,
> Wherein the light has flickered out and died.

Yes—a pretty good sonnet; but not what *I* wanted to say. Try again, sometime!

The poet in me tried again, stumbling, as was always his way, when he tried to think: *Ceiling and wall and whitewashed pillars of the low dance-hall are blackened with the fume of smoke, that mingles with the reek of beer to choke the hot close air. Dim-seen across the whirls of smoke, over the heads of lounging girls, stands a low platform where musicians once again begin to play. Quickly the groups of men break up, and each one finds his partner. Now upon the crowded floor there comes one couple more, that mingles in the mazes, turns and winds forever to the reeds' and brasses' time like all the rest. This is the girl I saw. A scarce eighteen I guess your age. The law proclaims you mistress of yourself, but I see deeper in those blue eyes like the sky, and name you what you are—imperious, wild, spoiled, rude, affectionate,—a weary child. I look into your eyes again, and see what all these men that look into them never yet have seen—doubt, questioning and fear. Yet if some good folk and austere should blame you now, you would not own the doubt—you would flash out and passionately declare you walked the way of your choice and found it fair. Give them the lie! Beat down within your breast the questioning, the torment, the unrest. Believe, in spite of all, spite of the faces floating in this hall under the smoke-wreaths hanging like a blight, that you have chosen aright.—Oh, I have looked upon your mother's face—or was it but the mother of your race? Mute, patient, stoical, more humble than a taméd animal, I saw her stand. She chose the other way, the way of resignation and of death. And who shall say you were not right to ask for deeper breath, for love and life and laughter, and what's called sin, if thereby you might win to freedom at last. Above the laws of God and man, and past even the neighbors' opinion, is the law that bids us seek for happiness. You saw the golden lights of pleasure gleaming over a marsh, and so you ventured in. And now—is this the end of all your dreaming? Is there not something fair and far to gain out of your daring and your pain? Perhaps, for you, that the wise world calls fool, according to its rule, the world is so much nearer to its goal of happiness and knowledge. You have dared, and you will suffer. Meanwhile, take your toll of pleasure, drink quickly, ere the wine turns stale—perhaps, who knows? God gave you leave to fail!*

I could have wished that God had been left out of it. But, if not quite poetry, this was better—nearer to what I was trying to think out.

On those spring nights I saw, around the street-lamps, thousands upon thousands of May-flies with shimmering wings, whirling around the light in a delirious mad dance that no one who has ever seen it can forget; and the next morning the street would be filled with great heaps of dead insects, to be swept down into the sewer. Because of a kind of heliotropism, they *had* to go toward the light. But, even though it served them badly when men put up street-lamps, their heliotropism must have been otherwise good for them— must have served some life-purpose! It must be a law of life. And the reckless impulse toward 'a good time' must be a law of life, too. The pretty little whores were obeying some law that was, in itself, good—it was Church and State and Property Institutions that had made the law go awry for them.

At this point the philosopher yielded to the poet, who broke, some-what incoherently, into utterance:

Heaps I found in the dust under the street-light at morn, drifting with every gust, dead and dusty and torn.

Here, at the fall of night, here was their life begun; an hour's wild dance in the joy of light—darkness, and all is done.

Flurry and madness and lust, whirling awhile in the light; broken, and flung in the dust—say, is it wrong? is it right?

What can we know, who have seen only the outward show?—death, and the whirling sheen? What can we know?

What of the flame within?—flame that would join with flame! What though we call it virtue or sin, give it an idle name?

Look at them, mad of the fire! Look at them, dead on the morn! Now can you spell desire—where and how it is born?

Oh, but if this were all, winds unceasing would bear the broken wings that fall, tenderly through the air—on to the pitiless heart of things, and pour them forever down, till in the sea of these broken wings God and His world would drown.

2

Of all the poets whom I read, the one who meant the most to me was Heine. Far from the greatest, and not even among the most admired, he was *my* poet in a very deep sense—because he was not a poet only. I enjoyed his prose, too, and responded to every quality of its style, the purpose of which I understood fully. He was my poet because he was also a critic, of art and of the political scene, and above all of life—and he criticised it from the point of view from which I wanted it to be criticised. He was mine because he wished, as one who had been a soldier in the Liberation War of Humanity, to have laid upon his tomb not a wreath but a sword; and because at the same time he was a gay and light-hearted lover. And he was mine, most deeply perhaps of all, because he was a Jew, and felt himself to be an alien in the civilization in which he had to live. As an alien, he could see that civilization in a way no smug native ever could—and more truly. But no smug native would know the depths of scorn there was in his drolleries—the hatred, prophetic of the lightnings of some ultimate destruction, in his wit. He was in but not of his world; and very much in it, however utterly not of it.

After the first flush of amazement and delight at finding myself a poet at all, it was not long before I began to consider what sort of poet I was. And in spite of natural prejudices in my own favor, I was not entirely pleased with what I saw. It was a curious fact that God kept getting into my poems. Banished very satisfactorily from my philosophy, God slipped into my poetic imagery, sometimes ensconcing himself so securely in a rhyme that he couldn't be got out without ruining a stanza and perhaps spoiling the climax of the poem, as in the one 'To a Butterfly':

> And if in bitterness and scorn
> I walk the ways my fathers trod,
> Thou, flashing through the perfumed morn,
> Shalt be my plea to God.

It is very disconcerting for a young Atheist to find himself talking about making a 'plea to God'. I didn't do it on purpose—it just popped out that way. And it might happen any time I wrote a poem. Sometimes the religiosity, and its accompanying sentiments, could be revised to suit my real view of life; but what a way to write poetry!

I did endeavor to educate my Muse, teach her something about Evolution, Socialism, and Biology, but she could not be trusted; she would presently revert to some earlier uneducated and sentimental stage in which she was more at ease. I drove her patiently through a course in Economics, but as a Revolutionary Working-Class Muse she was sadly tongue-tied. The effort to paganize her was a little more successful. At least I got out of her a poem entitled 'My Three Guests', which has some interest as a psychological document. It ran thus:

> I had three guests one summer eve,
> Covered with blood and dust,
> And these are the names men know them by—
> Envy, and Hate, and Lust.

> "The Christian folk, that dwell within
> The little town hard by,
> They hunt us out and hound us down—
> Now help us, or we die!"

> Now Envy was a clever lad,
> And Hate a husky brute,
> And the smiling lips of the hoyden Lust
> Were red as cherry fruit.

I brought them in and gave them food,
  And drink to quench their thirst,
And bade them make my house their home—
  I liked them from the first.

And in those friendly summer days
  I found that Envy's tongue
Had power to pierce to hidden truth
  With wit that probed and stung.

And I was glad to own the help
  Of Hate's hot strength, that bore
A firmness to my flagging limbs
  That else had toiled no more.

And Lust, that answered frankly back
  What Christian folk speak low,
Gave me a clue to all men's hearts,
  And taught me half I know.

So I proclaim them unashamed,
  As loyal friendship must;
And where I go, I take these three—
  Envy, and Hate, and Lust.

If I could have kept my Muse up to the mark of this in sincerity and wisdom, I should not have minded so much her technical crudeness. But why could my Muse achieve grace and dignity and beauty of phrase and rhythm only when uttering something on if not over the verge of sentimentality? I tried hard to make her speak for *me*. She sullenly and clumsily obeyed; but the first moment she got a chance, back she was at the old stand, ladling out syllabub, just as if she had never heard of Darwin, Marx and Haeckel. Byron had taught his Muse something; so had Shelley; evidently I couldn't. I should have been content with much less; if I could have achieved some of the lighthearted pagan sweetness of Herrick, I should have been happy. But my poetic treatment of love was intolerably burdened with idealism; and not a natural idealism, but an almost mystical idealism. What was I to think when I found that I had written this?—

But you, because upon your brow is set
  A sign that makes you different from these,
  No draught of theirs shall give you any peace:
Put by the cup, and fare on, thirsting yet.

If what I meant was that I had no intention of patronizing prostitutes, and could wait till I found the possibility of having a sexual love affair on terms acceptable to my mind, then I should have said so. But *brow—a sign—different from these—no draught of theirs—put by the cup—fare on!* Who was this but Sir Galahad?

3

It was, moreover, apparently, as a young poetic Galahad that I was befriended by women of what was to me the 'upper class', and welcomed to their drawing-rooms. I took my Socialism along with me, but that was to them a poetic vagary. They not only read my poetry—which was my passport—and praised it, but they discussed ideas and books and life with me. I needed their companionship, I needed to talk with people who had read books; and so far I had found what was the general rule in America—that women alone had time for such things, and interest in them. But I needed women's companionship for its own sake, too; the companionship of women older than myself, since I was still afraid of girls of my own age.

Mothering is an instinct hard to restrain. A kitten evokes it, and so apparently does a boy poet. A young poet (or even an old one, for that matter) is assumed to be something fragile and delicate, that needs to be protected from life. I must have looked the part. I was slender, with dark, rather long and disorderly hair, and a face that was supposed (erroneously, I believe) to resemble Shelley's, Keats's, and Byron's. Doubtless I could have got a haircut; but I had no wish to look like the efficient young fellows at business college. (I don't know when the 'yellow' hair became dark; perhaps it never was really yellow—but it was called so.) My way of dressing, which would have been slovenly in a business-college boy, was perhaps appealingly picturesque in a boy poet.

At that time I couldn't afford to wear a clean starched linen collar every evening, and I had learned that celluloid collars were not the thing to wear, so I didn't wear any collar at all, but wound a black silk muffler (an eighth-grade graduation present) around my neck and tucked it in my vest, declining to take it off when I came into the drawing-room. I couldn't very well take it off, because my shirt was collarless beneath; but it probably gave me just the final touch of authenticity as a Chatterton.

Not long before this there had been published a novel by May Sinclair, called 'The Divine Fire'. It told the story of a young poet, poverty-stricken, Shelleyan in appearance, idealistic, shy, incompetent in all worldly matters, and 'a genius'. He was a pathetic, beautiful and tragic figure—at least, many readers found him so, particularly women. . . . I myself, though admiring the book's great power, felt only disgust and scorn for its poet-hero, whom I considered merely a fool. When I found that *I* was being viewed in the light of that book, and was thus apparently regarded as a poor ninny like May Sinclair's hero, my indignation was privately obscene.

I might be bookish, but I wasn't a helpless incompetent. Nobody needed to shed any tears of pity over me. My idealism, moreover, was not a mush of Victorian sentimentalities and pieties, but the idealism of a boy who had read Ibsen and Bernard Shaw and the early Wells and the classics of Socialism. If I was girl-shy, it was (I thought) partly because there were so few girls who know anything about the things in which I was interested, and partly because I had no money to spend on girls; I had no mawkish notions about chastity, male or female—I would certainly not have anything to do with prostitutes, but I would like to have a sweetheart, and I would want to sleep with her, only she would have to be a girl I could talk with, too. That was my chief disgust with May Sinclair's hero—his ineffable chastity.

'A genius', was he, that hero of May Sinclair's? There was something suspicious about that word 'genius'. 'Ah, well, Mr. Smythe, I knew there was *something* you didn't do!' 'Genius', wherever the term was applied, seemed to mean, not special capacity, but special incapacity; this 'genius' of May Sinclair's couldn't do *anything* that other people could do—a divinely inspired booby, all *he* could do was write poetry!

That was not at all my notion of myself. At least, it overlooked the Socialist side of me. The vision of a world fit to live in could fling one headlong into a world from which a poet might shrink in dismay. As a poet I might be weak and forlorn outside the magic circle of words and rhymes; but as a Socialist I was arrogant and energetic. When I had delivered a Socialist lecture in the Negro church, pinch-hitting for the inexplicably absent Michael Kennedy, then, at least, I had not been a fragile, helpless, incompetent person.

4

Looking back at myself, I seem in truth to have been two different kinds of persons—two, at least; three, not forgetting the Stoic, who was still there, protecting me. Four, if one counts the student, who was at that time studying in the public library the things, of those I cared about, that I would miss by not going back to high school. Since the Socialist and energetic side appears to be a revival in new form of my earliest arrogant child self, it needs another name— Hero will do, if it is not taken too seriously. Stoic, Student, Hero, Poet—that might prove a troublesome combination to compose into an everyday working personality.

Perhaps it is only by love and imitation that we develop those parts of our personality which come into gradual existence and constitute a fairly harmonious whole—but a whole which is scarcely able to use the unexpected opportunities of life, and is still less able to resist its unexpected shocks.

But there seems to be another kind of character development— brought about by pain, coming suddenly, and making for disharmony of personality. The new partial selves thus evoked seem almost separate from the rest of the personality, which they may dominate, but into which they cannot snugly fit.

The complex personalities with which we face the world, and through which we get such happiness as we can achieve, seem thus constituted partly of almost separate selves, which are not developed gradually but are born full and entire out of the shock of catastrophe. They are not born out of nothing, but out of the shadowy poten-tialities of our nature.

It depends, to be sure, upon the world's demands and opportunities, as to which, if any, of these actualized selves can be exploited for happiness and usefulness. But these selves, once born, do not seem to dwindle and die even of neglect or starvation. They seem immune to the influences of the outside world. But they do seem sometimes to be knocked down, sat upon and held down by some other inner self—perhaps one evoked for that purpose from the vasty deep.

Can we call spirits from the vasty deep within ourselves? Indeed we can, Hotspur; and they will come, too. But they will not go! And if their presence imperils our life, liberty and pursuit of happiness, we must summon up a still stronger spirit to quell them. And there is, finally, the problem of creating some kind of family unity, if possible, among this strange crowd of fire-breathing genies and lotus-eating pixies and what-not within oneself. No serene love-developed harmony this will be, if it is ever achieved! And it may never be achieved at all. The chances seem rather against it. . . .

CHAPTER XII

HAIL AND FAREWELL

1

AFTER I had written a poem, I made several copies of it, or of a group of poems, in booklet form, neatly lettered, with a picture drawn on the cover, and gave them to my friends. I thus had the pleasure of immediate publication of my poems. Many years later, among some things my mother had saved, I found a handful of these booklets, dated 1904, when I reached seventeen, the year of my last term in school, my factory work, and my rejoining the Socialist party.

THEOLOGY

The Lord God spoke to me last night
Of debts of faith unpaid,
Of prayers unsaid and hymns unsung.
I answered unafraid:

'And though Thou be the greatest God
That e'er knew bended knee,
And though Thou madest heaven and earth,
Think who it was made Thee!

'For sure as heathen make their Gods
Of stock and stone and star,
So sure I raised Thee from myself,
Where the Eternal are.'

These stanzas are from a Socialist poem, 'The Builders':

The pharaohs and the satraps, they thought the deed was theirs,
And built these sand-swathed gardens, raised those sea-swallowed stairs;
But still behind their each caprice, working through hate and love
Was that slow subtle destiny that gave us good thereof.

* * *

106

The fierce barbaric hordes that came to burn and crush and spoil
But showed how strong must be the walls, how ceaseless be the toil.
And vanished, beastlike races that lived their unmarked span—
Behold, their work, despised, forgot, fits in the perfect plan!

When by some lingering haze of blood or dustclouds born of trade
Were hid the wide-strewn signs that long had grand intent displayed,
Then had the earth its dreamers, whose gaze was on the skies—
When dimmer sight found clods, they saw fair cloud-girt towers rise.

Slow was the toil and thankless, but perfect now they stand,
Those blood-baptised foundations, as in the first day planned.
And loftier, grander, lovelier than their most bold surmise,
Now lies the meaning plain at last to our maturer eyes.

But the next poem is in a different mood:

THE SONG OF EARTH

'Neath shifting sands of twice ten thousand years,
It lies, the lost Atlantis of my youth;
And this I have to show my sister spheres—
A dead dream, and these lingering tribes uncouth.

Not for the splendor of that ancient prime,
Nor for the deeds that still rejoice my soul
When I remember that lost flame-ringed time
That lights me yet on to my death-dark goal—

Not for these things I mourn: my bitterness
Recks not the cities and the gods forgot;
But their vast hopes, those dreams they could not guess
An hundred loveless centuries would blot.

All unfulfilled, they mock me, who did thrill
To those grand visions of my greatest race,
As I turn scornful to these, lingering still—
Masters of me by my contemptuous grace.

And here is still a third poem, and mood, on the same theme:

Give me to know these swift, dim days!
I understand not, and I fear;
How can these devious blood-wet ways
Lead up to heights serene and clear?

Their true intent I cannot see,
After the tears and toil and strife.
Can hell gain peace, machines go free?
Does death grope upward unto life?

It was, it may be remembered, the year of the Russo-Japanese war, and the year of President Roosevelt's re-election, a time of 'trust-busting' and 'labor troubles' and muck-raking; as the result of the Spanish-American war and the acquisition of the Philippines, the United States had become an empire; while to an imagination instructed by Jules Verne and the early H. G. Wells, the future of the machine age, with all its powers for good and evil, was sufficiently apparent. Though the young poet who wrote these lines had much to learn in other directions, there was not much to be learned in this direction until 1914 and 1917, neither of which years would be altogether surprising.

A sentence from a magazine article had profoundly affected my imagination; and it was set down beneath the title of a long poem I wrote that year entitled 'The Superman'. The poem is too long to quote, but these are the lines prefixed:

. . . "Of the time when the being that is yet within the loins of man shall stand erect upon the earth, and stretch out his hands among the stars."— H. G. Wells.

When not sociological, the themes at this time were likely to be theological, philosophic or ethical. Even when the subject was nominally the beauty of the world, there was another defiant theme in the background; one poem tells how a great king undertakes to 'take away everything' from someone who has incurred his enmity; but that one recounts the glories of nature, which no king can take away from him—and that same idea is behind this apparently simple nature poem:

TREASURE TROVE

Come, let us count our treasure once again:
The dim, hushed twilight woodland; and the river
Splendidly carpeted with sunset gold;
The moon agleam upon the crusted snow;
The lightning reaching vainly through the storm;
The blue sky mirrored in the silent pond—
The ripple shattering the vision all;
The fading pageantry of Autumn woods;
The changing mellow light a flickering fire
Casts on the ceiling as the day goes out;
The long black shadows writhing on the sand;
The full moon, touching with its crimson edge
The ribboned low horizon; the scant green

That dots the rain-soaked ground and tells of Spring;
The billowing clouds that drift down summer skies;
The eager wake frothing behind the keel—
All these are ours; all these—the world—is ours.

2

That summer I wrote a poem on the subject of adolescence; this—adolescence—I understood at the time to extend from twelve to seventeen. Subsequently, when I wrote a book on adolescence, and had to know what years it covered, I found that no two eminent authorities agreed upon its end-term, some placing it, for men, at 18, and others at 20, 22, 25 or later. Perhaps my notion was as good as these guesses. I was earning my own living, and I regarded myself as a young man. I was looking back upon my adolescence when I described it in my poem; and I should like to reprint it as a document giving an inside view of the matter—even though it is far from being a good poem. It was made up while standing at work in the factory. In the last stanza I said that it was unnecessary to tell what it was about; but when I found that none of my grown-up friends could guess, I added the sub-title:

THE GODS

A Song of Adolescence . . .

There is a garden where they go at times, and linger for a while;
And mortals, even I, may know the wine of Aphrodite's smile,
And hear adown the wakeful glade, with rosy-fingered Dawn's first kiss,
Resound a mellow fanfarade, the hunting-horn of Artemis.

I know them; courteous Hermes bade me welcome when I strayed therein
Unwittingly, my visage sad with pondering the might-have-been;
And straight my hand Athene took and led me down a wilding way,
And there within a sunlit nook I heard divine Apollo play.

And now so often gardenward and glad of heart my way I wend
That every gate they leave unbarred, and hail me for a welcome friend;
The jests that Aphrodite tells—the laughter-loving goddess, she—
Of mortals caught in heavenly spells, mar not our camaraderie.

Warm Aphrodite's lazy-light caress, that leaves one half-afraid;
And, like a cooling breeze, the white aloofness of the huntress-maid:
These know I well—the silent care of down-shod Ganymede; and
As lightly stirring in my hair, the comradely Athene's hand.

And Hermes holds much talk with me concerning commerce and the mart,
And of the days when his shall be more than a petty trickster's art;
He speaketh grandly of the time when greed for gain shall have no place,
But each shall deem this thing sublime, to serve the needs of all his race.

Oft past the smithy I have been, but of Hephaestus saw I naught,
Until I dared to venture in and marvel at him while he wrought:
His huge misshapen bulk divine loomed awful in the forge's glare—
Then saw I grace in every line, and craftsmanship writ in his air.

I watched the raw stuff changing turn 'neath his strong hand and cunning
　　eye.
And through the dim-lit smithy burn a miracle of symmetry;
That little last-touch was the clue to all the pride that swelled his heart,
And looking on him then I knew the joy of labor and of art.

Apollo, god of poesy, as human as the rest I find,
In that he striveth even as we that muse and choose and weave and wind,—
And so most godlike stands confessed in them that sing for us, the will
To utter of themselves the best, the sense of imperfection still.

And Ares laughs in boyish mood, and tells me tales of eager strife,
Until new daring fires my blood and gives me strange contempt for life;
Till I, peace lover though I be, would gladly stand before my foe,
And ward the swift blows off in glee, and smite him fair, and lay him low.

One morning as I wandered down the flowery river-bank, I heard
Close by a sweeter music blown than ever came from throat of bird;
And lying on a grassy bank whereby the silver waters ran,
While wild the reed-notes rose and sank, I saw the shaggy wood-god Pan.

The liquid ecstasy throbbed on, and surged throughout my tingling veins,
Now calm as some September dawn, now headlong as the July rains. . . .
And then on me there came a peace, the seeming that I was but part
Of them that dwell among the trees—the Creatures of the Tameless Heart.

* 　 * 　 * 　 *

Perchance if I should name it now, the name itself would keep some gleams
Of that pure splendor that I know—that very garden of my dreams;
But words at best are lifeless things (they spell the fact—they cannot spell
The glamor that about it clings)—so guess it, you who know me well.

It was very sensible of me, I think, not to let Aphrodite's divinely
smutty jokes ever mar our camaraderie; and there is a complete
characterization of my shy seventeen-year-old self in the description
of the two goddesses: *'warm Aphrodite's lazy-light caress, that leaves
one half-afraid; and, like a cooling breeze, the white aloofness of*

the huntress-maid'. Hermes is, as he should be, a Socialist, the trader revolutionized; and it is Socialism that introduced me into this garden where I first heard Apollo's lyre. Here is the comradely Nihilist girl-goddess, Athene, and a shy glimpse of laughing human girls, as divinely wanton as Aphrodite. It is the factory-world that I had wandered past before, not knowing till now that the grimy factory worker, Hephaestus, takes pride in his work. A poet, I had learned from Charles Eugene Banks, must criticise his own poetry and revise it—even Apollo must *'muse and choose and weave and wind'.* Perhaps it was Alexandre Dumas who, as Ares, told me tales of eager strife that fired my blood. And I think it was Walt Whitman's profoundly impressive Nature-worshipping poetry which gave me the sense of kinship with the Creatures of the Tameless Heart. But there are no authoritarian gods here, no hateful Zeus, no jealous and conventional-minded Hera. This is an Atheist and Socialist Olympus. I can imagine no happier or more fortunate adolescence than the one I described.

3

And, that spring, I had had the satisfaction of having my first poem printed, though to be sure only in one of the local newspapers:

MEMORIAL DAY

And this is their greatest glory, on whose graves our blossoms fall,
That the fathers tell the story, and the children forget it all.
Peace-bred children, they wonder at the strange old tales of war,
List to the battle-thunder faint-echoing from so far,
Scatter the blossoms of Maytime, tread softly, and speak low—
Then, with another playtime, the last of the memories go.
For yesterday the Blue and Grey, in deadly hate who met,
Slew, to make peace immortal—died, that we might forget.

I hoped the editor would read it hastily, and not really notice what the poem said; and, when it duly appeared on the editorial page on Decoration Day, I concluded that was what had happened.

That was one good thing about poetry; if it looked pretty, nobody knew or cared what it said.

Thus, to the loveliest of women I could dare give this poem, saying what I might not say otherwise:

THE GIFT

A perfect little ship I made,
    With patient hands, and eager heart—
From silken sail to carven keel
    The flower of boyish art.

I did not launch it on the bay
    That stretches calm and blue, so far
You wonder if it is a dream
    That any tempests are.

I came, and bore it in my hands,
    And kneeling, laid it at your feet—
Then rose to meet your glad caress,
    Than any thanks more sweet.

But now instead you strangely spoke
    Anent the little gift I brought,
Saying it showed an artist's skill,
    So craftily 'twas wrought.

The thirst I had not known was there
    Such words as these would never slake—
And it was worthless now, the gift
    You praised, but would not take.

If you had only glanced at it,
    And smiling, kissed me on the lips,
That rudely whittled block had been
    A marvel among ships.

But now, when you had turned away,
    Praising the skill of my mere hands,
In bitterness I flung it down
    Upon the ruined sands.

I tore the purple sail across,
    I snapped the polished mast in twain;
If it was but a thing to praise,
    My gift was given in vain.

And this, being a poem, could be presented without evoking
Candida's offensive speech to Eugene about their comparative ages.
But young girls continued to be to me an alarming prospect.

What! would you go with empty hands,
Unlaureled head, to where she stands,
And mark the look of sheer surprise
And easy scorn in her young eyes?
'Do you think that I will give,' she'll ask,
'My love to one who leaves his task,
Who shuns the field of combat, quits
The battle ere 'tis well begun,
And all the drowsy summer sits
Blowing his bubbles in the sun?'

Always there was with me in the land of the imagination a shadowy companion—a tender girl friend, rather than a sweetheart. Usually, in my poems, she was called 'dear friend'; but even when she was called my 'love', she was still a being almost without sex, yet faintly breathing the perfume of girlhood, the partner in a delicate and perfect comradeship, an unworldly and heroic comradeship. Always, too, she was a blue-eyed blonde.

O my love is very fair!
But to me
Not the sunlight in her hair,
Nor the touch
Of the strong and open sea
In her eyes,
Is a thing that I should prize,
Overmuch.

She is more than that to me,
She is youth,
And a challenge to be free,
And a brand
Searing from me all untruth,
And a friend,
Walking with me to the end,
Hand in hand.

4

But, in this matter of writing poetry, there is always a decision to be made. Is one going to be a Poet? That means—sacrifice everything else to poetry; and take what comes! Or is one going to write poetry for one's pleasure and to show to one's friends, and reject definitely the thought of giving up one's life to it? It makes a difference. And the decision must be made. The decision was already made, in my heart.

One has, as a poet, the sense of being the instrument of somewhat alien powers. One looks at a beautiful line: 'How could I ever have written that?' It is rather awe-inspiring. If somewhere in a beautiful poem there was one bad line, all the mental powers one might concentrate on it would never get it quite fixed up—unless, in that attempt, the ordinary powers of the mind were suddenly swept aside and the poetic powers took hold. To these poetic powers nothing seemed difficult; and they set themselves the most extraordinary hurdles to jump over, out of sheer exuberance. But it was nothing to them if the ensuing product were unintelligible, or ambiguous, or quite meaningless; they were satisfied—the thing had been done, if you asked *them!* Much they cared whether anybody understood it! They did not mind being silly, or saying things that were repugnant to the intellect. One could be in awe of such powers in oneself—but respect them, no! They would require to be wrestled with, as Jacob wrestled with the angel, before they would—if they ever did—become a means for the expression of one's whole view of life. And that took time and leisure; it was out of the question, when one had to earn a living. Nor did powers as recalcitrant as these were to promptings of the intellect promise much satisfaction as a means of making this a better world. The gift of poetry-making had better be divested of any such grandiose intentions, and cultivated as a private enjoyment. No one need be told about this decision. It would be too ridiculous to go around saying: 'I have decided not to try to soar above the Aeonian mount, while I pursue things unattempted yet in rhyme, and justify the ways of man to God.' There would still be poems to ease one's mind, poems to show to one's friends. Poetry was a thing that I could do, though not as I would; it was not me, and I could not submit to being its servant, its slave, its victim.

CHAPTER XIII

MY FRIEND FRITZ

1

HAVING ONCE had a job from which I had not been fired, that, according to the customs of the unskilled working class, was my trade. I was a 'prentice candy-maker. And it was in a candy factory that I now worked in Davenport. But among its intent, chocolate-smeared rows of aproned girls there would not be another Margaret. This was a large factory, floor above floor. I ran a 'vacuum pan' on one of the upper floors, getting there in the morning at half-past six, so as to have a batch of candy cooked and ready at seven. I fed a copper monstrosity with sugar and glucose in due quantities, so many times a day, and watched a recalcitrant steam-pump that kept the thing from exploding. The heat was regulated by a cock; when I hastily reached up to turn it, my bare arm was lucky if it didn't get burned on a steam pipe; it was hard to remember that steam pipe, and my arm was covered with half-healed burns. When a batch of candy was cooked, it had to be 'pulled' while hot—thrown over metal hooks in the wooden pillars, caught and thrown back, as in taffy pulling, only on a larger scale. It had to be pulled with the bare hands, and the first batch left eight blisters, one on each finger-tip; the next batch took off the skin from the blisters; after a week, callous skin had grown over the raw places. When more sugar and glucose were needed, I brought it from the cellar. I weighed a hundred and twenty-five pounds, and it was hard to pry a barrel of glucose weighing three hundred pounds out of a great pyramidal tier of such barrels that reached to the ceiling, without being mashed when the others came thundering down; and it was all I could do to roll that barrel up a three-inch step on its way to the elevator. At each day's end, the spilt sugar was swept from the dirty floor and put aside in a barrel of such sweepings, to be used in making horehound candy. On Saturday the floor was cleaned with hot water, spades and hoes; and then I had to scour my copper vessels clean and shiny with a rag soaked in tartaric acid, which got into my unhealed burns and scratches, hurting like hell-fire; and into my eyes, when I lay underneath the copper monster scrubbing its belly—but the acid, diluted with tears, lost its strength. Blinded and weeping, but rather pleased that I could stand it, I lay there, scrubbing the copper clean. The two candy-makers for whom I cooked were called 'Elephant' and 'Dutch'; I rather think it was I who gave 'Elephant' his name. The first week I was gravely told that it was the custom to 'wet' a new pair of overalls; this, it was explained, meant that the owner stood drinks for the crowd. "The custom," I said with equal gravity, "shall not be allowed to fall into innocuous desuetude." This was taken, as it was meant, as humor, and 'Elephant' went around repeating it. Before long, the phrase became 'knock-kneed steweytood', and was understood to refer to the clumsiness of the person to whom it was addressed. This transformation was assisted by my mispronunciation of the word 'desuetude'; my knowledge of words had been gained by eye and not by ear; many of the words which I used were ones which I had never heard spoken aloud. When I treated my fellow-workers, I did not know the ceremonial, but began to swallow my beer hastily, not liking the bitter taste, but not wishing to show it. "Well, here's looking!" said 'Elephant' hastily, and the candy-makers drank. When 'Elephant' proposed another round, I hastily hurried away.

2

One evening in that fall of 1904 there was a Socialist meeting on a down-town street-corner; and Michael Kennedy, who had not shown up at the Colored Baptist Church that spring, occupied the soap-box. I was in the edges of the crowd, an enthusiastic seventeen-year-old listener to Comrade Kennedy's speech, which told, among other things, of the growing forces of the revolutionary working class throughout the world, mentioning with especial pride the great German Social-Democratic Party. . . . Taking advantage of some pause, a burly stranger asked a courteous question—whether the speaker had ever been in Germany. The speaker had not; and it appeared that the burly stranger had, and had become well acquainted with the workings of the Social-Democratic party organization, and was willing to tell something about it, if requested. The invitation was heartily extended, and the burly stranger mounted the soap-box.

The German Social-Democratic Party, he said, was indeed a large and very efficient organization. But, he went on to say, it was not a revolutionary organization, and the Socialists here ought to know what it was like. It was a liberal and reform party, something like the Democratic Party in the United States. It had no hope of any revolution, nor any belief in one. At this point, Comrade Kennedy, who had been making agitated interruptions, mounted the soap-box beside him, and denounced him for the trickery by which he had gained possession of it. The burly stranger announced that he would continue his remarks on the opposite corner for all who cared to hear him, and then courteously gave the soap-box back to Comrade Kennedy. The amused crowd followed the burly stranger to the opposite corner, where another soap-box was quickly set up for him; and Comrade Kennedy found himself addressing only the dispirited committee of five or six who were in charge of the meeting. It was a poor evening for the Davenport Socialists.

But it was to be a fine evening for me. I maintained my stand among the faithful few, until Comrade Kennedy gave up his attempt to win back the crowd and bitterly went away. The rest of us joined the crowd at the other corner, and I listened in indignation to the malicious libels which were being uttered against my German Socialist comrades. The speaker then went on to discuss and confute Socialist theory. I was quite familiar with the Communist Manifesto, with Engels' 'Socialism, Utopian and Scientific', and other small books in red paper covers; and I had read some of the more readable parts of 'Capital'. When the speaker gave something as Marx's view, referring to 'Capital', I was quite sure it was not there, and dashed to the public library, a block away. Back I came breathlessly with Karl Marx's 'Capital' under my arm. I tried to break up this fellow's meeting with questions, as he had broken up the other, but he ignored me. Not until he had finished did I have a chance to challenge his statements, and offer him 'Capital' to find his proof in if he could; he smiled, and declined the opportunity. Furious, I told him he had lied about Marx; he snubbed me casually, and went away, leaving me in my chagrin.

But a big, florid man from the group of the Socialist faithful came over and talked to me; and presently, to my delight, I found myself invited to accompany the group to Turner hall for a glass of beer. I sat at a large table with five men who believed in another kind of world than the one we lived in, and were helping to bring it about— a world of justice and beauty and order. I drank beer with them. Beer, before that, had been a bitter drink; but now it was flavored with the splendor of talk and ideas. Afterward I walked with the big man to the place where he lived, and he asked me to drop in to see him the next evening. So began my great friendship with Fred Feuchter—Fritz, as I was proud to call him. He was a mail-carrier, a big, florid, dynamic man, large-minded and eloquent, and wiser in great things and small than anyone I had ever known.

The Socialist local, on his assurance, took me in as a member, though I was still a year too young by the rules. I thought the meetings dull, and no one disputed that; I was put on a program committee, and the meetings became lively, for after all I did know how to run a club. As fall turned to winter, I worked overtime at the factory, till nine; and I would hurry on the Friday evenings of our meetings from the factory to Turner hall, to be in time to take part in some discussion, or contribute an essay to the program. Our meetings had a large attendance, now that 'business' was not droned out boringly at indefinite length; wives came with their Socialist husbands, and a few Socialist girls showed up from high school. We discussed ideas, and my friend Fred Feuchter shone in that. If the energies of the Socialist local were, under the influence of my youthful enthusiasm, turned in cultural directions, there were none the less, and possibly more, votes for Eugene V. Debs—who was, I suppose, the candidate that year. I distributed literature at factories, and took a hand in odd jobs during the campaign. My friend Fred Feuchter had helped me magnificently in my program activities; and gradually I became his lieutenant in the practical and tactical management of the local. I discovered in myself a capacity for faithful henchmanship under an able leader, with no poetic shrinking from harsh measures.

A young enthusiast had his chance to try his hand at anything.

The youngest convert may aspire to leadership, and often does; but I never did. I did try, and fail, to be an efficient impersonal cog in the Party organization. I was financial secretary for a while; and it is doubtful if they ever did get the books straightened out afterward. It was conceded that I was better in writing platforms and manifestoes than in keeping track of vouchers.

My friendship with Fred Feuchter was the most important thing that had happened in my life. I had found a man whom I truly admired, and wished to follow, a man who had wisdom and courage, a man—and the first man—whose advice I could ask about anything. Not that I asked much advice: which was a good thing, for no human being could have been as infallible as I deemed my friend Fritz to be. But I learned many things from him of the greatest importance in the conduct of life. And it is interesting to me to note that these things did not concern ideals; I had read the same little red books that he had, already, and my ideals needed no improvement. What I learned from him were practical, sensible ways of dealing with the world—attitudes, rather than specific things, and really but simple common-sense. But common-sense was what I most profoundly lacked, and these simple acquisitions of wisdom were of prime importance to me. If one knows many recondite things, but does not know enough to go in when it rains, then that is a great piece of learning. Under his influence I began to learn not to attach to situations emotional values which were not there for the other persons involved; to live as though the outside world were real, whether I liked it or not; and not to pre-judge life, but to take it as it came and see it as it was. My father, no doubt, might have said to me: 'You have to consider the other fellow's point of view'; 'Facts are facts, you can't get around that'; and 'Don't cross your bridges before you come to them, my boy'—but these maxims would have carried no weight, they would have been suspect; yet these, not the maxims but the attitudes, were what I learned from my friend. He, at least, had no axe of respectability to grind when, after considering me in the light of the phrase 'intellectual proletarian', decided that I was more intellectual than proletarian, and would—he didn't undertake to say how—have a much better chance to make a living by using my brains than my hands; I would have less skilled competition in the one field than in the other, he assured me.

Since this was the first time anybody had ever taken serious note of my belief that I had to earn a living in factory work, his consideration of, and dismissal of, this belief was impressive. What my 'bourgeois' friends—I know that blessed word 'bourgeois' now—what they had tried to assure me was that I might have a great career as a writer; what he conveyed to me was that I didn't have a dog's chance as a factory worker.

I was, in fact, after the Christmas rush, fired from the factory. I got work in a job-printing shop, at a hand-press; but I had some objection to running the normal risk of having my right hand crushed to a mash in the iron jaws of the machine (my eldest brother had just lost part of another finger at the sash-and-door factory, leaving him a total of four whole fingers and one whole thumb on both hands); and I was transferred to the lithographing department. There it was my duty to feed beer-labels into a bronzing machine. I had also to breathe bronze-dust for eight hours a day. I became rather bitter about a civilization which could find no better task for a youth than that; a civilization in which the gilt on beer-labels—Very good, suggested Fred Feuchter, for a poem. 'But *you*—quit! Your family will not starve.' That was true; I had never thought of it that way. I did quit. It was now spring. I put on my best suit, and went to look for a job. Pausing to look at the new printing press in the windows of the Times, the idea occurred to me that I might get a job washing the ink off the rollers, or something like that. I went in. By one of those coincidences which make real life so utterly unlike realistic fiction, there had been, in the edition I had just seen run off, an advertisement for a cub reporter. It was supposed that I had come in answer to this advertisement, and I was sent to the city room, where I was given the job and told to report in the morning.

Although my friend Fritz had refused to prophesy the way in which I would be able to make a living by using my brains, this was the answer so pat that I felt as though he had not only pulled me out of a factory but pushed me into a newspaper office.

CHAPTER XIV

Cub Reporter

1

City editors are kind to cub reporters, or so I found mine. When no news was turned up on my 'beat,' 'J. C.' gave me an assignment. It was to find out about a Jewish holiday celebration; and as I knew nothing about Jewish holidays, I looked them up in the office encyclopedia, and so was able to ask intelligent questions of Rabbi Fineshriber, and write an intelligent piece about the event. Then I was sent to report the Rabbi's sermon; he had read my piece, and he invited me to come home afterward with himself and his wife and have a glass of beer and some conversation. So I made two friends; and I liked the Rabbi's sermons so well that I became a sort of member of his congregation, which consisted to a considerable extent of Gentiles, Socialists, Atheists and other heretics. The Rabbi was the best speaker I had ever heard, and the best orator I ever was to hear.

But cub reporters are on trial; and after a month I was fired; the proprietor had decided that I had no 'nose for news,' and that this was not what I ought to be doing. When other employers had made similar decisions about me in the past, I had always rather agreed with them. But if a newspaper was not the place for me, what was? The proprietor, if he knew, had not confided that to me. I was hit very hard. But I had two weeks' notice; and I decided to 'show them'—and to *make* them give me the job back, damn them! I began to turn in 'human interest stories' at the rate of two or three a day. Before the two weeks were up I had found a woman and several sick and dying children at one of the railway stations, with a story such that, when I asked 'J. C.' how much space I could have for it, he answered solemnly, "Seven columns." I did write about two columns, and the presses were held up for the last paragraph.

I had my job back. Life was incredibly like the Horatio Alger stories I had read in my childhood; but upon second thought, no—his heroes had never got ahead by sheer disrespect of their employer's opinions. It was more like 'Frank on a Gunboat'. 'Damn the torpedoes!' cried Farragut, and in a rain of shot and shell we swept past the rebel batteries to victory. . . . At any rate, life was not at all like realistic fiction, that was clear.

Nevertheless, after the glow of triumph had passed, the memory of this incident served as a warning that my hold upon this job, and upon the profession of reporting, was insecure. This was a job in a civilization which was not my civilization; not the exercise of my best capacities, but meeting the needs of newspaperdom, was my task; and it might be as irrelevant to anything I thought important as the gilt on beer-labels; it might, later if not now, be as contrary to my sense of decency as the job of making horehound candy out of sugar and dirt swept from the factory floor. To what extent had I anything to offer that a newspaper would pay money for? 'Human interest stories'—that was about all. My job hung by one thread; and that thread might be cut at any moment. I had, in fact, no future to look forward to. But I had a very interesting present.

I now lived several exciting lives. I was a Socialist, active in the local, and imaginatively stimulated by news of revolutionary uprisings in Russia; a poet in spite of myself, accidentally producing poems which were thought salable to magazines; a dramatic critic, writing reviews of plays at the German theater—not that I understood German, but that I liked writing dramatic criticism; a student of my favorite subjects at the public library; a friend, with golden hours to spend with Fred Feuchter, and Marilla Freeman, and the Fineshribers; and a newspaper reporter. At times the poet in me (for the Socialist did not mind such things) rebelled inwardly against going up to strangers in railroad stations and (tip hat) saying firmly and pleasantly and very rapidly: 'I beg your pardon I represent the Davenport Times will you please tell me where you are going. And what is your name please. S-m-i-t-h is that right? Mrs. H. J.? Thank you and your address. 1-4-5-2 Main street is that right? And you are going to meet somebody in Walcott. How is the name spelled. And you will stay how long. *Thank* you very much!"—tip hat; on to the next; forty people this train; over to the other station; eight trains today;—there's a bunch of society people seeing a girl off to college, they'll only snub you for butting in (and right enough they should), but here's the Old Man watching you, he'll give you hell if you don't tackle them—so carry the message to Garcia; what's anybody's privacy, what's your self-respect? nothing, the world's work must be done, and this is it, a perfectly fair sample of the kind of world we've always had and the kind of work that must be done in it, you get your pay envelope every week, don't you? you ought to be damn glad you're not breathing bronze dust—anyway, these poor fools want to get their silly names in the paper; and I can make them come across even if they don't want to, it's a technique and I've learned it, I can stick my nose into anybody's business without a blush, I'm a newspaperman, damn your eyes. . . .

2

In addition to these lives, a youth of eighteen is, very naturally, having some kind of love life. Perhaps it was some notions imbibed from my earlier Nihilist reading which set up a taboo in my mind upon Socialist girls, as if they were my sisters; I did not let myself fall in love with the girl comrades whose companionship I enjoyed. But on some evenings I stayed on duty late in the city office, and became enchanted with the warm friendly voice of the telephone operator on night duty in the telephone office. With nothing to do except read a little proof, I would neglect the 'History of American Class Struggles' that I had brought, and pass the hours in a long conversation with the night operator. When a call had to be put through she would tell me, and I would hang up; a minute later, the bell would ring, and our conversation would go on. And I, who had never had the art of small talk, who conversed, in however lively a way, always upon serious matters, and to whom the faculty of 'kidding the girls' was as alien as ventriloquism, became somehow an expert kidder. With airy nothings that I had not dreamed I should ever have at my command, the hours of the night glided by. And at last the time came when I asked for a date and was granted one.

At the hour appointed, I was at the counter of the ice-cream parlor most frequented by youth and beauty. I think I wore a red carnation in my button-hole, so as to be recognized. I waited expectantly, but no girl came. I waited half an hour—three quarters. Then two pretty girls strolled slowly by, looking in; a moment later, they had turned and were strolling past in the other direction. I rose from my stool at the counter. One of the girls squealed to the other, "There he is!" and both girls burst into peals of giggles, and fled around the corner.

I did not call that girl up again. My conversation lost from its range some airy touches it never recovered. And I have never liked using the telephone, since.

But that was not all of my love life. There was a girl whom I actually 'picked up'. Seeing her in some shop, and liking her looks, I waylaid her and made her acquaintance, and invited her to go with me to an amusement park that was situated on a small island in the river. She consented, and met me that evening. She was just as pretty as I had thought, and the island as we approached on the ferry was a golden glow of lights. Snatches of music from the dancing pavilions were wafted to us on the faint intermittent breeze, together with the damp smell of trees. I wished I could dance, and resolved to go to a dancing-class and learn. Since I did not dance, we took in the other amusements of the place, and imbibed ice-cream sodas. I felt not at ease. There didn't seem to be anything to talk about. I wasn't 'showing the girl a good time.' When I took her home, I thought she must be glad it was over. But she paused in front of the house and said, a little defiantly: "I go in the back way. This isn't my home, you know. I work here." I said that was all right, and felt miserable at not being able to give her any further reassurance. But why should she want to go out with me again? We just weren't good company for one another; I didn't dance and she didn't talk. I hoped I wasn't being snobbish; but when I thought of Margaret, who had been 'a factory girl,' I knew that wasn't it. We kissed one another good-night, and I felt ashamed of myself for having started something I couldn't go on with.

Then there was a picnic group that for a while I went on Sunday picnics with. I found myself regularly paired off with a tall, quiet, gentle, brown-haired girl; amidst a great deal of giggling, chatter and confusion, the girls in their Sunday clothes and the boys carrying enough food in baskets to feed a crew of threshers, we arrived by street car and walking at some wooded place, where we tried to do justice to the food, and sat around feeling stuffy the rest of the afternoon; at twilight the boys would lay their heads in the girls' laps, and there would be singing of sentimental popular songs; then, before it got too dark, we would go home. That was the routine picnic. But one Sunday somebody brought a new girl there, a beautiful, golden-haired blue-eyed girl. . . . And, our eyes having met, the rest of the picnic disappeared for me. I went to her, took her arm, and led her off dreamily into the woods. She went without question. We walked up the path, talking gaily, familiarly, like people who have known one another for a long time in dreams. We wandered in the woods until we came to a stream, and there we sat down on the bank and took off our shoes and stockings, and thrust our feet into the cool water. And there we stayed all afternoon, talking about heaven knows what, but very gaily and laughingly, utterly happy. I had forgotten time and place, and can only suppose that she had, too. Our eyes had hardly left each other's for a moment since our glances first magically met. I can only remember her blue eyes, her golden hair, her bare feet in the stream, and our happy laughter. But it grew twilight. We realized that we must have been gone a long time. We put on our shoes and stockings—*'Would to God your bare feet on the green grass trod and I beheld them as of yore'*—and walked back, silently and pensively, through the woods. Before we emerged upon the clearing, we stopped, and kissed shyly. Then we went to join the others. We were received in a curious way; everybody sat there and stared at us, and then everybody spoke at once, hailing us, and then there was a silence. I began to realize that we had not behaved in the way people should at a picnic. But then, I had just forgotten all about the picnic. Everybody jumped up, saying that it was time to go home. I found myself marching down the road between two of the other fellows, both of them very taciturn. I had the feeling that I was being treated like a criminal. Had it been so outrageous, to take a girl away and keep her all afternoon? We got on the street-car; but there was not the usual singing. My companion of the afternoon, seeming very subdued, evidently in disgrace like myself, got off the car with several others, with only the most fleeting farewell glance at me. Presently I found myself taking the usual girl to her home. On the front porch she said, with a little choke, the conventional words, "Thank you for showing me—such a good time today." I realized for the first time that I had hurt her feelings. I hadn't meant to do that! I felt frightfully stupid, and grew red with shame. I stammered: "I—I'm sorry." She said it was all right; I doubted if it was, and thought I ought to say something more. But I decided I had better go; so I said good-bye, and hastily slunk away. It all reminded me of nothing so much as being waked up from a trance in the factory, when a poem was being created in my mind, to find the foreman standing over me asking why I hadn't done something or other. It was the crashing in of a meaningless chaos of reality upon a beautiful dream; nevertheless, the meaningless chaos of reality was the world in which I had to live.

I never saw the golden-haired blue-eyed girl again; and I don't remember going on any more picnics.

I remembered my resolution to learn to dance. I went to a dancing class. I learned all the steps of the waltz in solemn solitary maneuverings about the sides of an imaginary square. *'One!* two, three' yes, I could do it perfectly. But when I took a pretty girl in my arms, and felt her live breasts touch my shirtfront, I lost the rhythm, became confused, and stepped on her feet. It was no use. I just couldn't seem to dance. I went to a second lesson, but it was too humiliating to be such a stupid blunderer. Dancing was not for me. I gave it up.

3

Poetry-making, though tacitly abandoned as a serious task, was stimulated by the gigantic revolutionary uprising all over Russia, and again I tried to deal with politics and social questions in verse. If I could be a Socialist poet, there would be some excuse for my taking myself seriously as a poet. I made many attempts, and all of them were failures. I remember a few lines from the poem I wrote when I read the news of peace between Russia and Japan, and the hasty return of the Czarist armies to crush the revolution:

'Odessa burns, a beacon in the night,
Riga and Kieff arm them in haste to smite,
And in the sunless capital the smouldering embers glare.
Beware! beware!

For still march in,
Like guests to some grim feast,
For slaughter of their kin,
The armies of the East.'

And the concluding lines:

'Unconquered ever! Thou art not such as we—
Thou art the symbol of eternal youth,
Awakened now and battling for the truth,
Bleeding at every vein, yet falling on Victory.'

Lines like these might be something more or less than a million miles away from the revolutionary odes of Shelley and Swinburne; but if I kept on, I might hope to do things which could bear comparison with my models. Yet what if I did? Who would read them? The year before, I had read in the Appeal to Reason some wonderfully eloquent and stirring appeals, first to farmers and then to beaten strikers, by an unknown writer named Upton Sinclair; then had come an astonishing and powerful serial novel called 'The Jungle,' which was now being published in book form and being read by everybody. Prose was evidently the medium in which to do what I wanted to do—prose fiction most especially. But then one must be a giant to swing the huge hammer of a book like 'The Octopus' or 'The Jungle,' and bring it down smashingly upon the thick smug cranium of the respectable world—such a giant as Victor Hugo had been. This was greatness; and I dared not aspire to it. My gift of poetry-writing was something which I thought of offering to the revolutionary cause; but I did not see how it could be of use.

That left poetry as a more or less private emotional satisfaction, allowed to go its own way, and devote itself chiefly (as it did) to love matters. It certainly in this field achieved more felicity:

When shall I cease to take delight
  In forms of transient grace,
Will-o'-the-wisps that all the night
  Flicker before my face?

Oh, sometime shall I not be less
  A creature of desire,
With gain of autumn happiness
  For loss of April fire?

Nay, I was sent a wanderer
On youth's eternal quest,
To go forever seeking Her,
Nor, ere I find Her, rest.

And all these forms so frail and fleet
Whereafter run tonight
My weary and enamored feet—
So dear they are, and bright—

Now, having lured me once again
O'er wild of hill and dale,
Shall this last foolish phantom wane,
This beacon fade and fail.

But past the phantom flames I see
The waiting face of Her
For whose high sake one well might be
Earth's weariest wanderer.

Sometimes a poem is prophetic, rather than reminiscent. At this time, also, I wrote a sonnet about the ending of a quite imaginary love affair; I cannot find the original, and I quote it here in a somewhat revised later version, in which a line or two has been changed; it prophetically described what were to be my actual feelings and behavior under such circumstances:

Dear, when you gave me your love, I signed no bond
To be forever worthy of that trust;
And if you think you have been overfond,
Take back your darling favors, as you must.
I will not bargain with you, knowing well
How futile were the effort to make over
Me, skeptic, vagabond, rebel and infidel,
Into the pattern of a perfect lover.

I was too crude, too arrogant, too cursed
With passionate candor, in our stormy past;
I made no promise even at the first,
And I will tell no lies, even at the last.
I love proud truth more even than I love you;
'Tis just you should dismiss me, Dear. Adieu!

Merely because I was known to be a poet and a writer of love poetry, even by those who had read none of my verses, I was now regarded here and there as a kind of young Don Juan—with, as I gathered in some surprise, a degree of admiration mixed with reprehension. This is the kind of reputation against which it is always vain to protest, since what people believe is what they wish to believe. However, though I had no wish to be a Don Juan, it was not on my program to remain what was called virtuous any longer than it took me to find a sweetheart who fulfilled my somewhat exacting terms. She must, just to begin with, be a girl to whom I was attracted both physically and intellectually—and this simple condition, not to go on to any others, was hard to fulfill. Besides whatever difficulties I myself was putting up to prevent my discovery of any such girls, there were really no very large numbers of girls whose ideas were not, to a youth who knew what ideas were, frightfully boring. And that devastating boredom in the company of girls whose ideas were all dully correct and proper (and, if improper, then improper in the dully correct and proper way), may account for such a poem as this:

IN VALLEY STREET

I

It was dark in Valley Street,
Where at evening I would meet
Lads and lasses not a few
Ever walking two and two.

Arms each other's waists around,
Glances fixed upon the ground,
They did not look up to see
Who was passing silently.

But I gazed in joy and pain,
Paused to look at them again,
Clenched my fists and shut my eyes,
Turned my face toward the skies.

For I walked down Valley Street
In the evening cool and sweet
With no sweetheart of my own—
Walked down Valley Street alone.

II

Now as down the street I go
With some girl I've come to know,
Arm in arm—again I pass
Maid and lover, lad and lass.

She is merry, she is fair—
And to lonely ones that stare
At the pair of us, I might
Very happy seem tonight.

Yet I sometimes wish that I
Might but put a twelvemonth by,
And go down the street alone,
With no sweetheart of my own.

I would gladly take the pain
If I might believe again
That there was a way like this
Leading straight to happiness.

But there are a number of poems which contain, in one form or another, the fantasy of the rescue or abduction (by intellectual conversion, it may be taken for granted), of some girl imprisoned in her tower of respectability, and her subsequent free and happy life with me in some kind of Sherwood Forest. Here is one:

From out each narrow room,
    Through windows locked and barred,
They look on flowers in bloom
    Here in the dewy sward.

We see their faces white
    At windows now and then,
Blinking toward the light
    And vanishing again.

They stare to see us pass,
    And wonder what we be,
That flash through flowering grass,
    Wood creatures wild and free.

Do you remember, Dear,
  How once you stood inside,
And yearned in hope and fear
  To the wild world and wide?

And how I bade you break
  The bars that stood between,
Burst from your cell, and slake
  Your throat with wood-winds keen?

The cobweb bars gave way—
  A step, and you were free:
Free to the light of day,
  The wooing winds, and me.

Who knows what hearts may burn,
  Deep in the sordid dark,
What souls may vainly yearn
  After the mounting lark?

Only, for us 'tis past,
  A dream of dark and drear,
And I hold you free and fast
  In the wind-swept stillness here.

And, finally, there is some anxiety about meeting this destined beloved:

TO AN UNKNOWN ONE

Where are you now, whom I shall surely find,
Some-time, I know not when, if soon or late,
But surely, surely—you, in body and mind
Lovely and strong and free and passionate!
Where are you now? For I this day have seen,
Walking in dream of you along the street,
Hands that I thought your dear hands might have been,
And eyes that seemed your own, so candid-sweet
They looked at me—me suddenly grown awake,
And wondering, "What if I should pass her by!"
Happiness of our two lives seemed at stake
One moment—then I knew it for a lie.
  And still you linger—truant, uncaressed,
  Unseen, unknown but of my dreaming breast!

CHAPTER XV

CIVIC EFFORTS

1

So, WITH several lives going at once, I passed from my eighteenth birthday toward my nineteenth; but before that was reached, a small Socialist monthly, the Tri-City Workers' Magazine, was turned over to me to edit. It was a chance for me to try my hand at Socialist journalism. But there were no local strikes to handle, and I could only find a few things to muck-rake, those that were under my nose.

Probably it did not advance Socialism much, but it gave me great satisfaction when I published in the Workers' Magazine an account of Nick Bingo's dance hall. In this article I sought to implicate the respectable classes of Davenport in the flourishing industry of making prostitutes. My generalizations were, I believe, sociologically correct; but my account of the clientele of Nick Bingo's dance hall may have been either incorrect or ambiguous, for I heard that the article hurt Nick's feelings: "Why," he said, "if I knew of any decent girls coming to my place, I'd of sent 'em home!" But it wasn't Nick I was attacking so much as the business men and the clergy of Davenport.

Even on a minor issue, I was glad to attack the intellectual and religious dignitaries of the town. Once, in the magazine, I violently denounced the public-library board for having crowded the children's department into a small hole in the corner of the basement, while letting the whole top floor go to waste as an unused auditorium; they were perhaps ashamed not to have thought of it themselves, and at the next meeting the change was unanimously voted; but, over and above the pleasure of doing something for the children and the library, it gave me a deep satisfaction to think of their intellectual and moral pomposities coming, as I learned they did,

to that board meeting all with copies of my intemperately disrespect-
ful opinions of them in their pockets.

As a reporter on a 'regular' paper, even above the level of meeting
trains, it seemed to me that one had to be an eye and an ear, an
organizing memory, a pencil and a pad of paper and two fingers
above a typewriter, rather than a person; my own opinions, feelings,
convictions and tastes had to be shoved out of the way so that they
would not interfere with getting people's confidence and eliciting
a story from them. Reporting was so devastatingly impersonal a
job, it reduced anyone to such a poor, unrepresentative wraith of his
individual self, that in order to recover the sense of being a particular
person with thoughts and feelings of his own, some reporters had
apparently to get drunk every so often; when they were drunk, they
were themselves, they were all they could not, must not, dared not
be as reporters; they could tell the world to go to hell, and pull themselves into some hasty, necessarily exaggerated but very refreshing
semblance of a living human being. My own Socialist journalism
was another kind of escape from, a different mode of protest against,
the horrible wraith-like doom of being a flitting reportorial eye and
ear, sans taste, sans guts, sans principles, sans feelings, sans damn near
everything that made life worth living. It was a spiritual relief to
me, even if it did not bring the co-operative commonwealth any
nearer.

But the magazine died in the violent local controversy over the
I. W. W.; and just before it died I was transferred by my paper to
a branch office out in Moline, where I could find nothing to muck-
rake except, literally, a noisome garbage dump. My articles in the
magazine were, of course, anonymous; but their authorship was
rather an open secret. My attack upon the library board had re-
sulted in a practical reform, to be sure; but a cub reporter was not
supposed to go around effecting civic reforms with a violent Socialist
magazine; it was a breach of reportorial tact, to say the least. A
clergyman might have called attention from his pulpit to what was
going on at Nick Bingo's, and that would have been correctly righteous indignation on behalf of the morals of Davenport; but what
business had a cub reporter bothering about such things?—except,
of course—as I was kindly advised by an older reporter—to use these

facilities furnished by the red light district to 'take my mind off sex'.

As a Socialist, I had come upon certain theoretical difficulties which were never properly straightened out in my mind, though I read all the literature which covered these difficult points. Any smiling Anarchist could ask, and several did, why I should work for the revolution if it were inevitable; and all I could reply was that he did not understand the Marxian theory. But that was conceded to be hard even for a bright youth to understand; and it did not matter if, in private, I wondered if I really understood the Marxian theory. It certainly threw a clear light into the pages of history— into the past. And it showed the workers as the only ones interested in overturning the present order. That was good enough Marxism for me. But I was emotionally inclined to agree with gentle Anarchist critics in their criticism of the restrictedly parliamentarian activities of the Socialist Party; that might be the result of my early Nihilist reading; indeed, there were grounds for suspicion in my own mind that I might be really a Utopian, and not, as I wished to be, a scientific Socialist. Again, that made no practical difference, since our local contained all kinds of Socialists, including Spiritualist Socialists. But when the members of the newly formed I. W. W. brought the same charge of parliamentarianism against the Party, and the other faction retorted with a charge of Anarchism, S. L. P.ism and Party-wrecking, I was glad for once to plead youth and ignorance. I privately suspected it was even worse than that; in these deep questions, my mind was only an imaginative and emotional organ, prone to error. I could follow a leader if I saw one; but I would never be a political thinker. The Party would have to settle this question, and tell me what to think.

Besides, in order to be—as I had been in a small way—a politician, and keep a good conscience, one must be *sure* that it was an impersonal end and not a selfish personal one that was being gained. What was obvious from observation was that other people were serving personal ambition in the name of the Party and the Co-operative Commonwealth. And one could trace that story right up to Briand, who had just been expelled from the French Socialist Party for joining a bourgeois ministry. The Socialist Party was a possible springboard to worldly success, and there could be no doubt that it was being used as such, though the persons using it might not know it. The Pope's Legate in Browning's poem checked them off sardonically: 'I have known *five*-and-twenty leaders of revolt.' All this was clear to me; there were plenty of humble and faithful Jimmy Higginses in the local; and my friend Fred Feuchter's capacities for leadership were not informed by any personal ambitions; but there were in the very substance of politics some motives that made me uncomfortable. I could, strangely enough, play that game, so far as ability went; but I could not stay in it—I had to get out of it, into a realm in which personal advantage could not be disguised as unselfish devotion to a cause. Politics was not for me.

2

Some of my poems had been sold, to Harper's Magazine, the Century, and McClure's. In one of these poems some editorial improvements were made. I did not know that editors, theatrical producers, literary agents, publishers, and other business folk who are frustrated creative artists, habitually stick their fingers into all the creative-art pies within their reach, because they just can't help it, and in the devout belief that in doing so they are helping the pies and the pie-makers—which, once in a way, may actually be true. But I stood in helpless anger while the editorial finger was delicately inserted into my poetic pie. Oh, not without my permission! I was young, and anxious to be published. So I professed grateful thanks, swallowing without making a face the black gall which exuded from my heart. Besides, the magazine paid fifty cents a line, and it would come in handy—when it came, for publication was a slow process, and poets stood in long lines awaiting their turn in the blessed spaces at the foot of articles or stories, from which jumping-off ground to soar above the Aeonian mount. The magazines, moreover, paid fifty cents a line not only for the poet's lines but also for those manufactured in their own editorial offices and published under his name—extraordinary generosity! The editorially manufactured lines were very instructive as to what poetic ideals of love were salable to the American intelligentsia:

> 'The flying glance, the floating hair,
>   The call and cry of One
> This flesh shall see not, though I fare
>   Onward from sun to sun.'

In other words, young Sir Galahad modestly asserts that no human girl is quite good enough for him. Not that this sentiment was alien to the spirit of my poem. It was a perfect criticism of my poem, an unconscious caricature. 'This is what you really mean, my boy! So out with it! Don't pretend that it is any fault of yours that these merely human girls don't suit you. You are not of this earth. Besides, you couldn't support any of these human girls, if you had them; you're just a poet, paid at fifty cents a line. Leave the human girls for vulgar business men to marry and take to bed— you go chase your Utterly Impossible She through the Cuckoo-cloud-land of rhymes!' And that was just what the poet in me would have liked to do. He could have written stuff like that—he *had* written it, God wot! He would have been quite happy turning out rhymes like that at fifty cents a line. What was there for a young man to do who harbored such a booby self within his bosom, except turn his other outraged selves loose on this one and give them permission to knock him down and kick him in the slats?

3

At the branch office to which I had been transferred, my boss, Jake, would not allow me to do any work as a reporter, but very amiably encouraged me to collaborate with him upon a musical comedy. This, of course, meant that it was only a question of time when I would be fired for incompetence. So in the meantime, besides writing lyrics and jokes for Jake's musical comedy, I read the complete earlier works of Frank Norris, and was aroused by some of his essays to the ambition to write a novel. In order to turn my attention more completely to prose, I undertook to break myself of the poetry-writing habit. It was a little bit like breaking oneself of the drug-habit; but I steeled myself against lapses into that absent, dreamy, intense, trance-like state, which would have been frequent during these weeks of day-long irresponsible idleness. When I felt a poem coming on, I turned my attention to outward and visible matters. And as a result of this discipline, I got so with poetry-making that I could take it or leave it. What happened was that the intense imaginative concentration, or whatever it was, became dissociated from rhyme and metre and was to some extent available for prose composition.

I began to dream and then to write a novel, while my strange job lingered on. My novel had an Episcopal bishop in it, and a farmer who has moved to the city, together with the farmer's daughter and son, the latter a youth who became a drug-fiend. The farmer and his daughter were based upon some neighborhood observations of social disintegration of rural families under town conditions—a theme which I planned to carry to its last extreme in an emulation of the Frank Norris manner; the young drug-fiend is perhaps explicable in terms of my experience in poetry-making; but why an Episcopal Bishop? The Bishop was to be engaged in well-meant social and religious reclamation work, in which he was to encounter the erring daughter; and in his attempt at effecting her moral reclamation, he was to become involved in the toils of emotions which would bring about his own moral disintegration and collapse. The young drug-fiend was to be a study in inability to face the world of actuality. An ambitious project, that novel, which did not get beyond the meeting of the Bishop and the fluffy-haired, sweet little baggage of seventeen, whose eyes looked so candid and innocent that even a hard-boiled Episcopal Bishop of fifty could not but believe that there must be, despite the appalling flagrancy of her record, something there worth saving. . . . I had never heard of the theory (except perhaps vaguely with respect to Shakespeare) that all of an author's characters are in some degree himself, representative of his own hopes or fears or impulses. It is amusing to think of these characters as being representative of their young author—particularly the Bishop. Indeed, a young Socialist has certain resemblances to a fifty-year-old Bishop, which perhaps no one who has never been a young Socialist or had one in the family could be expected to see. And young Socialists have frequently the habit of carrying their gospel into those haunts of sociological iniquity, the drawing-rooms of the upper bourgeoisie, where there are brands to be snatched from the burning in the shape of attractive young ladies, who seem too good at heart to be left in that world of hollow shams; in the attempt at their reclamation, moreover, such a young missionary may lose his Socialist soul. . . .

In dreaming of and working upon this novel, I did not think of either fame or fortune as a possible reward. I was doing it because it seemed to me the most interesting thing, as well as the hardest, that I could do. I had written a bushel of poems in the last three years, besides articles, essays and book-reviews; and I had expressed my views of life in conversation and letters. But in all these I had occupied a good many different points of view. A novel would require a point of view less narrow than any required by these brief and intense moments of vision. To achieve such a perspective would be to enjoy a kind of unification of my several diverse and contradictory attitudes. The separate attitudes would all be there, in some form, and able to speak for themselves—my Socialist self unconsciously but very mildly and tolerantly caricatured as the Bishop, and my poetic reality-fearing self as the young drug-fiend, while my pleasure-wishing self could have some scope and sympathy as the girl; and, in the novel, Pleasure could very soul-satisfyingly triumph over Duty, without the author being a whit the worse for it. Thus, in three separate characters of fiction, I would be able to set more completely at their ease the 'selves' which were being rather uncomfortably confined and not very successfully reconciled within the limits of my own skin. Then, too, I would be the philosophic manipulator of this tragic little drama, the god whose mind at once created and contained its violent and beautiful life! Or so it seems to me now.

My realization that I could not finish this novel came, not as might be supposed, from my ignorance of the private lives of Episcopal Bishops—I was prepared to dig up all the realistic detail necessary—but from my discovery of what had never before occurred to me, that a novel deals with the lives of people as they extend in the dimension of time. People are seen in a novel over a period of years, during which they change—develop—or disintegrate; and these changes are foretold, predicted, by small but significant events, as the years pass, before the final denouement. So, at least, it was in the novels I had read; so it was to be in my own novel. But I lacked observed data on this. I had never seen anybody change, or develop; and though I had seen a little disintegration, I hadn't seen it in its earliest stages, when it was merely the missing horseshoe nail through which the kingdom was later to be lost. I had never known anybody long enough to see much happening to them in the way of change. This was an accident of circumstances—I had moved from town to town, always seeing new people, seeing them very sharply and vividly, but leaving them behind in a year or two and never knowing what had happened to them. It was then that I began thinking of myself, and pressed my gaze backward for a little distance through the dark curtains which were between me and my earlier years, fold upon fold—enough to see a startling succession of Protean changes, not gradual at all, but sudden and utterly inexplicable. I did not know whether everybody was that way in growing up or whether it was just me; but it was not Darwinian and gradual enough for my fictional purposes, being more like the explosive 'mutations' of De Vries—and anyway it was an unpleasant spectacle to contemplate. It was like sorting through a bureau drawer full of old letters, theatre programs, unfinished diaries, souvenirs, newspaper clippings, manuscripts—one wants to burn the whole thing up and forget about it. My gaze lingered just long enough upon the past to reveal to me that I hadn't got as far away from it as I would have liked to think—that it was part of the muddle of my present character. Character? I had taken for granted that I had one, and a rather strong one, until I looked at it, and then it wavered, fluctuated, melted into a cloud of contradictions, and disappeared. My face assumed a grimace of distaste as I contemplated this preposterous mélange which appeared to be myself. It was an unpleasant occupation, thinking about what one was. Anyway, I was evidently too young to write a novel. So I would just stop bothering with it, and think about something interesting.

Before I quite dropped the dubious question of who and what I was, it occurred to me that my mixed personality might be the result of mixed ancestry. I knew well both the bad and the good side of the German 'character,' its crude insolence in power, its incredible meekness, its sentimentality, its order and neatness, its love of good living, its jollity, its sweetness and sanity, its love of music and ideas, of beer and philosophy, its dogged patience and thoroughness—and out of all these I hopefully selected order and philosophy and thoroughness as the German traits which I might possibly possess; these to stand against Irish poetry and mysticism and undependableness and insincerity and love of showing off—I couldn't seem, at the moment, to remember that the Irish had any good traits, except their habit of shooting British landlords. Like someone who has been to a fortune-teller and had a horoscope cast, I identified these supposed racial characteristics with the traits in my own nature. At any rate, I was not an Irish liar nor an Irish drunkard, and so, in spite of being an Irish poet, I might be saved by the plodding, reasonable, systematic Teuton in me.

4

Fired at last, as I had expected I would be, but most unexpectedly and delightfully given a better job on the other newspaper, The Democrat, by Ralph Cram, I took life a little easier. And one of my assignments was a strange one. The paper was about to celebrate its fiftieth anniversary, and there would be some harking back to the early days of the town. I was told with a smile to take the afternoon off and write a poem appropriate to the occasion. I went off and sat in the empty bleachers of a baseball park. The Muse, for all the rough treatment she had received at my hands, did not disdain to return. I discovered in myself a good deal of filial piety toward this city which had given me so many beautiful friendships, so much riches of mental and emotional life; and I returned with a poem on 'The Founders' which was set up in heavy type in the middle of the front page of the anniversary edition.

There was in Davenport a young reporter, two or three years older than I, named Harry Hansen, a tall, shy, sympathetic, straw-haired youth, then in spite of his shyness a very energetic and capable newspaperman, who afterward became literary editor of the Chicago News, and subsequently of the New York World and World-Telegram. In Davenport we walked and talked about poetry and plays in Fejervary Park, or I think it was called Central Park then. In his book, 'Midwest Portraits', he wrote these things about me: "Floyd Dell was in high school when I first heard of him; the story was that the high school had a freak poet, who actually sold verses to McClure's but who was eternally damned because he was a Socialist. Those who have read 'Moon-Calf' know today that Floyd's Socialistic activity was largely due to a lad's hunger for new intellectual contacts, a reaching out for new friendships to replace the inadequacy of association with mere schoolboys. I remember Floyd Dell of those days as a slight, diffident lad, who walked as if he were treading on eggs and who smiled faintly and deferentially at whatever was said, especially when he did not believe it, and then would disturb a gathering of callow high-school youths by opening a serious debate on whether the chicken or the egg came first." And again: "In the days of which he writes and in which I knew him, Floyd Dell was a lean lad with a bit of fuzz on his cheeks; rather negligent of his clothes and somewhat diffident in his manner; unobtrusive in a group, with a sort of smile which might be half interest, half disdain. And yet he was the best and most fluent talker of all if you hit his subject—though his subjects were hardly those that the average adolescent cares or knows anything about. Strange comment on philosophy; quotations from poets with unfamiliar names; stories from books with unconventional foreign titles. I remember a walk with Floyd Dell to that Vandervelde Park of which he speaks in 'Moon-Calf'—a walk that yielded my first acquaintance with Huneker, and through him with the dramatists who played so large a part in the early reading of Felix Fay; a walk that brought me my first glimpse of 'A Shropshire Lad'—quoted for the most part by Dell, to be read later with much searching of heart from his own little copy."

CHAPTER XVI

The Making of a Bohemian

1

In addition to the immense generosity of my friends, I was finding in Davenport an unexpected general tolerance for what were regarded as my rash but interesting youthful ideas, among people whom I regarded as my class enemies—the lawyers and other professional men whom I met as a reporter. To be sure, my own actual career as a manual worker had not lasted long; but my Socialist views were permanently fixed in my mind. I remained consciously an enemy of the class to which I now had, if I wished, the privilege of thinking that I belonged. Into this class I had a professional entrée of a sort which might, by a properly ambitious youth, be turned to good advantage. Much of a young reporter's work seemed to consist of making friends, upon any grounds whatever; and there was a friendly interest in me in unexpected quarters as a young poet and Socialist, where a properly impersonal cub reporter would have been just another nuisance. My ideas were inquired about, and listened to; and the listeners, though amused, said only in defense of the world which they represented that I would learn more as I grew up. One of them, who may have been forty-five years old, was so rash as to say to me that when he had been young he had had Socialist ideas, but that he had learned better when he grew up, and so would I. The reply which I made in verse was never shown him:

> Another taunt flung in my face by age!
> How long must youth sit quiet and submit,
> With insult for a shameful heritage?
> Scorning for scorning I will answer it.
> What is it that you said? That you had been
> Once young as I, and foolish as am I,
> And that like you to wisdom I might win
> And be as wise as you before I die?

> Hear this! If ever I become so old
> That I can taunt another with his youth—
> If my heart ever should become so cold,
> My soul so bitten by the wintry tooth
> Of age—then let the merciful lightning blaze
> And end the number of my empty days!

But these men were often sympathetic to my criticisms, remarking that I didn't know the half of it—and sometimes they told me bits of the half that I didn't know, of what was wrong with their world; their loyalty to that world seemed to consist in its actual advantages to them and in their conviction that, good or bad, it was permanent, and anything different a vain dream. Socialism, at least in a young reporter who was also a poet, was regarded as a kind of poetry; and also as a kind of intelligence which, when ripened by experience and disillusionment, would make me a useful member of the class which I now despised so heartily. A 'self-made' youth of energy and intelligence was, apparently, whatever I myself might think, on the waiting lists of respectable society. My youthful vagaries would not be held against me if I 'made good'. These men would be less tolerant, perhaps, of the youthful follies of their own sons, for whom after all they were responsible, and with whom they wanted to take no chances; their own sons must be, at all costs, groomed for their rôle in the world, scolded and praised and bribed into conformity with the regular social pattern of their class. But with regard to other promising youths there was an odd tolerance for nonconformity.

It was in these circumstances, of friendly and even affectionate treatment by older men who shared none of the ideals that made life worth living for me, that I wrote this:

> The dust whereof my body came
> Was ashes of an ancient flame,
> And rearisen ghosts of fire
> In me cry out with vain desire.
>
> Among these men of colder clay
> I wake by night or walk by day,
> And lift or lay my weary head
> Unfriended and uncomforted.

Only I con the tales of old
That tell me of my kinsmen bold
Who, laughing, broke the Law, and then
Went laughing forth as outlawed men.

Only I wonder when shall I
Go out beneath a stormy sky
Upon the road they knew so well,
An outcast and an Ishmael.

With every outward prospect, myself, of continuing in the favor of a city editor who found a variety of uses for my abilities, and excuses for raising my salary, I felt a profound lack of confidence in my own future. Though I had an outward air of self-confidence, and plenty of high spirits in company, I was depressed when by myself, lonely, and afraid. I wouldn't have given a nickel for any chances I might have in the world from the next day on. It made me smile to think that I was regarded by some people as a youth destined vaguely for success. I could get much comfort from contemplating the world's future, none from contemplating my own. It was dark and doubtful.

At the Socialist State convention, where I went as a delegate, I had met a beautiful Socialist girl of eighteen, with a quick and sympathetic mind. She and I began a correspondence, and it was my chief solace. On Saturday nights when I sat up alone in the office, to see the Sunday paper to press, I wrote her long letters of friendship. To her I wrote this friendship-sonnet:

Dear friend, we need each other, you and I!
The looks of understanding, words of praise,
The heart's quick language softer than a sigh,
That sweetens and redeems our empty days—
How much we need them, who are yet so few,
How must we cherish, who are all so weak,
The friendly presence that gives strength to do,
The friendly silence that gives heart to speak.

And we who singly are so frail, even we,
With your hand clasped in mine, and mine stretched on
Into the darkness where I cannot see,
But know another hungers, make a zone
Electric, a defiant coil unfurled,
That flashes fellowship around the world.

And presently, in my loneliness, and in spite of my curious feeling that Socialist girls were my sisters, I wrote her a love-letter, and it was responded to in kind. For a long time we exchanged voluminous love-letters. But I did not try to formulate plans for crossing the State to see her, in order to make good our paper kisses. Perhaps such plans would have been difficult or impossible to carry out; I do not remember. But I think I lived completely in the present, because it was all I had. I dared not, and did not, ever think of the future. I went on writing love-letters to her and being warmed and lighted by hers in the chill darkness that was wrapped around my heart for some unknown reason. Perhaps the reason is obvious. As a person with a living to make, I needed some kind of emotional or intellectual justification for the kind of work I did—the only kind, it seemed, that I could do. I had rejected my beloved Marilla's plans for me—I wasn't going to be a poet. What was I going to be? I had been fired from the other paper; when I was fired from this one, what would I do? Go to Chicago? How could I hope to get a job there? I had not a spark of courage with which to face the unknown future. My poems were too gloomy to be shown to anybody; I partly cut myself off from my friends, to whom I did not wish to confide my abject misery of spirit. My Socialist sweetheart's letters alone cheered me.

But with my father I maintained a genial companionship. By some people who knew how strong a Republican my father was, it was considered remarkable how well he and his Socialist son got along. We told one another humorously what we thought of the other's opinions, and no one's feelings were hurt. He went with me to a Debs meeting, and I did not mind his satirical comments afterward upon the audience. On Sundays I would go to the back door of a saloon with a pail, and fetch us back some beer. He would slice some rye bread, and cut some cheese, and pour out some beer into the thin glasses which he preferred, stopping just when the foam reached the top. He would hold up the glass to the sunlight and observe the color approvingly. "Here's how!" he would say. We would touch glasses, and drink. How good it was!

Of my mother's presence at this time I have no special memories. But when I think of her I remember that at this time a beautiful suicidal poem of William Vaughn Moody's—'Jetsam'—was so well known by heart by me, that I can remember now some lines which meant nothing to me then except that they were intolerably beautiful. It was supposed to be about the Moon:

> 'Oh, who will shield me from her? who will place
> A veil between me and the fierce inthrong
> Of her inexorable benedicite? * * *
> 'Once where I lay in darkness after fight,
> Sore smitten, came a little thread of song,
> Searching and searching at my muffled sense,
> Until it shook sweet pangs through all my blood,
> And I beheld one globed in ghostly fire
> Singing, star-strong, her golden canticle; * * *
> 'Then, since the splendor of her sword-bright gaze
> Was heavy on me with yearning and with scorn,
> My sick heart answered, "Yea, the little strife,
> Yet see, the grievous wounds! I fain would sleep." '

2

It is sometimes said, though now much more than it was in those times, that a young man needs a philosophy of life. Such a philosophy, if it is to serve his life-needs, should give him a guiding idea of his relation to the universe and to society—and this should be an idea that will set free his capacities for work and for affection. Had I such a philosophy? It seems to me that in reaching out to Socialism, I was possessing myself of the greatest intellectual and imaginative stimulus which existed in the world. It did give me a guiding idea of my relation to the universe, and to society; and this was an idea that set free my capacities for study. It also set free some practical political capacities, which had at first delighted and then had shocked me. So, though my philosophy set me free to be a politician, I could not be one. My philosophy, moreover, as long as it remained oriented to a Socialist Future, was an immense literary stimulus. But insofar as I had centered myself in the immediate political present, I was made to feel, as a writer, futile. Socialist propaganda offered to my talents as a worthy task only a kind of poetry which I could not write and a kind of fiction which, though I vastly admired it in Upton Sinclair and Frank Norris, I did not really wish to write. My talents were, if anything, poetic and psychological; and my philosophy, in its later propaganda mood, asked rather contemptuously what help poetry and psychology were to the Revolution. My philosophy had already nearly strangled the poet in me; and, since I had a living to make, I did not regret that; but, just because I had a living to make, I could not let it strangle the rest of my literary talents, even though they might be of no immediate and practical use in getting votes for Eugene V. Debs. I had to find some self-respecting way of making my living by the use of the abilities that I actually possessed; and my Socialist philosophy in its practical propaganda form furnished me none at all—it only discouraged me. Some youths, under these circumstances, as I later observed, threw their Socialist philosophy overboard at this point; others, I am told, have chosen to be politically rather than artistically creative; others, plain to see, went for many years, and promised to go on forever, in a state of internal conflict and outward confusion over this issue, trying to believe but never quite believing that their artistic products were somehow helping to overthrow capitalism; while a few managed to set their artistic talents happily at work in ways which seemed to them—though not always to their comrades engaged in practical political propaganda—to be ultimately useful to the cause of truth and freedom. As for me, I could never have stopped being a Socialist. My Socialism was too much a part of me, it was too invigorating to me as a student, too stimulating to my social energies, for me to dream of giving it up; as a person with a mere belief in Art, I should have been only an unhappy shadow of myself. I had to hold on to my Socialist philosophy, and yet somehow get from it the freedom to be an artist. In order to do this, I had to go back imaginatively to my earlier Nihilism, which set a revolutionary value upon Truth.

In my present world there were no Nihilists. But there was Bohemia, and it had a certain kinship to the Nihilist realm—at least the Bohemia did that I glimpsed in Bliss Carman and Richard Hovey's 'Songs from Vagabondia'. I became imaginatively a Bohemian. The Bohemian world of Murger did not please me; it was too pathetic—people were always dying in those garrets, and dying without an idea in their silly heads. The Bohemia I approved of was the one seen for a moment in every history of Parisian revolutionary uprisings, in which Bohemian students fought and died behind barricades in each crisis of liberty. Preferable to Murger's, because gayer, was the Bohemian realm of San Francisco, as amusingly reflected in Gelett Burgess's stories about it; his 'Queen Isyl' seemed to be a real person, and these Bohemians of his, however disguised in his fanciful fiction, had critical and rebellious ideas. San Francisco was already to me a romantic place, made so by Frank Norris's early books; and it became the home of my dreams. It glowed for me with a light that no other city ever had.

In Davenport, the working people I knew, Socialist or not, were all rather middle-class in their ways of life, with the possible exception of my friend Fritz, who combined the orderly habits of a civil-service employee with some mild Bohemian tendencies. I had to manufacture a Bohemia for myself. It takes some leisure to be a Bohemian; and accordingly it was in the middle class that I found one who was, in temperament, a fellow-Bohemian—a young married woman with a critical mind, who was so kind as to flirt with me. In her company I had my first experience of insouciant Bohemian companionship. Perhaps this companionship fixed in my mind, as a future Bohemian, a taste for some middle-class qualities in my Bohemianism—order, chiefly, and manners, and a certain degree of dignity; I never cared for or could abide disorderly, pig-sty, lunatic Bohemianism. The Bohemia I learned to like was, moreover, a quiet and seclusive place, not a show-off place; and a place with some outdoors in it—trees, flowers, streams, a sky; and all these remained a part of my notion of Bohemia. As a Bohemian, I did not ask of myself any regular, practical propaganda duties; my contribution to the Revolution would be such truth-telling as I could manage to do. And so I regained my self-respect as an artist.

As I sat with my fellow-Bohemian in the darkness of the summer-house, her lighted cigarette went up like a firefly on the bench opposite, paused, and turned into a glow that lighted up her face like a rose; the blooming of that sweet face out of the darkness was Bohemia. Soon enough, in that companionship, I forgot that I had ever been in the slough of despond. My poems were no longer filled with the murk of the abyss; they were amusing triolets and villanelles, begging for a kiss. And when, one day at the table where we were both guests, I refused the spring onions and she took some and passed them back smilingly to me, I knew that my beggar's plea was to be rewarded. My manners were considerably improved by her company. Hers were kindnesses I could accept, because they were not too maternal. She hardly agreed with any of my ideas; she had her own, but she sympathized with mine. And in her amused disagreements, with me, she afforded a companionship which had a profound solace. The companionship was for only an hour or two now and then; but it was so needed that the hours counted greatly. She was a teacher of an attitude toward life that in its gaiety included courage. The dark walls that had been closing in on me vanished. The future was still unknown, but that did not matter. Life was unexpected, and one followed where it beckoned. Anything might happen. Nothing was certain in this world, not even ill-luck.

I paid her the very sincere compliment, in a little poem, of bidding her, since for her I dared not hope: *For me at least hope this—that when I in love's luring darkness grope, with lips athirst for bliss, I may not ever in my blindness grasp a maiméd soul and mean, but hold irrevocably in my clasp You at nineteen.*

It is just possible that a flirtation with a handsome, intelligent, witty and kind young married woman is not a requisite and proper part of the education of some youths; but it seems certain that it is eminently desirable in the lives of all youths who are so unfortunate as to be poets. A young poet recklessly and helplessly puts more emotion and sincerity into living than ordinary life will bear; and in the gay extravagances, the pleasing insincerities, the playful overstatements and understatements and double-meanings of such flirtation, he learns something which extends far beyond the moment— it is nothing less than how to live safely and yet not too safely in a world which contains other people besides poets.

3

A society of freethinkers was to be formed in Davenport. I was invited to the first meeting, and there I saw George Cram Cook, the novelist. Three years before, I had been introduced to the Cook house by Marilla Freeman, my beautiful and adored librarian-goddess. George Cook was a poet and novelist, a romantic-philosophical novelist of whose reactionary Nietzschean-aristocratic conceptions of an ideal society founded upon a pseudo-Greek slavery, I as a Socialist had totally disapproved.

George Cook had found me at sixteen excessively bookish and rather 'inhuman'; that acquaintance had come to nothing. But we became re-acquainted at this freethinkers' meeting. George Cook seconded my proposal that it be called the Monist Society, and we were appointed a committee to draft a manifesto. Our common enthusiasm for Haeckel's philosophy enabled us to become friends.

This immediate and deep friendship took me out to George's farm at every opportunity. In our discussions he was converted from his Nietzschean-aristocratic-anarchist philosophy to Socialism, and brought by me in triumph to the local. He fell in with my admiring friendship for Fred Feuchter. And I, who had had Fred for my guide, philosopher and friend so long, found myself now serving in this same capacity, as mentor, to George.

Up and down in front of his fireplace in the country I tramped on Saturday evenings, making a new picture of the world for him; and he listened broodingly.

George had a nickname, 'Jig', by which at a later time he was universally addressed, but which was really his mother's pet name for him, a little-boy name which, I felt, scarcely fitted the great, tall, broad-shouldered, robust, slow-moving, serious, brooding fellow that George was in his early thirties, however much it might to a fond maternal fancy have ticked off some childish restlessness or versatility.

George Cook had always been temperamentally at odds with the world he lived in, and with the respectable class into which he was born. Apparently from 'Mammy' Cook, as she was called—a little, old, spry, efficient, mystical lady, very sympathetic to oddity in everybody—her son had accepted the rôle of 'man of genius'. But the 'man of genius' must accomplish something to prove his right to that title; and while awaiting the advent of powers mature enough to accomplish his masterpiece, he sinks insensibly to the fretful estate of an æsthete, who feels that his true home is in the Athens of Pericles or the Florence of the Medici. George Cook had gone through all that. He had played his violin to his English class in Iowa State University, and though it had caused official dumbfounderment, he would be romantically remembered for it by his students. Then, with the publication of his first serious novel, it was believed that he had the laurels within his grasp. But the next novel had found no publisher, and there had been none since. It is a miserable fate to be a non-producing 'man of genius' anywhere, but it is perhaps worst of all in one's home town.

George Cook wanted to live in a world which put truth and beauty first. He had tried to imagine one, with an aristocracy of poets and artists. But his Nietzschean Utopia was too vain a dream, and now, in a desperate quest for a new basis for his self-respect, he listened eagerly to my Socialist arguments. My energy, assurance, passion and dogmatism were very impressive to him. He was in need of a prophet, and ready to find one in the most unlikely figure. The fact that I was very young and mostly self-educated was all in my favor; the old, George knew, were silly, and as for colleges—he had studied at Harvard, Heidelburg and Geneva, and had taught in Iowa City and Leland Stanford, and he regarded all such institutions with an intense reprobation because of the way in which they had wasted his years. He was anxious to believe what I urged upon him, that his hopes for a happy and sane society could be realistically fulfilled only through a workers' revolution. He was glad to know that there really were other people in the world who wanted the same things that he did—millions of them, I assured him, in the Socialist International. George's painfully-groped-to criticisms of capitalist society had already been anticipated, and his political theories turned the other way around to better purpose. The theory of historical materialism, or economic determinism, was new to him, and gave him a fresh imaginative grasp of history, politics and social movements. He could not help regarding me, from whose enthusiastic lips he first heard this magnificent world-theory, with some of the awe rightfully belonging to Marx and Engels. George proceeded to take an active part in local Socialist activities, ran for office on the Socialist ticket, and began work on a Socialist novel, 'The Chasm'. The story of the novel was laid partly in Moline and partly in the revolutionary Russia of 1905.

The invigoration into action of a life that had for a year or more been sunk in lethargy and gloom, he regarded as due not only to these Socialist ideas but to the tonic influence of my confident, effervescent, talkative, arrogant, laughing, genially quarrelsome, unreasonably happy disposition. 'Mammy' Cook had remarked upon her big shaggy son going about with me: "Jig and Floyd—it's like a St. Bernard following a little terrier around." Our arguments were said to be the flying attacks of a ferocious terrior against a big, gentle St. Bernard.

George must surely have heard of all these ideas before, but perhaps he had been so completely immured in his early æstheticism that they meant nothing to him. His solitariness must have been broken through again and again, he must have had many rich friendships in the past, and yet the impression he gave me was of a person who had been lonely all his life. For whatever reason, he had never achieved independence and self-fulfillment; from ventures into the outside world, Europe, Mexico, San Francisco's Bohemian colony, he had returned to the comfortable paternal acres and the fond maternal presence. His great intellectual powers and rich artistic gifts had been expressed only in a surprisingly meager fashion, ending mostly in unfinished scraps. His talk of his past was of troubled and unhappy years; a struggle with drunkenness had been followed by an inward desperate battle to retain his sanity in a world in which everything, the shadow on the wall, a friendly greeting, the gesture of a man across the street, had come to have for him a secret Meaning— put there by God, for him to interpret and be guided by—this latter state the culmination of some frustrated love affair.

It was difficult to realize that so rugged a person as he seemed could be so sensitive; but he was painfully aware of what respectable Davenport thought of him. He had exiled himself upon the truck-farm, and shunned all his old friends. I, who felt that I had so many friends, felt sorry for George, who had so few, until I discovered that George's few were greater in number than my many; and when it turned out that some of my many friends were among George's few, from whom he had felt alienated without good cause, I reintroduced them to his trust and confidence, so that his life was enlarged by more than my society. Nevertheless he had times of brooding sadness, which did not yield to my blithe conversational assaults, and were sometimes unassuaged even by the violin which he took down from the shelf, seeking to heal his pain with beauty. Then he would sit and brood, and I would hover about, respectfully sympathetic, waiting for the fit to pass. It was an impenetrable mood, and a different man. When George was happy, he was, not only to my adoring young gaze, but to that of others, a figure of gigantic creative energy, superhuman, with a Promethean fire shining in his face. And when he lapsed

into sadness there was something lumberingly, lumpishly, hugely
Saturnian about him.

> 'Deep in the shady sadness of a vale
> Far sunken from the healthy breath of morn,
> Far from the fiery noon, and eve's one star,
> Sat grey-haired Saturn, quiet as a stone.'

That was George, at such times. He had one prematurely grey lock
which he twisted endlessly with a forefinger in those Saturnian
moods. What was he thinking about?

The past; of his past failures, in work and love; of the unpublished
novel that lay in his desk drawer; of his broken marriage. And, reflected in that glass darkly, the future; the new novel; the new sweetheart he was waiting to marry.

I had never read his rejected novel; I was willing to take his word
for it that it wasn't good enough. I had rarely seen, had never really
known, George's wife. To me it could mean little that the marriage
had gone to smash. At such rare times as George spoke of his marriage, he was, to my surprise, still bitter, still resentful, still hurt. I
had only his own account of the marriage, which therefore seemed
to me one which ought to have been ended earlier than it had been.
I could not realize it as a marriage begun with high romantic hopes,
nor think of their not coming true as a tragedy or a mystery. How
those early days of high romantic hopes had slanted on to the latter
days of soul-destroying quarrels was a question which it would not
occur to me that George might be pondering—whether it was some
mistake of his or hers, or perhaps some law of life too cruel for any
lover to believe. . . .

He was licking old wounds. He was thinking how his friends,
who had known him and his wife, could not accept the ending of
the marriage—could not sympathize with him in his new hopes.
Only this new young friend, who had not known his marriage, could
believe in his new love; the old friends, the most tolerant of them,
were sceptical, cynical, amused—the less tolerant were impatient,
angry, hostile. They did not know that to be without love was to
be dead. They joined with all the world to punish him. And the
pain of lost love wasn't enough punishment, it seemed; grief and
despair weren't enough punishment; the frightful abysses of melan-

cholia weren't enough punishment for having failed to make a success of his marriage:—no, there must be barriers put up between him and his new love; the doors must be shut and bolted between them; church and state must keep them apart; the bonds of the old marriage must be legally broken, with due formality; and meanwhile he must wait.

To my buoyant mind the matter was simpler than that. George had fallen in love with a pretty Anarchist girl, first seen in Chicago, who was now in New York, sub-editing a trade magazine—a girl named Mollie; and they were going to be married as soon as they could be. It would be lonely waiting; but they were having a correspondence that was voluminous and, judging from the scraps that were read to me, delightful. I, who at sixteen had been sufficiently critical of George, became during this later friendship protectively incurious about him; I managed to forget what I really knew. So that I did not by any means realize the chagrin of a man of thirty-three who has no means of livelihood which will enable him to be with the girl he loves. Nor was that all—the situation, if ever plumbed by one clear glance, would have revealed deeper depths of humiliation. And whether I was too boyishly incurious, or too boyishly admiring, or whether I knew already George's poetic helplessness too well to wish to see it clearly, I never took that glance at the facts. I did not ask myself why George, if he could not bring his sweetheart here, did not join her in New York. He supposed my youthful mind to be incisive, relentless, cruel; but it was never pressed against that poetic helplessness of his. When he spoke wistfully of the possibility of his getting a newspaper job, I was embarrassed; in that field, incompetent as I felt myself to be, I was toughened and hardened by the mere necessitous experience of earning a living in a way that I felt he never would be; newspaper work, at any level, was a rougher, more brazen, shrewd, unscrupulous and quick-witted affair than a poet like George could cope with; at twenty, I felt for George at thirty-three the impulse of protectiveness which the worldly, calloused, hard-boiled person feels for the person too fine-natured to endure the hard knocks of ordinary life. So I did not ask myself, ever, why, at his age and with his literary gifts, he should have been tied to a truck-farm. The answer would have been odd enough. Truck-farming was a part of George's theory of the artistic life; the idea was that a writer should not be economically dependent upon his writing, but should remain free to write what he chose. To be sure, in his untrammeled freedom, he hadn't written much. And, looking up one day from his accounts, he announced the discovery, overdue these four or five years but not made until that moment, that if he had to pay rent for the use of the family land and had to pay the wages of the family servant who was his farm-hand, he would be operating his truck-farm at a regular yearly loss! No, the reasons for truck farming could be really neither literary nor economic. He had a queer worship of Nature; he *wanted* (this was almost incredible to me) to be a farmer; he liked raising those onions, cucumbers, beans, tomatoes, muskmelons. 'Give all to love,' it has been written—'estate, good fame, friends, kindred and the Muse.' That would seem to include George's onions, cucumbers, beans, tomatoes, muskmelons; but it was to them that George was faithful, while he and his sweetheart languished apart.

The farm was at Buffalo, a village nine miles out from town. George's truck-farm itself was a small part of a country place such as I had never seen—to me a great wild park. And one could walk on the grass. I had never seen so much grass that could be walked on. . . . At seventeen, when I was working in a factory, I used to pass at dawn a big empty lot, in which there were, instead of the usual weeds and junk, some grass and flowers.—*Scarce fifty yards of grass and flowers, one tall, bird-haunted elm that rings at dawn; next summer these shall be among remembered things.* For somebody had said a factory was going to be put up there.—*Where careless goldenrod has poured its wanton treasure down the lane, a factory's length of dead brick wall shall vent its reek and stain.* A fine thing for the town, people said; but I, though theoretically approving the machine age as the blessed means through which the co-operative commonwealth should be brought into being, had mourned my lost 'breathing space' in stanzas of grief and indignation. . . . And here, out at George's farm, were endless grassy hills and valleys, a creek that slid murmuring under shady trees, a waterfall, deep woods, an abandoned granite quarry. Here was peace, here were the sights and sounds for which I was hungry, for which I went on long walks at night in town, to smell the flowers, the trees, the wet earth, to see the moon riding the clouds, to feel the night about me.

And here, too, in my friend's mind, were the fruits of a gentle leisure, despised now by their owner, and yielded willingly enough to me in return for what I could give, my Socialist ideas. I was happy to give them; but what I wanted from George was something gentler and more mellowed than my raw youthful brew of tonic ideas—the wine of an older vintage of thought, a more urbane and ironic and doubtful wisdom. I wanted the old books on George's shelves, among them the Mermaid Plays; I wanted to hear another voice than my own raised in the saying of old poetry; I wanted the thoughts of a mind that had been bruised upon experience, thoughts that were colored with pain and doubt. I as a Socialist had been prophesying woe to Babylon the Great; now I wanted to sit down by the waters of the gardens of Babylon, not to weep but to talk, with someone who had turned to behold wisdom and madness and folly; and whatsoever his eyes desired he kept not from them, nor withheld his heart from any joy, though in the end this also was vanity.

It was at this time that I read a very impressive American novel dealing with the subject of marriage, Robert Herrick's 'Together'. Though it was too New Englandish and fine-spun in its idealism, for my taste, it was a remarkably honest and able presentation of civilized people in a complex social environment. My admiration had hitherto gone to novels of an epic or a picaresque type; the reading of this particular American novel marked the emergence in my mind of a taste for psychological fiction. Though I continued to adore the epic qualities of the fiction of my favorite writers, among whom were Frank Norris, Jack London and Upton Sinclair, I found now upon re-reading them that Frank Norris's characters, though they had striking personal peculiarities, seemed to have no real individuality, nor any existence outside the scenes they occupied; I found that Jack London had an awkward boyish incapacity for depicting a woman or writing about love; and, though I was reluctant to admit such a thing, Upton Sinclair's characters, except when they suffered, were not human beings at all; while as for Victor Hugo, the grand master of them all, he was a glorified dime novelist when it came to dealing with individuals. Nevertheless, these writers had something in their books that was terribly important—the social scene, not in the static, placid, stupid Victorian sense, but in the dynamic, historical sense. This was so important that it overshadowed the delineation of character. Only Ibsen, so far as I knew, had achieved both truth of social situation and truth of individual character—and that had been a miracle which it did not occur to me to look for in fiction. But here was an American novelist attempting that difficult and important task! From that time forward, the novel became more interesting to me, less miraculously a matter of dazzling verbal gifts and more a matter of telling observed and experienced truths, a matter more in my line.

I had read very little fiction, at least as compared with the immense amount of poetry, science and history that I had read. It was a long time before I found any novelists that I could deeply admire, and even in the greatest of them I found failings that angered, disgusted or infuriated me. With regard to poetry, my taste was catholic; in fiction it was special, impatient, haughty, intolerant—I will not say unjust, because it is still my taste, unchanged in these characteristics, only more special, impatient, haughty, and intolerant. To satisfy so special and arrogant a taste, it would be necessary for me to write my own novels; even if nobody else liked them, they would be the sort of thing *I* wanted fiction to be. While I would read patiently and hopefully a dull Elizabethan play in the hope of coming upon a single golden passage, or would read anybody's complete poetical works and feel sufficiently rewarded by the discovery of one lyric nugget, the reading of fiction was for me increasingly hard work which I persisted in out of curiosity chiefly. So contemptious was I of most of the 'great novelists' whom I read, so completely alienated did I feel from the abominable mess of false standards which passed for literary taste, that I could never have dreamed of the possibility of my making a living as a literary critic; but I did intend to write a book of literary criticism, telling what was wrong with nineteenth-century fiction. And I did definitely see myself as a novelist—though I realized that I had a lot to learn about the technique of storytelling from the very writers whom I heartily despised as liars, hypocrites and charlatans.

CHAPTER XVII

ANTHOLOGY

1

BEFORE MUCH of my friendship with George Cook had been enjoyed, I fell in love with a girl who was to me one of the 'upper classes'. In spite of what seemed to me this vast gulf between us, I monopolized her society at our first meeting, forgetting everything else in the world but her, and took her home. I was invited to come and call on her; and, left alone with her at this second meeting, drowning in her eyes, I began to tremble all over. I did not know what to do; but she did. "Put your arms about me, Floyd," she whispered; "and kiss me." So I did. But I believe I recovered in argument subsequently the dignity I lacked at that moment. We argued a great deal about love and marriage, and she disagreed completely with all my views. She had a suitor, with whom she had quarreled, whom she had dismissed in anger; a fine young man, from everything she said about him, except that it seemed to her that she had been thrown at his head by her family. What she liked about me, it seemed, was that she could talk about such things—about anything—to me; and I discussed them sympathetically, thoughtfully considering her happiness. I could make no claim upon her, and would not have dared to think of doing so, on account of my poverty. And, in her eyes, marriage with me was out of the question, because, as she said gravely, she was three years older than I was. So it was made clear at the start that our sweethearting had no future; but it went on, in the midst of our arguments. In our arguments, she was a realist; she banged me mercilessly and smilingly with the common word, the brutal phrase. In some discussion I spoke of 'the child of a free union'. "What other people call a bastard, I believe," she remarked; and when I flinched at the word: "They do, you know!" From these verbal wars,

158

in which she defended convention, and I urged the claims of freedom in the abstract, we turned with no sense of strangeness to the joyous enchantment of kisses. And that enchantment lasted until her suitor returned to press his claims of honorable matrimony. She was troubled; she really loved us both, she said. But she couldn't marry me, and she could marry him. It was a sufficiently humiliating position for a lover to be in, though she was very sweet about it, and grieved and tender. But I was used to giving up things. And I wanted her to be happy.

I did not know how much of a pattern this was in the life of an impecunious young poet. I was not marriageable, but very companionable; and besides the desire to be married, it would seem that some girls have also the desire for a companionship in which they can be frank about themselves. It is a genuine kind of love, which a girl clearly differentiates from the kind of love which is a basis for marriage. I had not been able to make the distinction in my own mind so clearly; I had wished to God I could marry her. But she had been honest with me, and there was nothing to reproach her with. My heart was not quite so just as my mind; it wondered how she could have done it. But my hurt and my loneliness only made me the sooner, and this time unbidden, put my arms around another girl and kiss her; and to my astonishment she returned that unpremeditated, impulsive kiss. It seemed that I had, as a young poet, an attractiveness to slightly older young women whose more serious emotions were temporarily disengaged. But George, I think, regarded me, with a little surprise, as a more emotionally frivolous fellow than he had supposed, when I brought a new girl out to the Farm one Sunday.

The new girl was light-hearted, intelligent, and affectionately critical of me. I must not be, she told me, like my friend George—who had neglected to shave in honor of a young-lady visitor, and who had worn his old corduroys. I must have my shoes well shined and my trousers well pressed when I came to see her, if only for the benefit of her parents: "Let *them* think you are a respectable young man, anyway!" She mocked at my idea that I belonged to the working-class; "you have the typical bad manners of the aristocracy," she said. My ideas of conventional life seemed to her very funny: "But that's only what people *say*—that's not how they really act!" And she defended what I regarded as bourgeois hypocrisy, on the ground that it gave people much more freedom than any other arrangement would: "As long as people know what to say, and how to keep up appearances, they can do pretty much as they please in this world." From the first, I mixed my attentions with arguments. I intended them as abstract, and should not have been so bold if I had realized that they were taken very concretely and personally; but they were not taken at all in ill part. However, she had strict principles: right was right, and wrong was wrong; but, once that was conceded, I gathered that in her opinion the heavens would not fall if a girl did something that she knew perfectly well was wrong. That still, to my mind, left room for much argument. I was not a seducer; if a girl were to give herself wholly to me, it must be with a clear conscience; she must believe that what she was doing was *right*. "But it *isn't* right!" It was equally against my principles to take advantage of a girl's momentary helpless passion; and I lived up to my principles. My nobility gained me her respect; or so she professed. But my own self-respect was not increased by that nobility of mine. I did not know why I was ashamed of myself; but I was. It seemed to me that there was perhaps something in love that was not included in my theories. Was it, or wasn't it, absurd to boggle over a word? But so merely sociological was my knowledge of these further reaches of love-making which I had been discussing, that I sought preliminary instruction of my poetic ignorance in the learned pages of a scientific treatise, translating its Latinate erudition into a quite unaccustomed boldness of thought and intention. Or was my second thought too late? A mocking rhyme out of Percy's 'Reliques' sang in my mind:

> 'There is a flower that gleameth bright,
>   Some call it marygold-a,
> And he that wold not when he might,
>   He shall not when he wold-a!'

2

The girls whom I brought out to the farm seemed to George very conventional and not very interesting young ladies; for so they behaved. That was annoying. But what disturbed and puzzled me was what they thought of George. It seemed like mere bourgeois prejudice; when he appeared carefully groomed, his loose bow-tie was commented upon. They said he was charming. But—there was always a 'but', not at all intelligible. "Are you going to be like that thirteen years from now?" one asked me. I had never thought so far ahead. Thirteen years! I could only seem to imagine myself at thirty-three as a bum begging for a nickel to buy a cup of coffee, Mister; my imagination ran most readily to such images when my future was up for my consideration. What was the matter with George? "Nothing. He's fine. But why does he stay here in Davenport?" I said he was writing a novel, but the answer did not seem to be satisfactory.

These unreasonable feminine moods were explicable, however, when I reflected that they did not know the George whom I knew and talked with; he declined, or was unable, to put himself on exhibition for them. His deeply wise and poetic mind wasn't on view. But perhaps they wouldn't have valued, as I did, the power to reach into the past and into the future and make oneself consciously a part of some great world-process of change and becoming. Perhaps they would not have valued, as I did, the effort to put down in words on paper for other eyes and minds that vision of the world-process. I thought of him as a seer and poet. And perhaps young ladies do not like seers and poets of thirty-three; though at twenty it can be regarded as a delightful youthful folly.

But later I remembered that suggestion that he ought not to stay in Davenport. I was surprised to find him hurt and grieved by the mild allegations of quite nominal 'cruelty'—if I remember rightly, his neglecting to shave was included—which had to be in the divorce charges, with a requisite coloration of wifely indignation to prevent the technical suspicion of any such illegal thing as collusion having occurred. His father was a leading citizen and a distinguished member of the bar, the suit would be heard before one of his father's old friends, and conducted pro and con by lawyers with whom as a youth George had gone to school; and George felt ashamed at the thought of their bandying such matters back and forth. The respect of people for whom *he* had no respect, meant a lot to him. The divorce was being conducted in a quiet, dignified way, according to the most polite upper-class Davenport pattern, in a way to spare everybody's good name; but it took a long time. If he felt so keenly his position here in Davenport, why did he stay here? Still, I could understand his not wanting to leave the Farm. And one needed leisure, to write a novel. His sweetheart was in New York; but—I knew nothing about New York, of course—I couldn't imagine him there. He belonged here, as the master of this idyllic spot. He had spoken, once, a little wistfully, of getting a job. But his job was to weave the glories of the mind and of the visible universe into words of light and power. Poets should be exempt, I felt, from the hateful necessity of doing other silly jobs.

3

Sooner or later, with one girl or another, at this rate, it was inevitable that even so stubborn-principled a youth as I was would find himself really a girl's lover. When that happened, it seemed as though a new dimension was added to my sense of life. Now the hours of companionship in love, less argumentative, had infinite new depths of delight and meaning and beauty. These were the furthest shores upon which the widening waves of life had broken. It was a magical experience to take a girl utterly into my mind and heart and senses and imagination.

But what is a large freedom for honorable and innocent American-style sweethearting is a crowded, hedged-in and irritating parole-system for real lovers. The first barrier that had to be broken was the implicit, taken-for-granted word-of-honor which every American youth and girl were supposed to have tacitly given not to take any base advantage of their freedom; and, though we had actually given no such promise, and could have no real respect for a law which youth had no hand in making, we nevertheless would be regarded, if found out, as disreputable violators of a sacred parental trust. In being true to our love, we had to be, if only to protect it from instant destruction, liars and hypocrites to the world. My sweetheart, who had the gift of happiness, and a knowledge of the limitations under which it could be exercised, was very sweetly sensible in her recklessness; she had no qualms of conscience about deceiving her parents, regarding it as the proper business of parents to guard a daughter and the proper business of a daughter to evade their watchfulness; while parental 'trust' in her, she well knew, was merely a convenience to them, in lieu of shutting her up—a mere shadowy lock to be picked, an open window to climb out of to meet her lover. The secrecy of the affair was normal and natural to her; since when had daughters been what their mothers supposed them to be? More likely, for the sake of peace of mind, a mother only pretended to suppose her daughter to be an angel; if a mother supposed the contrary, what could she do about it, after all? The mother of daughters has a hard life, and it is a day of thankfulness when she sees the last of them respectably led from the altar by a husband who can take care of her. Thank God, that's over!

All this, though evidently a well-established part of American mores, was strange territory to me, who had got my ideas of love chiefly from advanced literature. I would have felt more comfortable in a situation in which my right, and the girl's right, to love without marriage could be frankly stated, sincerely defended, and coura- geously acted upon. But that was quite out of the question. I had no place to take her, no protection to offer her; and besides, she wouldn't have gone. We had to take, and be satisfied with, the love we could get by lovers' cunning and lovers' lies and lovers' curiously innocent and shameless hypocrisy. It was hard to manage, in our supposedly trustful but still rather watchful American world; we had to sneak away to hiding places; but, if lovers are in earnest about it, there are always plenty of such, secure as a desert island, in the midst of a world apparently full of parents, relatives, neighbors, strange busy-bodies, policemen, and street-lamps. The American earth had taken no oath of allegiance to that section of the Constitu- tion which guarantees the chastity of the daughters of the respectable middle class; the earth, still pagan at heart and as hospitable as ever it was of old to lawless young love, gave us a green soft bed. And, if the plays of Shaw and Ibsen had not prepared my mind for such love as this, the poems of Heine and Herrick had done so. The Elizabethan lyric poets had celebrated just such loves as this, loves stolen and beautiful, in defiance of all the social order of the world, and with only the more ancient earth and sky to understand and bless them. These lyrics in the English tongue were full of echoes of the Greek anthology; then it was, say the professors, in the Alex- andrian period, that lovers began to be romantic about their mis- tresses—a strange fact, rather incredible, and probably not quite true; but then, it would seem, and not earlier, there was struck in poetry the romantic note that was to vibrate down the centuries. It was not mere metaphor and simile when the Alexandrian poets claimed earth and heaven as sponsors of their loves; these mistresses of theirs had begun not to be, as in older times, bought and paid for. The suspicious face of mother, duenna or jealous husband (her Owner!) lurked around the corner in these poems; the girl only ceased to be owned when she gave herself in love; only became a person when she stole herself out of the safe-deposit vault of the parental home, or the domestic strong-box of marriage, where she was being kept to breed and nurture lawful heirs. This stolen love was personal love, romantic love at last, passion that had nothing to do with dutiful domesticity or child-breeding; and earth and sky accepted it, if society could not. The American moon and stars, just as in the lawless youthful loves of old Alexandria, were the lamps that shone beneficently upon our nuptials. I did not know how like I was to those old-world poets to whom love was necessarily and as a matter of accepted fate a joyful secret companionship outside of lawful wedlock, a companionship necessarily impermanent, knowing its doom from the beginning. She and I, in America, were living the old-world love life of a poet and his mistress, for the same old reason of youth's poverty and the same old social fact of lawful marriage being a matter of child-bearing for her and wife-support for me.

What earth and sky might not have understood in this situation but only grandly and indifferently tolerated, was that the impersonal, elemental, irresponsible fire of sexual love, when given the privilege or obligation of having no fruition in children and domesticity, could become a kind of passionate friendship, a recognition of the truth that each was, beyond sex, a person. It was the discovery that could be made in the serenity that had been achieved in each other's arms— a grateful, tender and enthusiastic discovery of the enjoyment to be had in each other's separate, unique self. It was as though these individualities, truly liberated into fearless existence by our happy love, had been born of our embraces.

Persons we might have seemed before to each other; but what had seemed in each other's eyes our marks of distinction, she from other girls, I from other youths, were superficial, negligible when true, and mostly false, being part of the masks we habitually put on to face the world in. I had seemed to know everything out of books and be an amazing explainer; but beneath this, more real and deep, was the intoxicated learner of living wisdom, endlessly eager for that sharper and sweeter knowledge, boundlessly appreciative of it—another person quite, who only dared to exist through her happy encouragement. She had been remarkable to me at first as a girl interested in books, because at our initial meeting we had found and clung to desperately in conversation the one partly illusory literary enthusiasm we seemed to have in common. That girl, whom I had thought I loved, scarcely existed; but our love brought out of its discreet concealment all her real nature, joyous and brave, humorous and tender, with depths below depths of candor for me to explore. The only trouble was that our talk and love and being together outdoors didn't begin to use all the possibilities of companionship with her. There must be a million beautiful things for us to do together, and it would take a lifetime to do them. That wouldn't bear thinking of: but, as it was, I had her curious words and thoughts to feed my mind on, her tones and accents to hear thirstily, her laughter to delight in, and the radiant glances from her eyes, or their way of letting me into their depths, all the magic of our intimacy to fill my heart brim-full; there was peace for a fevered head against her soft breasts, there was wholeness of being in her arms.

It might seem impossible that love, so strictly forbidden to dream of any future, could be truly without reserve. Reserved to the present it certainly was, as a fish is confined to the water in which it swims. Stone walls do not a prison make, nor iron bars a cage, when all that one can wish is inside. Perhaps young lovers only plan for the future because they are so continually and firmly urged to do so by others who have houses to rent, baby-carriages to sell, and so on; furniture-factories would close in Grand Rapids, mail-order houses topple in Chicago, clergymen would starve, city clerks would have to go to work washing dishes in restaurants, and poets who make a living writing those poems that begin, 'When you and I are old, Mary', would commit suicide, if young lovers did not think of 'the future' instead of 'tonight'. The future often seems to exist not for its own sake at all, but only to cheat us of some present and real joy. It makes promises of its own; but are they true? The future itself is an unverified hypothesis; maybe for neither you nor I will there be any future. How many credulous lovers have talked about 'next

June' to whom it never came? The world will go on; it has a future. But we? A mental reflex of secure and undisturbed social habit, the future is all right for other folks to think about; but some would rather not. Some must get along without a future, and find their eternities of love in such brief but authentic hours as they actually have together.

For most people, who had to have a lifetime of marriage and a well-furnished house for their love, and then seemed to achieve in all that time and space nothing more than a dull and mean respectability, I had a youthfully arrogant scorn; though she assured me that I still had something to learn. From them?

The word 'pagan' had not been spoiled, then; it meant free, natural, fearless, unashamed, joy-loving. Pagan she was, for me. But for me the word 'mistress' had been spoiled; to my mind it connoted the despicable exploitation of the daughters of the poor by gilded youth. I did not realize that an impecunious poet may have a mistress, and that I had one. I did not realize that a girl of what I thought of as the upper classes might find a certain kind of freedom only as the mistress of an impecunious poet; and I missed entirely, in my Socialist scorn of the word 'mistress', its connotation of that proud self-ownership and self-disposal which I knew well enough as the very essence of my sweetheart's love for me.

Such old-world lover-and-mistress-ship as we enjoyed was considered not to have the right to exist in America, where in good democratic theory there was no obstacle to the honest, open marriage of a girl with any youth, however impecunious or poetic. There was, indeed, no irremovable obstacle to our lawful matrimony, except in the minds of both of us; she did not wish to be the distraught wife of a youthful poet with no prospects, nor did she at all wish me to change from what I agreeably was into the more practical fellow who might manage to support her and the babies she would have in marriage. Her views, very candidly expressed, corresponded exactly to my own profound but less candid and far less self-respecting attitude. Certainly I could not support a wife and children, and I had no prospects which would warrant me in dreaming of becoming my sweetheart's husband; but these certainties were obscurely humiliating, never as frankly faced by me as by her. In our holiday love, as she called it, there was for me, and I fancied for her too, always the shadowy wish for impossible things.

But why cry for the moon? It had been wonderful to find, in this absurd and mean chaos of a world in which I had secured a precarious foothold, that little lives of friendship and love, full of beauty and truth and goodness, could be built somehow shiningly up among all the ugliness and falsehood by which youth was encompassed; but these little lives were at the mercy of that world in whose drab alien chaos they were built up. The world that called itself real, the world of ruthless money-making and timid respectability, sweeping on so hastily toward its doom, might in accident or malice smash our happiness at any moment. Not in such a world as this could youth's happiness have more than an evanescent existence. So make the most of the moment!

And it was soon ended.

We go to choose. Now under the low gate where fragrance of sweet peas clings close, and delicate tendrils sway in the night wind, on through the length of the lane whose uncropped hedges blacken to either side, and almost meet above to weave a pattern on our path of perfumed shadows and magical moonlight blent—and yet a little further, by the oak whose leaves hold ghostly talk high in the air— then open road. The brown and barren hills on that side stretching out beneath a sky set with scarce, lonely stars; and over here, the mellow wheat-fields flaunt their happy gold, and, golden in a haze of gold, the harvest moon slants heavily to earth, a honeycomb that drips with summer's sweetness. Behind us now the wages and the hearth, laughter and kisses, and the lamplit room. Before us now the night. And useless as the foam spat from the wave, I go. But you, smiling the lore of old nations whose child you are, seeing farther still perhaps than I, turn to the mellow moon, and to the fields that yield their harvest treasure tamely up, and to the four walls lighted from within, and close with lives and loves and hates and hopes. And in your smiling, unbelieving eyes, the quiet scorn of struggle that has built the four walls of the world, stone upon stone—I see it, and it half dismays me now. But for a while the friendship of the stars, the poignant beauty of the face I pass knowing that I shall never behold again. . . .

But it was not so easy as that. As I wandered, an exile from paradise, remembering her, I mourned not only all our love had been to us but all it might have been. It began to be hard not to see its ending as an act of treachery. That experience of first love, so happy and good, was being made ugly and evil in my mind. The old pattern of hate and scorn was there for me to take—if I left out the truth, if I could pretend that all had been as all was not. Then I could have believed her a heartless wretch and myself a pathetic fool. . . . What was it one of my poets had said about giving his heart to a woman? She trampled it underfoot, she broke it all to pieces—and each piece was a clot of hell. That was just how I felt. Each little piece of my heart was a clot of hell—filled with venomous writhing snakes that hissed and spat their poison at the beloved image. It was not only my loneliness, the ache of empty arms wanting her, that I must endure, but—oh, intolerable! The little snakes hissed and spat at her image. The tenderness, the truth, the sweetness that had been mine, must never have been real.

But there were other voices, too; I had to silence those other voices if I listened to the little snakes. All I had ever believed in, every civilized thought about women, every generous emotion, every unselfish wish, everything that had entered into my Utopian philosophy of life, spoke against the serpents. 'You do not own her,' said the voices.

And, when I listened to these voices, the serpents stopped hissing and spitting. So I listened while the voices said their say, and the pieces of my heart were not clots of hell any more. 'What she has hurt,' said the voices, 'is not your heart but only your pride. And that will heal.' And slowly in my mind all the beauty and goodness were restored to her image. I had that now, to keep always. 'You will be lonely for me for a while,' said the voices, 'but you can bear that pain.'

CHAPTER XVIII

Last Days in Davenport

1

At the age of twenty-one, I remembered not very much about my past life. It had been immensely long and varied, and full of excitement, hope, and pain. But over it a series of soft dark curtains of oblivion had fallen; as a new life opened in front of me, the curtains of forgetfulness had drifted down behind, blurring and veiling the past. Soft dark curtains were falling now. I faced again an unknown future.

I had been fired from my paper—for insolence to the proprietor, they said—and I had gone out to stay with George on the farm. Nineteen-seven had been a panic year; things might be better in the fall of 1908, when I was going to Chicago to look for a newspaper job.

While George worked on his novel, I, to pass the time, wrote one too; and even though mine was no good whatever—there was no disagreement among any of its half-dozen private readers about that, though some said it was so bad that it was good, particularly the bathroom scene—in despite of its worthlessness, George envied me my literary facility; words came slow and hard to him.

Besides writing the novel, I did some short stories, which George admired. We lived in the little cottage, where, in the long evenings, in George's study, by the little stone fireplace, with our corncob pipes, there would be the most delightful discussions. Our talk ranged through poetry and science and history and world-politics. It was a time of serenity and leisure such as I thought I had missed by not going to college. And now George told me of the time when a college education was to have been offered me, and how I had turned it down. "I think it was a good thing you said what you did," George told me; "but how do you feel about it? Do you wish you had gone

to college?" The public library, the homes of my friends, the Socialist local, newspaper work, and now a truck farm—these had given
me whatever I had in place of a college education, with all my friends
as teachers. "I think I've had something much better than college
could have given me," I said. Perhaps it was only my egregious
egotism which made me think that the things that happened to me
were better than the things that happened to other people; but I
regarded myself as an exceptionally fortunate youth.

Sometimes we tramped the nine miles in to Davenport, and went
to call upon our friends—Fred Feuchter, or Dr. Fineshriber, the
eloquent young Reform Jewish rabbi, or 'Maj'. Marilla, my adored
librarian goddess, had gone from Davenport to another city. We
called also upon Susan Glaspell, a young newspaperwoman who had
begun a brilliant career as a novelist. She read us some of her just-
finished novel, 'The Glory of the Conquered', the liveliness and
humor of which we admired greatly, though George deplored to me
on the way home the lamentable conventionality of the author's views
of life. Susan was a slight, gentle, sweet, whimsically humorous
girl, a little ethereal in appearance, but evidently a person of great
energy, and brimful of talent; but, we agreed, too medieval-romantic
in her views of life.

Among other things, as I remember, we discussed the question of
why Davenport was—as it was—an extraordinarily literary and intellectual town. I had formerly felt that the goldenness of my years
in Davenport was a special miracle performed by a suddenly kind
universe for my especial benefit; but now I thought of it as the result
of definite social forces. Davenport was what it was because it was
so largely German and Jewish, with an 1848 European revolutionary
foundation, and a liberal and Socialist superstructure. There was also
some native American mysticism in the picture, a mysticism of the
sort which blossomed in the '30s and '40s, a curious religious expression of romantic libertarian ideas. George's mother had such a libertarian mysticism, unintelligible to us; what I did not realize was that
there was a good deal of it in George, too, not least of all in his passionate poetic-philosophical attempt to solve the riddle of sex, and
synthesize in words and in action his yearning for an ideal and perfect constancy in love with his yearning for an ideal and perfect
freedom in love.

We discussed free love at Susan's. George was going to marry an Anarchist girl, and Anarchists believed in free love, and so, in some vague and uncertain fashion, did George and I—at least, we did not believe that love could be promised, contracted for, and legally or morally enforced; and if the simple Anarchist ideal of free love was perhaps too beautiful a dream to be quite true, it was also too beautiful a dream to be scoffed at. I think that my own feeling about such freedom was far from its being a permission to follow every romantic or sexual impulse, but rather, in the first place, a declaration that such impulses were good in themselves, though they might be un-fulfillable because of inconsistency with more important impulses; and, in the second place, this mutually conceded freedom of love might, in some marital situations, serve to conquer the demoniac emotions of jealousy and lead to a happier outcome, whether of recon-ciliation or of separation. For some reason I thought of freedom as a right granted to the loved one in unselfish and understanding love, not as a privilege to be exercised lightly or casually by oneself. I was rather solemn about it. These views were uncertain in my mind, a pious hope that people could be so generous, rather than a formal belief that they ought to be. What I did believe very dog-matically and as a plain civilized matter of course, was that mutual love created its own obligations, and that the attempt to impose such obligations by legal force or moral terrorization was a tyranny which no one was bound to respect. As for children, I was convinced that there were too many of them in the world, and that people ought to wait until they were quite sure they were well married before they had them. George added the footnote that enlightened under-standings of one sort and another were not uncommon at the outset of marriage, but that the process of living together usually somehow abrogated these preliminary understandings and left the couple quar-reling over their troubles as bitterly as those whose views were quite oldfashioned.

Spring came, the divorce went through, and George left for Chi-cago to meet, marry and return with his Anarchist sweetheart. I was to wait to welcome them before going back to town.

2

George's new bride, Mollie, was a little girl with dark hair and a

round face, twenty-two years old, happy and sparkling and delightfully talkative, much in awe of her godlike husband. She was also
prepared to be in awe of me, about whom George had written to
her in such enthusiastic terms; but that was not necessary, for I did
not stand upon my presumed dignity, but, as a country boy, was
immensely curious about the metropolitan New York world from
which she had just come. There was a dinner, at which she talked
of literary Bohemians in New York, and of various restaurants of
which I had never heard—Mouquin's, the Gonfarone, the Lafayette,
the basement of the Brevoort—which began to take on a romantic
significance as she talked. The life of her friends in New York
seemed to be somewhat like that which went on in the San Francisco
Bohemia of which I had read and of which George had talked to me.
It was all very fascinating; that was, I vaguely felt, my world—at
least, a world in which I could be at ease in thought and talk and
love, without having to be on guard.

I had expected to go back to town to look for some kind of job
for the summer; but George now invited me to be his hired hand
for the spring season; so I stayed on. The spring vegetables which
had been nourished in George's greenhouse until they were past
danger of freezing were now replanted in the garden in holes made
by a finger thrust in the barely thawed soil, and there was a culti-
vator to be pushed between the rows—there were various anxious
things to be done for those wretched vegetables, which seriously interrupted conversation. George liked to bend his back and nourish
infant vegetables into marketable adolescence: it gave him a sense
of creative power which his labors with words on paper did not
quite yield. As for me, the more I became the nursemaid of vegetables, the more my imagination turned toward literature. Finding
a lost knife at the other end of the garden, I held it up, chanting some
words which the wind blew away; and George, coming up, said with
resigned tolerance to his literary hired hand, "I presume, from your
Tennysonian gesture, that you were saying, *'Clothed in white samite,
mystic, wonderful.'* " On a trip to town with the first-fruits of the
garden, in two wagons, starting before the dawn so as to be at the
Davenport grocery stores when they opened, George relaxed from
his georgic preoccupations (it had amused me very much to find
that George meant Farmer in Greek) enough to chant antiphonally

with me back and forth from wagon to wagon, in the dawn-light, the stanzas of Sappho's Ode to Aphrodite. It was mostly for the sound of the Greek words, of course, but the words meant something too, and both of us were praying, for reasons which we scarcely understood, praying the wile-weaving daughter of God not to afflict our hearts with love's pain and grief. . . .

Meanwhile, the rush of the season over, I bestirred myself about the muskmelons, which George had given up for lost. These had been his most profitable crop last year, and he had put the largest part of his ground into them this year. But the stripe-bugs were killing the vines. Insect-murder engaged my furious energies for weeks; but an emulsion strong enough to kill the stripe-bugs killed the vines; one way or another, the vines died. The U. S. department of agriculture had nothing helpful to suggest. I tried killing the stripe-bugs one by one, working from dawn till dark, smashing them between a callous thumb and finger as if they had been so many counter-revolutionists. But the stripe-bugs bred faster than I could slay them. How I hated to admit that I had been beaten by those damned bugs! But, exhausting and despairing, I at last gave up the struggle.

George's father and mother were out at the Cabin now. Mollie's name for 'Mammy' Cook was 'Ma-mie', pronounced *à la Française*. We all took dinners at the Cabin. Davenport friends began to appear for week-end visits. The Anarchist girl wife was critically inspected. Someone was horribly shocked by her going around in overalls and bare feet. One would have thought from the talk that there was something vulgar about bare feet. I laughed; Mollie's bare feet were beautiful. But George's feelings were hurt; he wished Davenport would let them alone.

George now spent most of his spare time working on his Socialist novel. Mollie, not wishing to disturb him, talked to me instead. Besides, George had heard most of her stories already. . . . She was the daughter of a picturesque and wonderful (I had not yet learned to translate, in these daughterly accounts, 'wonderful' into 'irresponsible') father. In mid-adolescence she had found in succession the Vegetarian cult and other Nature and Health cults, and finally there in Chicago a brilliant Anarchist group—just as I had found the Socialist group. She had had a year or so at college; and various inter-

esting jobs, including posing for a great sculptor for one of the figures
in a famous sculpture (but this must be kept a secret from respectable
Davenport, for it was a nude figure), and acting in a road company.
Though she was a much more adventurous person than myself, I
recognized in her the same necessity for boldness in facing the world,
a courage born of poverty. She had the same temperamental power
that I had surprisingly found in myself for breaking the bars of cir-
cumstance and finding the riches of beauty and truth in an unpromising world. Perhaps there was something idealistically piratical in
both our dispositions. Freebooters both, we had never for long
stopped to be sorry for ourselves, nor had the patience to wait for a
revolution, but had taken our own happiness where we found it in
this Other People's World that we wanted to destroy. I did not think
all these things; but I felt an encouragement in a sense of our kinship,
our likeness.

I told her my life story as she had told me hers; and from her implicit acceptance of me as a person like herself, there was more to in-
spirit me for my coming struggle with Chicago than in the sober
counsels or sympathetic reassurances I had received from my other
friends, particularly my women friends. Mollie did me the honor not
to think of me as a fragile, poetic youth who needed to be protected.
She thought I would get along all right.

At Mollie's suggestion I sent some things to the Anarchist magazine
in New York, which were eventually printed there—a short story, a
poem, and a brief essay on 'the terminology of sex'; in this essay I
criticised as highfalutin and evasive the romantic language in which
sexual lovemaking was described in books of fiction when it was
described at all; I suggested that the increasing freedom of women
and their way of talking about sex would provide writers with a
simpler and more adequate language; the literary language, I said,
is based upon the language of polite conversation, which in turn is
determined by the taste of women; and women's way of talking about
sex—with probably a mingling of what now seemed forbiddingly
erudite scientific words and what now seemed vulgar slang—would
become the accepted language of literature. I was considerably
amused to get back an enthusiastic letter from Alexander Berkman,
addressed to 'Miss Floyd Dell' on the envelope, and beginning 'Dear
Floyd—' and telling me that I sounded like 'a very interesting girl'.

Mollie and I talked and laughed together happily; and neither of us guessed how mournfully superannuated a husband in his middle thirties could feel as he looked from his study window and saw his young wife with his young friend, a girl with a boy, eager, happy, care-free. He brooded, twisting his forelock.

Suddenly, after some revelation of his feelings to her, I found myself deprived of her delightful society. She never had time to talk any more. She was very housewifely—and very wifely. Her attention was given entirely to her husband. She hardly spoke to me, except in casual, necessary, polite table-remarks, or, occasionally, humorous matron-like speeches addressed to me as a juvenile guest. No more confidences, no more enchanting tales of Bohemian life. I wondered what I had said or done to hurt her feelings. I racked my memory for something in my talk or behavior which could have offended her Anarchist idealism, and have caused me to be thus thrust forth into the outer darkness.

After enduring chagrin and bewildered anxiety for a while, I began to see a new Mollie here, a domestic, tamed, conventional Mollie, anxious not to offend the standards of Davenport. Mollie, indeed, was just finding out that she was married to Davenport in being married to George; perhaps it had not been so nominated in the bond, but there it was, and she was doing the best she could about it. She was really an adaptable person, she had been an adventurer because she had to be, but she wanted security, and was glad—if that was what George wished—to be more his wife and less the symbol of Freedom. But George didn't know what he wanted, and hers was a difficult rôle. I did not understand any of this, but saw only that marriage had tamed this wild bird. I felt rather bitter about it, and in reply to her humorous matronly patronage I made ironic remarks in which my disillusionment was expressed. These remarks of mine were not so much resented as made the opportunity of more pointed chaffing. We began to quarrel about irrelevant things, the pronunciation of a word, the validity of the whole-wheat-bread cult, or the nature of the Buddhist religion. Neither could scarcely say a thing but the other would take exception to it. We quarreled a lot, more or less amusingly, and with sufficient Bohemian and Socialist politeness (which is different from middle-class politeness) but with some obvious emotional animus. George rather complacently remarked:

"Anybody would think, to hear you two quarreling, that it was you who were the married couple."

I began to inveigh against Anarchist ideas, including incidentally the theory of free love. Mollie remarked that I was getting conservative in my old age. George said, a little gloomily, that there was little to look forward to if there was no hope that mankind would be able to get rid of the morbid passion of exclusive possessiveness in love—somehow. I said, yes, in heaven there would be no marrying or giving in marriage; but here on earth—. The arguments never got anywhere, of course.

The season was over, and I went to Davenport to look for work. After a few odd jobs, I was invited back to the Farm for the rest of the summer. I went back. We tasted the muskmelons which had ripened on the dead vines; they looked all right, but they tasted like dust and ashes. George, at this juncture an Iowa farmer and not an idealist, was determined to sell them anyway. We took to town two wagon-loads of this Dead-sea fruit, and disposed of them to unsuspecting grocers; but on our next trip we found no buyers.

Presently Mollie confided to me that she was going to have a baby. She looked happy about it. She looked like the cat that has swallowed the canary and doesn't care who knows it. "You want a baby, don't you?" I said, taking in that idea. "*Yes,*" she said. So girls like Mollie *wanted* babies, then, really; it wasn't just something that was put over on them by their husbands, or conventions, or Nature! "I'm glad you're having a baby, then," I said.

One day soon afterward there was a sudden summer storm—with a blinding flash, as if the lighting had struck the house, and a clap of thunder that seemed to shake the earth. Mollie screamed, jumped up, stood trembling; and I put my arms about her awkwardly to comfort her. It was then that I discovered that I was in love with her; and the discovery was so disturbing that I decided to go back to town.

I had a week's work canvassing for the city directory, and then, though I tramped the streets looking for work, I could find nothing. After paying my family's rent, and something on the grocery bill, I had only twenty dollars left with which to go to Chicago, above my railroad fare; I hoped to increase it. My eldest brother, who had been sick, was back at work again, and the family would be able to get along; I was told not to worry about them when I went to Chicago, but to look out for myself. I tramped out to the Government Arsenal, over the bridge that I had crossed so often in my poetry-making days. I saw the Commandant, and he told me there was no work. His military hauteur angered me, and, after thanking him politely, I made up this poem as I walked back across the bridge:

TAMBURLAINE

Shepherd of thoughts, by day and night
My watch upon the hills I keep.
The Captains scorn me, passing by—
A simple tender of the sheep.

But scorn for scorn I give them back,
And in my heart I think of this—
They shall bow low, when I shall ride
In triumph through Persepolis.

3

That fall George said he wanted to take Fred Feuchter and me as his guests to the next meeting of the Contemporary Club. A young lawyer and poet—whose somewhat Shelleyan poetic drama, 'The Breaking of Chains', I had read and reviewed (a little snootily)—would read a paper on The Use of the Injunction in Labor Cases; and there might be a chance for an argument.

The Contemporary Club, as I knew, was an organization supposed to contain the leading male intellectuals of the town; it was conservative, with a sprinkling of liberals like Dr. Fineshriber; mostly lawyers, divines and editors. George, of course, was bringing Fred and me there to put the conservatives to rout and the liberals to shame with devastating Socialist argument.

The evening came, and George ushered Fred and me uncomfortably into that quiet, refined, courteous atmosphere of—as George had called it—genteel intellectuality. It *was* an atmosphere calculated to congeal any normally passionate intellectual conviction. Nobody ever raised his voice here, apparently; nor ever expressed any thoughts which were such as to raise the voice about. If anybody had such thoughts he suffered once or twice in silence, like George, and then stayed away.

The tall, slender, handsome young poet-lawyer read his paper. The Three Musketeers could scarcely credit the evidence of their ears. It was a recital—accurate, they took for granted, and a masterpiece of concision, for all they knew—of the ways in which the injunction had been used in labor cases. But not a word about the social significance of that class-use of the courts. No criticism, no attack, no defense, no comment. An informative piece, no doubt; useful, perhaps. But as a 'paper' read in a club for intellectual discussion? Was *this* the intellectual pabulum of Davenport's brightest and best minds?

George was not surprised; he had known it would be like that. We waited for somebody to start the discussion. . . . An eminent judge arose, beamed upon the young lawyer, and complimented him upon a—hrrmp!—very able presentation of the subject. There really was nothing to say, after that. At least, nothing else to say; so somebody else got up and said it again. And then, very casually, as if they hadn't known all the time that George was bringing in his Wild Men—attention focused upon us.

George got up. But it wasn't the George that Fred and I knew, who got up. It was the George who belonged to respectable Davenport, hated it, feared it, was morbidly sensitive about what it thought of his eccentricities—the George who had been brought up as a gentleman, whose father was there looking on and wishing to be proud of his big, handsome, brainy son—it was *that* George, never clearly seen by Fred or me before, who got up, tried to modulate his voice to the right tone, a tone implying that it wasn't anything to be excited about, the tone of an amiable, academic discussion between gentlemen—got the tone, lost it, and then said his say like a schoolboy in the presence of his father with the family clergyman looking on. However, embarrassed as he was, his sentences had form and substance. He did make a brief criticism. It was listened to curiously, tolerantly, benevolently, and there were elderly nods of apprehension. There *was* that point of view, of course, and the Contemporary Club was open to the expression of all points of view, said the nods. George, as he sat down, looked hopefully at me and Fritz.

Fritz ought to have the last word, so I got up, and spoke. But my remarks, which I had intended to be scornful, sounded to me, as I spoke, merely ill-tempered, bad-mannered, foolishly rude. I was, moreover, getting incoherent. Sweat burst out on my brow. I went on desperately. My voice became high and shrill. . . . This was awful. . . . Somehow, I finished, and sat down. I had merely made a fool of myself. Fritz, save the day!

Fritz got up—Fritz the masterly, the giant in debate, the genial crowd-compeller. Fritz spoke. . . . He sputtered. He grew ponderous. Then, overcome by righteous and ineffective anger, he burst into vehement broken English. I tried not to listen. He ended in furious unintelligibility, sat down, and wilted.

They were all very polite about it, the Contemporaries. They behaved like the lady into whose lap the fowl has slipped, at a dinner party, under a clumsy carver's knife—as if nothing had happened. The young poet-lawyer, who would have rather liked to be friends with these three lunatics who were so angry about his paper (what in the world did they expect?), looked after us rather wistfully as we trailed out, then saw that his father was waiting for him. "That wasn't bad, Arthur," he said severely.

Mr. Cook, who was getting old and gentle, wished that he could say something comforting to his son George. George was always a sensitive boy. . . . Why should he think this mattered?

"Come on," said George. "Let's find a saloon," said Fritz. "I'm afraid the institutions of America will survive the attack we made on them tonight," I said. "I should have known better," said George. The glass of beer helped a little, but not much.

We caught a street-car and rode down the hill. George asked us to come in and have a glass of wine. Fritz said no, he had to go to bed. I went with George.

Mollie met us at the door. "Well, did you and Floyd and Fritz overthrow the capitalist system?" she asked gaily. "We met the enemy and we are theirs," said George gloomily.

Mammy Cook was waiting up. And there was a young woman there, small, attractive, dark-haired, who taught something in the high school, a new teacher. Her name was Margery Currey. George told the story of the débâcle. The dark-haired little girl made amusing and comforting comments. Her round face was dimpled in each cheek. She wore her brown hair like a coronal. She had a sturdy, plump little body. I liked her playful conversational style. I took her to her boarding house, and upon my recommendation she prom-

ised to read Engels' 'Socialism, Utopian and Scientific'. She had
heard that I was going to Chicago, and she said her home was right
there in Evanston; she would be there for Thanksgiving, and I was
invited to spend that holiday there. She thought her father and I
would like one another, she told me. And I said I would be glad
to come.

CHAPTER XIX

First Days in Chicago

1

AFTER casting my vote for the Future, as represented politically by that perennial candidate, Eugene V. Debs, I went to Chicago, armed with a letter of introduction from Marilla. And I was met at the railway station by a friend of Marilla's, a young man from the 'Commons'—a settlement house. He inquired about Davenport, and Dr. Fineshriber, and Ralph Cram and others. Then I recognized him as Graham Taylor, whose lectures in the extension series on sociological problems I had attended and reported. Marilla had told him that I was the reporter who gave their series such good stories. I was taken to a street-car, and we went half-way across Chicago. At an intersection of busy and dirty little streets rose a gracious and homelike building. I was to stay there until I got my bearings. . . . I thought of how my eldest brother, years before, had made a brief, reckless and defeated invasion of Chicago. How different this was—a cheerful little room, that gave me a sense of ease and security in this great chaos of Chicago; and I was to meet the Head, Dr. Taylor, and the residents, at dinner. It seemed strange; I was being treated so well—too well. I must not let myself get to living in a Fool's Paradise. . . .

In a day or two I was a boarder in the home of a friend of Mollie Cook's. I had met Mollie's picturesque old father, Dr. Price. I was looking for a job and seeing the town. I find a sheet of paper with brief notes:

FIRST IMPRESSIONS OF CHICAGO (Nov., 1908)

——Arrival in Chi; dark—crowds—big buildings.
——Meeting where I saw Jane Addams; her voice and eyes.

——Anarchist meeting anniversary of death of Haymarket victims; Voltairine de Cleyre.

——Nazimova in 'The Comet.'

——Zangwill's 'Melting Pot.'

——Meeting Margery; the vegetarian restaurant; the chop-suey place; walk on the beach at Evanston; Vedder's 'Rubaiyat' etc.

——Lincoln Park; the flowers.

——Thomas Concert (Margery).

——Grand Opera (M) [I didn't like Grand Opera].

——Damrosch recital of Debussy and Maeterlinck.

——Public library; Arthur Symons' Poems.

——The lake [It was grand].

——McClurg's book-store.

——Newspaper office.

——Job-hunting.

——Olympic Music Hall; skit key to Congreve & Wycherley.

——C—— on [her friends] 'the radicals'—Harmon "the incubus" [Moses Harmon was the leader of the Anarchist group]; Barnard the poet [the chief artistic adornment of Anarchist society], the man who won't work, and his early tragedy (?), etc.

——The Price house [Mollie's father's] on Indiana Avenue; Bohemian plan, meals, etc.

——Mrs. [Elia W.] Peattie's home [she was the literary critic of the Tribune; and she read me a play of Synge's, my first knowledge of him]; child poet.

——Dining with [Martin] Johnson at German cafe; at his room, his books, his projected novel, his poems. Personality [the Aesthete].

——Chicago Daily Socialist.

Each of these notations brings back a vivid memory; but I pause to wonder how a youth who came to Chicago with twenty dollars in his pocket, managed to take his girl to a Thomas Concert and the Grand Opera. His girl must have stood treat; and I would have had no conventional masculine objections to her doing so, since she had the money and I hadn't.

Mrs. Peattie's reading of Synge's Irish play drew my attention presently to Synge's poems; here was a way of writing poetry that I wished I had known about when I was young and a poet—an earthy, simple, sincere kind of poetry, into which no highfalutin' false idealism could creep. In this style, and in a mood of homesickness, I wrote a little poem, during that first year in Chicago:

> I wish I had my father here,
> And I'd send out for a pail of beer;
> A loaf of good rye bread I'd get,
> And slice it up and butter it;
> Brick, Swiss, limburger, any of these,
> So that we had a hunk of cheese.
> He'd set us out the glasses thin,
> And pour the foaming liquor in,
> Then stop his pouring, quick and right,
> And watch it crown the glass with white;
> The color and the glow he'd note
> Before a drop had touched his throat.
> We'd lift our glasses up, and clink
> Brim against brim—'Here's how!'—and drink.

I wrote no poem to my mother; but I did, in earliest Chicago days, write a short poem in which I was thinking (without any good excuse) about Jesus and His mother:

> Can you not leave me for awhile,
> O traveler by my side?
> I gladly went with you a mile,
> But now our ways divide.
>
> Detain me not, for I must go
> On my appointed way;
> I loved—I love you yet, but lo!
> I walk alone today.

I wished I had my father here; but to my mother—not letting myself think it was she that I addressed—I said, 'Can you not leave me for awhile?'

Early in these Chicago days I saw Isadora Duncan dance. She was very beautiful then, and her dancing was a revelation of the full glory of woman's human body. The beauty of it was terrific and blinding; it created one's soul anew with its miraculous loveliness, the loveliness of youth and joy.

During those early days I was quickly disillusioned in the Anarchists, toward whom I had felt drawn by many temperamental Nihilist sympathies. I did not like at all what I had heard in Chicago about the conventional Anarchist cult of 'free love'. As for Socialism, I attended one meeting of my branch Socialist local, and found it afflicted with the same kind of hum-drum and boringly long-drawn-out 'business procedure' which I had enthusiastically and at least temporarily reformed back in Davenport; but I had other fish to fry now.

I looked for a newspaper job, apparently in vain; and my twenty dollars would not last forever. But a check came from a magazine for some poems just as my money ran out. My letter of introduction from Marilla was to Charles Thomas Hallinan, an editorial writer on the Evening Post. Not being able to get me a job on his own paper, he went around with me and introduced me to all the city editors in town. I made the editorial office of the Post my camp during my campaign, and got well acquainted there. Suddenly I was given a reporter's job.

2

When I was sent out on some assignment to some unknown place—'the Annex', for example—I went and asked a policeman where to find it. But my human interest stories, and especially my occasional turns at dramatic criticism, seemed to please the city editor and managing editor. I had learned a certain trick of whimsical humor that made almost any subject yield a readable story—a way, too, of introducing, at times, serious matter in a playful disguise, into news-stories; and that happened to be the manner, or something near the manner, which the paper was trying to maintain—the tone of 'urbanity', I think it was called, though it gave me scope for the pulling of unexpected laughs. But I had caught it from Margery's letters and Margery's conversation, which had a graceful lightness of their own; the image which it had called up to my mind was that of the butterfly shimmering in a sunny landscape which has a smoking volcano in the background. The world was, to my mind, the volcano, though I had no notion at all of the way in which it was presently to prove itself such—a volcano, in my thoughts, merely as a vague general promise of hell to pay; and the butterfly was the way the mind could, in thought and talk, catch and reflect in an idle winged dance the glints of sunshine in that landscape. That was the way her mind worked, and it fascinated me. I had earlier been disappointed because she hadn't read 'Socialism, Utopian and Scientific', which I so earnestly had lent her; but she had read the 'Bab Ballads', and her thoughts went to its tunes, taking for granted that the world was a pretty terrible place, and seeking to get some gaiety even out of that fact, in the way that Gilbert turned the horrors of cannibalism into the innocent-seeming jungle of 'I am the cook, and the captain bold, and the mate of the Nancy brig.' She did not really wish, as I did, to find order in the universe; she was at home on her terms of whimsical humor with an essentially chaotic universe, of a sort that would have terrified my more law-seeking mind. Where I wanted to know the reason for everything, she did not really believe there was a reason for anything, and only wanted to see the humor of everything. A jest was better than any argument, to her. And my imitations of her manner served me well in newspaper work.

I had for some time lived, in my private world of friendship and love, among people who were usually about ten years older than myself, with very few exceptions; in interests, tastes and habits there was less discrepancy between me and that older age-group than there was between me and almost all youths and girls of my own age. It was to such a world that I was best adjusted; and, since girls of my own age, when they did not frighten me, did hurt me, it was with young women of this older age-group that I would find it easiest to fall in love. In Davenport, after the breaking-up of my serious love affair, I had a love affair which was conducted mostly by correspondence with a young woman of this older group; and now I was in love with Margery, and we were together during all her holidays. She was a girl of twenty-one in looks, and I was a man of thirty-one in mental powers, tastes and habits. We found no discrepancy to bother us in our friendship or in our love, and cared no more for that indicated by the calendar than we did for what anybody else might think about us.

She had been right in saying that her father and I would like one another, though again it was the attraction of opposite natures. A delightful, gentle, whimsical, sensitive man, he had withdrawn his interest, except such as was barely necessary to make a living, from the contemporary world, and fixed it upon the past, in two fields chiefly—the England of Dickens, whither I could not follow him despite his conversational gusto for English chop-houses and such; and the early history of Chicago, which, as he talked of it, became in my mind the scene of a novel which I invented in great detail but of which I wrote only a few chapters. He was at work upon a 'History of Chicago'; and when he invited me to contribute a chapter to it upon some aspect of the town that interested me, I wrote upon 'Socialism and Anarchism in Chicago', centering in the Haymarket story. The attractions which I felt for him, and for his daughter, were attractions to a sweetness and humor which I greatly needed, being myself in mind rather too hard and reasonable. That I should have been attracted by their qualities seems natural, but, if there is no sense in asking why a girl falls in love, that still leaves me wondering why her father should have been so pleased with me and so fond of me from the first; perhaps protectively both, since sweetness and gentleness and humor have so much strength in them, and hardness and reasonableness so much weakness. I learned much from them both; but they did not wish to learn anything from me; they wanted to love me, in spite of any pain it might cost them—as anybody with half an eye could have seen that it would, sooner or later.

I fell heir to somebody's class in English literature at Hull House, and became acquainted with various of the residents there. I observed that besides those I should have expected to find, people who were performing, so far as possible, all the primary social services for their neighborhood and city, there were some aesthetes sheltered there who ministered to the needs of the neighborhood for beauty, in the theatre, for example; I knew from my own English class how deep this hunger for beauty was. And I wondered if some of the monasteries and nunneries of the Middle Ages had not been refuges for people whose qualities were weakness in the outside world and yet strength and service once within those walls. I did not compare myself to any except the aesthetes; I recognized in myself some kinship to them, but I did not know exactly what it was, for I had forgotten most of my own history; but I thought myself not so thin-skinned, and better able to stand the hard knocks of the outside world. I wrote a children's play in verse for some theatre-group there, but I think it never got performed.

I was living now in a kind of co-operative apartment on Canal Street, with genial old Dr. Price, Mollie's father, and a disappointed middle-aged inventor turned trade-magazine editor, and a gentle middle-aged postal employee who was accumulating clippings—he

had great boxes full of them—relative to his great projected book
upon some kind of more or less Socialist solution of all economic
problems. One of us cooked until he got tired of doing so; anybody bought any kind of food he thought appropriate, at any time;
when Dr. Price was cook, he cooked a peck of potatoes all at once,
and we lived indefinitely upon cold boiled potatoes (and very good
they are, too, with butter, pepper and salt). Harry Hansen in his
'Midwest Portraits' quotes someone's reminiscences of my Canal
Street home: "In the midst of this Floyd had a room—a funny
little post, with a lot of dust and disorder about. It was sparsely
furnished, but attractively, and on the chiffonier and at those Canal-
street windows (imagine—of all places!) were Japanese runners,
dug up from some basement bazaar and put to a use that was to
become popular later. And, of course, lots of books about."

Here I fell sick with something which threatened to be pneumonia, and was rushed to the County hospital. I was surprised and
pleased to find myself an object of concern to the managing editor,
who wanted me put in a private room; none was available, and I
was happy in the big ward, getting over what must have been a
touch of the 'flu'. Never did anything taste so delicious as the cup
of strong tea with milk and sugar with which I was awakened at
five o'clock every morning. The head-nurse was a perfect beauty—
just to look at her made an invalid feel that he was getting well.
And people came to see me—Hallinan, and the boys from the city
room, and people from Hull House and The Commons. My pay,
I was told, would go on while I was getting well. It was wonderful
—everybody was so kind. Could this be Chicago? Or was it a
dream?

I was well enough to leave the hospital, and it seemed to me that
Hull House and Margery were benevolently competing for the
privilege of looking after me while I recuperated.

When I was back on the job, I spent my leisure time loafing in
the editorial room, contrary to the habit of reporters; and sometimes
I turned in a column on something or other for the page. It was
an interesting group there. My friend Hallinan—Hal, he was to
me now—was a slender, youngish-oldish man, perhaps then arrived
at thirty, with an immense sociological erudition, a Socialist and
social-settlement background, and a well developed skill in present-

ing an enlightened point of view acceptably in the columns of what was supposed to be a conservative paper. Hal would have seemed almost as boyishly youthful as I did, except for his erudition, the sense of humor with which he restrained his intellectual passions, and the premature grey with which his hair was brushed at each temple. Hallinan and I had liked each other at once; perhaps in me he saw a younger edition of himself, with more unrestrained enthusiasms, less knowledge and more apparent energy. (For, as to energy, it was fortunately not my shy and helpless self that I brought to Chicago; at least, under Hal's friendly encouragement, there came out of that shell my other vastly confident, voluble, easily friendly, somewhat arrogant and rather bumptious self. Bumptiousness, or self-assertion, seems to be up to a certain point an engaging and refreshing quality.) The chief editorial writer was a good-looking, well-set-up young man, with a Yale background, vaguely apprehended good-family connections, a distinctly conventional way of dressing, and a quiet, well-bred voice, all of which set him rather apart from my sympathies as being too 'leisure class'. A long, thin, elderly, vastly experienced, gentle and quite unconsciously cynical newspaper man, was the other member of the editorial staff. Adjoining the editorial office was the cubicle of the literary editor, a short, stocky young Irishman, Francis Hackett, a brilliant youth of twenty-five, whose quizzical face appeared sometimes at these editorial scenes. The managing editor, the tall, middle-aged, courteous, anxious, physically nervous, appealingly amiable ringmaster of these intellectual performers, stopped in to bestow a benediction, or offer a suggestion, or hint a warning now and then. The fact was that the Evening Post had a tradition of intellectual brilliance which, in lieu of sensational qualities, was an important part of its stock in trade. Besides that, it specialized in financial news, and the reading of it was an established habit among the best people. But intellectual brilliance was of some importance, and it was to be had only—in those days—from employees whose views were not conservative at all. So there was always the task of catching your brilliant writer and getting him to be content to be brilliant within reasonable limits. No wonder the managing editor was anxious and nervous from day to day! The chief editorial writer was genuinely a liberal-conservative, hitting always the right note; and the elderly editorial writer was unimpassioned, descriptive, non-controversial. But my friend Hallinan, who had devoted an immense care to learning how to say forbidden things in innocent and unimpeachable ways, kept the managing editor on the edge of his chair; Hal had never spilled over yet into the impossible, but an anxious eye was kept on every word he wrote. And the literary editor, Francis Hackett, took full advantage of the presumed freedom of literary matters from editorial policy, and wrote in a way that did not even pretend to square with the conservative policy of the paper. That would have been all right, if literary matters had kept their place, but they had a way of being social and political matters, too. But Hackett had an incisive way of writing which had given him great prestige among intelligent readers. He resented the merest shadow of interference; and the only thing to do was give him enough rope and hope he wouldn't hang the paper with it. Just now quite a lot of brand-new rope was going to be given him—the literary page was to be turned into a supplement, like the New York Times Literary Review. But the problem of getting out a brilliant paper would, by all accounts, have been easier if it hadn't been for the owner.

The owner of the paper, though I had seen him—a small, shy, imperious, bright-eyed Jew—was otherwise a mythical figure. The things which were said of him hardly fitted together to make a plausible human being. Was he really a Baptist, or had he merely given money to some Baptist cause? Was he a fanatical prohibitionist and teetotaler? Was he, though miraculously uncanny in the stock market, as ignorant of everything else as he was reputed to be? It was said by his employees that the trouble was that he *could* read; sometimes he read his own paper, and then there was hell to pay. Then the managing editor had to explain to him that the doctrine of evolution was quite respectable nowadays, that lots of Baptist ministers, even, believed it; or else that the piece to which the proprietor's finger pointed did not mean what it seemed to mean, but that, when read calmly, it showed that God was in His Heaven and all was right with the world. I did not know how much of all this to believe; I thought it was rather a joke, though it was clear that the proprietor was not in sympathy with the actual intellectual content of his paper. There was always an implicit warning of 'The Bogey Man will get us if we don't watch out'—and an earnest, unflagging effort to let no day pass without putting a fast one over on the Bogey Man. It was the object of the intellectuals on the staff to make the best possible use of the means which the proprietor provided to spread ideas of the kind that he was known to deplore. The task had its obvious difficulties, but the risks made it exciting.

I reviewed a book for the literary page, and soon afterward was told by Hackett of the plans for a literary supplement and offered a job on it as his assistant. "That means," said Hackett, with grim jocularity, "that you will have a hell of a lot of books to review—unsigned stuff—all the dirty work. You will wash up the dishes in the kitchen, while I sit in the parlor and discourse enlightenment to the suburbs." Even so, the opportunity was wonderful enough.

3

The supplement, begun in March, was called the Friday Literary Review—and, in smaller letters—of the Chicago Evening Post. And Hackett was better than his word about the privileges of his assistant; he gave me an opportunity from time to time to shine in long signed reviews, and even to appear occasionally upon the front page.

It did seem ridiculously like a Horatio Alger story of success, and Hal chaffed me about it. "The unknown youth comes from the wilds of Iowa and gets a job as a literary critic on a Chicago newspaper before he is twenty-two." Indeed, it required some accounting for. Luck might account for half of it. But it seemed symptomatic of something that was happening in the United States, in the regions of thought and taste, a social change that was manifesting itself in literature. In Davenport, a few years before, as a cub reporter, I had constituted myself the dramatic critic of the German theatre there, despite the fact that I did not understand the language, for the sake of writing about drama and ideas and life in a way different from the way affected by the regular dramatic critic of the paper. I had written about these things in what I thought of as an intelligent and civilized way. That intelligent and civilized way of looking at things was getting to be in demand. And that was a portent. To my friend George, back in Davenport, the conservative literary tradition had seemed a discouragingly solid edifice. He had told me that Frank Norris, Upton Sinclair and Jack London, even with David Graham Phillips thrown in, did not make a new literary era. Respectability still stood with shotted guns behind the literary barricades, he had warned me. But now it began to seem certain that the time was soon coming when the literary sansculottes would swarm over the barricades. . . . As for myself, doubtless the fact that I could 'review' briefly from thirty to a hundred books a week, and still have time to read one book and criticize it, had something to do with my having this job. Another thing that was apparently in my favor was that, in spite of my wide reading, I did not know too much about literature, and did know something about other things, history, sociology, science, ideas in general.

But there was still another reason, unsuspected by me, why I was presently regarded with favor by the managing editor. Hackett went to New York on a trip to see the publishers, and mailed back a review in which he argued with some heat against race prejudice against the Negro, and, in one paragraph, against the current shocked attitude about 'miscegenation'. When the paper was on the presses, the managing editor had just got around to reading the proof of this review. He appeared in the literary editorial room, pale and trembling, a strong man in anguish, holding the proof in his trembling hand, asking me: "Why the hell didn't you show this to me? We'll have to stop the presses!" I looked where his thumb was. "Oh, I cut that out. The review was too long for the page," I said. With the look of a man reprieved from death, he said, "Oh—you did?" He took a long breath, looked at me, and nodded. "Better show me the proof next time," he said, and smilingly added: "Miscegenation is not yet a part of the Evening Post's editorial policy." Hackett was not so much pleased when he returned, but I argued that he should not expect me to pull his chestnuts out of the fire for him in his absence. I thought little of this incident, and did not know that in managing-editorial eyes I was regarded as a young man of great discretion, a young man who could be depended upon, a young man with sterling qualities, a young man with a future.

CHAPTER XX

IDYLL

1

IN THE summer of 1909, Margery and I were married, at her home in Evanston. As a mild gesture of defiance to conventionality, and because of our fondness for Rabbi Fineshriber, we asked him to come up from Davenport to perform the ceremony. He used a very beautiful old Jewish form, in which we drank one after another from a goblet of wine—an excellent burgundy selected with care by the bride's father; it symbolized the life we were to share. It was a rather large goblet, but I conscientiously drank my full half; the bride, who had been rather nervously afraid that the groom was absent-mindedly going to swig it all, received the goblet with relief; her symbolic experience with goblets of wine was in the Episcopal communion service, and so she politely took only a sip. However, and despite what her Episcopalian Evanston friends might think of the irregularity of a Jewish wedding, we were now married. And in the spirit of tolerant levity in which alone a legal and religious transaction of this sort could be taken, I composed the following

EPITHALAMIUM

For licensing we did not shirk
To give two dollars to the clerk;
We gave a preacher proper trouble
Making our singlenesses double:-
Would lovers all did emulate
Our true regard for Church and State!

The idea of our being married, when we first discussed it, had seemed to me economically hardly feasible, since my wages were not such as a wife could be supported upon; but Margery did not wish to be supported—she would keep on teaching school and get a position in Evanston or Chicago. I had always thought of marriage as so utterly beyond my means that I could scarcely believe it possible now. But it worked out on paper. And soon we were actually settled in a four-room-and-bath apartment in a new apartment-building up in the Rogers Park district, only a few blocks from the Lake and a short walk from the El. There was furniture in it, a bed and a couch, tables and chairs, a bookcase, and dishes, and linen—Margery had some money saved up from teaching, and I, to my surprise, found that I could get credit at Marshall Field's. The apartment and furniture were ours! I had never dreamed it would be so easy. Something so remote and improbable that I had not allowed myself to think about it, was here, now, actual, mine. I was married and living with my wife in an apartment of my own. That seemed to me much more remarkable than being an assistant literary editor.

The front room and the dining room were really one room, united by an archway so wide there was space left only for formal indications that this really was a partition. In the dining room there was a round table that could be enlarged by putting in a leaf or two; we would have some parties, and enlarge it. In the front room was a small library table; it had a shelf underneath that would be in the way of my legs if I tried to sit at it and write; I would just have to learn to sit sideways. And, also in the front room, a small couch. I thought of the small couch in George's study at the Farm, where he lay down to think. He reminded me of the heroes of so many Russian novels, who, whenever anything has to be decided, throw themselves upon the couch and think. . . . Twin beds in the bedroom; apparently nobody ever bought anything but twin beds nowadays. I had tried to argue with the clerk at Marshall Field's about it. When, I had asked, had double beds gone out of style? They had been out of style for several years, he assured me. I asked if it was because American husbands and wives no longer enjoyed sleeping with one another; or whether it was the symptom of a growing sense of individuality, insomnia, or feminism; or whether it was just because two twin beds could be sold for more than the price of one. The clerk seemed bewildered; all he knew was that everybody bought twin beds. In the bathroom there was a shower as well as a tub; I did not mind a cold shower but I hated a cold plunge; so I took a cold plunge every morning; at least one was thoroughly awake after emerging from that icy tomb. In the front room, too, was the bookcase; I was accumulating a library. Reviewers could take their review copies to McClurg's and sell them for half-price—the only pay they got; and I had done so as a reviewer; but now that I was an assistant literary editor and being paid a salary for my work, I felt that that would not be either honest or dignified; but I would take home and keep such books as were the accessories and instruments of my job. . . . And there was the Lake, two or three blocks away, invitingly cool in this frightfully hot summer weather; when we got home from our respective jobs, we put on bathing suits and dressing gowns, went down for a short swim—in my case a dip, since I had never learned to swim—and came back to lounge about and drink iced lemonade. . . . When I took the El in the mornings and emerged from one of the stations just over some railroad tracks, with the air full of clouds of steam, Chicago seemed mysterious and romantic, and I myself in a dream. "Am I really here?" I would ask myself. Did I have a job, a salary, a future in newspaper literary criticism? Did I have a wife, and an apartment in Rogers Park? Or was it just a dream, and would I wake up to find myself back in Davenport, fired from a job? Would these seeming realities waver and disappear? I must not let myself believe in them too much. . . .

Under Francis Hackett, the Friday Literary Review was giving expression to a growing youthful body of American literary taste, which had nourished itself upon the very best European literature and had civilized modern standards. That growing body of taste had hitherto been almost voiceless, and was supposed not to exist. Literary criticism was almost entirely either academic or mere puffery; to be alive and to have any knowledge of literature was a combination almost unknown; to bring social ideas to bear upon aesthetic products was something very new indeed. The smug provincial minds in the seats of power in American publishing, respectable magazinedom and criticism had not the slightest notion of the revolution in public taste which was going to overthrow them in a very few years. The newer, modern taste which already existed in youthful quarters would by the mere passage of years become power-

ful, if in the meantime it were not discouraged and weakened by
the sense of its impotence. The Friday Review, a pioneer in modern
civilized criticism in America, gave encouragement to this taste,
helped to formulate it, helped to lead its enthusiasms in the right
directions and to direct its resentments against the proper objects of
its enmity. And Francis Hackett was an extraordinarily intelligent
and able editor, who conducted this campaign with unflagging zest,
good humor, judgment and skill. The response which came from
readers all over the country was encouraging; the Friday Literary
Review had a circulation of its own; and since *it sold books,* the publishers respected it; only in its connection with the paper itself was
there occasion for discouragement and the threat of possible ex-
tinction; if the owner chanced to find out what it was doing, this
light might be snuffed out at any moment.

After a year's apprenticeship, my name was posted up in the
box on the editorial page as 'Associate Editor'. And, at the same
time, Hackett told me that he had no expectation of dying of old
age at this literary-editorial desk; some time I could have the job
myself. Hackett and I had in certain respects gone through the
same mill of experience; when he came from Ireland at the age
of seventeen, after some job in a law firm in New York, he had
come to Chicago, where he was said to have been discovered selling
neckties in Marshall Field's basement; he had got a job as reporter
on the Post and was said to have been so poor at that that he was
promoted into the editorial department at the age of twenty-three.
He had been apprentice literary editor, and had just become literary
editor the year that I came to Chicago. His point of view was
distinctly sociological, and represented an extreme liberalism; he
had achieved a much better unification of his artistic and intellectual
interests that I had—or would have at twenty-five, his age then. I
could be, and was, very useful to him in his job; he had no reason to
complain of my industry or zeal, and if I did not understand what
the devil he complained of in my style, at least I was always willing
to re-write a criticism and try to make it better. He never did succeed in making clear to me what he didn't like about my reviews;
perhaps he thought me better as a lieutenant than I would ever be
at the helm of the Friday Review. If so, he was right, though it
did not make any fatal difference. Though he helped me, trained

me as well as he could, gave me every encouragement to make the most of this opportunity, he had toward me the distrust which one brilliant Irishman feels toward another; and I certainly distrusted him on the same grounds—quite unjustly, as events made clear. What one clever Irishman thinks of another—too often with the best reasons in the world—is that he is out for himself, in spite of all his pretensions of ideals and principles. Any Irishman knows how perfectly selfish and ruthless the next Irishman is. It was taken for granted among his colleagues that he would make a brilliant marriage; the pork-packing aristocracy had all the money it wanted, and a young literary star, if not quite so good as a Grand Duke, was nevertheless a desirable acquisition and adornment; and this idea about my Boss did not shock me, nor did I ever question that it represented the probabilities. What kind of dubious self-advancement my Boss thought his lieutenant was going to achieve, I do not know, but he certainly believed me to be a hard-boiled, selfish, ruthless lad, in spite of my poetic airs. So we got along very well, and did some good pioneer work on behalf of modern American literature.

Necessarily, the books which I reviewed were not all ones of my own choice, nor had I an opportunity to review some I would have liked to handle; but in those first two years I find that I reviewed or wrote on Jack London, David Graham Phillips, Hilaire Belloc, James George Frazer, Hewlett's poems, Frank Norris's 'prentice work, O. Henry, Alice Meynell, William Blake, Gelett Burgess, the Journals of Emerson, James Oppenheim's poems, Gertrude Atherton, Helen R. Martin, Eden Philpotts, Francis Thompson, George Meek 'the Bath-Chair Man', Granville Barker (whom I disliked heartily as a Puritan), Nietzsche, Emily James Putnam (from whom I learned a great deal about the history of women), Ezra Pound, Anna Hempstead Branch, Georg Brandes, Arnold Bennett, Maurice Baring, Gustav Frenssen, Ford Madox Hueffer, Upton Sinclair (whom I scolded for his wrong views on genius and sex), Bernard Shaw (whom after a long period of idolization I violently repudiated as a prophet, because of his Puritanism—the most dogmatic and silly piece of 'criticism' I ever wrote in my life), Arthur Schnitzler, Frank Swinnerton, Ellen Glasgow, G. K. Chesterton, George Moore. . . . Some of these writers I immediately had interesting letters from, and others, years later, I found remembered my reviews with a pleasure which was very flattering to me.

My journalistic disguises had dropped off in the field of criticism, where sincerity had some rights. I was as dogmatic as I had ever been. I wrote, in reviewing the translation of Brandes's book on Ferdinand Lassalle: "And so, on August 31, 1864, the baresark lover faced his opponent with a pistol at fifteen paces, and was shot dead. An unworthy ending, says Brandes, to such a life. Perhaps not. He had failed in the first crucial test of his will. He had failed, because he was not, after all, a man of action, but a man of thought trying to be a man of action: Hamlet trying to be Fortinbras. As he failed in love, he would have failed—it is easy to believe—in politics. He would have been used as a tool by Bismarck for reactionary purposes. A weak man pretending to be strong, he was exquisitely adapted to play a part of infinite folly. Happy his fate, which permitted him to die before he had betrayed his cause." But there was some irony kept for other themes; thus, of Brandes himself: "There is in Brandes's writing all the charm of mid-nineteenth-century conviction. He assumes no airs of Olympian detachment. He does not ask, like Pilate and the Agnostics, What is Truth? He knows very well what Truth is. He and his friends have captured and caged it in a party-platform: hear it sing!"

The dogmatism is there upon all political topics; writing of Nietzsche, I said: "Well, the aristocracy has betrayed the magnificent confidence he reposed in it; it has never even read its own philosopher. And the mob, instead of remaining content, as he wished it to do, with its doctrines of renunciation, has embraced to a large extent what is a Nietzschean creed: the revolutionary proletariat everywhere regards itself as an aristocracy, and arrogates to itself instinctively every defiant characteristic of the 'master-morality'! Nietzsche himself is especially cultivated by anarchists, while Tolstoi, the renunciator, has found most of his real followers among the aristocracy. But another fate more astounding still has befallen Nietzsche's philosophy. He sought to provide the European aristocracy with a goal— the Superman; and with a code—adventurous and intense living. But on account of his obscurity this gospel has fallen into the hands of a class of self-appointed interpreters who are, in the main, inferior, dull, and base. So we have the spectacle of the splendid writings of Nietzsche—having the splendors of both great prose and great thought—being championed by heavy-handed oafs whose best feat is to imitate Nietzsche's mob-baiting in a kind of greasy Billingsgate."

Those were days in which criticism and discussion of marriage, already begun in the American novel, were beginning in criticism; this, from my own pen, was a very mild and good-humored example of it:

"If most European marriages are marriages of convenience, most American marriages are marriages of inconvenience—relative misalliances, mismatings of a thousand degrees of recklessness, experiments of which some are carried through triumphantly while others are proved failures in the divorce court. The way lads and lasses woo and wed is, despite the embroidery of our romancers, a simple matter; but the process of adjustment of mature men and women, of different breeding, different ideals, different notions as to what constitutes a joke—this is endlessly various, endlessly entertaining."

'Entertaining', I wrote, in complete sincerity—not 'sad', much less 'tragic'. Entertaining was what I found it in my own experience. Marriage was a much more satisfactory arrangement than I had ever supposed a person like myself would find it. It certainly had none of the dissatisfactions or faults of marriage as pictured in contemporary American or English realistic fiction. There was no tyrannizing—we were equals, each contributing to the support of the home. Nor was there any subjection to an artificial social standard—we had our own friends, who were not involved in middle-class social life at all. There were not even any bickerings—we had nothing to bicker about. If my wife had, as school-teacher and home-maker too, a double burden, I was assistant cook and bottle-washer, expert in making a salad, lobster Newburg, and other dishes—I was assistant home-maker, and very much on the job. I was living very happily as the result of an arrangement, unknown to my earlier life, in which a wife worked and earned money and shared in the support of a domestic establishment. I felt grateful to this arrangement, and was enthusiastic about it as a solution of the problems of young love in our present society. I was an ardent Feminist.

Meanwhile, as for Socialism, the question which I had been unable to settle in my own mind back in Davenport, that conflict between parliamentarianism and direct economic action as preached by the

I. W. W., had not been settled by the Party; on the contrary it was tearing the Party asunder, and every year that passed made the split wider and deeper. The most invigorating Socialist writer in the language, for me, was G. K. Chesterton, whose reactionary religious and other social tendencies puzzled me; yet back in Davenport days I had valued his criticisms as a corrective to my enthusiasm for Bernard Shaw, and in his most reactionary and most bigotedly religious views I felt there was some kernel of common-sense that I needed. The world of forward-looking ideas, once unified in my mind under the aegis of Socialism, was splitting up and scattering in different directions—and I had to keep in sympathy with the most diverse and irreconcilable conceptions of the Future, in order to feel that it was a Future in which human beings could live and enjoy life. But Feminism was in the air as well as in my mind—men and women were thinking about it, and eager to read about it. The criticism of existing society in literature, which had gone some distance along economic lines, was turning toward sexual arrangements. Those problems which worried most novelists—the conflicts between the need for social stability and the need for individual freedom—did not worry me, who was a contented young husband, in whose heart no wayward impulses had arisen. The whole immense and hardly known subject of sex did interest me greatly, and I was reading Havelock Ellis's monumental work in stray hours at the John Crerar library. The only problem of marriage which I faced was that of adjusting myself to a girl who had a different background, and a different attitude toward life. I had read in Jack London's 'Martin Eden' of the young workingman who makes a writer out of himself, and is in love with a 'bourgeois' girl, who was castigated in the novel as conventional and cowardly. Well, I was such a young working-man-become-writer, and I was married to a 'bourgeois' girl, and she was not 'conventional' in any socially objectionable sense, and not at all cowardly—on the contrary, very courageous. She did try to improve my table and other manners; and I accepted the corrections. Bad manners were not a sacred part of my personality; I was willing to lose them—if I could, which was not so certain. No conflict existed there. No conflict existed at all in our relationship, but a good deal of necessary adjustment went on, in which my pride, I think, suffered less than hers. I knew well that I needed more capacity for enjoyment of actualities like food, clothing, colors, the whole world of simple and sensuous existence—I was grateful to be humanized by my wife; she, however, who among materialistic and frivolous people had always been by contrast the idealist and the deeply thoughtful one, was not so pleased, and was rather bewildered, at finding herself in what appeared to be, again by contrast, a materialistic and frivolous rôle as a wife. But these adjustments were made with good humor, and added to the zest of life.

Our circle of friends was chiefly made up of people whose interests and ambitions lay within the field of the seven arts. Through Lucy Huffaker, a friend of Susan Glaspell's, we met Mabel Reber, society reporter of the Tribune, at whose home we were to find many friends—and first of all her sister, Edna Kenton, a writer. Edna Kenton's conversation, with its marvelously analytic story-telling gift, charmed us and added not merely new information about people, but new depths to our knowledge of life. Through Edna Kenton and her sister we came to know Martha Baker, the miniaturist. At Martha Baker's studio one day, learning from her that she had not had a nude model since she left Paris years before, Margery and I posed for her, happy to be of use to an artist, and quite approving of nudity. She gave us a small pencil drawing of ourselves, giving it a Paris date as a protection against scandalized minds, which seemed to us an unnecessary thing to do, since we knew nobody silly enough to be scandalized by such a picture. It was framed and hung somewhere inconspicuously in our apartment.

Through Martha Baker we came to be friends with Ephra Vogelsang, a beautiful girl with a beautiful voice, who hoped to go into grand opera. Presently we were happy to know Marjorie Jones, who had been and was again to be an art photographer; an enthusiastic listener to poetry. And there were others, who wanted to write, act, or paint. Always before I had been a guest at other people's houses, with never a place of my own where I could be host to my friends; and I enjoyed immensely the assumption of this new rôle, though I always forgot most of my general obligations in the intensity of some conversation, and left the running of the party to Margery as hostess.

Our dinner parties were small and gay affairs, with a good California wine to enliven the conversation, and some simple meal upon which we had both collaborated. My wife's father, who enjoyed such company, was usually among the guests. We all talked about ideas, and found a great deal to laugh at in each other's flow of wit. In contrast to much that I have seen in Suburbia since then, those dinner parties had an Arcadian simplicity; but in contrast with the duller, stodgier Chicago dinner parties of almost everybody that all of us knew, they seemed of an unrestrained Bohemian abandon. It was true that they were very amusing, and sparkling; and the idea that anybody would drink too much was unthought of. The combination of temperaments which my wife and I represented was, on such social occasions, very successful—her gifts created an atmosphere in which ideas could dance and sparkle.

2

The summer after our marriage we planned to go to Davenport on our vacation and see my family, and, of course, George and Mollie. George had written me about literary collaboration with Susan, and I reflected what a fortunate thing that might be for them both, since each had something the other tremendously needed—Susan's humor, story-telling capacity and sheer literary expertness, conjoined with George's magnificent ideas and brave truthfulness, should make a masterpiece. If Susan could put her remarkable gifts at the service of truth instead of romantic illusion, if George could have at his command words that raced and danced instead of groped and stumbled, that would be a book! Never were there literary needs which had a happier fulfillment than in such a collaboration, I thought. Mollie wrote, a little oddly, while rebuking me for the silly things I had written about Bernard Shaw: "I find myself growing Puritanical. I have little patience with my former deification of passion. I think the value of sexual love is very much overestimated, and holds too consuming a place in the scheme of things. The old-fashioned God of Repression has a wise purpose behind him." A strange way for Mollie to write.

When we got to Davenport that summer, we went out at once to the Farm to see George and Mollie. I wandered off into the pastures with George, and Margery stayed with Mollie, and we heard the two sides of the same upsetting story. George wasn't in love with Mollie any more; he had come to realize that he had been in love with Susan all along, without knowing it. People, of course, can't help such things, and it does no good to be morally indignant about it, especially if you believe in freedom; but it is humanly very sad. And as for me, while I loved George, and knew how hard he was taking it all, I had had my feelings very badly hurt by Susan before I left Davenport, and hadn't been able quite to forgive her, so that I wasn't the most sympathetic possible person with respect to George's emotional predicament. A few years before, when his first marriage had broken up, I had been the only person who could sympathize with him. Now I was among the others, too. I know what he was thinking that day as we lay there by the waterfall talking, because, brushing the tears from his eyes, he spoke of a mullein stalk in front of us—"It's like a Corinthian pillar," he said; and in a poem of great beauty, 'Though Stone Be Broken', that he wrote a few days later, there is the mullein stalk lifting its "Corinthian column": the whole scene is there, and what he could not say to his hard-hearted friend is there. The waterfall is there, wearing away the rock year by year:

> 'And somewhere there on the yet uncrumbled floor,
>   I know the point must lie,
> Where the receding waterfall shall pour
>   The day I die.
>
> 'Death does dismay, but even more than this,
>   Heart's hunger lacking food,
> Tense melancholy's perilous abyss,
>   Black solitude,
>
> 'Immuring barriers, bolted doors held shut,
>   The hostile world's deep guile,
> The stiffened knots of circumstance uncut,
>   Cold chains to file,
>
> 'Disintegrating grief, heart-sapping care,
>   All things to make us old,
> Darkness of faded hope, and heart's despair,
>   And love grown cold.'

The prayer that we had prayed, chanting antiphonally from wagon to wagon in the dawnlight, to the wile-weaving daughter of Zeus, not to afflict our hearts with love's pain and grief, had been in vain, for him.

But there was the baby, and the other baby that was coming. Mollie, the Anarchist girl, who believed in freedom, was being as noble as she could about it all. I thought about the babies; I didn't want to have any children of my own—I had no hope of being able to support any, and felt no urge toward parenthood. But I felt that if these were my babies, I couldn't ever leave them. . . . But then, I was still rather in love with Mollie, and couldn't see how George could be out of love with her.

At my own home, I had the impression that my mother, though very polite to my wife, didn't like her; perhaps because Margery was older than I, and a mother finds it easier to give up her son to one whom she does not think of as a rival to herself. My mother showed me a large bureau full of old manuscripts and newspaper clippings: I took a sheaf of poems, and told her to burn the rest. The bottom drawer was full of letters from my Socialist sweetheart of a few years ago. I stared at them, remembering May and the comfort of those long letters. When had we stopped writing to each other? Why had I never gone to see her? I could not remember. It had seemed so impossible then that within a few years I would be a literary critic in Chicago. Life was strange.

CHAPTER XXI

PREMONITIONS

1

GEORGE COOK's novel, 'The Chasm', was published that winter. Hackett made a face at the philosophizing in it, but praised it warmly. "It is a novel with great ideas in it. It is a novel with that peculiar sincerity which thrills the reader like a quick look of understanding or a sudden burst of sunshine after rain. It is a novel written out of the writer's heart." And, the Socialist Party having failed to buy this Socialist novel—as I could have told George if he had asked me—he came to Chicago and worked on a dictionary, while Susan, who had been in Chicago, went on to New York. George seemed doomed to that kind of waiting, in absence from his beloved, until the divorce courts gave him leave. He lay upon our couch in Rogers Park and twisted his forelock, just as I had imagined him doing.

He showed me the poem he had written, 'Though Stone Be Broken'. In it were these stanzas:

> 'Love lasting until death—is it a dream—
>   Is it a dream alone?
> Shall no love last here while the unceasing stream
>   Wears out the stone?
>
> *   *   *
>
> 'Shall anything endure where rock decays
>   Beneath the raindrop's weight?
> Shall Love prevail against the flood of days
>   Swept on by fate?
>
> 'We know not; but we know that only Love
>   Can keep our hearts alive:
> For this—the best that we have knowledge of—
>   We live and strive.

'Love's yearning hope forever to endure
     Endures, and yields no jot.
Loves fail: the unshaken soul of us makes sure
     That Love shall not.

'Loves fail: but as we face the corroding powers
     That test all loves and try,
My faith gleams diamond-hard that this of ours
     Shall time defy.

'Lo, I am yours—by life's profoundest forces
     Flooding man's heart and brain,
As waters in the thunder of their courses
     Follow the rain.

'Love, dearest love, whom bitter barriers keep
     In loneliness afar,
O bear it till the surging waters sweep
     Away the bar.'

I was again drawn by my friend's charm, his sweetness; but I wasn't
going to sympathize with his suffering. And when he asked me
very simply to believe in his love for Susan, I answered: 'All right,
I will, then. But how many times are you going to ask me to believe in your eternal love for some girl?' He twisted his forelock.
"I was going to say that this will be the last time. But I remembered
something that was said to a friend of mine. He had said that the
love problem was settled at last, for him. And the man he was
talking to, said: 'The love problem will be settled for you, when you
are dead.' " We laughed, and let it go at that. And Edna Kenton
has told me of an even more frightfully cruel thing I said to him,
one evening when he had been telling her the story of his life,
ending: "So you see, I have climbed up with pain and agony out
of the chasm"—at which I am told that I said: "Yes, George, you
have climbed up out of the chasm; but you have climbed back up
on the same side you were before." Presently George wrote a sonnet.
It was called, 'To Certain Renegades', and it appeared to be about
the Socialist leaders who had deserted the Party. But I knew, from
the way he showed it to me, that it had something to do with *me*.
I didn't get the point at first. I hadn't deserted Socialism for
Capitalism, that I knew of; but maybe he thought I was getting

conservative in my new job. Afterward I saw what he was saying to me—and other renegades.

> 'You, whose uncaptured youth gave you the dream—
> I need not name it—destined, when men deem
> Rightly thereof, to renew the decadent world;
> You, whose bright hope strong circumstance hath furled,
> And set you on the hostile walls, you see,
> Better than those who never have been free,
> Flaws in the mail you shall not wear again;
> And well you see the staggering of men
> Lame in the fight you watch from shielded towers;
> Your own souls teach you well the flaws of ours,
> And let you magnify them in the gaze
> Of scornful enemies who give you praise.
>
> 'But tell us—for your own old ardor dead,
> For your old joy in a great purpose fled,
> For the old thrill of oneness in the fight
> With all the brave old bringers of the right,
> For the lost vision of the goal immense—
> Tell us, O friends, have you found recompense?'

Yes, there were a whole flock of birds killed with that one stone—all the renegade Socialists, and me, too, once a believer in freedom, but now one who mocked at my friend, lame in the fight that I watched from the shielded towers of my little apartment in Rogers Park. There is no doubt that I was hard and unsympathetic.

2

The months passed, and Hackett, under constant harassment from the management of the paper, grew restive, and decided to quit his job and write a novel. He said, "Well, you can be literary editor now," and departed for New York in the fall of 1911. And now I was able to give George a job on the Friday Literary Review as my associate editor. How strange it seemed—that I, who had worked for George on his truck farm back in Davenport days, should now have him working with me in Chicago!

George wrote very beautiful and very thoughtful critiques for the Friday Review. And I felt at liberty to adopt a somewhat lighter tone in my criticisms. I should have felt a little more at ease as his helper than as his boss. He looked more the part, too—I felt my mere twenty-four years as a difficulty in occupying the rôle of literary editor. It was true that people, meeting me, expressed surprise at my youth; I was to take that as a compliment, no doubt—how surprising that one so wise should be so young! I had certainly laid down the law on all sorts of subjects with an air of authority. And now I had to go to New York to meet the publishers. They would think me too young to be criticising their books. In preparation for that trip, I commenced growing a moustache, and got a pair of nose-glasses. I felt, in that disguise, a little bolder.

On the paper itself my position was very secure. As the successor to that firebrand, Hackett, great confidence was felt in me. And I proceeded to demonstrate my attitude by giving a front-page review to an extremely radical novel on adultery and divorce, in which I praised all three, including the novel. I was congratulated by the managing editor upon my splendid review, and handed a twenty-five cent cigar. I was a little surprised, myself. But the author of the book was Joseph Medill Patterson, who, though a Socialist, was one of the Chicago Pattersons and destined to be the owner of the conservative Tribune, when he had got through sowing his intellectual wild oats. And the book was published by a Chicago publisher. There is money in radicalism, sometimes, and I was being a great help. The plot is even thicker; but there is no need to go into it. Suffice it to say that I evidently knew on which side my bread was buttered, and could be depended upon to say the right word at the right time. All my radicalism would be viewed with a kindly eye. Never did a young literary editor start out under more favorable auspices.

Hallinan and I had lunched together at one of our favorite basement Greek restaurants, and had gone for an afternoon glass of ale together, almost every day since I came to Chicago; and now Hal, George and I made an incessant trio, eternally delighted in each other, practising in conversation the ideas we were to put into the paper. George complained that I stole some of his ideas and wrote them before he had a chance to; but after the miscegenation of ideas that went on at those luncheons it was difficult for one to tell which were his own brain children. But my view of life had been very deeply affected by George's talk ever since our friendship first began. In a deep friendship between an older and a younger man, the older man feels concerning the younger: 'My lost youth!' and sooner or later, beneath his gratitude, the younger feels: 'There but for the grace of God go I!' And for George I had by turns both of these feelings, since in some odd respect I always felt myself to be the older in that relationship—I felt in George my own lost youth; a youth I had taken infinite pains to lose, but which I valued in George and wished to protect. Once Hal remarked, at one of these luncheons, that he sometimes indulged in the day-dream of having a million dollars. George and I said we did, too. Hal said that in his day-dream he endowed certain people, so they could go ahead and do what they wanted to, without having to worry about money. George and I said we had planned exactly the same thing in our day-dreams; and I went on to confess that in my day-dream I had endowed George with a weekly sum for the rest of his life. "Damn your impudence!" said George, glaring at me; "why, I planned to endow *you!*" Hal said *he* had endowed us both. I found that I privately resented the idea of George endowing me, as much as he seemed to resent such imaginary beneficence from me; I did not mind taking Hal's gold at all.

Margery and I went to New York—our first visit; we spent all our savings, seeing the town; and I bearded the publishers—or perhaps I should say I moustached them. In moustache and pince-nez glasses they took me for a regular literary critic.

Edna Kenton was an enthusiastic admirer of Theodore Dreiser, and I had read 'Sister Carrie' at her bidding; after a long exile in magazinedom, Dreiser had returned to literature with 'Jennie Gerhardt', and I had just hailed it on the front page as a great novel. In New York I was invited to a luncheon to meet Arnold Bennett; Dreiser's publishers were the hosts, and I suggested to one of the firm that Bennett be asked what he thought of Dreiser. "Oh, he's never heard of Dreiser," was the publisher's reply. But I had read Arnold Bennett's criticisms in the 'New Age' for years, those published under the pseudonym of 'Jacob Tonson', and I found it difficult to believe that there was anything under the sun Bennett didn't know about. So I leaned over and asked him. He instantly replied: "Dreiser's 'Sister Carrie' is the best novel that has ever come out of America."

I found my lost youth again in another poet, who sent me some

verses from Springfield, Illinois, and then came up to Chicago to
see me. His name was Nicholas Vachel Lindsay—an ungainly
youth, a youth in spite of his being then thirty-six years of age; a
mere boy, with his heart full of beautiful and preposterous dreams.
He had a 'gospel of beauty'. And he had written of his home town,
in defiance of the hopes of all its real-estate dealers:

'Let not our town be large, remembering
    That little Athens was the Muses' home,
That Oxford rules the heart of London still,
    That Florence gave the Renaissance to Rome.

'Let us build parks that students from afar
    Would choose to starve in rather than go home;
Fair little squares with Phidian ornament,
    Food for the spirit, milk and honeycomb.'

He was planning to go on a tramping trip and trade his rhymes for
bread. He got out little private editions of his poems, and gave them
to his friends—no publisher was interested in them. He illustrated
them with his own drawings—quaint pictures of moons and ships
and bubbles, in an Aubrey Beardsley style with all the diabolism
left out, and watered down with milk from the nursery. He had
been an art-student at the Chicago Art Institute and in New York;
and since then he had lived at his mother's home in Springfield, not
earning a regular living; he tramped about a good deal, and he made
Socialist speeches, and also took part in the Anti-Saloon League
campaigns; his mind was full of the rich barbaric color of raw
America, its churches and dance-halls, its cities and farms, white
folks and black—he had looked on at everything; but none of this
elemental interest in life came into his thin sweet verse. We discussed the possibility of a publisher for his poems, and I wondered if
Thomas B. Mosher, who had found a small audience of intense poetry
lovers in America, would be interested in bringing Vachel's poetry
to their attention. I did not mind its lack of elemental interest;
its message—and it was all message, except what was quaintly boyish
fantasy—touched my heart:

'Let not young souls be smothered out before
    They do quaint deeds and fully flaunt their pride.
It is the world's one crime its babes grow dull.
    Its poor are ox-like, limp and leaden-eyed.

> Not that they starve, but starve so dreamlessly,
> Not that they sow, but that they seldom reap,
> Not that they serve, but have no gods to serve,
> Not that they die, but that they die like sheep.'

He wanted to see my own poems, and returned them with a list
of titles, some of them marked with one or more hearts, thus—♥.
One heart meant he liked a poem, three hearts ♥ ♥ ♥ meant
that he liked it a lot. He thought it strange that I did not want to
publish them. I did, then, print some of them, anonymously, on the
editorial page of the Friday Literary Review, among clipped matter,
as 'Poems of a Young Man'; but they looked thin, pale, and out of
key with the new, robust literature which we were finding to praise,
even in America. Once or twice Vachel went on picnics with some
of us up on the lake shore, and we recited poetry.

George and I, who knew that poetry should be read aloud and
not merely with the eyes, had been much interested in W. B. Yeats's
insistence that poetry should be chanted. Yeats had given the
musical notation for one of his poems, and we had Ephra Vogelsang
play it on the piano while we tried to chant the poem. It didn't come
out very well, but the idea haunted us, and we kept trying to find
the right 'tunes' for various poems. I had fallen in love with G. K.
Chesterton's 'Lepanto', which had been published in an English
weekly, and I chanted that loudly, with all its

> 'Dim drums throbbing in the hills half heard,'

and its

> 'Strong gongs groaning as the guns boom far—
> Don John of Austria is going to the war—
> Stiff flags straining in the night-blasts cold,
> In the gloom black purple, in the glint old gold,
> Torchlight crimson on the copper kettle drums,
> Then the tuckets, then the trumpets, then the cannon, and he comes—

*   *   *

> '*Vivat Hispania!*
> *Domino gloria!*
> Don John of Austria
> Has set his people free!

It made a loud, glorious chant. And then Vachel, who had all the barbaric music of America locked up in his memory, now in his turn, there on the beach, whispered into the night:

> 'My sweetheart is the girl beyond the Moon,
> For never have I been in love with woman,
> Aspiring always to be set in tune
> With one who is invisible, inhuman.'

Well, Vachel had made his choice; I was glad he had made it that way, because some youths ought to choose poetry instead of a girl; but I was not sorry I had chosen the way I had. I wished I could help Vachel find a publisher; but who cared about moon-poems? Few enough. I felt so much older than Vachel. . . .

Being an editor makes one feel old. Here was Brander Matthews writing in to argue with 'the editor of the Friday Literary Review' about spelling reform. I had poked a little very gentle fun at the enthusiastic hopes of the spelling reformers—hopes with which I sympathized, but which did not seem to me very realistic. And the sixty-year-old Brander Matthews wrote in the vein of a reckless youthful reformer to the staid, urbane, wordly-wise editor of the Evening Post's Literary Review. It was funny. There seemed to be nothing left to do but write back: Yes, I was a youthful reformer once myself, Brander! But when you get to be as old as I am, you will realize that the world is slow to change its habits. I said this jestingly to George, and he replied thoughtfully: "Do you remember, Floyd, how you once wrote a sonnet, saying that if ever you became so old that you could taunt another with his youth, then you hoped that the lightning would mercifully blaze and end the number of your empty days? You may have been joking about Brander Matthews, but that is all the same to the Gods. You have taunted Brander Matthews for his youth—and now look out for the lightning!"

Martha Baker, the painter, died. I was one of the pallbearers; and I thought, as I sat there in the church, some of the things that people think when their friends are dead. The painter Sorolla had called Martha Baker 'the greatest living miniaturist'. In her latest work there had been a sudden change—the dark and inquisitive portraiture of her earlier pictures had given place to something bold and joyous, seen at its best in some of her young-girl portraits, frank delineations of that fervor of adolescence which gives a wild beauty to young faces.

How many years it had been before she could reach that lyric rapture in her work! And then, death, as she stood on the threshold of this new world of achievement! A coffin, even if carried by six friends, is heavy. Death—and the world goes on. The preacher had been talking about an immortality in which none of us believed. Death— the world went on, but one that had been living and unique was not here.

3

The lightning which George had predicted for me blazed in a premonitory way. There was a girl; and we kissed. And then, suddenly, I was in a realm more real to me than the world I had thought of as real—which had now become a shadow, a dream, something remote and dim. I was happy and free; not a literary editor; not a husband; only myself. All the values in my universe were suddenly transvalued. I felt like a wanderer, long absent in alien lands, who sets eyes again upon his native place. Why should I have ever imagined myself that stranger, worn that uniform? This, the realm of liberty, was one in which I could be at ease. There need be no effort here to be what one was not, only infinite sincerity of oneself to another, in love and talk and laughter. We made love happily and solemnly.

It was not until I had kissed her good-bye, and gone down the steps, that I realized what it meant to go home and have dinner with my wife.

I had to put this out of my mind. I was going back into the other world—the world in which I was a husband—and, if I could remember rightly, a literary editor, or something like that. I took a street car.

It is, at best, in Chicago, a long way from anywhere to anywhere else. I was taking the longest possible way. The journey lasted a thousand years.

I had a great deal to think out. I had not shared some current views, considered 'modern', as to the permissible liberties by which the old-fashioned institution of marriage could be made tolerable to adventurous people. I did believe in freedom, and never for a moment had given anybody who knew me intimately the right to suppose that I believed in anything else; but I had always taken it for granted that love, to have precedence over marriage, must be of a desperately serious nature—no mere sudden natural impulse, such as this had been. I couldn't think that impulse wrong. I didn't think it wrong. But I did not wish to be tossed into the maelstrom of such impulses; I did not wish to lose—I wished desperately not to lose— the peace and order and stability which I had so miraculously achieved in my marriage. Now, under the threat of these impulses, my little apartment walls, in my imagination, seemed to shiver and melt away, leaving me in some vast darkness. I was afraid. I did not want to be the sort of person who had a lot of idle sexual experiences at every opportunity. And now I realized how multitudinous the opportunities were and would be. Sex was something too important to be taken that way. And yet I was, and now I knew it, one to whom such intimacies were beautiful, good in themselves, seemingly a part of the enchanting intimacy of mutually self-revealing talk; I should have felt a coward, been ashamed of myself, if that hour's intimacy of talk had not been made perfect and complete. It belonged to me; never could I repudiate it, or regret it. And yet it did not fit into the structure of my life's peace, order, stability. It was not a memory that I could bring to a marital dinner table. Some time I must think it all out. But just now I had to put it out of my mind.

And so, going back into a world in which it had no possible place, I tried to shut my mind against thoughts of what had just happened. I looked out of the window, trying to concentrate my mind upon the consecutive blocks of Chicago. My eyes, however, refused to see what was before them. Someone left a newspaper in the seat, and I picked it up eagerly. The headlines made no sense whatever, nor did the text, even when the same sentence was read over three or four times. The funny-pictures were better—they occupied my mind for a long minute or two; and then the thoughts were back again. Was I going to be like this when I got home? Wouldn't I be able to pay any attention to anything, hear what was said to me, or answer sensibly, because of what was on my mind? A line or two from Robert Burns popped up in my memory:

> 'The minister kissed the fiddler's wife,
>   And couldna' preach for thinkin' o't!'

I smiled; but I felt, for the first time, sympathetic to that preacher. Poor devil! I looked around the car. A great many men were unfaithful to their wives. Did they have this difficulty of not being able to get it off their minds? Did they read their papers, and think what were the chances of the Red Sox, just as if nothing had happened? Some of them might be ashamed of themselves; they would wish it hadn't happened; I couldn't do that. I wasn't ashamed. What had happened was right, in its own realm. It just didn't belong to this other world. And—that was the trouble—I was going home to dinner.

Now I was the young man who lived in that nice little apartment, who sat on one side of a little round table, at dinner. That was all real. I had forgotten that. It had been vague a while ago, but now it was the most real thing in the world. A while ago I had been just myself, somebody who could do what he liked. Now I was a part of a marriage. I could not think of myself now apart from my marriage. Yet into that reality of my marriage there would intrude the image of that girl; the memory of our lovemaking would wing its way through my mind like a blazing arrow. Was that a picture to bring to a dinner table? Already it was a barrier between me and the girl sitting opposite at that dinner table. I felt as if she could see the whole picture in my eyes. Would I ever be happy with her again, having this thing on my mind? . . . I reflected that an ordinary citizen does not take these things too seriously. What's past is past, he says, and looks at the baseball news. . . . Should I tell her? No, that would just hurt her feelings. But it would have been a relief to think that I could tell her. Theoretically, a modern husband and wife could tell each other things like that; that had been our explicit assumption: actually, one didn't tell. It might spoil everything for her. It hadn't made any difference, really. It wouldn't, if she didn't know. . . . I wished there were somebody I could tell it to—so as to get it off my mind. I could understand how a good Catholic would wish to rush to a priest. If I told any of my most intimate friends, they would only envy me, and think I was boasting. I just had to keep it to myself. . . . I wanted life to be simple. And all this was too complicated. Too frightfully complicated. . . . And what explanation would I give for being so late? This street-car was crawling. And I must not, on some sudden impulse, give this thing away. I must be sensible. Only it would be clear that something had happened to me. I was apparently a poor hand to keep secrets. If this was the sort of thing that happened to people, then they ought to be able to accept it as something that belonged in their lives. How could two people really be intimate and have secrets? Well, they did. They might go through this kind of mental agony the first time, but after a while they got used to it and took it easier. I couldn't imagine myself ever going through this again. No—I would choose between taking such a happiness and not taking it; but if I took it, it would be only because it was deeply important to me, and there would be no secret about it. I could stand anything—the worst that might happen —better than trying to fit together a dream and a reality that didn't fit. . . . But just now what I had to do was stop thinking about it. That was all.

Having gone through this round of thought, I went through it all over again. The end led back to the beginning. It was like a tread-mill. Round and round and round. No, I couldn't go through this again. This would be the first and the last time, so far as idle secrets were concerned. I would take my choice. . . . I had formerly been living in a simple and ingenuous world. Now I saw it with new eyes. I recognized the possibilities in my life that I hadn't known. I had just now been for an hour in a realm of freedom in which I had been happy and at ease. That realm lay on every side of me, a flowering wilderness, behind the solid walls of custom and habit— and those walls were not solid: they melted and vanished, and one was in the flowering wilderness. It was beautiful; it was only the coming back that was the trouble.

A new thought occurred to me: I would make a story out of this— change the circumstances, disguise the characters, and get it off my mind that way. . . . And in my mind's eye I saw the ending of the story. Mrs. Oxten—it was a woman who was going through all this, because no reader would ever believe a man so absurd as to agonize over such an adventure—Mrs. Oxten, then, would return home from her six weeks at the seashore, with all these thoughts going round and round in her mind. She would ring the bell, and run up the steps. Her husband would open the door at the top, and stand waiting for her. He would be smiling, and that would make her feel better. They would kiss, and everything would suddenly be all right. The familiar place would evoke familiar thoughts. She would say the expected words. Life would go on as usual.

It was something like that, in fact. And the story of Mrs. Oxten was written, which I have now changed back, as nearly as possible, into fact. The story was followed by several others, of an imaginative sort. Ever since I had been in Chicago, I had carried a notebook, into which I jotted ideas for stories, none of which had got written. Now I began to write stories. One of them was based upon a newspaper account of the beating of some girls by the matron in a state reformatory. Another was about a girl who ran away from home to join a side-show in a cheap circus. All the stories were of young people, and were filled with sympathy for them, taking their side against the world, against law, against convention, against their elders. One of these stories I gave to the New York International, two others were sold to the Smart Set, some were published later in The Masses. And I began to read with immense enthusiasm the unfinished trilogy of the life of Jacob Stahl, by a new English writer, J. D. Beresford—the story of a young drifter of artistic temperament, whose marriage had broken up, at the end of the first volume, and who, at the end of the second volume, was about to go off and live with a girl with whom he was in love, without benefit of clergy. But in the excitement of producing stories I had found a flowering wilderness of fancy which for a while left me with no eyes for the one which lay about me behind the brick walls of custom and habit.

4

In the year 1911 there were signs that the world was on the verge of something. It was thought to be new life. The London Athenaeum—we quoted it in the Review—said: "Few observant people will deny that there are signs of an awakening in Europe. The times are great with the birth of some new thing. A spiritual renaissance may be at hand." The Contemporary Review said: "We are face to face with a new world teeming with wonders unknown", and prophesied a "European renaissance", "a thing of wonder and beauty, a supreme achievement". And George Cook, writing in the Friday Review, expressed the hope that America, as an intimate part of modern life, would be "moved by the same new perception of the beauty and wonder of the world, and not be voiceless".

Something was in the air. Something was happening, about to happen—in politics, in literature, in art. The atmosphere became electric with it.

And I, re-reading the Conclusion of Pater's 'Renaissance', was moved to make some New Year's Resolutions, which the following New Year I remembered, and recommended to others in the Review, with the warning that the trouble with New Year's Resolutions is that "one sometimes keeps them". I lived—so I reflected—in an interesting time, full of its own peculiar scenes, with sounds and colors all its own; and yet I had been content to read about it in the newspapers. If I had been in Freeport in 1858, I would probably have waited to read about the Lincoln-Douglas debates in the paper. I was living as if I had a thousand years to live! And so I resolved to break up some of those regular habits which had kept me in a path, as it were, between my apartment and the El, the El and the office, the office and the restaurant. I would resist that instinct of conservatism which had been keeping me in a pattern and making me old before my time. I would use my faculties, see and explore life, and so 'on this short day of sun and frost, not lie down before the evening'.

CHAPTER XXII

Nineteen-twelve

1

The year 1912 was really an extraordinary year, in America as well as in Europe. It was the year of the election of Wilson, a symptom of immense political discontent. It was a year of intense woman-suffragist activity. In the arts it marked a new era. Color was everywhere—even in neckties. The Lyric Year, published in New York, contained Edna St. Vincent Millay's 'Renascence'. In Chicago, Harriet Monroe founded Poetry. Vachel Lindsay suddenly came into his own with 'General William Booth Enters Into Heaven', and commenced to give back to his land in magnificent chanted poetry its own barbaric music. 'Hindle Wakes' startled New York, as it was later to startle Chicago. The Irish Players came to America. It was then that plans were made for the Post-Impressionist Show, which revolutionized American ideas of art. In Chicago, Maurice Browne started the Little Theatre. One could go on with the evidence of a New Spirit come suddenly to birth in America. But perhaps the most impressive of all, from a certain point of view, was that the New York Times Literary Supplement published in its sacrosanct columns this utterance: "Now, let us understand each other—you, the mob who are shouting the names of every latest and maddest and most foreign writer, and we who dare to refuse to join the mob. We are not mediocrities or mollycoddles. We are not senile nor supersensitive. We accept Wilde and Ibsen and Shaw, Von Hoffmansthal, and Strauss, Matisse, Van Gogh"—oh, the New York Times Literary Supplement accepted everybody! And the Friday Literary Review, which had been thought rather 'young', was in the middle of a movement. Our reviews sold more books than ever—an impressive fact. We published a list of recommended books at Christmas, and the bookstores were sold out of them in a few days; one docile customer bought the whole fifty books, others used it as a check-list. Something was happening—no doubt of that. But what it was seems now less certain. Looking back now, it seems almost as if the world had had an icy premonition of its impending doom, and was seeking feverishly to live in the last days still vouchsafed to it.

One who is in the midst of such a happening does not see it all—he is partly occupied with what is happening to himself. I was seething and bubbling with stories. And there was an enchanting music to be explored in prose. One story told of a sister and a brother, each anxious for the other's safety, who proceed to escape from each other's watchfulness and endanger themselves to their heart's content, he in a forbidden airplane race and she in a forbidden love affair. And at the end of the story the sunset sky 'was like a banner flung out over some magnificent adventure. "Look!" whispered the man, and pointed upward. But the girl lay motionless upon the grass, silent, with closed eyes, breathing slow, deep breaths, while overhead there sounded, clear and clearer in the twilight stillness, the throb of a motor, like the beating of an indomitable heart.' Those consonents were orchestral music to my ear: KLR!—KLR! sounded the thin sweet horns—*clear and clearer in the twilight stillness*—and then the rumble of the drums, TBMLR!—TBMLR!—*the throb of a motor, like the beating of an indomitable heart*. To a mere reader it might be just a sentence, but I could not say it over to myself without tears of joy in my eyes.

2

Hackett had left me a small note-book containing the names and addresses of reviewers, and comments upon them. One name was that of Lucian Cary, set down as an English instructor in some college, with the comment: "very brilliant, but hard to get anything out of him". One evening when Martha Baker was having a birthday party at her studio, a young Tribune reporter had arrived, asking if there were a story in this; I said no, but offered him a drink, and invited him to join our party. I might have offered any Tribune reporter a drink, but the invitation to join our party was a token of friendship at first sight. He said he would like to, but he had left his wife down at the corner drug-store. It was not, to the best of my knowledge and belief, customary for Tribune reporters to take their wives with them when they went out on a round of evening assignments; but it appeared that they were fond of one another's company. So we all said, "Bring her, of course!" He said he would, and told us his name—Lucian Cary. He introduced his wife, Augusta, a girl with beautiful ash-blonde hair. They were henceforth part of our circle. Lucian was from Madison, Wisconsin; he wanted to write realistic novels; he had very much the same view of life and art as the rest of us, though more Shavian perhaps, and less Socialist; and Hal, George, Lucian and I became a foursome upon all occasions. Augusta was going to have a baby, and was soon unable to get away from her apartment, so we were there a good deal, of evenings; she was for a long time very shy and silent in the presence of such tremendous intellectuals as Hal, George and me, remaining a sweet and sunny presence in the background; but when she finally did talk, it appeared that she had lots of opinions of her own—challenging opinions. Her name was familiarly shortened now to 'Gus'; and Gus, besides feeding the hungry intellectuals bountifully, and listening to their endless reading of poetry, became one of the most amazing talkers of us all. Talk was almost the chief interest of our lives; and it lasted longer and longer into the nights. Sleep, we all discovered, could almost wholly be dispensed with, and some mornings saw us all going back to the day's work without having been to bed at all; strong coffee in quantities became a prime necessity of life. When George, his legal probation over, departed for New York to get married, Lucian Cary became my associate on the Friday Literary Review. Hackett's little note in the note-book had proved his acuteness as a describer; Lucian Cary was very brilliant, and as hard to get work out of as he was brilliant. Hackett had made me sweat as his assistant; but George Cook and Lucian were not 'assistants' but 'associates', and they lived up to the term very literally. I was charmed with the company of both, and—oh, well, I could do the work myself. Now it was Hallinan and Lucian Cary and I who lunched together every day, and went out for a cup of coffee or a mug of ale at four o'clock in the afternoon, to renew our eternally unfinished discussions of life and art. These were golden days. Once, at sixteen, I had written a little poem saying that if I had one wish it would not be for power or fame or gold or long life, but for the privilege of reaching out to some unknown one in the crowd and saying: 'Be thou my friend!' That wish the Gods had immediately granted me. I had done that in Davenport days, and now in Chicago was doing it again; and at twenty-four just as at seventeen, it was the richest part of life.

3

It was commented upon me by my friends that I never spoke of my past, of my childhood, or of my family; I might be an orphan for all they knew, so they remarked. And that stuck in my mind. I was ashamed of not being able to send my family more than a little money, irregularly; I had a sense of being in a different world from them. My mother was happy to have me in this world; but I should have liked to do something more for her. Thirty-five dollars a week, however, even if one's wife keeps up her share of the domestic establishment, is no fortune; and my mother always said in her letters that they were getting along well. As for my earlier life, I had forgotten it almost completely.

I kept up my education, while a literary critic, by reading new books which informed me of the latest views in astronomy, biology and other matters. Also I kept on reading books from that immense list of great novels which I had not yet read. Tolstoi's 'Childhood, Boyhood and Youth' was one of these. I was struck by the vividness of Tolstoi's memories of his childhood, and asked myself whether it were possible for a man to remember things so clearly and so far back. I set down all that I could remember about my own childhood; three sheets of paper sufficed. But it was enough to startle me. Had I really been a boy with long yellow curls? I tried to trace some sort of development in my mind from the child I glimpsed in the past on down to me in the present; it was a strange story, and perhaps one worth telling. I thought of making a novel of it. New memories cropped up in my mind.

Arnold Bennett, suddenly made famous by his novel, 'The Old Wives' Tale', after many years spent in the writing of undistinguished fiction, was a figure of special interest to some of us, perhaps as an example of industry and perseverance rewarded with success. Gilbert Cannan also appealed to some of us, as a young man of extraordinary accomplishment. Bennett, Cannan and J. D. Beresford were writing more simply and honestly than any American writers except Dreiser, and a young American who wished to write realistic novels could learn much from them. Helen R. Martin and Ellen Glasgow were writing of the rebellion of women and children against the patriarchal family in Dutch Pennsylvania and the South, and I admired greatly what they wrote, only I wished they knew more clearly what they were doing. Samuel Butler's 'Way of All Flesh' was an intellectual acid that was slowly eating through the traditional family sentiments with which our genuine emotions were coated over. And Somerset Maugham's 'Of Human Bondage', when it was published a few years later, would be for us the great example of realistic fiction in English. I admired greatly the realistic novels of Gustav Frenssen and of Martin Anderson Nexo; and I joined in the universal admiration of Romain Rolland's 'Jean Christophe', at least with respect to the earlier part of that work. Tolstoi was on our shelves, and Turgeniev; and Dostoievsky and Chekhov were new enthusiasms. There was, for any young American writer, no lack of good models. We theorized immensely about the technique of novels, short stories and plays.

When Arnold Bennett was in Chicago I went to see him at his hotel, and had a long talk with him. He asked me whether I had been born in Chicago or in a small town. In a small town, I said; and then he assured me—though I hadn't asked him—that I could write novels. He went on to say, however, that it was growing up in a small town that gave one the knowledge of people necessary for novel writing. A novelist, he said, learns everything he knows about people before—I think he said twenty-one years of age, possibly earlier. That might be true. But—I reflected—I hadn't grown up in one small town, I had grown up in three small towns. Somewhere I had heard, or perhaps I invented it, the maxim: 'Always make a merit of your defects'. I remembered that, and thought: I will write the story of a youth whose character was formed by his having been uprooted from one environment after another; such a youth would not be a settled and regular person—he would be me. I began to have a conception of the character of my 'hero'. I rather disapproved of him, but he interested me a lot.

All of us were going to write novels. It was to us a way of escape from the essentially humiliating situation of being, as newspapermen, the hired hands of ignorant, mean and base employers. We knew quite well that some day this job would explode. We had no hope of being rewarded for scattering as much intelligent thought as we could. In the meantime, the Friday Review was doing its job well. There would be nothing to be ashamed of in the way we handled the opportunity to give encouragement to the young creative intelligences, or the older ones either, in the America that we reached.

4

The Little Theatre which Maurice Browne started, up in the top of a building on Michigan Boulevard, opened with a play of Yeats's, 'On Baile's Strand', and I was enchanted with Raymond Jonson's deep grave voice as Conchobar or Cuchulain, I forget which, I think the former; and some of the speeches of the play have stayed in my mind to this day. One of the high arguments of that play was over the question of whether a man desires a son; and it was singularly thrilling to me; I never expected to have any children, because I was too unsure of being able to support even myself, and it would be too rash to give such hostages to fortune. But I loved the young sons of one of my women friends with all the fondness of a bachelor 'uncle'. And this speech of old Conchobar's to the younger man reverberated to the depths of my emotions:

> 'You play with arguments as lawyers do,
> And put no heart in them. I know your thoughts,
> For we have slept under the one cloak, and drunk
> From the one wine cup. I know you to the bone.
> I have heard you cry, aye in your very sleep,
> "I have no son," and with such bitterness
> That I have gone upon my knees, and prayed
> That it might be amended.'

And there were two other speeches in the play that were to stay in my mind. In one of these speeches, Cuchulain, the younger man, is defending 'that fierce woman of the camp', the Queen Aoife, his one-time lover, from the older king:

> 'You have never seen her, ah! Conchobar, had you seen her
> With that high, laughing, turbulent head of hers
> Thrown backward, and the bowstring at her ear,
> Or sitting at the fire with those grave eyes

Full of good counsel as it were with wine,
Or when love ran through all the lineaments
Of her wild body—although she had no child,
None other had all beauty, queen and lover,
Or was so fitted to give birth to kings.'

It became a picture into which any girl whom I loved henceforth
had to fit in my mind. And the third speech, Cuchulain's again,
was this:

'I never have known love but as a kiss
In the mid battle, and a difficult truce
Of oil and water, candles and dark night,
Hillside and hollow, the hot-footed sun
And the cold, sliding, slippery-footed moon,
A brief forgiveness between opposites
That have been hatreds for three times the age
Of this long 'stablished ground.'

This speech was in complete contradiction to my whole philosophy
of sex, but it may have spoken for the fear of women still lurking in
my mind.

Schnitzler's 'Anatol', as presented by the Chicago Little Theatre,
was enjoyable; but its gentle mockery of the egotism of the philan-
derer and the emptiness of 'light love' was something I had already
savored in the printed play; I agreed too well with its 'moral' to be
moved by it. The great emotional triumph of the Little Theatre was
its magnificent and heart-breakingly beautiful presentation of Gilbert
Murray's translation of 'The Trojan Women' of Euripides. Miriam
Kiper's wonderful voice as the leader of the chorus shook my heart.
And Elaine Hyman as Andromache, in her scene with the child
Astyanax, about to be slain, her beauty and tenderness and the tragic
loveliness of her voice, were profoundly moving. The funeral of the
slain child made this the deepest experience of the art of tragedy I
had known.

The young actress, Elaine Hyman, whom I came to know, was
richly talented; she was an artist with an extraordinary gift for the
expression of beautiful and romantic emotions in design and color,
and her voice in the singing of old ballads was as moving as in her
speaking on the stage; as an actress she was perfectly fitted to the
poetic drama.

I think it was in the year 1912 that 'The Yellow Jacket' came to

Chicago; it burst the traditional boundaries of the theatre for me. The best scenery, I realized, is that which is created by the spectator's imagination; and a small wooden board was a better baby for stage purposes than a realistic doll, while a real baby would have shattered the make-believe of the plot utterly. I wondered what a puppet theatre would be like, reviewed Gordon Craig's ambiguous but stimulating book on the theatre, and had a long, interesting letter from the author. 'Sumurun' appeared, with the original German company, to reveal new depths of fantastic and sensuous beauty in stagecraft; and I was told by the managing editor please to leave dramatic criticism to the dramatic critic—who was Frederic Hatton, a very able and very earnest young man, whose only fault, if it were a fault, was his sternly 'highbrow' attitude toward the drama, his exalted scorn of anything frivolous in the precincts sanctified by Ibsen, Shaw and Granville Barker; if anybody had told us that Frederic Hatton was going to be the author of a successful farce entitled 'Getting Gertie's Garter'—well, we just wouldn't have believed it.

When I first came to Chicago, I had attended the opera, and had been bored and angered by the wretched acting, the bad scenery and the soupy music; nothing would ever convince me that this preposterous mélange had any artistic validity—it was obviously a leisure-class cultural tradition only. But when I attended the Thomas concerts, and was put to sleep by the greatest music of the nineteenth century, I concluded that my mind was closed to serious musical enjoyment, a misfortune which might not be repaired and had better be accepted without pretense. But now I found that there was one kind of music in which I could take the deepest enjoyment. This revelation was afforded by the Fuller sisters, Rosalind, Cynthia and Dorothy, who sang old English ballads to the harp. I went happily mad over old English ballads, and the Fuller sisters, especially the enchanting Rosalind, whose voice never ceased to vibrate in my memory. A whole new field of aesthetic enjoyment was opened up to me; I found that I loved all kinds of simple music, the ballad music of every country, seventeenth-century music, Gregorian chants, primitive music, and especially Negro spirituals, which were beginning to be reproduced on phonograph records, as sung by the Tuskegee Singers—'Go Down Moses', and that whole magnificent range of choral songs. There were even, embedded in the alien artifice of opera, bits of this older, simpler music, not spoiled by the complicated technical elaboration which constituted the peculiar and to me unintelligible glory of nineteenth-century musicianship—bits of folk-music which rang out clear and true and beautiful.

5

The starting of the magazine Poetry by Harriet Monroe revealed the presence of poets hitherto unknown. Eunice Tietjens, who was on that magazine, was one of these, much admired by me; I thought her translations of Baudelaire miraculously faithful to the music as well as to the meaning of a poet who, in all other translating hands, lost his glamor utterly; it was later that she wrote and contributed to The Masses the poem 'The Drug Clerk', which remained one of my favorite American poems; but she had already shown the possession of the Elizabethan phrase-magic. Another girl poet whom I greatly admired was Helen Hoyt, who captured better than anyone else the simple romantic truths—as distinguished from recapturing the traditional romantic attitudes—of bodily human love. A girl poet who wrote under the pseudonym of 'Eloise Briton' contributed to The Lyric Year a very beautiful poem which I loved and knew by heart:

> 'Dear vagrant love whose heart is scarred
> By the deep wounds of passion's war;
> Whose every kiss, a blood-red rose,
> From seed of dead desire grows,
> And kisses gone before;
>
> 'Dear love, whose arms sure magic know
> To kindle all the form they hold;
> Whose hands are sweet against my breast
> Because of others they have pressed,
> And love-lore learned of old;
>
> 'Dear, I have left you, ere the flame
> Should cease to leap from lip to lip;
> Ere my white limbs should lose their power,
> Or into that last pallid hour
> Love's waning moon should slip.' * * *

This note, struck more lightly and with a mocking charm, was to become familiar and dear to the heart of America within ten years; in this poem it was struck for the first time in American poetry.

Yes, there were young men poets, too, in Chicago; one of them, a friend of mine who shall be nameless here, wrote a solemn Whitmanesque love poem of which the prize lines were:

'Spontaneous thou!
And instantaneous me!'

Amidst all this burgeoning of poetry, I could not help remembering that I had been a poet once, myself; and my lost youth shone to me never so appealingly as out of the eyes of girl poets. Their youth, so full of genius and so fearlessly dedicated to the difficult and thankless rôle from which I had shrunk, made me feel very old. I was being a sensible person, reviewing other people's books for a regular weekly stipend, instead of starving in a garret. I envied them. One evening, as I sat playing at *bout rimes* with a girl poet, we swiftly produced these two sonnets upon the rhyming words we had handed each other; and it seemed characteristic that her imagination should hurdle the words *drouth, cold* and *old* into something hopeful, while I managed to get something sad out of the words *stray, day,* and *play.* Hers was called

BEFORE SPRING

'Autumn long past with blazing forest drouth;
Winter so full of bitterness and cold
That even the throbbing Heart of Time grows old,
And shivering satellites of warmth fly South:
When men forget the very thought of youth,
Comes a day splotched with little gleams of gold,
With faint mist on the hills above the fold,
And soft sweet wind-kisses upon one's mouth.

'And trees and hearts that had been cold and bare,
Touched by a soft wind and a little trust,
Grow warm again and delicately fair,
And all the starving cold and winter must
Depart at last. Beauty is everywhere,
And Life will rise, where Death had been and dust.'

Mine, middle-aged and mournful, was called

DELPHI

'I hear prophetic voices from the deep
Heart of my youth, where all has been so still
That nevermore I climbed the ancient hill
Of memories, or laid me down to creep

Into the secret grottoes that still keep
The fount of life, the hidden source of will,
And all the waters that refresh and fill
The gardens on the hither side of sleep.

'For now the world encompasses me round,
My soul is tethered so it cannot stray;
Ah, what avails the Apollonian sound,
The voice oracular that bids me play
Upon the hill where stars like flowers abound,
The glorious child of an immortal day!'

6

One of our reviewers, who became one of our friends, was Llewellyn Jones, a remarkably erudite youth; he afterward became the Post's literary editor. Fiction-reviewing was done largely by women and girls; some of them wanted to make a little money by selling the books at half-price to McClurg's; others wanted a light task to solace their domestic idleness; and to others it was a possible gateway to journalism or creative writing. Some of them were, from an editor's point of view, pretty hopeless, but some were promising, and these I labored to instruct in the art of book-reviewing. 'In heaven's name, *don't* tell the story of the book! Bring to bear upon the book, in aesthetic terms, your attitude toward life'. So attitudes toward life were discussed, as well as English rhetoric, in our editorial conferences. One of my young book reviewers, Fanny Butcher, subsequently became, and is now, the literary editor of the Chicago Tribune. Another, Augusta Cary, Lucian Cary's wife, succeeded him as literary editor of our Friday Review. Another of our reviewers was Margaret Anderson, the beautiful and very young literary editor of The Continent, a religious weekly; her position there did not necessarily imply that her views were conventionally religious; but her views, as expressed in 1911, had been, in fact, austerely idealistic, matching her starry-eyed, unearthly young loveliness, which was just too saintlike. She wrote well, if more enthusiastically than anybody had ever written before in the whole history of book-reviewing; and an editor could not argue with her, for she stared him down with young limpid blue eyes which knew better than all his crass cynical wisdom; so we had printed her enthusiastic tribute to an ultra-idealistic novel, 'The Iron Woman', by Margaret

Deland—and then we had got a friend of George's to write us a review of the same novel two weeks later, in which a modern point of view was expressed. The novel dealt with the theme of renunciation; a wife, utterly unhappy in a marriage, refused to leave him even when her husband offered her a divorce so that she could be happy with her lover. This celebration of renunciation moved Margaret Anderson to write as follows: "It's a glorious, flaming thing! It strikes a moral height that hasn't been struck so stirringly and convincingly for years. . . . No review can express the power of the thing; no criticism can do justice to an art that produces a novel like 'Helena Ritchie' and then transcends itself in a sequel of even greater proportions. We might say that it places Mrs. Deland with the immortals—and then know that we had said an inadequate thing." The counter-review, under the heading of 'Second Thoughts', two weeks later, said: "There is something tight—fixed—at the core of the spirit of this beautiful writer. She has employed all her art in an attempt to make beautiful a thing that is hideous; we greatly admire the art; we do not find the hideous thing in the least beautiful." It had seemed a pity that young Margaret Anderson should be committed to a kind of 'Paul and Virginia' ideal of literature and life. But all this had been back in 1911; and this was 1912, and Margaret Anderson was presently to appear as the editor of the Little Review, which was destined to be, as the sponsor of James Joyce's 'Ulysses', more modern than us all. When, years later, I read Margaret's autobiography, I was amazed, and touched, to read: "I liked Floyd— which means I liked his conversation. Liked it enormously." I had supposed she despised me, regarding me first as a crass mocker, and later as an old fogey. I note also her description of me in this sentence: "Mrs. Dell (Margery Currey) had created a sort of salon for Floyd, who was so timid that he would never have spoken to anyone if she hadn't relieved him of all social responsibility and presented him as an impersonal being whose only function in life was to talk."

It was a beautiful year, a year of poetry, and dreams, and of life renewed and abundant. We were all full of ideals, illusions, and high spirits. We were young, and the world was before us. The parties in the little Rogers Park apartment were gayer than ever.

And always Margery's gentle old father was there, delighted to be in the midst of so much abounding young life.

But I have to record one regrettable thing, that with the advent of cocktails one young man got tight one evening. I walked him sternly around the block seven times to sober him up, and he asked me, in shame at his condition, if I thought his wife would leave him. It *was* a pretty frightful thing, getting drunk, but I felt that she might forgive him.

CHAPTER XXIII

LAST DAYS IN CHICAGO

1

THE YEAR 1913 started off very excitingly with, among other things, the Irish Players. What a wonderful experience it was to sit in the gallery night after night and see the rich world of Synge and Lady Gregory! One evening just after the Irish Players' arrival, I was sitting alone in a restaurant, finishing my coffee, when in came Maurice Browne of the Little Theatre, and with him a tall, slender, distinguished-looking young man whom I had last seen in the Contemporary Club in Davenport—Arthur Davison Ficke, of whom I thought now more favorably as the author of some very beautiful poems in an early number of Harriet Monroe's magazine, Poetry. They came to my table, I drank more coffee, and we talked of the Irish players. They said how grand it would be to invite Sara Allgood and some others to supper, and I agreed, and asked, Why didn't they? One of them had been introduced to her upon some occasion, but he was too much in awe of her to proffer such an invitation. Immensely pleased at finding two men shyer than myself, I offered to do the asking—"if you will pay for the supper, Arthur?" He would; and they watched with admiration one who was not afeared of goddesses go to the telephone (I was really scared to death) and return with a pleased acceptance from Miss Allgood and her friends. The supper was duly given, and much enjoyed, and it led to an immediate friendship between Arthur and me. He came up to our apartment in Rogers Park, and was at the gayest of our dinners; and later he let me see his just finished 'Sonnets of a Portrait Painter', of which I became an enthusiastic admirer, and which I soon knew by heart, and recited upon all occasions. They seem to me, now as then, one of the great achievements of the new era in poetry. Always

Arthur was one whom it was a delight to sit up with till all hours in talk about everything in the world.

2

Those who associate with artists come to envy them the spaciousness and simplicity of their studio homes. We did not want a painter's studio with a north light and everything, but we did want something in the nature of a studio; a double studio, or perhaps two studios side by side, something less cramped than our Rogers Park apartment—at least, that was the reason we gave ourselves. The regular studios were too expensive; but there was in Chicago, besides such studio buildings, a place where artists lived, down on the South side, by Jackson Park. There, on Stony Island Avenue fronting the Park, and on both sides of Fifty-Seventh Street, were what had once been rows of small shops, in temporary structures built at the time of the World's Fair, only one story high, without basements, and with broad plate-glass windows on each side the door; these had never been torn down, and were now mostly inhabited by artists. The rents were very cheap; and when that summer two of them fell vacant, around the corner from each other, we left our Rogers Park apartment and moved in; Margery's place was on Stony Island Avenue, and mine on Fifty-Seventh Street, with the back doors adjoining. These places each consisted of one very large room, which could be separated into two by a temporary partition. Hers had the luxury of a bathtub, but in mine the bathing arrangements were more primitive—one stood up in an iron sink and squeezed water over oneself with a sponge. We were delighted with this Bohemian simplicity; and, with so many good restaurants, there would be no occasion to do any cooking except when there was a party. In my studio there had been left by the previous occupant a huge round wooden model stand, like a turntable in the railroad switch-yards, which could be set up on a small table and made to accommodate a remarkable number of dinner guests.

Our neighbors, the Nordfeldts, were interesting—they occupied the corner studio between us. B. J. O. Nordfeldt, the painter, was a small, gentle, smiling, restless Swede, with a little goatee; his newer paintings were in the bold Post-Impressionist style, and his portraits, simple and decorative, conveyed intensely the personal quality of people whom I knew. He asked me to sit for him and I was immensely flattered. On the other side of my studio was that of Ralph Pearson, an etcher and art photographer. Kathleen Wheeler, who did portrait busts, lived around the corner and across the street; and next to Margery's place was a studio of metalcraft, taught by two University of Chicago students, Annette Covington and Blanche Manage. Across the street lived a beautiful apple-cheeked girl whom I had first seen, eager and buoyant, a few rows away, at a matinee of the Irish Players; I said to Lucian Cary, indicating her, "There's Ann Veronica," a reference to the heroine of H. G. Wells's latest novel; afterward I was embarrassed to find that my remark had been overhead by her companions, and that she was being chaffed about it; she was Ernestine Evans, and she wanted to write. I have forgotten where Mary Randolph, a sculptress and a friend of the Nordfeldts, had her studio; but she asked me to pose for a head, and I did. The head was done over several times and then abandoned as unsatisfactory; apparently my head did not lend itself to sculptural treatment; but I shall never forget the sensation of sitting on a model stand and being stared at by a handsome sculptress. A man is used to having a prolonged meeting of his eyes with a girl's mean something; and it is hard to get used to meeting a girl's wide-eyed, impersonal stare. Her liquid, starry gaze embarrassed me. And, as the gaze continued, piercing me, probing me, seeing me with calm indifference, I became uneasy and almost afraid—I wanted to look away, but that seemed cowardly and evasive, so I kept on staring back, until those grey eyes of hers seemed profound gulfs over which I hung, dizzy, tottering, about to drown. And then, saying "Mm", she would turn to the clay head, and put a tiny pellet of clay on the end of the nose. She had not been searching my soul, but only considering just how long my nose was.

Being painted by Nordfeldt was a less nerve-racking ordeal, for it was all over in one sitting—and there it was, me to the life; and much food for thought in what I saw. But the trouble was, the portrait was exhibited in the window of Thurber's Art Gallery, and was food for thought to a good many other people. They seem to have said, a good many of them, grimly, "So this is what we are coming to, with all this modernism!"

For in the meantime both the Friday Literary Review and I myself had apparently become in some eyes symbolic of all that was either inspiriting or alarming in the 'modernity' that was rising in such a flood. Too symbolic of 'modernity' for the comfort of either the Review or me. But something and someone must stand as the symbols of a change that is welcomed by some and feared by others. I cannot see myself from the outside, and am rather incredulous of things that I have heard about myself. Apparently a kind of cruel wit I had was not always harmlessly confined to the circle of my friends. Probably there were traits in me which lent themselves to this kind of symbolic use. And, the more the Review became of service to the cause of modernity, the more it was looked upon in certain quarters with a baleful eye. My position was becoming as harassed as my predecessor's had been. And in mid-year the Friday Review lost the dignity of its tabloid independence and was reduced to a mere double-page in the body of the Evening Post, in an attempt to discipline its wilful modernism.

Under hostile nagging from my superiors on the paper, I still retained editorial good humor and judgment. But it must have been under this hostile pressure that I went to sartorial extremes—which were now set before the eyes of Chicago in my portrait. Yet if my get-up was wrong it was due to Charlotte Perkins Gilman and Michael Carmichael Carr, for it was their idea. I might have been able to resist a man's arguments about what I should wear, but in these matters I had a naturally trustful attitude toward women. Charlotte Perkins Gilman was a pioneer Feminist, the author especially of some satirical and philosophic Feminist verses much admired by me; and my wife was her agent as a lecturer. Then there was Michael Carmichael Carr, who had dropped from the sky into Chicago, an extraordinary person, thin, with a little pointed beard, a man highly talented in stage decoration, who had worked with Gordon Craig and had known Isadora Duncan—one whose stories would be listened to with fascination by Americans in the spirit of 'And did you once see Shelley plain?' The three of us, Charlotte Perkins Gilman the Feminist, and Michael Carmichael Carr the Artist, and me an impressionable young literary editor, were sitting at luncheon together in a Chicago restaurant, when they decided that I should wear a high collar and black stock, and carry a stick and gloves. It does not seem to have occurred to me to dispute such authoritative counsel. Besides, I thought of myself as having a long neck, which a high collar and stock might hide; and perhaps it was an unconscious reminiscence of the black silk muffler I had once worn as a boy poet in Davenport. But it did attract a lot of attention, especially when my portrait was put on exhibition.

There was a Browning centenary meeting in some public hall, and I was one of the speakers. I was enthusiastic about Browning as a poet, but wondered why he was praised as a philosopher, since, I said, "the shallow optimism of 'God's in his heaven, all's right with the world' had never been equalled by anyone with a pretension to thinking." Some people felt that this was not the sort of thing to say at a centennial celebration.

My first book was published that year—a collection of essays, reprinted from the Friday Review, on Feminist leaders, beginning with Charlotte Perkins Gilman and going on to deal with Mrs. Pankhurst, Jane Addams, Olive Schreiner, Isadora Duncan, Beatrice Webb, Emma Goldman, Margaret Dreier Robbins, Ellen Key, and Dora Marsden of The Freewoman. In the introduction I noted that "we have as the motive behind the rebellion of women an obscure rebellion of men". The assertion was also made there that the author was devoid of the spirit of 'Romance' or 'woman-worship', an assertion contradicted by each of the book's eloquent pages. I was, and remained incurably, romantic about women. I thought them perfectly wonderful, and would never cease to think so.

Never a lawyer at heart, Arthur Ficke left the law business in Davenport at every opportunity to come to Chicago to attend Japanese print sales—he was a notable collector of Japanese prints— and to go to the theatre and to visit the Art Institute; so I saw a good deal of him. He found in our exciting Chicago world a stimulus to some change in his own career—he was at the time uncertain whether it would turn out to be his liberation as a poet from the imprisonment of Davenport, or his ruin as a respectable citizen and lawyer of that town, or both; and in that mood he wrote these

'LINES TO AN OUTRAGEOUS PERSON

'God forgive you, O my friend,
For be sure men never will;
Their most righteous wrath shall bend
Toward you all the strokes of ill.

'You are outcast—Who could bear,
Laboring dully, to behold
That glad carelessness you wear,
Dancing up the sunlight's gold?

'Who, a self-discovered slave,
As the burdens on him press,
Could but curse you, arrant knave,
For your crime of happiness?

'All the maxims of our life
Are confuted by your fling—
Taking dullness not to wife,
But with wonder wantoning.

'All the good and great of earth,
Prophesying your bad end,
Sourly watch you dance in mirth
Up the rainbow, O my friend.'

I was not really having quite as good a time as all that.

3

At some time in those Fifty-Seventh-Street days, I met Carl Sand-burg, and he read some of his poems from manuscript. They were all impressionistic, misty, soft-outlined, delicate; I remember liking particularly the one about the fog that 'comes on little cat feet'. Carl Sandburg had not struck yet the note he was soon to strike in 'Chicago—hog-butcher of the world'. I saw something of Theodore Dreiser, who was in Chicago for a while; he said I was the best critic in America; but I had said he was a great novelist, so it was only natural for him to think well of my critical powers. And Dreiser told me of a Chicago lawyer named Edgar Lee Masters, who was a poet; America would hear from him soon, said Dreiser. I looked up Masters's previous volumes of verse, but they were unpromising, so I did not take any stock in Dreiser's prophecy—and so missed a chance to be one of Masters's 'discoverers'. A new, hitherto unknown novelist swam into my ken, Sherwood Anderson, with the manu-script of a novel, 'Windy MacPherson's Son', which I immensely ad-mired; it had things in it about the Middle West which had never got into fiction, and a soul-questioning quasi-Dostoievskian note in it too which I admired devoutly—more then than later, for I was then in a soul-questioning state of mind. Sherwood Anderson worked in an advertising agency, and loathed it. At one of Margery's parties I met Sherwood Anderson's wife, Cornelia, a slender, delicate, self-contained, warm and understanding person; she wore, I remember, what someone called 'her sole recognition of evening dress', a Dante wreath about her hair; she talked to me of her three children; she soon afterward became a school-teacher, and worked her way up to a principalship. At another of these parties I saw her friend, Tennessee Mitchell, who became Sherwood Anderson's second wife. Professor George Burman Foster, a distinguished liberal theologian and professor in the University of Chicago, was brought by Llewellyn Jones to a studio party; and I remembered how a book of his had upset Davenport just after I left that town. The book was one which the conservative library board had refused to allow in the library; and the free-thinkers and Socialists had made an issue of it; the Democrat was filled with letters pro and con, George Cook and Susan Glaspell leading the epistolary war; business men, I was told by Rabbi Fineshriber, stopped in the morning to argue about it on the street-corner, and noon found them still arguing; Dr. Foster was brought to town to address a huge meeting; the issue of freedom of thought became the chief one in the municipal campaign, and a new mayor was elected on a pledge to appoint a library board that would put Dr. Foster's book in the public library. Susan Glaspell had made a magazine story out of it, and it sounded fantastic, but it was true. Where else could such a thing have happened but in Davenport? And there was a meeting in Margery's studio at which Margaret Anderson set forth her plans for the new modern magazine, the Little Review. . . . Life became like that—parties, people, new people, new friends; it was rather dizzying. "Reminiscences of those days flower whenever two or three are gathered together," Harry Hansen later wrote in his 'Midwest Portraits' of these and later times: "Most of the time they met in Margery Currey's big rooms, once the habitat of Thorstein Veblen—perhaps they were even called 'studio', for in that day, ten years ago, the word had not yet fallen into disfavor through commercialization—and Margery was the hostess whose gift for hospitality, for friendship, was as genuine and effective as that of Madame Nodier or Madame Adam or the Marquise du Defand in Paris of other days. These ancient store-rooms house a shrine . . ." I think Margery liked it more than I did. Only in a smaller and more intimate group of friends was I ever at ease.

The Post-Impressionist Show came to Chicago. I wanted to write about it, but I had been repeatedly warned that I was *not* the political editor and the dramatic editor and the music editor and the art editor of the Post, but simply and solely the literary editor; so I had to review a book as an excuse for writing about the great event at the Art Institute. There was, very conveniently, a book by C. Lewis Hind, on Post-Impressionist Art; unfortunately, there wasn't a copy of it in Chicago. But I reviewed it anyway, on the front page of the Friday Review; and after giving Mr. Hind due praise for his doubtless valuable and informative book, I went on to deal with the Post-Impressionist Show. Harriet Monroe wrote me that it was the best thing that had been written in America on the subject. It might have been, at that; modern art was as new to all except a few people in America as it was to me. Post-Impressionism exploded like a bombshell within the minds of everybody who could be said to have minds. For Americans it could not be merely an aesthetic experience; it was an emotional experience which led to a philosophical and moral revaluation of life. But it brought not one gospel, it brought a half-dozen at least, and from these one could choose what one needed. What I needed, and what I chose, was the gospel contained in the bold color and primitive simplicity and serene vitality of Gauguin. This was the furthest from what I was; I felt that I could go a long way towards that extreme and be the better for it.

I had been thinking a great deal about Nordfeldt's portrait of me. It was considered by some of my friends to be somewhat unsympathetic, rather a caricature of me; but it was not as unsympathetic as I began to be toward the personality I found myself exhibiting, of which my stick and gloves, and my high collar and black stock seemed, though superficial, yet faithful manifestations. I accused myself of being inadequate to the job of living—most of all inadequate in love, in not being capable of any deep and lasting love. I criticised myself fiercely for being too timid, too intellectual, too afraid of serious emotion. I wrote a sort of short story, called

'The Portrait of Murray Swift', which was a vivid description of the Post-Impressionist Show and the effect it had upon many of our minds; also containing a slightly fictionized version of my own portrait, which gave me an opportunity to criticise myself. Here is my description of that portrait:

"And then he saw himself, drawn with an exquisite and mordant irony, with stick and cigarette, uncertainly halting before earth and sky, the head tilted back with a quirk of inquiry, the face curious and evasive, with something that was almost boldness in the eyes, something that was almost courage in the chin: Murray Swift, observant, indecisive, inadequate, against a rose-colored background."

4

Our circle of friends was enlarging swiftly, as though it were a standard to which the young and bold in spirit could repair. And what I had thought of as my own special difficulties in solving the problems of life and love, my reckless ventures, desperate shifts, compromises, hopes, ideals, were more general than I had supposed. The old and broken-spirited came, too; men and women talked to me as to one who could understand and sympathize; they told secrets for which they needed the relief of a confessional. A very respectable gentleman cried as he told me the story of an illegitimate baby of his, buried in some Chicago cemetery; he went there sometimes and put flowers on the grave; I could see him, in my mind, coming, stealthily, with his posy, to look down on this pledge of his lost youth and its illicit romance, buried there in that grave; I could see him, in my mind's eye, going furtively back to his home, his career, his respectability, home from that secret, pitiful tryst—the symbol of an age that was passing. Now, it seemed, candor was more in fashion; only that didn't solve everything. It didn't solve anything. It didn't heal the cruelties of love. . . . I had been considerably occupied in my reviews with the discussion of 'genius' and 'egotism' ever since I came to Chicago. I had repudiated the notion of 'genius' being entitled to special privileges, and I deplored the self-centered life of the egotist. I was trying not to be a selfish egotist; and I think that at least I succeeded in being much less of a selfish egotist than I easily might have been. In the world which opened before me, poets seemed to have special privileges with respect to their love affairs; these affairs had to be condoned or over-looked, if they could not be admired and envied. The poet's irre-sponsibility was taken for granted. I could have the rôle of poet if I chose; though when a publisher offered to publish a volume of my poems, I had declined the honor, and suggested that he publish my feminist essays instead. But not poets alone had these special privileges in the matter of love affairs—'genius' in every field had them, and exercised them in the shadow of the most respectable insti-tutions, as I learned (though perhaps erroneously) in some detail. I had always felt myself entitled to no special privileges, but had held what was perhaps felt to be a more socially subversive doctrine, that everybody was entitled to all the rights there were—whatever these rights might be, of which I had never been sure.

I had become less sure, as I became involved in more than intel-lectual and literary adventures. My private life became a bewildered and inconsistent one. I fell in love, and very seriously; and my wife, however hurt, was kind and generous, and willing to end our mar-riage. It was I who refused to give up our marriage, and, after desperate attempts to eat my cake and have it upon one theory or another, I gave up my love affair to keep my marriage—only, against my will, to fall in love with another girl, and give up that love; and then with a third, given up in turn. If my marriage was already shattered, I did not know it, and could not believe it. My wife's love was as patient as it was humanly possible to be, and more generous than anyone could have asked. She was wise enough to decide that our marriage had already come to an end. And when this decision was made, I was hurt and incredulous; and only after some bewildered days did I awake to the realization that this ending had been inevitable.

The going-to-pieces of a marriage is often a painful spectacle for friends to watch. But there were in this case no public quarrels; no advice was asked from anybody by either, and no distressing confidences given to anybody by either. What was still more re-markable, there were no private quarrels, and no reproaches or recriminations. This way of dealing with domestic tragedy did not pretend to be 'natural'; it was an attempt to be 'civilized', and it succeeded in being perfectly well-mannered and good-humored. In a domestic landscape where in the background there stood a smoking volcano, there was still sunshine, and butterfly-wings to reflect its glints. And after the break-up of our marriage, we continued to be friends.

Domestic tragedy was not unknown in conventional circles in Chicago, as any city editor could testify; and as for my breaches of the seventh commandment, of which I have given here a complete enumeration, it was a paltry record in comparison to that of any of Chicago's really enterprising sinners. Public decorum had been preserved. The only thing to attract attention to this private do-mestic situation was its incredible urbanity. Quarrels, threats, 'scenes', could be understood, sympathized with, and, after being relished in gossip, hushed up; the world stood ready to include any domestic tragedy short of murder in its benevolent conspiracy of putting the best face on things. 'Too bad! Well, such things do happen!' But a break-up which gave no opportunity for the pro-nouncement of 'Too bad!' was alarming. If man and wife could separate peaceably, live around the corner from one another, and still be friends, appearing amiably at the same parties, and evincing some fondness for one another, what was the world coming to? It was a terrifying threat to the status quo. And besides, could it really be true, my dear, that they had a picture up on their walls of the two of them without a stitch of clothes on?

It was at this time that my friend Arthur Ficke wrote a poem entitled

'LINES FOR TWO FUTURISTS

'Why does all of sharp and new
That our modern age can brew
Culminate in you?

'This chaotic age's wine
You have drunk, and now decline
Any anodyne.

'On the broken walls you stand,
Peering toward some stony land
With eye-shading hand.

'Is it lonely as you peer?
Do you never miss, in fear,
Simple things and dear,

'Half remembered, left behind?
Or are backward glances blind
Here where the wind

'Round the outpost sweeps and cries—
And each distant hearthlight dies
To your restless eyes?

'I too stand where you have stood;
And the fever fills my blood
With your cruel mood.

* * *

'Into that profound unknown
Where the earthquake forces strown
Shake each piled stone,

'Look I; and exultance smites
Me with joy; the splintered heights
Call me with fierce lights.

'But a piety still dwells
In my bones; my spirit knells
Solemnly farewells

'To safe halls where I was born—
To old haunts I leave forlorn
For this perilous morn.'

* * *

As for the love-affairs, those dreams which would not fit into the realities of my life as a married man, they were at least beautiful dreams. I don't think any of us quite knew what we believed about love and 'freedom'. We were in love with life, and willing to believe almost any modern theory which gave us a chance to live our lives more fully. We were incredibly well meaning. We were confused, miserable, gay, and robustly happy, all at once. Perhaps we were groping hot-bloodedly toward friendship; perhaps we were in a desperate scramble after a lifetime's happiness; we hardly knew, and would never know. Love is, as Bertrand Russell said of mathematics, a subject 'in which we never know what we are talking about, nor whether what we are saying is true.' But I should like to live in Utopia, where one could write harmlessly about such things. We were intensely alive; we inflicted blind unintentional cruelties upon those we loved; but there was no meanness and no cynicism in our hearts; and there was beauty, and trust, and candor, and forgiveness.

A serious love affair is a matter of so much importance in anyone's life that a wholly true account of such a life would present the story in detail. That, for all sorts of reasons, I have no intention of doing in this book with regard to some love affairs that were to me of the most profound emotional significance. The story of my life here given is the less true for those omissions. But upon such a young intellectual as myself a serious love affair might be expected to have certain dynamic effects; first, it would shatter with its reality any intellectual theories with which it had been approached, and reveal in blinding glimpses something truer about love, and perhaps more terrible in its splendor, than was set forth in any philosophy of freedom; and then, by its gifts of pain and heartache and tears, never to be forgotten, it would create new emotional dimensions for a timid soul to explore when it gained the courage—since there is nothing like the endurance of pain to teach us the nature of life and the satisfactions it has to offer. Some hearts, at least, if not all, must be broken, and broken again, and again, just as some minds must be disillusioned again and again, before they are much good for the simple purposes of life and love. And girls seem to know it. It would have been too much to expect me to be wholly grateful at the time; but the time would come when I would be infinitely grateful not less for the pain and disillusionment than for the half-understood glimpses of an archaic glory.

But these were lessons which it would take years to find out that I had learned.

5

I went to New York to visit the publishers for my paper. And there I had news from Chicago. The proprietor of the paper had, I was informed, read my latest review, which began:

' "Will you have a cocktail?" asked my friend. "No, thanks," said I, "I've just been reading Jack London's 'John Barleycorn.' " '

The review went on to give a very sympathetic account of the book, which was a vivid autobiographical tract upon the evils of drink and the need for abolishing the saloon; my own view was that of one who expected national Prohibition soon to come and would welcome it when it arrived. But the proprietor read no further than the first sentence, and rushed, it was said, to the managing editor, purple with wrath. "Look! he boasts of his vile habits and low associates!" With trembling fingers the managing editor took the review, which he read with a clearing face; he pointed out to the proprietor that it was an argument *for* Prohibition. So, I was told, my job was saved; but the proprietor's accumulated wrath needed expression, so he had proceeded to fire several of the other departmental editors, whereupon the managing editor had resigned, and my friend Hallinan had followed his example. So I wired in my resignation, too.

I came back to pack, and found the new managing editor anxious to retain my services. But I thanked him, and suggested that he give my job to Lucian Cary, and let him have his wife Augusta as assistant, which was accordingly done. I made my plans for going to New York. There was a farewell dinner for me, at which Margery Currey announced that she had a job on the Daily News. And so I left Chicago, with no money, and no job awaiting me.

I had been happy in Chicago; never would it seem to me a grey and ugly city. I loved the Lake, Michigan Boulevard with its open vista and its gleaming lights, the Parks, even the preposterous loop district with its sudden architectural leap into the sky; I had seen beauty there, enough to fill my heart; there had been days and nights of talk and laughter; the years had passed in a golden glow of friendship; and it was a city haunted everywhere by the memories of love, its pain and its glory. It had been a generous city to a young man. I would always be grateful for what it had given me.

CHAPTER XXIV

Greenwich Village

1

Several of my friends lived in New York, and most of them in Greenwich Village, or in Provincetown, Massachusetts, a tiny seaport which appeared to be a sort of summer suburb of Greenwich Village. Other friends came from Chicago in the next few months or years, until most of the old group were here. I was no stranger in the Village.

Later I made up some rhymes about the beginning of Greenwich Village:

> Not mine to tell of those old times
> When, haunted by immortal rhymes,
> With leaking shoes upon his feet,
> Poe lived and starved in Carmine Street
> And life was short and love was sweet:
> All this is true, so I daresay—
> But it was long before my day.

It seems that as New York expanded hugely northward, this fashionable nineteenth-century residence district was deserted and left to decay into a picturesque twentieth century slum, in which only the north side of Washington Square still held its head above the mire; and this slum, for economic reasons, became increasingly the home of artists and writers.

> There was a Greenwich Village then—
> A refuge for tormented men
> Whose heads were full of dreams, whose hands
> Were weak to do the world's commands;
> Builders of palaces on sands—
> These, needful of a place to sleep,
> Came here because the rents were cheap.

The rents were cheap because the rush of traffic could not make its way through the little twisted streets that crossed and recrossed each other and never seemed to get anywhere else. Seventh Avenue was now being slowly cut through, and the West Side subway was being extended southward; but Greenwich Avenue still, like a barrier flung athwart the Village, protected it from the roaring town all about.

> Where now the tide of traffic beats,
> There was a maze of crooked streets;
> The noisy waves of enterprise,
> Swift-hurrying to their destinies,
> Swept past this island paradise:
> Here life went to a gentler pace,
> And dreams and dreamers found a place.
>
> And here, safe out of change's way,
> The houses crumbled to decay—
> Crumbled, yet stood; the rooms inside
> Were high and stately, deep and wide,
> Memorials of vanished pride:
> No modern inconveniences—
> And who would live in rooms like these?
>
> Who but the men of paint and rhyme?
> Here, out of space and out of time,
> They dreamed their dreams and had their day,
> Such as it was, of work and play:
> And some were sad, and some were gay—
> But no one in the world a word
> Of 'Greenwich Village' ever heard.

That Greenwich Village which was still unknown to the outside world, I had heard about from Edna Kenton and Vachel Lindsay. The Greenwich Village into which I came was a different Village, still unknown to the outside world, but not long destined to keep its happy privacy.

When I came, in the fall of 1913, the Liberal Club was just about to move down to Macdougal Street, and Polly Holliday was to run a restaurant in the basement. The Liberal Club and Polly's restaurant were to be what there had never been in the Village before, a common meeting place. There had always been tiny cliques and groups of artists and writers, mutually indifferent or secretly suspicious of each other. Each person knew his own little crowd, and that was all; of the rest of his neighbors he was no more aware than if he had lived in an apartment block uptown. But the moving spirit of the Liberal Club was Henrietta Rodman, a high-school teacher, and a very serious young woman, who had an extraordinary gift for stirring things up. Incredibly naïve, preposterously reckless, believing wistfully in beauty and goodness, a Candide in petticoats and sandals, she was laughed at a good deal and loved very much indeed, and followed loyally by her friends into new schemes for the betterment of the world. She was especially in touch with the university crowd and the social settlement crowd, and the Socialist crowd; and it was these, many of whom never actually lived in the Village, who, mixing with the literary and artist crowds in the Liberal Club, gave the Village a new character entirely, and one which was soon exploited by real-estate interests; it was not any longer a quiet place, where nothing noisier happened than drunken artist merrymaking; ideas now began to explode there, and soon were heard all the way across the continent.

And Polly Holliday, who came from the staid town of Evanston, Illinois, and looked very madonna-like, presided with benignant serenity over the wild and noisy horde of young people who began to collect in her restaurant, seeing to it that these truants and orphans were properly fed. Her right-hand man in this enterprise, cook, waiter, dishwasher and chief conversationalist, was Hippolyte Havel, an Anarchist, with fierce moustachios and goatee, a gentle soul with occasional volcanic outbursts. 'Bourgeois pigs!' was his favorite term of invective.

The first evening I was in the Village I was taken to call upon a beautiful girl dancer who kept a pet alligator in her bathtub; she bade me let it bite my finger, saying it wouldn't hurt me; I obeyed her trustfully, but offered the alligator the little finger of my left hand, just in case—; and the amiable reptile nipped it very gently. The next morning Henrietta Rodman came to call, and asked me to write a play to produce at the housewarming of the Liberal Club; Jack Reed was to have done one for them, but he had just been told he was to be sent to Mexico as a war-correspondent. So I said I would; Arthur Ficke and I had invented one together at lunch before I left, called 'St. George of the Minute', a satire upon 'modern' ideas, and I would do that one.

I wrote a little piece called 'Mona Lisa and the Wheelbarrow', about Leonardo da Vinci and the 'two great riddles of the world today—machinery and women'. It recorded the awe I had felt as I looked, back in the Crerar Library in Chicago, at the reproductions of Leonardo's notebooks, with their 'drawings of wings of birds and of tentative bird-like machinery which illustrate his attempt to discover the secret of flying. And while I looked I heard through the open window the throb of motors in the sky. Before me were the facsimile sketches, torn and thumb-marked by dead hands, of Leonardo's uncompleted dreams—a great mind's guesses at the mystery of mechanism; and outside, while thousands waited and watched to see him die, Beachey was breaking a record.' I went on to say that the fateful question about Woman was whether she would ever 'achieve conscious and purposeful control over her terrible biological potencies', or whether she would go on as always and submit to being 'the victim of Life even as the Moslem submits to being the victim of Death.'

The little piece sold to Harper's Weekly for enough money for me to live on for a whole month. I visited the Smart Set, where the editor, Willard Huntington Wright, very flatteringly told me that my story, 'Jessica Screams', had caused more cancellations of subscriptions than any other story they had ever published. By Berkeley Tobey, who was the business manager of The Masses, and my boon companion, I was taken to the office of that magazine, and there I met Max Eastman, the editor, and John Reed. Max Eastman was a tall, handsome, poetic, lazy-looking fellow; Jack Reed a large, infantile, round-faced, energetic youth. The magazine had been started by a group of Socialist artists and writers; it had run out of money, and stopped; then they had read in the papers something that Max Eastman, a professor of philosophy in Columbia University, had said; he was evidently a Socialist, and they wrote a letter and asked the professor of philosophy if he would like to edit their magazine. He quit his professorial job, raised some money, and now the magazine was going again.

Now as it happened, when the magazine had stopped, the business manager, an enterprising Dutchman named Piet Vlag, had taken its moribund remains to Chicago, and had there united it with a Socialist and Feminist magazine published in Chicago by Josephine Conger-Kaneko. I had been at a meeting where the merger was made, and I had been made an editor of The Masses; but that had all been illegal, and I didn't mention it to Max Eastman or Jack Reed. But when they asked if I had any stories, and I asked them how long, and they said about six hundred words, I said I hadn't any of that length but would write them one; and the next day I wrote a story of that length called 'A Perfectly Good Cat'; the magazine didn't pay for anything, but it was a great honor to have the privilege of contributing to it; the story, when published, was to evoke more letters of protest from shocked contributors, including Upton Sinclair, than anything The Masses had ever published up to that time. That Smart Set story and that Masses story would seem very tame now; but readers were easily shocked in those days.

I did not find a job, but I managed to keep going for the rest of the year by selling a few things to the magazines. Then, in December, one noon as I was walking down Greenwich Avenue, I was called into Gallup's restaurant to a gathering of some half dozen editors of The Masses, and was told that I was to be an editor, and get paid twenty-five dollars a week for helping Max Eastman get out the magazine; I said that was fine, but strictly on condition that I got my salary with never more than one week's delay.

Life seemed extraordinarily simple and happy in Greenwich Village; one even got a job without asking for it!

In the Village there were to be rented, for thirty dollars a month, whole floors in old houses, each with two enormous rooms—high-ceilinged rooms, with deep-embrasured windows, and fireplaces—and a hall bedroom, a kitchen with a gas-range, and a bathroom. In one of these apartments I lived very happily for several years with a girl with whom I was deeply in love. It was a companionship of two artists, which we knew might not last long, but which we hoped would last forever. Those were beautiful and serene years.

My job on The Masses was to read manuscripts, bring the best of them to editorial meetings to be voted on, send back what we couldn't use, read proof, and 'make up' the magazine—all duties with which I was familiar; and also to help plan political cartoons and persuade the artists to draw them. I could submit my stories and poems anonymously to the editorial meetings, hear them discussed, and print them if they were accepted; and I came to run a regular department of literary criticism, mostly written by myself, in the back of the magazine, besides articles upon current matters. The play which Arthur Ficke and I had invented, and which, renamed 'St. George in Greenwich Village', I produced at the housewarming of the Liberal Club, had been a great success, produced 'in the Chinese manner', without scenery—also without a stage, curtains or footlights. The Village enjoyed being satirized, and this was a satire upon everything in which the Village believed.

2

Upon coming to New York, I stopped wearing my high collar and black stock; I wore a flannel shirt instead. It was a place where one could dress as one pleased; and one might wear a necktie for a belt, without its attracting any attention. The people one passed along the streets were people that one knew; at least, if one went along the street, one did pass half a dozen people that one knew, and it made the Village seem to belong to oneself. When I ventured out of the Village, into the Uptown world, I felt alien and a little frightened; but I reassured myself by staring at the big stores and saying under my breath: 'Probably on the verge of bankruptcy'. That took them down a peg.

The Masses was presently indicted for criminal libel at the complaint of the Associated Press, for saying that it suppressed the news in the Colorado strike; the case was afterwards dropped. The magazine, among other news, told of Frank Tannenbaum's being arrested for leading homeless men into a New York church to sleep. Jack Reed was sending vigorous, realistically beautiful short stories to us from Mexico. I was thrilled when John Sloan drew a picture of a girl being beaten by the matron of a reformatory, to illustrate my story, 'The Beating'. Among The Masses' literary editors, Louis Untermeyer, who had written about poetry for the Friday Review, was a friend already; we were interested in the same things, and lunched together frequently to discuss the universe. At the monthly editorial meetings, where the literary editors were usually ranged on one side of all questions and the artists on the other, I saw Horatio Winslow, Mary Heaton Vorse, William English Walling, Howard

Brubaker; and Art Young, John Sloan, Charles A. and Alice Beach Winter, H. J. Turner, Maurice Becker, George Bellows, Cornelia Barns, Stuart Davis, Glenn O. Coleman, K. R. Chamberlain. The squabbles between literary and art editors were usually over the question of intelligibility and propaganda versus artistic freedom; some of the artists held a smouldering grudge against the literary editors, and believed that Max Eastman and I were infringing the true freedom of art by putting jokes or titles under their pictures. John Sloan and Art Young were the only ones of the artists who were verbally quite articulate; but fat, genial Art Young sided with the literary editors usually; and John Sloan, a very vigorous and combative personality, who was himself hotly propagandist and felt no desire to be unintelligible, spoke up strongly for the artists who lacked parliamentary ability, and defended the extreme artistic-freedom point of view in their behalf. I, who had tried to get up a rebellion against Max Eastman when I first came on the magazine, over some high-handed proceeding of his, had soon become his faithful lieutenant in a practical dictatorship. Once the artists rebelled and took the magazine away from us; but, as they did nothing toward getting out the next issue, Max and I got some proxies from absentee stockholders and took the magazine back. It stood for fun, truth, beauty, realism, freedom, peace, feminism, revolution.

I hardly realized at the time the nature of the problem The Masses group was trying to solve—co-operation between artists, men of genius, egotists inevitably and rightfully, proud, sensitive, hurt by the world, each of them the head and center of some group, large or small, of admirers or devotees; now it seems to me an extraordinary triumph that so much good-humored and effective co-operation was possible between them. Nobody gained a penny out of the things published in the magazine; it was an honor to get into its pages, an honor conferred by vote at the meetings. Max Eastman and I did get salaries for editorial work; but that was regarded as dirty work, which ought to be paid for. We were actually a little republic in which, as artists, we worked for the approval of our fellows, not for money. I think that the practical success of the experiment—it never made money, always had to be subsidized, and the success to which I refer is its enthusiastic continuance under these conditions—was due chiefly to Max Eastman's tact and eloquence; he could talk anybody into doing anything. .

Margaret Sanger had begun her work on behalf of women's freedom from unwanted pregnancies; she renamed the prevention of conception 'birth control', and under that name it began to get attention in the newspapers. This propaganda went on under the threatening shadow of a federal statute, passed under the influence of that strange moral monstrosity, Anthony Comstock, which classed such information as 'obscene'. In New York City a woman police spy, pretending to be a wife desperately in need of birth-control information, got a pamphlet from William Sanger, and he was arrested. The Masses published articles in defense of him and of Margaret Sanger, and the magazine was immediately flooded with thousands of letters from women, asking for information about the methods of birth control, and giving the best as well as the most heart-breaking reasons for needing such information. These letters, as associate editor, I answered, saying that we were forbidden by law to give the information; then, as a private individual, I carefully turned over all these letters to other private individuals, who mailed this information to the women; and in this law-breaking I cheerfully and conscientiously participated. I believed then, as I do now, that it is a moral duty to violate evil laws. In the words of a favorite poet of mine, Whittier,

> 'When Law, an unloosed maniac strong,
>   Blood-drunken through the blackness trod,
>   Hoarse-shouting in the ears of God
> The blasphemy of Wrong'—

then Law had to be violated; and I should have been ashamed of myself, I could not have endured living in the same skin with my conscience, if I had not violated that evil law, and given those women the information which no one had the right to deny them. Some of them, to be sure, were Comstock's spies, some were spies of the Roman Catholic police force, and good men were in prison now for breaking those evil laws; but that was my lookout. A world in which such a frightful tyranny was enforced against truth was already a prison, and all America was living in it. Nor did I consider that my lawbreaking was on a par with the lawbreaking of corrupt magistrates and policemen, who broke their oaths for private gain and advancement and made America a worse place than it was; my law-breaking was in accordance with the implicit oath which I had taken as a rebel against tyranny, it made America a little better, and it gained me only the approval of my conscience. Such lawbreaking is for an intelligent person a necessary condition of keeping his self-respect.

If I write about this matter in moral terms, it is because I was and remain in this respect a moralist, a believer in good and evil, in right and wrong, with a religious duty of serving righteousness and hating and fighting evil. I should like to believe that there is a special hell for policewomen spies who betray the cause of humanity, of their own sex, and of justice, for dirty money.

I had brought the manuscript of Sherwood Anderson's novel with me to New York, trying to find a publisher for it. At last I sent it to England. But before I did this, I took another look at the last chapter. Sam McPherson, the man who was wandering about seeking Truth, had come upon three children, whose mother didn't want them. Sam told her: 'I know a woman in the East who would take them and raise them.' This was Sam's wife, who had no children. So the deal was made, and Sam, 'with the little girl in his arms and with one of the boys seated on either side of him', started back home. I liked that. I felt that, in a world in which Truth was hard to find, children were a very acceptable substitute. But the chapter did not end there. Sam picked up another child on the way home, and then another. I forget whether it was five or seven orphans that Sam McPherson brought back to his wife. I thought that was overdoing it. Some people might even think it funny. But I did not want to argue with the author about it. I just cut one of the pages in two with a pair of scissors, and pasted it on a blank sheet of paper, so that the book ended with Sam taking the three children to Sue; the rest I put away in a drawer of my desk; the author could do as he pleased about it when he read the proofs. And it was thus that I sent the book to England. Grant Richards wrote back that he would like to publish the book, but war conditions made it impossible. I asked him to send it to John Lane Company, whose manager enthusiastically accepted it, and brought it out through the American branch of the company. I never told Sherwood Anderson what I had done about his last chapter; I remembered how hurt I used to be when people tampered with my poetry, even with the best intentions.

3

My old friend George—everybody called him 'Jig' Cook now—seethed with ideas and ambitions; he corresponded with university men about the organization of a college teacher's union, which to some people then seemed absurd, but which later came into existence. But he could not seem to write stories which would sell to the magazines. This was partly because the magazines wanted, in the main, something rather ignoble; but it was also because his stories, so magnificent when he talked about them, were not magnificent when he wrote them. He was discouraged. But among his Provincetown friends, Mary Vorse, Wilbur Steele, John Reed, Hutchins Hapgood, he saw fine talents which had managed to make some kind of honorable and successful terms with the existing literary market; and that was what he was trying to do.

Shortly after I came, he told me he had begun a novel about me. I reflected that if there was a novel in me, I really ought to do it myself. I thought about it, and named the youth who had been myself 'Felix Fay'; and then a title occurred to me—'Moon-Calf'. And I set to work and outlined the first chapters. When I sketched out some very painful memory, it was a great relief; but it was slow work.

George found it slow work, too, and dropped it. Susan Glaspell, in her book, 'The Road to the Temple', published a page from his unfinished novel about me. 'Nathaniel Burleson', the scholarly gardener, is George; 'Winifred Curtis', the librarian, is Marilla Freeman; and I am 'Allan Dorr'; the page is from a chapter entitled 'Running Up the Flag':

'Allan told Winifred Curtis, the librarian, about his leaving school and going to work in a candy-factory. She was concerned at the length of his work-day, and wondered how he could have any life left for his evenings in the library. She remonstrated when he told her he often sat up until twelve or one, writing.

'Before long she carried home this writing. . . .

'Next morning when Nathaniel Burleson, having sold his vegetables, came in from his wagon, in blue shirt, and corduroys, with some books to exchange, Winifred made him sit down and read the poems.

' "A sixteen-year-old boy?" he echoed. "Here in Davenport? And you say you discovered these poems last night?"

' "Even so," beamed Winifred.

' "Then how," demanded Burleson, "do you explain the fact that you have neglected to run the flag up over the public library of this city?"

'Winifred looked dazed. "A stupid oversight. I'll have the janitor attend to it at once. You don't think it will hurt him, do you?"

' "Hurt him? Oh, by swelling his head! Well, I wish some one had tried to damage me like that!"

'Looking back from his wagon as he drove off toward the country, he saw the flag go up for Allan Dorr.'

A lovely fancy of a generous mind; but, if he had any such notion, I am glad 'Winifred Curtis' did not carry it out. But what really happened, I think, was that when I was a boy-poet and George a married man trying to keep his marriage from going to smash, I— as his Lost Youth—made him uncomfortable. One's Lost Youth in another person is always an anarchic and socially liberating (or disintegrating) influence. Now the odd thing is that George was also *my* Lost Youth. And when we both needed that influence, we became tremendously friends, and got, besides, what else there was to get from that friendship—George taking my Socialism, and I his rich, deep, human knowledge of the world. But now both of us craved stability, we didn't wish any disturbing, anarchic, liberating influences, we profoundly hoped to settle down—and we were rather afraid of each other. We didn't know why; but we were too much alike in our romantic weaknesses of character—and in the other as in a mirror each could see too clearly a picture of himself that he didn't quite like to look at. We didn't want to spend the rest of our lives getting ourselves mated and unmated and mated again; we wanted to stay mated and use our literary talents in some way that would be of some use in the world. George needed terribly some literary success, for he felt that he had to justify the break-up of his marriage. Mollie had taken the children to California, where she was going to teach school and support them; meanwhile 'Ma-mie' Cook was helping her with money. George sat and thought about his children a good deal, twisting his forelock; he had a bad conscience. He was happy in his love, happy as he had never been before; but the cost of getting it had been a terrible one that he would never cease to feel.

When Sherwood Anderson's book was published, I saw that he had added a few more pages, but had left the rest of his orphans out—it was only three, not five or seven, that Sam brought home to Sue.

Sherwood Anderson came to New York, happy with his first appearance as a novelist, and immensely hopeful of the book's success. While here, he gave me some very helpful advice about certain chapters of my own beginning novel; each touch, naturally enough, made my 'Felix Fay' a little more like his own typical characters, and less like me—particularly in his suggestion that I have 'Felix Fay' always dreaming of future literary success, which I had never done. It was his idea that young 'Felix' should have been day-dreaming in school of a brass plate put up on his birthplace to mark the place where a 'great author' was born. He enthusiastically urged that 'Felix', having heard the false story of his having tried to rescue his beloved books from the fire, should finally come to believe it himself; I could not quite go that far, even in fictionizing 'Felix', who was, after all, me, and no lover of falsehood at any age.

'Windy McPherson's Son' did not sell very well. It was a few years too early; after the war, it would have found a wider popular favor. It was the true pioneer of all the newer Middle-Western realism, and has, I think, great importance as an effort of American life at self-understanding. We began to publish Sherwood Anderson's short stories in The Masses, the ones which were subsequently collected in the volume, 'Winesburg, O.' And Sherwood Anderson was married to his second wife, the beautiful and spirited Tennessee Mitchell.

4

In Greenwich Village, though there was a very general sobriety, I saw more drinking among presumably intelligent people than I had ever seen before. I saw whiskey drunk for its quick effect, which shocked me. I saw guests, when the host's supply of liquor was exhausted, send out for more, which seemed to me abominable manners, especially when I was the host. And once I came home late at night from the studio of some artist, whom I had been persuading to draw certain pictures for the magazine, but doing it—for artists are funny that way—so that he would think it was all his own idea; and when I got home, none of my keys would fit the street door. I tried them over very patiently, and still they would not fit; it was not until I had tried them over a third time, that, in mild annoyance,

I broke the adjacent window with my fist. It broke with a crash like thunder, and instantly a policeman appeared a half a block away. I turned and started to walk in the other direction in a dignified manner, as if I had nothing to do with it; but the policeman called, 'Hey, you!'—so I stopped. At this moment I realized that I had made a slight mistake about which house I lived in, that was all. But I was sunk in an abysm of shame; I had never thought I would be in this condition. The policeman, however, seemed to think all the better of me, after that. A strange way to secure the approval of policemen! I was still ashamed, horribly ashamed. And I am yet, for that matter.

It was not thus that I liked to get drunk. I preferred to get drunk on ideas, on talk, on argument, or in any kind of play. I remember one occasion when Eunice Tietjens was in New York, and a group of us, including Theodore Dreiser and Nordfeldt and several girls, went into Polly Holliday's to get a drink. But the little basement room was crowded, and the waiters were busy, and we got no drink. It was Eunice, I think, who asked us if we knew how to play 'Up Jenkins!' We said no, and she proceeded to teach us. If you don't know how to play "Up Jenkins!" you can find out from some child's book of games. But four hours later—it was nine o'clock when we arrived—we woke to the world, and found ourselves alone in that room, whence all but us had fled. We had been completely immersed in that childish game; our wild shrieks and roars of laughter had driven away the roomful of people who had come to experience the solemn joys of the dry Martini and the gin fizz; the sounds of our abandoned revelry had drawn three policemen from blocks away; Polly had locked herself upstairs with a headache, and finally sent word to ask us if we wouldn't *please* go home; otherwise, no doubt, we would have stayed till morning.

Some of us used to go to Staten Island for evening picnics in the summer. We would choose a secluded place on the beach equally distant from the lights of civilization in each direction, and go in bathing without any clothes on, which is really the only way to enjoy being in the water. One night the water was phosphorescent, and the bodies of the girls in swimming, dripping white fire in the darkness, were the most beautiful sight I have ever seen in my life. After a swim, we would build a bonfire, cook a steak and eat it, and sit about its embers reciting poetry. Those were beautiful evenings.

There were Greenwich Village masquerade balls, given by the Liberal Club. I was on the committee which picked Webster hall for the first ball; and I suggested Pagan Revel or Pagan Rout as a name for it, the latter being chosen. But I was the most miserable person in the world at these balls, for I did not dance. I finally got so as to be able to dance with my sweetheart without stepping on her toes; but that only made my situation worse—if I were seen dancing with one girl, I would naturally be expected to dance with the others; nobody would credit my explanations. So, at these scenes of gay festivity, full of color and music and laughter, which were beginning to advertise Greenwich Village to New York as a place of jocund merrymaking, I slunk miserably away to keep company with the other men who could not dance; we lined up at the bar and drowned our sorrows. Once I seem to remember climbing one of the pillars to the ceiling and unscrewing the electric light bulbs (by way of making a slight contribution to the general good time). I would have given anything to be able to dance. I *knew* how to dance, all right; but, like the unhappy youth of some story that I heard, 'the music confused me and the girl got in my way'.

In a little piece called 'Alcoholiday', printed in The Masses, I wrote that I had learned 'the secret of drunkenness': 'It was at Province-town, in a cottage on the edge of the sea, where we had sailed and bathed and sat on the sand all day—that sea to which my friend [whom I had just quoted as praising alcohol for the courage which it gave to rebels, so he said] and his friends and I myself had been irresistibly drawn, as to the bosom of a great and universal mother, for rest after a hard year's work. In that seat there was something elementally peace-giving, and there was a strange comfort now in the dull boom of the tides on the shore as we sat around H's fire-place drinking and talking.

'It came over me at the height of the evening that drunkenness was an elemental thing like the sea; a universal mother upon whose breast we sank for comfort and rest. The unintelligible precision with which J. had been elucidating his mystical philosophy, the flaming hatred of injustice which shone in H's splendid drunken eloquence, the extraordinary and satisfying lucidity of S's silent

thinking, the abandon of the two girls, were a release from the expression of the hateful, necessary arrangements of a civilization
against which something in them was in revolt. As in the embrace
of the sea, so in the embrace of those vast tumultuous tides of the
older soul, down to which alcohol leads us with a strange certainty,
there is release and rest.

'But Revolution? Not that way.'

—These were my friends, so I was being very poetical and polite
in my diagnosis. I could not say, without being dismissed as a
Puritan, that I thought drunkenness a refuge for souls too weak to
cope with the actualities of life.

CHAPTER XXV

War as a Background

1

I WAS ON vacation in Provincetown when the European War began. George Cook and I tried to apprehend what it might mean. I recalled H. G. Wells's stories of such a war. I couldn't envisage this one.

It was horrible; but one watched to see what would happen; the mind couldn't take it in. The Socialists in the warring nations became patriots and joined in the war. Our magazine protested at the British notion that all Germans were militaristic, but editorially hoped that the Allies would win. John Reed and Boardman Robinson went to Europe to write articles and draw pictures about the war. The magazine printed an article by Roger W. Babson, on 'Peace as a Matter of Business'. Nobody knew what to think, what to hope for, or what to fear. Minds, trying hard to think, were dazed. Meanwhile we kept on being as intelligent and as civilized as we could. I wrote some articles, and more Younger Generation stories. Frank Crowninshield invited me to contribute to Vanity Fair, which I took pleasure in doing. And I kept on writing and producing short plays. The world's future could reveal itself only from day to day, microscopically and meaninglessly. The mind adjusted itself quickly enough to mere slaughter; that was only a form of death, and death had always been going on. Until the plot of the horrible drama was revealed, it was scarcely interesting, now that the strangeness was over. Life went on, there were parties, there was gaiety. Laughter is a hardy weed; it blooms anywhere. It was against this background of War that our lives had to be lived. One could not stop living just because there was a war going on. These were still our lives.

I saw, next spring, a blossoming branch, cut from an apple tree, adorning a house. The blossoms didn't know they would bear no fruit; and they were just as lovely. I thought: perhaps civilization has been cut off, like that branch; but we don't know it—we can only go on being what we are.

As I write now, there is a war going on in China; it may—it logically will—involve the United States in a war with Japan; but it doesn't seem to affect us much in the meantime. The war in Europe was like that, at first, except that more people took sides and said silly things about 'the Huns'.

2

Besides, we had troubles here at home in America—the same old stupidities, bigotries, injustices; and there were the same things as ever to fight for—among them, woman suffrage. We had an issue of the magazine devoted to that, and I put in my best efforts in behalf of Votes for Women. It was only in the privacy of our Liberal Club little theatre, amongst ourselves, that I made fun of the suffrage movement; I would not have thought of doing so in Vanity Fair; in public, I made fun of the anti-suffragists.

Alice Duer Miller's suffrage rhymes, with their wonderfully amusing satire upon the antis, were among my favorite reading, and still seem to me among the very cleverest, wittiest and most eloquent political satires ever written. But all this did not keep me from poking fun at the whole votes-for-women campaign amongst ourselves. I enjoyed doing both things; as an editorial worker on behalf of woman suffrage, I was being a useful citizen; as a mocking dramatic commentator upon the movement, I was harmlessly expressing another truth. I was not to blame for the fact the two truths might seem to collide if placed in the same plane; I kept them in the planes where they separately belonged.

The Village quite understood this attitude; it wanted its most serious beliefs mocked at; it enjoyed laughing at its own convictions. And for a while I was the satirist of the Village. A movable stage, curtains and footlights had been provided at the Liberal Club. There was a group of amateur actors and actresses, including Jo Gotch, Will Pennington, Louise Murphy, Marjorie Jones, Berkeley Tobey, Justus Sheffield, Griffin Barry, Laura Tobey, and Kirah Markham.

Jean Untermeyer designed our costumes. Every few months there would be a bill of three one-act plays that I had written. Some were romantic and poetic, but most of them were satirical little comedies making fun of ourselves—sometimes making fun of the ideas which I was earnestly propagating in The Masses. One of these little plays was a rowdy farce, with a suffragette as heroine, a farce bearing the same title as that of an earnest woman-suffrage book—'What Eight Million Women Want'. It shocked Henrietta Rodman dreadfully, and she called a meeting about it in the Club. But all the women except Henrietta, and they were just as good suffragists as she was, enjoyed it and approved of it.

All sorts of 'modern' and 'radical' behavior was satirized in these little plays. 'The Perfect Husband' dealt with an amiable 'civilized' triangle situation in which husband, wife and lover are all 'good friends'. And masculine 'modernity' was ridiculed even more pointedly than the feminine kinds. A comedy called 'The Idealist', a satire upon sexual idealism, was a mocking footnote upon the behavior of myself and various of my friends, who in our search for 'eternal love' went from one wife and sweetheart to another. One of the hero's most fatuous-sounding speeches, about 'keeping sweet and warm one's friendships with women without letting them turn into love' was a plain statement of the effort I was making sincerely then, that I would be sincerely making all the rest of my life; in the play it was a mocking reminder of the romantic tendency I had which would always make that effort difficult and sometimes impossible. I lived, then and always, naively, earnestly, hopefully, believing that I had solved or was about to solve the riddle of how to be happy and stay happy in love; but the mocking imp that popped up in my mind and wrote these comedies, saw all my weaknesses. 'The difference between friendship and love, for you,' wrote the mocking imp, 'is about three weeks'. The imp saw, moreover, a selfishness in women to which my romantic eyes were blind, and was highly amused by it. That mocking imp was as separate from some other parts of my personality, as the poet in me had once been. At nineteen I had dreamed a three-scene play entire, with dialogue complete, and had hastily written it down when I awoke. It was different from anything I had ever done; it was called 'Sinners All', and satirized the whole sexual morality of all the world I knew. I sent it to Upton Sinclair, who wrote back that it represented a society more corrupt even than that which existed under capitalism; and my friend George Cook paid me the immense compliment of saying that it was very like the plays of Congreve and Wycherley, which I hadn't read. There were no more dream-irruptions of that mocking imp from his abyss of cynicism, but when I wrote comedies he was there at my service, ready to stick his finger through the tissue-paper of my most precious ideals. And the uproarious enjoyment of Greenwich Village audiences, composed of high-minded idealists all, seemed to show that the satire struck home there, too.

But George Cook didn't like this kind of satire. Our attempts at intimate talk revealed embarrassingly discrepant attitudes toward the problems of life. Susan didn't understand why we couldn't be the same close friends we had been. But George flinched from my kind of talk, although I endeavored to temper the wind to the shorn lamb. I had left no children behind me in my broken marriage; and I could bear to think of the past, and about what I had done, the unhappiness I had caused—it was not too great a load for my robust conscience to bear, and I could analyze my habitual weaknesses and laugh at my favorite illusions; while George, who in the pursuit of happiness had taken upon his sensitive conscience a load greater than it could ever bear in any peace, suffered too much when he thought about the past, and never dared think critically about himself any more. He wished to romanticise and glorify and justify himself; that was his best escape from the dark avenue of thought, at the end of which he would sit, in black and silent gloom, twisting his forelock, facing Failure. But he had been unable to effect any self-romanticization in writing. He tried sculpture, then playwriting—he and Susan collaborated upon a little comedy called 'Suppressed Desires', in which they attacked psychoanalysis as the enemy of marital happiness; he tried acting, and liked it, and the Provincetown group started a little Wharf Theatre. And then in Provincetown he found an unknown young playwright, Eugene O'Neill, whose little one-act plays were superb and beautiful romanticizations and glorifications and justifications of Failure. And now George's life had what it needed; his life was henceforth lived under the ægis of Eugene O'Neill's plays, which he dreamed of bringing to the Village and producing there. The belief in the triumph of his own kind of good over all the evil of the world, which he had got from one youth back in Davenport in 1907, as Socialism, had collapsed in July, 1914; and now from another young man, in Provincetown, he had learned another gospel, of the beauty of failure, upon which he founded new hopes—strangely enough, hopes of success. If the world were ready to hear this new gospel, Failure would be Success.

CHAPTER XXVI

TIME'S CHANGES

1

GEORGE COOK brought the Provincetown Players to New York in 1916, and a theatre was made out of a stable on Macdougal Street. There was a play of mine, 'King Arthur's Socks', on the first bill, and three others later. I sympathized deeply with George's hopes, though for the life of me I could not share his profound admiration for Eugene O'Neill, whose plays seemed to me obviously destined for popular success, but whose romantic point of view did not interest me. As for a chance to work in a little theatre, that was an old story to me; I had had my own little theatre in the Liberal Club for two years—I had been playwright, stage designer, scene painter, stage manager and actor; it had been great fun, but I could not make a religion of it, as George seemed bent upon doing. But I was sufficiently an idealist about the little theatre to be shocked by the ruthless egotisms which ran rampant in the Provincetown Players. I saw new talent rebuffed—though less by George than by the others—its fingers brutally stepped on by the members of the original group, who were anxious to do the acting whether they could or not—and usually they could not; but I need not have wasted my sympathy, for the new talent, more robust than I supposed, clawed its way up on to the raft, and stepped on other new fingers, kicked other new faces as fast as they appeared. It was all that one had ever heard about Broadway, in miniature; but nobody seemed to mind. There was devotion and unselfishness, a great deal of it, in the group, from first to last; but these qualities were only what I expected. And what did astonish and alienate me was the meanness, cruelty and selfishness which this little theatrical enterprise brought out in people, many of them my old friends, whom I had known only as generous and kind.

265

The internal wars of The Masses were conventions of brotherly love compared to the eternal poisonous rowing of the Provincetown Players. But over this crew of artistic ruffians, seething with jealousy, hatred and self-glorification, George ruled, with the aid of a punch-bowl, like one of the Titans. He really believed in the confounded thing! And his vision it was that held this Walpurgis-night mob together in some kind of Homeric peace and amity. Drunk and sober, he whipped and hell-raised and praised and prayed it into something that—though this was not what he was aiming at—did impress Broadway. Many fine talents got their chance in that maelstrom. George prided himself upon his efficiency, and, so far as I could see, hadn't any. It was my impression (which may have been inaccurate) that he could not delegate authority; he thought that nothing could get done without his doing it himself, and he ran hastily from one thing to another, and nobody was allowed to drive a nail if George were there to do it—only, under the circumstances, he couldn't be everywhere, and things did get done after a fashion by others, subject to his mournful disapproval. He fell madly in love with one toy after another—when a wind-machine was acquired, hardly a word of dialogue could be heard for months, all being drowned out by the wind-machine; and the 'dome' became a nuisance, it was so over-used; when I was too busy to stage-manage a play of mine, he turned it over to some new enthusiast with lunatic ideas, who put the actors on stilts, so that nothing could be heard except *clump, thump, bump!* Nothing was too mad or silly to do in the Provincetown Theatre, and I suffered some of the most excruciating hours of painful and exasperated boredom there as a member of the audience that I have ever experienced in my life. George tolerated everybody and believed in everybody and egregiously exploited everybody; and everybody loved him. He was the only one, it would seem, who could have presided over this chaos and kept it from spontaneous combustion. His own play, 'The Athenian Women', was noble in idea and conception, but somehow not dramatic, though I tried to persuade myself that it was at the time. Another play of his, 'The Spring', had a moving idea in it, muffled in an awkward plot; George's father had died and left him some money, and George took and blew in a great hunk of it, putting his play on Broadway, where it hadn't a chance; I thought that plain egotism, and vulgar anxiety for 'fame', and rank selfishness, in not considering the needs of his children—all of which may have been unjust, but which is what I, his old adorer, thought of him. And then his mother, 'Ma-mie' Cook, came to New York to be with her big boy, and sewed costumes for the Provincetown Players, and mothered the theatre. To me, the justification of the Provincetown Players' existence—aside from discovering Eugene O'Neill, a mixed blessing—and he would have been discovered anyway, I thought—was in two plays: one was Susan Glaspell's 'The Inheritors'; a beautiful, true, brave play of war-time. In this play, moreover, Susan Glaspell brought to triumphant fruition something that was George Cook's, in a way that he never could—something earthy, sweet and beautiful that had not been in her own work before. To much that was praised in her plays I was not responsive— 'Bernice' was not for me. But to my mind 'The Inheritors' was a high moment in American drama. And I like to remember beautiful Ann Harding, first seen as the heroine of that play. The other play in which the Provincetown Theatre fully justified its existence was Edna St. Vincent Millay's profoundly beautiful 'Aria da Capo', a war-play too, in its own symbolic fashion, and full of the indignation and pity which war's useless slaughter had aroused in her poet's mind and heart.

I did not like George Cook during this period; he was a Great Man, in dishabille; and Great Men, whether on pedestals or in dishabille, tended to provoke only irreverence from me. But then, I did not like Eugene V. Debs to talk to; he orated blandly in private conversations, taking no particular note of whether he was talking to Tom, Dick, or Harry. I did not like Mother Jones, either; when she came into The Masses office, I retreated behind a desk and looked longingly at the fire-escape. I am sure I should not have liked Tolstoi, Gœthe, Dr. Johnson, or Paul Bunyan. And how could I like Jig Cook when he was being Tolstoi, Gœthe, Eugene V. Debs, Dr. Johnson, Mother Jones and Paul Bunyan all rolled into one? Once, when I felt impelled to offer him some useless personal advice upon the conduct of life, I apologetically remarked that once we had been great friends;— "Shake on that," he said, and warmly grasped my hand, and listened in troubled silence; but his life was, it seemed from the outside, hardly within his own control; it was as if he were being driven on by a daemon to some unknown goal.

For Susan Glaspell my respect and admiration grew immensely; it is a difficult position to be the wife of a man who is driven by a daemon, a position from which any mortal woman might, however great her love, shrink in dismay or turn away in weariness; but it was a position which she maintained with a sense and radiant dignity.

2

Theodore Dreiser, who had been living uptown, moved down into the Village, and I saw a good deal of him—a large, cumbrous, awkward, thoughtful, friendly person, with no small talk except a few favorite joshing sillinesses, but with a great zest for serious conversation. A Teutonic sentimentalist at heart, I thought him, as the author of the chorus of his brother Paul Dresser's song would be——

'The moonlight sleeps tonight along the Wabash,
From the fields there comes the scent of new-mown hay' . . .

And, equally at heart, a brave lover of the truth, and a rugged, stubborn and gallant fighter for it. I respected him deeply, and laughed at him—a combination which he found it hard to understand; the suppression of 'Sister Carrie', the hostility of a conventional world of criticism, and the admiration of a faithful few, had given him some of the traits of the martyr-hero, which rather oddly consorted with his Balzacian ambitions. I admired the things he could do in writing which nobody else could do—the simple and poignant truths of life; and I thought his philosophic notions bosh and his historical ideas mere uneducated ignorance. I found that he did not agree with those critics who praised him for the immense amount of bricks and mortar that were visible in his towering structures of fiction—the multiplicity of details which such critics called 'realism'. He was not especially interested in the details, but was using them, and perhaps over-using them, earnestly in trying to achieve beauty. He once told me with honest tears in his eyes that a novel had no excuse for existence unless it was beautiful. And by beautiful I knew that he meant true to the deep emotions of the human heart, not to the mere visible surface aspects of life. Once Edgar Lee Masters—the lawyer-poet he had told me about in Chicago, who was now publishing some very remarkable things in Reedy's Mirror, called 'The Spoon River Anthology'—came to New York, bringing with him a two-volume

work by a Scotch professor upon Greek poetry; and one evening when
I was at Dreiser's, Edgar Lee Masters and Dreiser took turns reading
aloud, very solemnly, the chapter on Sophocles. Perhaps Dreiser
noted my mischievous smile, for he wanted to know what I thought
about Sophocles. I said it was all very well to admire the 'impeccable
perfection and flawless beauty' of Sophoclean art, but that in America
something less would satisfy me very well—something which hastily
captured the spirit and the aspect of our rapidly-changing world, before it was overwhelmed with its new destinies; and, without mentioning them by name, I described as well as I could the work of
such American writers as Theodore Dreiser and Edgar Lee Masters:
that, if not Sophoclean, was good enough for me, I said. But Theodore Dreiser and Edgar Lee Masters shook their heads sternly; they
would be content with nothing less than the impeccable perfection
and flawless beauty of Sophoclean art. They were both haunted by
the somber Sophoclean chorus: "O ye deathward-going tribes of
men, what do your lives mean except that they go to nothingness?"'
Dreiser kept scrap-books, in which he was always hunting up some
favorite poem; and once, in looking over a scrap-book, I found a
poem of his. I said, 'I didn't know you wrote poetry!' He snatched
the scrap-book out of my hands. 'It's too late,' I said, 'I've learned
that poem by heart', and I recited it to him very solemnly. He
groaned, as well he might; the poem was very boyish, incredibly
sentimental. (I know it by heart still.) Dreiser was publishing his
long novel, 'The Genius', at last, but the publisher wanted it cut; and
he hired me to cut it. I would take a large hunk of that mountainous
manuscript, and go through it, crossing out with a light lead pencil
such sentences, paragraphs and pages as I thought could be spared;
and when I returned for more, there sat Dreiser, with a large eraser,
rescuing from oblivion such pages, paragraphs and sentences as he
felt could not be spared. Yet he had no narrow vanity of authorship;
it wasn't because they were *his* sentences that they were so precious,
but only that he thought they were needed. When, at one spot, I
complained that a short passage was needed for structural reasons,
he said with gigantic tolerance, 'Well, if you think it's needed, go
ahead and put it in.' I was being paid, so I went ahead and put it in.
If one short passage, true in psychology but remarkably inaccurate in
certain architectural details, is ever discovered in that book by the

sort of people who devote their lives to that sort of thing, Dreiser should not be blamed for a lapse in realism. We had a curious argument about 'Bill Sykes'; I didn't think Dreiser should describe one of his own characters by saying he was a Bill Sykes in appearance. "But he was," said Dreiser, "just exactly like Bill Sykes." "I know, but Bill Sykes is just a character in another novel—not a figure in the world of reality that all novels are about." To Dreiser, however, 'Bill Sykes' was as much a part of the world of reality as the Washington Monument; and when I pointed out that his readers might not have read Dickens, he said, "Well, they ought to, then." I told Dreiser that Arnold Bennett had said that 'Sister Carrie' was a perfect novel except for one flaw: the chapter titles were in metrical verse, whereas, according to Bennett, a prose novel should be written wholly in prose. Dreiser said, "My God!" I asked Dreiser if he thought a novel could be written while the author was holding down another job. He said: "I never could do it."

Among my friends at this time, seen at the Liberal Club and conversed with eagerly at a side table while the dancing was going on, was Herman Simpson, a gentle and wise Socialist editor and lover of literature; although I knew many people who were abler than I, there was only one whom I regarded as wiser in any important respect, and that was Herman Simpson, whose judgment upon literary matters and upon life was something which I profoundly respected. The person to whom I felt nearest in my attitudes toward life and art was Louis Untermeyer; though I disagreed violently with most of his views on poetry—he was one of those who, along with Harriet Monroe in Chicago, were laying down the rules as to what modern poetry must and must not be, all of which I was happy to see triumphantly broken by Edna St. Vincent Millay and Arthur Davison Ficke. Louis pronounced the funeral oration over 'thee' and 'thou' and all such archaic turns of speech; while Harriet Monroe, if I am not mistaken, declared the sonnet an archaic form, unfitted to modern times; and both of them rather thought that poetry ought to deal with machinery, skyscrapers, strikes, lynchings, and such serious matters, rather than dally with roses, moonlight, love and other trivialities; fortunately, they did not live up to their theories too well. Louis Untermeyer and I shared a passion for Heine's poetry, of which he became a translator, while I retained in safe unpractised theory the notion that only I was perfectly fitted to the task of making Heine seem like poetry instead of doggerel in English. Both of us were thoughtfully concerned with the problem of living a life of reason while practising a creative art—something which most of our friends found too difficult. Vachel Lindsay would send us his new poems and—which is rare in a poet—take our advice about revisions and rearrangements. But when Vachel came to New York and recited his poems at the Liberal Club in a dress suit and boiled shirt, Louis preceded him on the program with a parody of a Vachel Lindsay poem, 'The Fourth of July', and Vachel was very much put out. Vachel did not like a piece I wrote suggesting that he had first learned his new manner from Chesterton's 'Lepanto', as recited by me on the lake-shore in Chicago; he said he learned it from William Rose Benet's 'Merchants of Cathay', if anywhere. I took, then and always, so much pleasure in Vachel Lindsay's poems, and the recitation of them at brief intervals became so important a part of my happiness in living, that I should not be begrudged the notion that I had a little something to do with bringing them into existence, with the help of Chesterton and Yeats. Louis Untermeyer, who had early corresponded with J. M. Synge about Synge's poetry, used to quote Synge's 'Preface' upon all occasions, until I said, "You will end by believing you wrote that Preface yourself, Louis." He said, "I almost do."

At this time I knew very intimately a young man who was subsequently accused of being a Government spy in the Socialist movement; and I later puzzled myself vainly with trying to decide in my own mind, on psychological evidence gained from a hundred intimate talks, whether that young man could ever have become a spy. It was a strange world in which we lived, one in which almost anything was possible; and one learned to talk in a friendly way to enthusiastic radicals while keeping well in mind that they might be agents of the Department of Justice, as some of them certainly were.

3

My friends and I often talked about what the Village meant. It was more than a place where there were cheap rents; more than a place where struggling artists and writers lived. It was more, and less, than a place where people were free to 'be themselves'. It was, among other things, very conspicuously to an insider, a place where people came to solve some of their life problems. Some people who had been desperately unhappy threw up their hated jobs, came to the Village, got along somehow, found something they liked to do, and then renewed their contacts with the outside world. Later we saw them go back into the outside world, more capable of dealing with it than they had been before; but even now, in two years, we could see the curve, plot the graph in our minds. Some people had to stay in the Village; they were permanent Villagers—and already we could see them settling down to be the Swiss innkeepers and Tyrolese bell-ringers of our mountain health-resort. A moral-health resort—that was what it was. Work and love were both concerned. People who found in themselves inadequate emotional motives for sticking to their jobs or their marriages in the outside world, and were cracking under the strain, dropped everything and came here, found peace and tolerance, and a chance to discover what they were like and could do. For young people of talent it was a paradise; youths could have love affairs without having to 'marry the girl', and without finding themselves fathers of families long before they were grown up themselves; and girls of talent did not have to wonder, as back in the home town, whether it was true that losing their virginities would help in the development of their artistic abilities—nor engage, as back in the home town, in intrigues of the most elaborate furtiveness and most desperate secrecy, backed up with frightful hypocrisies maintained even in the face of their 'best friends'. It was a refuge from Mother's morality. But it was not, except for some, a permanent refuge. One hoped to find out what one was like, what one could do happily in the way of work, and straighten out one's love life. Being free to have all the love affairs that one might wish, was a means to the end of finding one love affair that suited, that could be permanent. That was how some of us figured out Greenwich Village. To others it meant other things, of course.

We had various friends who lived in the outside world, and came to see us in the Village. We learned how they kept on with jobs they hated and marriages that no longer interested them. Drinking was their chief solace in doing hated jobs; and secret, brief love-affairs their solace in maintaining marriages that bored them. Husbands took girls to hotels, and dropped them in alarm when the girls became too possessive. Wives took vacations from domestic duties, and it was a poor vacation that did not include an 'affair'. We thought the Village morality better. In open-and-aboveboard trial-and-error love affairs, something might be learned; the other sort of thing was an attempt to disguise failure, that was all. Despite our fondness for some of these friends of ours in the outside world, we rather despised them, certainly felt scorn and pity for them. And we knew they envied us; if we stopped being in love, we could say so. One Chicago friend of mine told me: "My wife meets me at the door, always, with the question, 'Do you love me, darling?' And for ten years I have been wishing to God I had the nerve to say 'No, darling.'"

But when such people, cracking under the strain, came into the Village, it took them time to become acclimated. They were rather shocked to find that Village girls, after having had enough love affairs, wanted to get married. They were still more shocked to find virgins in the Village, some a little ashamed of being such, and hoping to find some lover who could persuade them not to be. Girls, however, enjoyed in the Village the freedom to live their own lives; and some of them lived their own lives exactly as they would have done in the home town, were courted and married, and saw in the Village only a better place than the home town to find husbands in. All this was bewildering to the newcomer, who thought he knew what Greenwich Village 'freedom' was, and found that he was very much mistaken.

Lucian Cary came East. After being the editor of the Post's Friday Literary Review for a while, he had become editor of the Chicago Dial—that staid old literary weekly had become 'modern' too. Then, if I remember rightly, it ceased to exist, or perhaps the job exploded, as jobs have a way of doing; anyway, Lucian set up a work-room in an attic, and started to write short stories. Or rather he started in to write a short story. Every day for weeks and months he came to us with a new version of the same short story, and handed it to us to read, and we said sadly but firmly, 'No', and he went back up to the attic. Finally he came down with a few pages, and we said, "At last!" So he finished it, and sold it to Collier's, and then got an editorial position on that magazine, and kept on writing short stories; and his wife, Augusta, in Chicago, turned over the Friday Review to Llewellyn Jones, and came to join her husband in New York.

Sherwood Anderson came to New York on a visit. And I think

it was then that he first appeared to my gaze wearing a high collar and black stock; he had always, since I knew him, carried a stick, but the black stock was a new feature. It seemed to me a quaint, old-world, eighteenth-century masquerade. I wondered why Sherwood Anderson should have done that. What was the idea? And then, dimly, as in a dream, I remembered that once, in some previous life, back in Chicago, *I* had rigged myself out in a high collar and black stock. Yes, I had! But I could not remember why.

I wished that Sherwood Anderson had gained a popular success; he was centered too narrowly, I thought, in the Little Review crowd, who gave him an adulation which seemed to me less good for a writer than the impersonal tribute of strangers who pay two dollars for a writer's book. He was writing a semi-mystical prose-poem about himself in the Little Review. He had suddenly become an admirer of Gertrude Stein's unintelligible prose. And there were qualities I did not like in his latest stories—the beginnings of a new manner which was to gain him fame, but which I never liked, because it seemed to me an abandonment of simple truth. When he asked me why I did not like his new work, I tried to explain. After he went back to Chicago, he wrote to me, reminding me that he had said he was going to dedicate his volume of stories to me when it was published; he sent me the proposed dedication for my approval. Except that it was to occupy the page where a dedication is placed, it had no resemblance to a dedication. It was in the form of an anecdote about me, and it was untrue. Floyd Dell—he wrote—had once had a fire at his house when he was a little boy; and Floyd Dell had rushed in through smoke and flames to rescue his beloved books; but when Floyd Dell saw that no one was looking, then Floyd Dell threw the books back through the window, and Floyd Dell waited until there was a crowd gathered, and then Floyd Dell rushed in to rescue his beloved books all over again.—I took this unfriendly caricature of a dedication to be Sherwood Anderson's way of ending our friendship; I wrote back to him telling him not to publish it and not to dedicate the book to me at all.

Isadora Duncan brought her school of young dancers to New York; and I saw her and them, in a great loft on lower Fifth Avenue. She seemed a curious combination of old washerwoman and Great Mother of the Gods. The school, with its beautiful young tunic-clad dancers, dazzled me; and having seen them dance for the first time, I wrote:

> This is the morning of the world, and these
> Stars from the burning hand of God outflung
> In gorgeous constellations; goddesses,
> The first born of the heavens, strong-limbed and young,
> Walking beside the amaranthine streams—
> Touching our hearts with terrible loveliness!
> Or figures seen within the bower of dreams,
> Whose meaning the waked mind dare never guess.
>
> It is a poem and a prophecy—
> A glimpse across the forward gulf of time
> To show our dazzled souls what life shall be
> Upon the sunlit heights toward which we climb:
> A flaming challenge to a world benighted—
> A lamp of daring in our darkness lighted.

I was trying to finish my novel. It went slowly and painfully. In the meantime my sweetheart and I had become estranged, for reasons clear to neither of us at the time, and presently I fell in love with somebody else. The companionship thus ended had been a beautiful and happy one; and if a companionship between two artists had been all that either of us asked of love, it might have lasted forever, instead of three years. It had been understood that we would, when that time came, part without quarreling. And there was no quarreling. There was one talk, sad and tender and friendly. We both cried a little when we said good-bye. We told each other how happy we had been. Like frightened and lonely children, we kissed and parted.

4

My ambitions as a poet suddenly revived, in the now-popular free-verse form. One day I wrote:

> This morning I went to Heaven, where I have not been for a long time.
> I did not stop to see the sights—
> The glassy golden driveways and the great gates of pearl,
> Where all the tourists come, reading out of their guide-books:
> "The first is jasper, the second sapphire, the third chalcedony," and so forth.
> I made no stay for the show-places,
> But took the first street-car out to the factory-district,
> And got off at a corner well known to me in the old days

When I was a wage-slave in Heaven.
There in the middle of the block stood the old red-brick building
Where I had slaved and sweated—God, how I hated it!
Well, I went in—
In at the big door marked "No Admittance—Keep Out."
The faces were strange to me as I rode up in the freight elevator,
And when I entered the old work-room, the noise and smell were terrific,
And the lighting was a disgrace.
I just came in to look round—it was honestly all I came for.
But over at the window by his tiny forge
I saw a man I knew at work,
Shaping with strong and delicate blows
A poem on the anvil.
I went up suddenly to the foreman,
A seraph named Abdiel.
He was a quiet, stubby little man in overalls,
And he remembered me.
I said to him, I said,
"I'd like to get my old job back."
He looked at me, and then at a splinter he had run under his nail.
"You know," he said, "the processes have changed since you were here.
Everything's done different."
"I know," I said, "I think I can handle the work."
Confidently—just like that.
He looked at me, and then at his splinter, and said as if annoyed,
"Come around at eight in the morning."

   Well, I suppose I'm a fool.
But when I saw that fellow at work at his anvil,
My fingers ached for the sledge handle,
And I could feel the hard-soft metal yielding itself,
Taking the strong and delicate impress of my thought.
So here I am—again a shaper of poems,
Doing the poorest-paid work in Heaven,
Where I have not been for a long time.

   But, after an outburst of free-verse, I went back to rhyme. And
one day I wrote a poem about a lovely sight I had iust seen:

> Morning sun
> And morning shadow
> In the green valley
> That dips from the meadow,
> A cry of delight
> From the hidden pool,

A splash
In clear depths mountain-cool—
A girl's laughter,
And between the trees
The dancing glimmer
Of white knees.
Startled and fearless,
A girl at play—
Let the swift hours
Their flight delay!
Her lips are as cool
As a dewy blossom.
Who shall stir the peace
Of that unstirred bosom?
Who is he,
The lucky youth
Who shall take the kisses
Of her laughing mouth?

In the Trobriand Islands, I have since read, poetry is magic; when the youth makes poetry-magic, the girl is put under its spell, and comes. So it was here. I, to my infinite astonishment, was that youth whom I had envied in my poem.

CHAPTER XXVII

Hopes and Fears

1

In 1916 the infamous Anthony Comstock died and went to hell, and an obscure person named John S. Sumner took his place as the hired agent of a private organization which, in cahoots with a corrupt police force, exercised an unofficial Censorship over American thought, and art, and literature; and a cowardly and hypocritical American public allowed this tyranny to go on. The Masses, which had fought Anthony Comstock, continued to shed light upon the fanatical terrorism exercised by his successor. The magazine, to help pay its expenses, maintained a book-shop which, among other things, sold the most enlightened books that existed upon the subject of sex. One day the new censor, John S. Sumner, a lean, sharp-nosed man, came snooping into The Masses book-shop, to see whether we were selling Forel's 'The Sexual Question'; if so—since he was the judge of these matters—somebody could be sent to prison for it. I talked with him; the discussion was amiable enough at first, for I was curious to know what kind of mind could be brought to engage in this dirty work. I tried to find out *why* he thought Forel's book so objectionable, for I thought it a very wise and good book: it was, it appeared, because Forel expressed sympathy for homosexuals—or, as Sumner put it, "approval", which, as I remembered the book, was not true. We began to quarrel over the meaning of a technical term, concerning which, strangely enough, Sumner was quite right and I was quite mistaken. "Young man," he said with great dignity, "I know what I am talking about." Whereupon I replied with some heat that he knew nothing, was a fool, an ignoramus, a liar, a coward and a sneak. He then marched out of The Masses office.

By this time the situation had become much more clearly defined for us on The Masses. Allied propaganda was dragging the United States into the war, in spite of the re-election of Wilson on the promise contained in the slogan, 'He kept us out of war!' Nearly all the American Socialist leaders, from Upton Sinclair down, had joined in the pro-war hysteria. Eugene V. Debs alone among familiar Socialist names stood for Socialist principles; and Bill Haywood of the I. W. W., who had been expelled from the Socialist Party. Socialism seemed a broken reed; but the Pacifist movement looked stronger and more courageous than had been expected. I had to consider whether I was a Pacifist or not; I wasn't sure—if there were hope of Revolution, I wasn't. But the masses of Europe seemed to be going like sheep to the slaughter; Revolution seemed a vain hope.

2

The breaking-up of a settled though illegal domesticity in Greenwich Village appeared to be as great a shock to the community as the breaking-up of a home in any other part of the United States. A social centre which had been a gathering-place for our friends had been suddenly destroyed; and its destruction was resented. Moreover, although there were those men in the Village who indulged in passing love affairs, something better was expected of me. I was an earnest young man, doing serious work; and I was, though I had not realized it, an example to newcomers, one who could be pointed out as proof of emotional stability in our little world. It was as if a deacon had commenced to go astray. Moreover, there were, as I now found out for the first time, classes in Greenwich Village—two sets of class cleavages, in fact. One class division, though deeply existing, had no name, but could be very well described by the popular American terms, high-brow and low-brow. My former sweetheart and I had belonged to the high-brow class—very much so. All those who had intellectual distinction, and some of those who had artistic talent—but not all of the latter—belonged to the socially superior group. It was a curious classification, and one possible to define exactly, though not without some elaborateness; not all people with artistic gifts belonged to it, some of them being regarded, by the high-brow group, merely as pigs or bums, regardless of their talents; conscious and deliberate control of one's life and restraint of one's sexual impulses, were part of the high-brow standard—one's sexual impulses were indulged, not impulsively or at random, but in the light of some well-considered social theory, which might be of almost any kind but had to be thoughtful and consistent; and manners were a part of that high-brow standard—there was something more gentlemanly and ladylike and less bohemian about high-brow manners, in every respect, than about low-brow manners in the Village. And this high-brow class was the one to which I belonged; these were not merely their standards, they were my standards. If I had chanced to fall in love with a girl who belonged in this group, I should have been, at least, sympathized with. And there was the other profound class division in the Village between the old settlers and the immigrants. Within the three years that I had been there, beginning the year that I arrived, a definitely new Village had come into existence—and my former sweetheart and I had been among its first families. We had come over in the Mayflower, so to speak. I had always known that the attitude of my old friends toward the uptown people who strayed into the Village with money to spend, was the attitude of the poorer British aristocracy toward wealthy greengrocers; and now I found that the attitude of these same old friends toward the young people who were coming into the Village from here, there, and everywhere in the name of freedom, art and a good time, was, in the main, the attitude of the Boston Back Bay toward the immigrants landing on the pier. I had, apparently, violated all the most ancient and sacred traditions of the Village aristocracy. Worst of all, I was apparently seriously in love with this girl. Our love affair was subjected to a thorough and ruthless ostracism. I later observed this process from the outside, in the lives of some of my friends, when I was the only person of the old group to accept a friend's new sweetheart as having any rights, the only one not to treat her as an offensive intruder; and I agreed with one of these girls in her view that Greenwich Village was, considering its reputation, an extraordinarily snobbish and sanctimonious place. I, an offender against all its standards, was still welcomed into the society of my old friends; but my new sweetheart was not welcome there.

In resentment at my treatment by my old friends, I abjured their society as readily as I should that of any Presbyterian suburb; but lovers cannot spend all their time alone in each other's delightful company—a love affair has to have some kind of social milieu; and so I acclimatized myself as best I could to a new and to me unknown society, that of the younger Villagers. It was an interesting realm, though I never felt at home in it. I found that I was regarded by these younger people as one of the pillars of a hated Village orthodoxy. The Masses, and subsequently the Liberator, though regarded by the rest of America (wherever it was known at all) as daringly modern in its pictures and poetry, was thought of by the younger Villagers as tame, old-fogy, stupidly conservative. The contributions offered to the magazine were passed upon by the assembled editors in meeting, but I was the one who wrote 'Sorry, F.D.' in green ink on rejection slips; and so I was regarded as the one responsible for the condemnation of so much youthful genius to oblivion. I had been told that young writers sat about in basement cafés and cursed me; they were too polite to do so in my hearing, but I now for the first time went to those obscure cafés, heard their talk, and gathered that they regarded me somewhat as George Cook used to regard Richard Watson Gilder and Robert Underwood Johnson. From their point of view, they had good reason to think of me as a moss-backed conservative, since the Cubist and Futurist pictures they produced under the influence of the Post-Impressionist Show were, to my mind, too often only ugly and silly; and their modernist prose and verse too often incompetent, unintelligible, and uninteresting.

3

I had become a good deal disillusioned with regard to this confused welter of 'modernism' in art and literature, despite the fact that out of it came some few works of creative genius; and I was impatient of the incoherent and semi-mystical thinking that accompanied it. I would have liked to see this modernism criticised from a conservative point of view, but the conservatives were seldom capable of anything but cries of rage or despair about it. The only ones in the conservative ranks who were attempting to think out the problems presented by the chaos of modernism were the so-called 'humanists'. These were obsessed with a quaint philosophical phobia of Rousseau, they shrank with academic aversion from the creative spirit, they were bigoted; nevertheless, they were trying to say something which seemed to me to have at least a grain of truth in it. The new young leader of the humanists was Professor Stuart P. Sherman, of the Illinois state university. In 1917 he published a book 'On Contemporary Literature', which I read with great interest, and with some amusement at finding myself not so hostile even to the Professor's freaks and follies of judgment as I was entitled to be, so sympathetic was I to something in his point of view.

O. Henry (I remarked in something I wrote about the book) had told the story of two Kentucky families who spent their lives laying for each other with guns, in the quaint Kentucky fashion. Then young Harry Montague went to New York, and right there on Broadway whom did he see but his deadly enemy, old Colonel Capulet! Here was his chance—he had long intended to shoot the old scoundrel on sight. But—Harry was feeling lonely in New York. And Colonel Capulet was, after all, a fellow Kentuckian. So he bought the old gentleman a drink.

I offered no such affront to the academic dignity of Professor Sherman, but I confessed to a certain pleasure in this literary meeting. I had been told that he was a reactionary old duffer, and I had expected, as a member of the younger gang, to take a shot at him in my review. But—the fact was (I said) that I was not entirely in rapport with the generation to which I was supposed to belong. Much of the time (and especially when they were discussing the convictions which we were supposed to be fighting for) I didn't know whether I agreed with them or not, because I didn't know what they were saying. It was a relief to find someone talking in a way which I could understand. Mr. Sherman was so lucid that one knew at once how much one disagreed with him.

My not unsympathetic review (written but never printed) expressed my own emotional need for finding order in a chaotic universe. At this time there rang in my mind a line from one of Chesterton's poems, the dedication of his 'Napoleon of Notting Hill':

'We have found common things at last, and marriage, and a creed.'
I had found my creed long since, in Socialism, and it was not shattered for me by its betrayal all over the world by its leaders and followers; this betrayal had always been a danger implicit in its parliamentary formulation, and the gigantic debacle of the Second International, if a huge and frightful disillusionment, could be no surprise; out of the horrors of world war would come some new, or old, more realistic, more militant and ruthless Socialism—what, I could not imagine

until it came, for I was no political thinker, but revolution was my creed and I wanted to find no new one. But I did want to find 'common things at last'. And I did want to find marriage. I said to myself that I did not care if my new sweetheart were not an intellectual. Her beautiful breasts were perfect for the suckling of babies. But I did not wish to add to my mistakes the one which I had seen my friends make—not one friend, nor two friends, but a dozen of them—I wanted to be a father to any children I had, not a romantic begetter who proceeded to wander away over the face of the earth in pursuit of some new illusion. How could one be sure love was not an illusion, ever? At least, one could wait and see if it endured a few social trials. I felt quite sure now that I did not want to be married to a girl artist; I wanted to be married to a girl who would not put her career before children—or even before me, hideously reactionary as that thought would have seemed a few years ago. One artist in the family, I was convinced, was enough. And, since all intellectual and artistically creative young women seemed (though perhaps this was only my notion, in defiance of what was before my eyes) hell-bent upon careers, perhaps it was only with a girl as simple and natural as a South-sea islander that I could find the kind of permanent happiness I wanted.

My boyhood's Socialist hero, Jack London, had died in 1916, no hero any longer in my eyes. A few years earlier, sent to Mexico as a correspondent, he came back singing the tunes that had been taught him by the American oil-men who were engaged in looting Mexico; he preached Nordic supremacy, and the manifest destiny of the American exploiters. He had, apparently, lost faith in the revolution in which he had once believed. His death, as a tired cynic, to whom life no longer was worth living—according to the accounts of his friends,—was a miserable anti-climax. But he died too early. If he had lived a little longer, he would have seen the Russian Revolution. Life would have had some meaning for him again. He would have had something in his own vein to write about. And he might have died with honor. As it was, the ending which seemed to belong rightfully to his life came to another life, that of a young man who was in many ways like Jack London—Jack Reed.

CHAPTER XXVIII

LIFE AT THIRTY

1

THE RUSSIAN Revolution of March, 1917, brought glorious new hope; but soon it was apparent that Kerensky was trying in the name of Socialism to lead Russia back into the shambles. And failing;— a failure which seemed to require American cannon-fodder. The Masses stood, according to the best of its bewildered lights, for peace, Socialism, and revolution; it told the truth, which just wasn't being done in America. William English Walling and other pro-Ally editors denounced us as pro-German and resigned. But new editors and contributors joined us. And most of the artists stayed with us; and the art-for-art's-sakers became among the most boldly propagandist of all.

2

What I had been finding out, in my private life, was that there may be such a thing as incompatibility of temperament between two people who love each other deeply. I took up writing one-act plays again, and in one of these, 'Sweet-and-Twenty', without having the least idea that I was writing about myself and my new sweetheart, I presented a young man and girl who, after they fall in love, find that he is interested chiefly in Socialism and she chiefly in dancing. He offers to lend her books, and she to teach him to dance, and each declines the other's offer. They quarrel, and turn their backs upon one another:

'HE. It appears that we have very few tastes in common.
'SHE (*tapping her foot*) So it seems.
'HE. If we married, we might be happy for a month——
'SHE. Perhaps. (*They remain with their backs to each other.*)

'HE. And then—the old story. Quarrels. . . .

'SHE. I never could bear quarrels. . . .

'HE. An unhappy marriage. . . .

'SHE (*realizing it*) Oh!

'HE (*hopelessly turning toward her*) I can't marry you.

'SHE (*recovering quickly and facing him with a smile*) Nobody asked you, sir!

'HE (*with a gesture of finality*) Well—there seems to be no more to say.

'SHE (*sweetly*) Except good-bye.

'HE (*firmly*) Good-bye, then. (*He holds out his hand.*)

'SHE (*taking it*) Good-bye!

'HE (*taking her other hand—after a pause, helplessly*) Good-bye!

'SHE (*drowning in his eyes*) Good-bye! (*They cling to each other, and are presently lost in a passionate embrace. He breaks loose and stamps away, then turns to her.*)

'HE. Damn it all, we *do* love each other!

'SHE (*wiping her eyes*) What a pity that is the only taste we have in common!'

Back in the earliest days of my life in the Village, I had seen a young man of great earnestness and high intellectual and creative capacity begin a love affair with a very beautiful, delightful and frivolous young woman; and he had started in to educate her. It used to be one of the amusements of some of the more sardonic of us to make calls upon them, to see what deep book A. was reading aloud to R. this week. It was always sociology, economics or history. And R. sat there, beautiful and bored, but patient and wistful, her feet up on a chair, smoking one cigarette after another, while A. earnestly read on, page after page, chapter after chapter, volume after volume. Well, I was not going to commit that folly. But, though I hated to admit it, I was, apparently, an intellectual snob. The counsel offered to the bewildered lovers in my little play, 'Sweet-and-Twenty', by the mad real-estate agent, was this:

'THE AGENT. If you are wise, you will build yourselves a little nest secretly in the woods, away from civilization, and you will run away together to that nest whenever you are in the mood. A nest so small that it will hold only two beings and one thought—the thought of love. And then you will come back refreshed to civilization, where every soul is different from every other soul—you will let each other alone, forget each other, and do your own work in peace. Do you understand?

'HELEN. He means we should occupy separate sides of the house, I think.

Or else that we should live apart, and only see each other on week-ends. I'm not sure which.

'THE AGENT (passionately). I mean that you should not stifle love with civilization nor encumber civilization with love. What have they to do with each other? You think you want a fellow student of economics. You are mistaken. *You* think you want a dancing partner. You are mistaken. You want a revelation of the glory of the universe.

'HELEN (*to George, confidentially*). It's blithering nonsense, of course. But it *was* something like that a while ago.'

In real life that was no solution. And this new love affair at last came to an end. It had been no light love affair to me, whatever anybody might think. And it had a much deeper significance for me than was expressed in the trivial verses with which I tried to comfort myself at its ending:

> And now we know what they say is so—
> O hide your tell-tale eyes!
> We are fools who follow and fools who grasp
> At beauty as it flies.
>
> The wingéd joy we capture so
> Only a moment lingers—
> A stain of delicate golden dust
> Upon our eager fingers.
>
> But shall we then withhold our hands
> And stay our foolish feet
> When, next, illusion flutters by?
> I wonder, O my Sweet!

It had been the most serious love affair I had ever had—because it was the first in which I had dared to think of my sweetheart as a girl whom I wanted to be the mother of my children. For several years, the sonnet which I found most heart-breakingly beautiful of all those in my friend Arthur Ficke's 'Sonnets of a Portrait-Painter', was this:

> 'We needs must know that in the days to come
> No child that from our summer sprang, shall be
> To give our voices when the lips are dumb
> That lingering breath of immortality.
> Nay, all our vision compassed not such hope—
> Nor did we, in our flame-shot passagings,
> Push the horizon of our vision's scope
> Toward regions of these far, entangled things.

We knew not such desire; but now I know:
O perfect body! O wild soul aflower!
We, wholly kindled by life's whitest glow,
Turned barren from our life-commanding hour.
Now, while I dream, sweetness of that desire
Lies on my heart like veils of parching fire.'

But I had thought that was just poetry. Now I wanted to fulfill that poetic wish in serious reality.

I often pored over a book of pictures by Carl Larssen, a Swedish artist. The pictures showed an old house beautifully made over, and filled with happy, healthy, romping children. I wanted a home like that.

I wrote another chapter of my novel. And then I fell in love again; it began, for me, with a dazzling romantic passion which faded and went out within a few weeks; so deep and genuine had it seemed, so much had I believed in its reality, that I was dismayed by its swift waning—more so, apparently, than the girl, to whom this masculine changeability was already known and by whom it was accepted philosophically, without bitterness. She, in that brief intimacy, had had the relief of telling the story of her life and last unhappy love affair to a sympathetic listener. And, though this was a failure as love, it seemed, curiously enough, a success as a friendship; it had tenderness and beauty, and it broke down the barriers of fear between two people who were shyer and lonelier than they seemed.

Now I was seeing Bohemia for, as it seemed to me, the first time. I certainly felt a secret snobbishness in its midst; I felt like the Spanish officer in 'Carmen' who goes off with the gipsies. But in this snobbishness about my fellow-Bohemians I was not at all unique. I found, upon further acquaintance, that all of them had a similar or, usually, more extreme snobbishness of their own about their companions. Each of these young fellows felt that he was a gentleman and scholar consorting with gipsies; all of the girls felt that they were young women of genius condescending to enjoy life among this gipsy rabble. Each one felt that he—or she—was only playing at Bohemianism; though each, to the others, seemed really Bohemian. Almost everyone, indeed, had a background of the most unimpeachable respectability; there were clergymen's daughters here, and college dignitaries' sons; they were almost invariably the children of people of some importance in the home town. Anyone coming upon them at a noisy gathering in 'The Working Girls' Home' or 'The Hell Hole', two of the Village's favorite saloons, might never have guessed it. Their favorite song, of which they never tired, but of which I got sick to death, was 'Frankie and Johnnie'. These youngsters would in a very few years, if they stayed here, inherit the Village, and be its old settlers, looking down in disapprobation upon a younger crowd. But now they were disdainful youth.

In this Bohemia I saw something of love without marriage from the outside, and learned things about it that I had never known— things which had not been written in any of the learned books that I had read. First of all, girls wanted to be married, not only for conventional reasons, but also because sexual relations outside of marriage aroused in them feelings of guilt which made them miserable. There were three ways in which these feelings of guilt were commonly exorcised—first, and most completely of all, by the emotions of self-sacrifice. If a girl were moved to pity and compassion for her lover, she would gladly sacrifice herself to give him happiness, and find her happiness in that sacrifice. One saw a good deal of that. Any tenth-rate free-verse poet could find a capable and efficient girl stenographer to type his manuscripts, buy his meals and his clothes, pay his rent and sleep with him; the maternal emotion sufficed instead of a marriage ceremony. There was one poet in Greenwich Village, an ugly, dirty youth, who was a malignant caricature of a human being, with a heart full of venom against all who befriended him, of whom it was said that he worked Pity as a racket, ruthlessly exploiting every person within his reach; and the astonishing thing was that girls of whom one would have expected more spirit and intelligence were helplessly the victims of their feelings of compassion for such cry-babies. Being something of a Nietzschean myself, I despised pity, and did not like it to be mixed up with love. I certainly did not wish to be pitied by any girl. The other spiritual hocus-pocus which sufficed instead of a wedding-ring to give a girl a good conscience, seemed to consist in quotations and arguments from Edward Carpenter, Havelock Ellis, and other modern prophets, arguments designed to show that love without marriage was infinitely superior to the other kind, and that its immediate indulgence brought the world, night by night, a little nearer to freedom and Utopia; I had once believed something like that, and had been sufficiently eloquent along that line, at twenty, but I just didn't believe it any more. All I had to offer to salve any girl's conscience in what would be to me a trial marriage, was companionship, talk, laughter, poetry, picnic suppers beside a bonfire, the beauty of the countryside—I had a little house in New Jersey—and the music of the phonograph. There was a third very popular way of reconciling a girl's conscience to a love affair, and that was by giving her a lot to drink; but I didn't like to have alcohol mixed up with love, any more than pity. If a love affair couldn't get along without alcohol, pity, or Utopian theory, I would have to get along without the love affair.

Friendly talk between a lonely and unhappy youth and a lonely and unhappy girl might easily lead to lovemaking, without even the illusion of permanency. A few such incidents opened up to me the vista of a life spent like that. But there was something too profoundly important about the sexual relation for my emotions to accept it as a natural part of the process of getting acquainted with a girl; it involved for me emotions absurdly incongruous with my rational attitudes in such a passing relationship—the wish for self-sacrifice, for lifelong devotion, violently romantic feelings, which were defeated and made rather ridiculous by the mere facts of the case. However mismated we obviously were, in these two or three instances, however impossible it was that our relationship should continue, it had seemed to me strangely like a marriage; and when we had had breakfast at a Village restaurant and kissed each other good-bye on the street-corner before going our separate ways to work, with no expectation of continuing with what had so accidentally and impulsively begun, it was like a strange divorce, bewildering and distressing to me. But part of my mind accepted these situations readily enough, and uttered its manifesto in a little poem:

> Blue eyes, brown eyes, green-and-gold eyes,
>   Eyes that question, doubt, deny,
> Sudden-flashing, sweet young bold eyes,
>   Here's your answer—I am I.
>
> Not for you and not for any
>   Came I into this man's town:
> Barkeep, here's your golden penny—
>   Come who will and drink it down.

I'm not one to lend and borrow,
I'm not one to overstay—
I shall go alone tomorrow,
Whistling, as I came today.

In another mood, remembering that I was supposed to have some connection with a revolutionary movement, if indeed any such existed now in the world except in mere idle talk, I wrote ironically:

Leave my sword alone, you hussy—
There is blood upon the blade.
Dragon-slaying's but a messy
Sort of trade. Put by the blade.

Take my knee and—O you darling!
One forgets how sweet you are. . . .
Snarling dragons—flowing flagons—
Devil take the morning star!

I lived in various parts of the Village, and for a time occupied a basement room in a house on Charlton Street made over by sweet and gentle Elizabeth Prall, who ran a bookshop, and whom Sherwood Anderson came courting and who became his third wife. My friends seemed all to be getting unmarried and re-married again. I thought a good deal about marriage, but less critically of it as an institution and more critically of myself as a person ill adjusted to its responsibilities. The problem of reconciling the real or apparent need, whichever it was, that people felt for the invigorating and revivifying experience of love affairs, and the profound wish for emotional stability and unity in marriage, was an old problem; and none of my modern theories solved it. Least of all could I believe in the theory of a marriage which genially encouraged outside love affairs—I had seen too well how that worked out. An artist was supposed to have a special need for love affairs; I could well believe that he had a special inability to resist them. But if that were an artist's privilege, it amounted in the end only to being an unhappy and frustrated human being.

I was troubled to think of the sort of person I was apparently becoming—of which I saw some examples in the Village, whom I heartily (and perhaps unjustly) despised. I did not want an endless succession of 'light' love affairs. Yet I could easily be that sort of person—for I had enjoyed deeply each love encounter, had valued the briefest of them, finding even in a passing intimacy the riches of companionship, mutual self-revelation, beauty to remember, newness to be charmed by, and joys that were none the less real because they had no tomorrow—that seemed even more poignant because they were of the moment only. Perhaps I *was* that sort of person. But I did not want to be that sort of person. My life would be a failure if that were the best I could make out of it.

Back in Chicago I had read for the first time, and now read again, Burton's 'Anatomy of Melancholy'; I had written in the Friday Literary Review that it yielded a peculiar pleasure that was too little known—in the contemplation of all the maladies to which the soul is subject. The section of Burton's book on Love-Melancholy fascinated me, as it had fascinated so many others, my favorite poet Keats among them. Burton had led me to the reading of Freud and his disciples, though I did not understand some of these writings, and misunderstood much that I thought I grasped. Everybody in the Village had been talking the jargon of psychoanalysis ever since I came. We had played at parlor games of 'associating' to lists of words, and had tried to unravel dreams by what we supposed to be the Freudian formula. And I had been for years remembering odd bits of my childhood and trying to fit them into some pattern—trying to find out what I was really like.

Should I go to a psychoanalyst? And if so, what, precisely, for? I was thirty years old, and I had not found myself yet either in work or love. Thirty seemed a decisive age. It was, I felt, time to do something about my life. The world might be going to drown itself in blood, but I had my own life to live. If I had known there was to be just one year to live, I should still have wished to solve my own life problem before I died. I was as little satisfied with such literary accomplishments as one-act plays, poems, short-stories and book-reviews, as I was with little love affairs. I wanted to be set free to love deeply enough to get married and have children; and I wanted to find in myself the powers necessary for completing my novel.

I talked to my dearest friend and former sweetheart, and she encouraged me. So I decided to be psychoanalyzed.

CHAPTER XXIX

A New Idea

1

War was declared against Germany, and a populace which had just voted for peace was exhorted, clubbed, censored and when necessary lynched into acquiescence. Debs, Emma Goldman, Haywood and the I. W. W. leaders were arrested. The respectable leaders of the pacifist movement counselled doing nothing in particular. Under cover of patriotism, every form of reactionary brutality had free scope. The business men began to graft millions of dollars on war contracts, and were happy. Labor got its slice of the boodle and was happy, too. Civilization in the United States toppled into the abyss of war.

None of us on The Masses believed that Revolutions are 'made'; but if we had believed that a revolutionary situation existed, and had known how it could be precipitated into revolutionary action, some of us would, I believe, have been glad to join in that effort. For what was left of Western Civilization was now something that belonged to the junk-heap of history. But Revolution in the America that we knew seemed utterly and ridiculously out of the question. All that could be done was, in a world gone insane, to keep alight a little flame of intelligence—to keep on telling the truth, as long as we could.

Yes, and the flame of beauty, too—it was our job to keep that alight as long as possible. The 'Renaissance' that had been predicted in 1911, that had begun in 1912, was still—fantastically!—going on. The war did not stop it. The war only made it bloom more intensely. And The Masses became, against that war background, a thing of more vivid beauty. Pictures and poetry poured in—as if this were the last spark of civilization left in America. And with an incredible joyousness, the spirit of man laughed and sang in its pages. It is strange to look through the files. So much good humor, sweetness, happiness is there! A few of us could be sane in a mad world.

Best of all I liked, in that outpouring of beauty and wit, Frank Walts's gay cover designs, Hugo Gellert's naked girls and mountain-climbing goats, Lydia Gibson's Polynesian girls in black and white, C. E. S. Wood's 'Heavenly Dialogues', Charles Wood's dramatic criticisms, John Reed's news and other stories, and Boardman Robinson's superb political cartoons.

I wrote on my draft card, 'Conscientious objector against this war' —against any capitalist war, I meant. I was just within the draft age; and I would be among the later ones to be called up. Meanwhile, in the magazine, I praised conscientious objectors, and argued that political objections were conscientious ones. I expected to be some sort of 'conscientious objector'.

2

I hadn't much money to spend on being psychoanalyzed, but the analyst whom I picked out was willing to do the work for the pittance I could afford. Later, my analyst repudiated the whole Freudian theory, but at that time he was orthodox. My work on my novel, which had already resurrected many buried memories of childhood, made the task easier; and so did my familiarity with the technique of 'associating' to words. There was no time lost in resistance to the process. Memories, dreams and associations poured out of my mind in a never-ending torrent. The analysis, which went on through 1917 and 1918, was much interrupted and was never completed. But from the first moment it became for me a matter of tremendous interest, and gave a new emotional center to my life. It did not interfere with any of my duties, and I wrote better than I ever had before; but for a long while I tried, and partly succeeded, in having no love affairs, preferring to wait until my emotional problems had been solved, so that I could love with a whole heart. Besides the new view which I was getting of myself, I gained from this psychoanalytic experience a new view of the whole world. These psychoanalytic ideas affected literature, criticism, education, love, family life, child-rearing, and provided a basis for a new view of history, not supplanting the Marxian one but supplementing it. Here was an idea of the same importance as the Copernican idea, the Darwinian idea, the Marxian idea—destined, like them, to revolutionize human thought in a thousand ways. My mind leaped to grasp the multiform significance of this new truth. And for me the dying old world became young; mankind would survive, at whatever frightful cost, this madness of war; sometime, certainly, the workers would learn their lesson, take up the sword of revolution, and achieve peace, security and justice. And then the world would have to go on learning—how to live, how to love, how to be happy. I had never been at home in politics, and was but a poor stick as a revolutionist; but I was a student at least, and I could learn this new knowledge.

In knowing myself, as I had at last begun to do, there was generated a new happiness and self-confidence. My character was not made over; far from it; but I could see it in its habitual operation, note how it worked, see why it worked thus, catch it at its silly tricks, understand it to the core. I did not expect to become a new person; but I did expect as the final outcome of this self-knowledge a better balance of interior forces. And I was in no hurry for that to come about; I had to see myself as I was, first. But I did have new powers, already; I was not the blind victim of unsuspected motives; I was happier and freer, even in my follies, of which I was to perform a plenty. And I understood other people in a way I had not before; I knew why they acted as they did, and what they would do next, and—most magical-seeming of all—could read their hidden secrets when I needed to do so, much to their astonishment. This was an accomplishment which could be carried to the point of folly, and was so carried by me. In the intoxication of this new knowledge, I talked too much about it, of course. But most of my friends were presently being psychoanalyzed, and we could talk together without being thought mad.

When one apparently possesses such knowledge as I was learning, he becomes an object of curious, awed, incredulous interest to all his friends, who come to see him as if to a fortune-teller, relating their dreams, telling their painful secrets, asking for advice, which it is hard not to give; but the temptation to become a parlor psychoanalyst is checked by the fact that one's friends, having told something they are sorry for, turn and rend one savagely. So one gets to evading confidences, and pretending that one doesn't see anything except what is right on the surface. Even so, one is suspect, as a kind of practitioner of the Black Art. One knows too much!

My psychoanalyst gave me no interpretation of my dreams, but let me interpret them myself; nor did he tell me I had a terrific mother-complex, and was narcissistic, had a great deal of unconscious homosexuality, and a variety of other frightful-sounding traits; I found all that out myself, and told him. He offered me no advice upon my private life; it was my own idea that I should not have any love affairs while I was being analyzed—though this decision was not carried out with complete consistency. I formed a very happy friendship with a beautiful, spirited and extremely intelligent girl who was engaged to be married, and whose fiancé was on a job in some remote part of the world. She and I went everywhere together for months, and I fell deeply in love with her, but I did not tell her so or behave in any but a friendly way; I dared not touch her hand for fear of betraying myself. She had told me all about the young man's romantic courtship of her, and I felt that I could never forgive myself if I did anything which might spoil that romance. I loved her, but my love was too uncertain a thing to offer any girl. No, I would not say or do anything that might upset her. But I told her all about herself and love and psycho-analysis and revolution. When we went on picnics, with my room-mate for a third, I recited poetry, and we carved all our initials, including those of her absent fiancé, inside a heart cut into the bark of a tree. It was a beautiful and happy friendship, and I was glad I had enough self-control to keep my emotions to myself. When at last the young man came, my roommate and I invited the two of them to dinner; he was a tall, handsome, romantic, adventurous fellow, whom my roommate and I admired vastly. We thought her a very lucky girl, and could not understand why she should act as though she were ashamed of him. After their marriage I used to call on them, and was puzzled to see her treat her handsome husband as if he were something the cat had brought in. The marriage broke up eventually, and I thought it too bad, considering that I had exercised such nobility and self-restraint on its behalf. Some years afterward, thinking about it as one of life's ironies, it occurred to me that perhaps the girl had got so used to me, in those months, that she was trying her fiancé in her mind by the standard which I represented; if she had tried me in her mind by the standard which he represented, I should have cut a sorry figure, of course. Should we have denied ourselves that happy friendship? We had both meant well, and by all ordinary ethical standards had behaved admirably. Perhaps there is a moral to this, but I certainly do not know what it is.

For a while my assistant on The Masses was Dorothy Day, an awkward and charming young enthusiast, with beautiful slanting eyes, who had been a reporter and subsequently was one of the militant suffragists who were imprisoned in Washington and went on a successful hunger strike to get themselves accorded the rights of political prisoners; she wrote a delightful novel, 'The Eleventh Virgin', about those days, in which fact is mingled with I do not know how much fiction. I think that I recognize 'Hugh Brace' in her book as intended for me: "a tall, slightly-built youth who was thirty-three and looked twenty-three. There was a look of great delicacy about him, an appearance of living in the night-hours and sleeping during the day. As a matter of fact, most of his work was done at night, not only his own writing, but his editorial work on the Flame, a monthly magazine. . . . You did not notice the color of his hair or eyes. They were contradictory eyes. They were curiously detached and yet luminously sympathetic. During the course of the lunch, June noticed that his clothes as well as his manners had the same awkwardness. It came, she thought, from extreme shyness, and remained with him even when he forgot himself in the heat of discussion. Behind his writing desk, he had poise. With a pen in his hand, he was gracious as well as graceful. He lost neither his dignity nor his train of thought when interrupted. . . . In back of his apparent softness there was a streak of iron and he was never ill"— a very flattering portrait. The novel also contains the quite true story of a very delightful though unusual summer household, of which her heroine, 'June', was a member:

' "You cannot possibly live and clothe yourself on ten dollars a week," Hugh told her thoughtfully. "Besides, a salary of such dimensions savours of capitalistic exploitation. Daniel and Kenneth and I, as you probably know, have rented a furnished apartment from a friend of ours for the summer at practically nothing so as to keep down our own expenses. And we've decided that the only thing lacking around there is a woman. Kenneth sleeps on a couch in the dining-room and Daniel and I have separate couches in the living-room. Besides a kitchen, there is a big hall bedroom which is quite unnecessary, so why don't you come down and live there? Your only responsibilities, my dear, will be to be silent in the morning and fairly agreeable in the evening. We'll all take turns at cooking and bed-making. Yes, even the dish-washing."

'This was the beginning of the "ménage au quatre" which miraculously worked from inception and was their boast to friends and even acquaintances. Hugh's theoretical love-making, Kenneth's vicious pipe, Daniel's lectures on chastity and June's almost irrepressible desire to sing before breakfast did not seriously disturb the friendship of the four. And the arrangement continued until the "Flame" with many other radical publications was abolished by the government in the fall of that year.

'Breakfasts were at eight every morning and June for courtesy's sake was conceded the first bath. She always felt so fresh after her cold plunge that it usually fell to her to run around the corner to buy the papers and go to the little French bakery and buy the brioche. By the time she had returned, the others had jumped in the tub and out, had set the table and made the coffee. Immediately scrambled eggs and tomatoes had been established as the staple breakfast food and these Daniel prepared. Hugh made the coffee and it was Kenneth that set the table. He acknowledged that he was worthless as a cook but June comforted him by saying that he was the only man she ever saw who could set a table properly without forgetting anything that was necessary.

'They ate with newspapers propped before them and cigarettes near at hand to add the finishing touch to the meal. It was an attractive breakfast room. The table had been painted bright orange and the chairs were black. There was matting on the floor and a wide low couch was the only other furniture of the room. Japanese prints and old brass candlesticks and lamps were the only ornaments.

'In the evening when one of the four brought home guests, which happened practically every night, it was understood that he should bring with him extra food. There was always steak. That Hugh insisted on for he often worked all night and went to bed after breakfast. June contributed strange-looking vegetables which no one knew how to cook and the recipes of the Italian grocer were seldom satisfactory. Kenneth favored complicated pastries of Greek, Turkish or French origin and Daniel saw to it that there were sensible and well known things such as potatoes and salad.

'The meals were always successful. There were editors and authors, and artists who always had to be prevented from drawing on the attractive surface of the table.'

The heroine's mother comments on it in the novel in these terms:

' "As for those three boys, Hugh and Daniel and Kenneth—they're perfect dears. And the apartment is a lovely one. I don't blame you for preferring it to a furnished room," she had said. "Of course your friends think nothing of it and neither do their friends. But think of the world. Not your world, I suppose, but my world. If any of my friends ask 'where's June living now', and I say, nonchalantly, 'with three men over on Waverley Place,'—what do you suppose they'll think? Not that I'm likely to answer them in any such way." '

3

The Masses, harassed by the post-office authorities, was suppressed in October, 1917, by the Government, and its editors were indicted, myself among them, under the so-called Espionage Act, which was being used not against German spies but against American Socialists, Pacifists, and anti-war radicals. Sentences of twenty years were being served out to all who dared say this was not a war to end war, or that the Allied loans would never be paid. But the courts would probably not get around to us until next year; and we immediately made plans to start another magazine, The Liberator, and tell more truth; we would stand on the pre-war Wilsonian program, and call for a negotiated peace.

The Russian Revolution of November came—Kerensky was overthrown, the Bolsheviks were in power. This was a Socialism that meant what it said! The mind was incredulous at first—could this really be happening? Could it last? Jack Reed went to Russia to write for the Liberator. And then there was Brest-Litovsk—and Germany at last seemed to some of us, to me certainly, an enemy, because German militarism threatened the existence of Soviet Russia.

4

I started in to work on my unfinished novel. But the Provincetown Players wanted some one-act plays from me; I had two on hand, not yet produced, which I was reluctant to submit to their mercies, after the frightful things they had done to the last one of mine they had produced—the one where all the actors had been put on stilts, which an author would shudder to remember. I could imagine George Cook tossing a new play of mine to some lunatic amateurs who would think it a bright idea to have all the characters standing on their heads; but one suffered in silence the wounds dealt by an old friend, and one could deny nothing to George. At least, while I had no job, I would have time—if I took it from my novel—

to stand over my play and see that it was not mangled. One of my plays had a scene laid in Washington Square, the other a scene laid in a cherry-orchard; and I hated to think what kind of pseudo-realistic sets would be provided for these plays by the Provincetown experts. So I designed the sets for both plays myself, and painted the scenery. Naturally I was pleased with the result; but so was the audience, and each time the curtain went up on my cherry-orchard scene, there was a burst of applause. A single cherry-bough with blossoms painted on a flat blue-green backdrop, with the same branch repeated on the two blue-green screens that masked the sides of the scene, composed the cherry-orchard, in the center of which there was a bench; its simplicity, after the incredible fussiness into which the Provincetown Players had descended, made it seem very beautiful indeed.

A girl was needed to play the ingénue part in the first of these plays, 'The Angel Intrudes'. In response to that call, a slender little girl with red-gold hair came to the greenroom over the theatre, and read 'Annabelle's' lines. She looked her frivolous part to perfection, and read the lines so winningly that she was at once engaged—at a salary of nothing at all, that being our artistic custom. She left her name and address as she was departing, and when she was gone we read the name and were puzzled, for it was 'Edna Millay'. We wondered if it could possibly be Edna St. Vincent Millay, the author of that beautiful and astonishing poem, 'Renascence', which was just this year published in a volume of her poems, under that title, though it had appeared in 'The Lyric Year' back in 1912—a prize poetry competition in which, judges being what they are, it had *not* won the prize.

And indeed it was she. Having just been graduated from Vassar, she had come to New York to seek fame, not as a poet, but as an actress: for who could expect to make a living writing poetry? She had another string to her bow, being a musical composer. She had set some of her own poems to very beautiful music, including her poem, 'Mariposa', which is perhaps better recalled by its first stanza:

> 'Butterflies are white and blue
> In this field we wander through.
> Suffer me to take your hand.
> Death comes in a day or two.'

Perhaps somebody can persuade her to publish this singularly lovely musical setting of her poem.　She entered upon the scene, in the second of my little plays, 'Sweet-and-Twenty', singing a song which I had written, to music which she composed—music which made it sound like one of the old English ballads of which it was an imitation.　I transcribe it here, for the pleasure of remembering her voice as she sang it:

> When I was a girl, my mother would say,
> 　　"April—May!
> These are the months to beware of the moon.
> 　　May—June!
>
> "And the blackbird singing upon the spray,
> 　　April—May!
> Beware, my child, of the blackbird's tune."
> 　　May—June!
>
> When I was sixteen no more than a day,
> 　　April—May!
> I met a young man in the flush of the moon.
> 　　May—June!
>
> His step was light and his manner was gay,
> 　　April—May!
> And he came from afar, by the dust on his shoon.
> 　　May—June!
>
> I looked at him once and I looked away,
> 　　April—May!
> And my heart it asked but a single boon.
> 　　May—June!
>
> "I love you," he said, "for ever and aye!"
> 　　April—May!
> For ever and ever—the blackbird's tune!
> 　　May—June!
>
> I could not leave him or send him away,
> 　　April—May!
> So we walked in the wood by the light of the moon.
> 　　May—June!
>
> I had clean forgot what my mother did say,
> 　　April—May!
> But I learned it all and I learned it soon.
> 　　May—June!

Early in our acquaintance, during the first rehearsals, I spoke of her astonishingly beautiful poem, 'Renascence', written at the age of nineteen; and it came out that part of it was written at the age of eighteen. "I don't suppose," she said, "that anyone could tell where the two parts are joined together." I confidently bet I could; and she scornfully bet I couldn't. The next evening I pointed out the two lines which were the end of the earlier and the beginning of the later part. She admitted in surprise that I had succeeded. "Moreover," I said, "these first lines of the second part were written later than all the rest of the poem, and replace some lines by which the two parts were originally joined together"—a longer passage, or a shorter, I forget which I said. Whichever I said, it was really the other way about; but the passage was written at a later time than all the rest of the poem and did replace some earlier lines joining the two parts together. She was greatly astonished, and a little in awe of my uncanny critical powers. I was a little astonished, myself, though I had been quite sure the night before, reading over the poem to myself and 'tasting' the mood and style and rhythm of its lines with some alert inward sense, that there were these three temporal divisions in the poem; but it was the first time I had ever set my critical sense so delicate and apparently difficult a task.

I heard Miss Millay read poetry, her own and other poetry; and I had never heard poetry read so beautifully. It was like the girl's voice she describes in 'Elegy':

> 'But your voice,—never the rushing
> Of a river underground,
> Not the rising of the wind
> In the trees before the rain,
> Not the woodcock's watery call,
> Not the note the white-throat utters,
> Not the feet of children pushing
> Yellow leaves along the gutters
> In the blue and bitter fall,
> Shall content my musing mind
> For the beauty of that sound' . . .

Her reciting voice had a loveliness that was sometimes heart-breakingly poignant. I fell in love with her voice at once; and with her spirit, when I came to know it, so full of indomitable courage. But there was in her something of which one stood in awe—she seemed, as a poet, no mere mortal, but a goddess; and, though one could not but love her, one loved her hopelessly, as a goddess must be loved. Perhaps because she was one's Lost Youth one felt sorry for her and worshipped her at the same time. The lonely, unreachable, tragically beautiful, inhuman, remote and divine quality in one who was, at moments, a scared little girl from Maine, and at other moments an austere immortal, was something which drove everybody who knew her to writing poetry in the attempt to express that recognition of her lovely strangeness. Arthur Davison Ficke came nearest to expressing the feeling which one had about her, in this sonnet:

'For Beauty kissed your lips when they were young
And touched them with her fatal triumphing,
And her old tune which long ago was sung
Beside your cradle haunts you when you sing.
Wherefore there is no light in any face
To win you from these memories as you roam;
Far though you seek, you shall not find a place
Wears the mysterious twilight glow of home.
You are an exile to those lonely lands
Far out upon the world's forsaken rim
Where there is never touch of meeting hands,—
Always you must go on through spaces dim,
Seeking a refuge you can never know—
Wild feet that go where none save Beauty's go!'

And it was this same paradoxical feeling of awe for the immortal and pity for one's own Lost Youth in her, that I tried to express in this sonnet, which was published in the Liberator as a 'book-review' of her volume of poems, with a preliminary explanation in the Petrarchian fashion:

(The octave is a sympathetic disquisition on the subject of youth, which, as is but too well known, seeks after the impossible. The sextet is an exordium on the same subject from the standpoint of sober and experienced middle-age. The sonnet thus has the merit, so much prized by the judicious, of presenting both sides of the subject.)

Child of the lightning, alien to our dust,
We seek you in the tempest—you are there,
Drenched with the storm of beauty, gust on gust
Of poignant sweetness only you can bear.

Startled, you vanish in the darkness, fleeing
The too-close human handclasp; you are fain
Of the caresses native to your being—
Strange joys that wound intolerably with pain.

But all in vain your hands to touch the sky
Reach up, in vain your bosom to the thunders
Bared—there is only you and mayhap I
And the old commonplace authentic wonders
Of food and fire and bed. There's no use trying.
So back you come, and yet—Why, you are crying!

The appearance of one's Lost Youth in so gallant and beautiful a form is a disturbing thing in anyone's life. One does not see 'Shelly plain' without some hurt. To know a great poet is a precious but painful privilege. Upon me, perhaps because I was in the process of being psychoanalyzed, it had presently a curiously stabilizing influence—to this girl poet, as to one to whom it rightly belonged, I yielded in my mind the right to the heroic egotism of genius, and for myself I decisively staked out a claim in the field of more ordinary and happier humanity.

Meanwhile we came to be good friends, and I became acquainted with the girl poet as a human being, whose society I enjoyed in all of her moods, grave and gay. She lived with her sister Norma in a room on Waverley Place; then her mother came from Maine, and her sister Kathleen from Vassar, and they had an apartment on Charlton Street. The three sisters could sometimes be persuaded to 'harmonize' an old song of their own, Edna taking a throaty baritone:

'Oh, men! Men! Men!
Oh, men alluring!
Waste not your hour
(Sweet hour!)
In vain assuring.
For love, though sweet
(*Love, though so sweet!*)
Is not enduring.
Ti-di-dee and ti-di-da!
We must take you as you are,'
Etc.

A pleasant scene to remember. I heard the poet recite the poems which were subsequently printed as 'A Few Figs from Thistles', and saw the discouragement which greeted their return from magazines which a few years later would have worn them as the proudest feather in their cap. She acted in a number of Provincetown Theatre plays—without pay, of course—and presently got a part in one of the Theatre Guild productions. She had great hopes there, and when she did not get a hoped-for part in the next play, she cried like a heartbroken child. She kept on writing beautiful poetry, and getting it back from the magazines with rejection slips. Later she did hack work for some of the magazines under a pseudonym, to keep the wolf from the door.

Always the teacher whenever I had the slightest excuse, I earnestly discoursed upon Pacifism, Revolution, Soviet Russia, and Psychoanalysis to her. She was very much a revolutionary in all her sympathies, and a whole-hearted Feminist. Inez Milholland had been her heroine in college days; that militant leader of the struggle for women's freedom had been suspended in shocked disapproval from Vassar, but had since then become its pride and boast, as Edna Millay herself was to be, after herself being suspended for some trivial infraction of a silly rule. Once I idly gave to Edna Millay a bronze button which had been left in my room, one of those which were awarded to the women and girls who had suffered arrest and imprisonment during the militant suffrage campaign. Tears came into her eyes. "I would rather have the right to wear this than anything I can think of," she said.

From her and her mother I learned casually a good deal about her earlier life. Later, on some walking trip, I was in Camden, Maine, and saw in the neighboring village of Rockland the house in which Edna was born, there between the 'mountains' and the sea. Mrs. Millay was in Camden for the summer, and I went to call on her. On the porch were baskets of apples, branches of pine, and there were bunches of herbs strung up to dry—herbs of which I do not know the names, but which were a part of the earthly lore that Edna Millay learned from her mother as a child. The place was fragrant with the mingled odors of apples, pine woods and herbs. It smelled sweet and strange, like Edna Millay's poetry.

She kept always in herself a good deal of childhood; and so it was easy to imagine her as a little girl in Camden. Not an ordinary little girl. A kind of gipsy child. The Millays were poor, and upon

Mrs. Millay fell the burden of supporting three daughters. She worked out as a practical nurse, and the children at an early age ran the house and fended pretty much for themselves. Edna was the eldest, and somewhat the boy of the family. Her mother had expected a son, and when the child was a girl, she brought her up, she told me, like a son—to be self-reliant, fearless and ambitious. She was called 'Vincent' rather oftener that 'Edna'.

It was not all work and no play for the children, by any means. There was a lot of wild, free play outdoors. Vincent was very much a tomboy—and would always remain so, on one side of her nature: a delightful, impudent, freckle-faced, snub-nosed, carroty-haired gamin. There was a lot of imaginative play indoors, too—charades and acting and singing, the girls making up their own dramas, songs and music. There was much reading of books. The housework was often neglected in favor of more interesting things. There was a carefree Bohemian slatternliness about the housekeeping, interspersed with fits of New England neatness. Vincent, the tomboy, would tie a rag around her head and be a severe and spinsterish little housekeeper for a few days. She still had that in her personality in Greenwich Village days—the New England nun.

Her mother knew this wasn't an ugly duckling, but a young swan. Mrs. Millay valued learning, and taught Edna to value it; and she was a poet, and encouraged her daughter's interest in poetry. All the old poets were read and reread. The girl's first creative efforts were recognized as meaning something. The flame of her young genius was tended and guarded. And she was encouraged to discipline herself in the form and technique of verse. At fourteen she won the St. Nicholas gold badge for poetry; the poem was rather conventional, not an inspired bit of juvenile free verse. She learned the molds first, into which she later poured her emotions while hot. Her mother put more emphasis upon her respecting the conventions of art than the conventions of behavior. She never did learn to respect the conventions of behavior; though sometimes she played at observing them, in a not very convincing grand-lady style, exaggerating them as a gipsy child would.

It was a gay and courageous poverty, with no self-pity in it; making terms with necessity, but not with appearances; asking a lot from life, and getting a lot out of it; with always the woods, the mountains and the sea for comfort from life's hurts and humiliations; for life does hurt sensitive people; love hurts and bewilders them as they grow up—and they have to go on past the hurts to get happiness.

Once Edna Millay swam out, on an unfamiliar neighboring beach, toward a lovely green island; it was further than she could ordinarily swim, but she bravely hoped to make it. Her self-confidence waned before she could reach it; but she did not want to turn back. With a tremendous effort she reached the lovely green island—and it wasn't an island, it was just a mass of floating sea-weed, and no foothold. Now her strength was all gone, and it was only with the courage of despair that she swam back. Her tired body wanted only rest, and each stroke was a long agony, but her will drove her on and on, and courage brought her home.

At eighteen to twenty she wrote 'Renascence'. The first part is full of the pain of life. The second part, under its mystical disguise is, if I may interpret it upon no authority but my own—a suicide fantasy, with the conclusion that life for all its pain is too sweet to give up. Never has the simple beauty of the earth been more poignantly captured in words than in this girl's poem: never, I think, in all poetry. And the decision the poem utters is one that was implicit and explicit in all her writing from that time on—to seize upon life fearlessly with both hands, even if it hurts.

The publication of this poem in 'The Lyric Year', brought her recognition from other poets and lovers of poetry. The twenty-year-old girl in Camden received letters from and entered into correspondence with many people, and began in that way a series of emotionally significant friendships. She had a gift for friendship. People try to draw a distinction between friendship and love; but friendship had for her all the candor and fearlessness of love, as love had for her the gaiety and generosity of friendship.

One of these correspondents was my friend Arthur Davison Ficke. He had read that poem by an unknown poet, was amazed by its beauty, and wrote her an enthusiastic letter of praise and admiration. The self that she revealed in her letters to him wasn't the girl mystic that he had rather expected. She had made her decision about life. She was now a frivolous young woman with a brand new pair of dancing slippers and a mouth like a valentine. The attitude toward life that was to take the younger generation by storm in 'A Few Figs from Thistles' had already been formulated in Camden, Maine.

At Vassar College, to which she went later, her life was enriched by the friendships she formed there, and saddened by the death of one of her dearest girl friends, memorialized in six lovely and tender elegies in 'Second April':

> O loveliest throat of all sweet throats,
> Where now no more the music is,
> With hands that wrote you little notes
> I write you little elegies!'

Edna Millay was to become a lover's poet. But with some of her poems she was also to give dignity and sweetness to those passionate friendships between girls in adolescence, where they stand terrified at the bogeys which haunt the realm of grown-up man-and-woman love, and turn back for a while to linger in the enchanted garden of childhood. One to whom friendship is love and love is friendship could explore and interpret the beauty of this tender friendship-love of girlhood. 'My heart, being hungry, feeds on food the fat of heart despise'.

When she and then her whole family came to live in Greenwich Village, its Bohemianism was not strange to them; without realizing it they had been Bohemians and Greenwich Villagers in Camden, Maine. Mrs. Millay cut her hair short like the rest of the girls, wrote poetry, sewed costumes for the Provincetown Players and acted in one of the plays. The mother of a girl of genius has a difficult rôle to play in life; and she played that part gallantly and nobly.

Her one-time Davenport poet-correspondent showed up during the war-days wearing a Sam Browne belt and puttees—Major Arthur Ficke, carrying dispatches from Washington to General Pershing, and meeting her now for the first time. Arthur Ficke, Edna Millay and I sat on the floor and ate pickles and sandwiches and talked gay nonsense. The next morning, on shipboard. he wrote some silly little verses, beginning:

> 'This pickle is a little loving cup.
> I raise it to my lips, and where you kissed
> There lurks a certain sting that I have missed
> In nectars more laboriously put up.'

And then this:

> 'Yet, lest with too much taunting of the gods,
> They should grow angry that I torture so
> Their beauty into devious periods,
> I will speak truth one moment ere I go:
> I will confess that loveliness has stirred
> Like a long music through me many a time
> When all my courts and fountains with some word
> Of yours were echoing in a silver rhyme—
> That when the apes and peacocks all have done
> With prancing in the portico, there shall be
> A recollection, safe from sun to sun,
> Within the dark high-vaulted halls of me—
> And one tall window, dearer than the rest,
> Whose prospect is your open golden west.'

During these Greenwich Village days I took Edna and Norma Millay to call on Eugene Boissevain and Max Eastman; it was for some reason a stiff, dull evening; everybody was bored. I was annoyed with the girls and disgusted with our boorish hosts; it was impossible to guess that Edna Millay and Eugene Boissevain would one day be married to one another; they were certainly not in the least interested in one another that evening! . . . To conclude the story, I was present at their second meeting, some years later, in Croton-on-Hudson. We were all playing charades at Dudley Malone's and Doris Stevens's house. Edna Millay was just back from a year in Europe. Eugene and Edna had the part of two lovers in a delicious farcical invention, at once Rabelaisian and romantic. They acted their parts wonderfully—so remarkably, indeed, that it was apparent to us all that it wasn't just acting. We were having the unusual privilege of seeing a man and a girl fall in love with each other violently and in public, and telling each other so, and doing it very beautifully.

The aftermath was equally romantic. Edna Millay's health had broken down in Europe, and she was really a very sick girl when she came out to the country for a week-end. The next day she was all in; Eugene took her to his home, called the doctor, and nursed her like a mother. His care at this time perhaps saved her life, for her condition, as shown by a subsequent operation, was very serious. When she was well enough they were married.

Eugene Boissevain had been the husband of Inez Milholland, Edna Millay's heroine of college days. He himself, an adventurous man of business, was in private life a playboy with incredible energy, romantic zest, and imagination. Moreover, he had really enjoyed being the husband of a gallant Feminist leader; his pride hadn't been hurt by her dedication to a cause, and her not remembering to darn his socks. A divinely ordained husband, it would seem, for a girl poet, who would certainly not remember to darn his socks, either!

Edna St. Vincent Millay was a person of such many-sided charm that to know her was to have a tremendous enrichment of one's life, and new horizons. It was something that one would always be glad to remember.

CHAPTER XXX

On Trial

1

THE LIBERATOR, with Max and his sister Crystal Eastman as editors-in-chief—and my old friend Hallinan, now in London, as one of the contributing editors—came out in February, 1918. Soon we were printing the utterances of Lenin. There was true revolutionary leadership now in the world—if we could only understand it. At least we could tell the truth about Russia. Socialism that meant what it said, took back its old name—Communism. There was a new International coming into existence. In America, the rank-and-file Socialists had under the impact of war stood by their Socialist principles, though deserted by most of their leaders—but not by Eugene V. Debs, who said: "I am a Bolshevik from the crown of my head to the soles of my feet." But Socialism in America would take a long time finding out where it stood.

The trial of the Masses editors was set for the middle of April.

2

One of my most-loved war-time friends was Randolph Bourne. He had, as I think, the best intellect of any of the younger group in America; a mind always clear, poised and just upon the issues about which the rest of us wavered or went to emotional extremes. He had written a book on the newer education; and now he was one of the very tiny anti-war group, at a time when even Professor Dewey had fallen headlong into militant patriotism and was 'doing his bit' by attacking the meagre handful of brave conscientious objectors in the pages of the New Republic week after week in the name of Pragmatism. I remember that, because it was my indignation against Professor Dewey and my description of Pragmatism as 'convenient surrender of principles to force majeure', at some Village party, which made Randolph Bourne my friend. He had been associated with Van Wyck Brooks, Waldo Frank, Louis Untermeyer, James Oppenheim and Paul Rosenfeld in the editorship of the Seven Arts, until its subsidy was withdrawn because of its anti-war attitude. Then he found it almost impossible to get any of his writing published in any of the supposedly liberal weeklies. It was in the latter part of 1917 and through 1918 that I knew him. He seemed to like, and even to envy, the intemperate and blasting way in which I expressed my opinions in private conversation, just as I envied the temperateness and justice of his writing. In talk, each of us had a good deal of sardonic wit, which we heartily enjoyed in each other. Upon one occasion Randolph took me around to call upon Waldo Frank, who was working on a novel, and teased him to read aloud a page or two, hoping to engage Waldo Frank and me in a literary argument. The novel was modernist in style, and I asked him why he did this and that, because I didn't know, but our discussion was amiable enough. Waldo gently said to me: "I should think you would want to write in the experimental modern way, and not in the old, formal Victorian way," or something to that effect; and I, thinking of my unfinished novel, said: "By the time you have triumphantly demonstrated the virtues of the new way of writing novels, I hope to have learned the old-fashioned way of writing them." But upon other occasions, with a better opportunity, Randolph succeeded in evoking the argumentative fireworks he had been hoping for, which he relished with a huge, diabolical grin.

Randolph Bourne's friends were used to his appearance, and forgot about it, thinking of his beautiful mind; but at first sight he was very startling. He had been born dreadfully misshapen, with a crooked back and a grotesque face, out of which only his eyes shone with the beauty of his soul. He forgot this outward aspect, or succeeded in pretending to himself that it did not exist; he hated to be treated as any other than a wholly robust and ordinary person, and if anyone took his arm in going across the street, the touch would be shaken off fiercely. He intended to be a conscientious objector, and was prepared to face any ordeals which might ensue; prison, to be sure, and being mobbed, was an everyday possibility in the lives of any of us, but no one of Randolph's friends dared to remind him that he could not pass the physical examination when he was called up for service, and would be exempted from military duty. He lived within some kind of protective illusion in that respect; no one would have been so cruel as to remind him of what he had succeeded in ignoring. And concerning this I have a painful memory, which it will ease my mind to tell.—I had written a short autobiographical novel, afterwards destroyed because it was too literal for publication, about life in Chicago; Randolph Bourne read it, and was enthusiastic about it, though he said, "It is not Chicago, it is the Bagdad of Haroun al Raschid." I told him of my unfinished novel, 'Moon-Calf', and he wanted to read that. Some friends suggested that he read some of it aloud to the group, and he agreed. On that evening, then, he took my manuscript, and in his beautiful voice read aloud the early chapters of my book. It was an occasion such as makes a young author happy, for Randolph Bourne, in whose judgment I had the greatest confidence, showed approval of all he was reading. He came toward the end of the section dealing with 'Felix Fay's' life in Maple, as I called the town of Barry, Illinois; and he had just started to read a certain paragraph when I awoke from my trance of listening, to an unhappy realization of what was in that paragraph. It was too late to do anything; and I sat there paralyzed, while he read aloud, in a voice that he managed to keep in its usual key, the following:

'Once her nephew came to stay with her for a while. He was a cripple, and was sent from one to another among his relations. His name was Dick. He was twenty-one, and he could do nothing but whittle; there was something the matter with his back. "Get me that stick there," he would say to Felix as they sat together on the wide porch. Felix would bring him a piece of soft wood. Dick would bend his brown head over it, and his face, which was thin and strained, would become composed and beautiful as he worked. When he finished, it was a turtle or a mouse or a bird—delicate and sure in its carved contours. Then, after Felix had admired and handled it for a while, he would say, "Give it back!" And then he would destroy it. He would take his knife and chip off a bit here and there, his face lighted with an ugly, evil pleasure, as if he were tormenting a live thing. When at last it was only barely recognizable as the thing it had been, he would toss it carelessly out into the grass.

' "Why do you do that?" Felix would ask curiously.

' "I'm playing that I'm God," he would say, and laugh heartily, as though it were the greatest joke in the world.

' "What do you mean?" Felix would persist. "I don't understand."

' "You will some day," Dick would reply, and then he would whistle beautiful melodies.

'Dick went away, and when Felix asked the old woman about him a month later, she told him Dick was dead.'

Randolph came to the end of the episode, and laid the manuscript aside, and everybody volubly talked of something else. I felt sick.

Randolph Bourne died in December, 1918, of pneumonia, leaving only a fragment of his book on 'The State'; and America lost one of its most greatly gifted minds, imprisoned in that frail and pitiful body.

3

At ten-thirty in the morning of April fifteenth, five of us—Max Eastman, Merrill Rogers, who was the business manager of the Masses, Art Young, Josephine Bell, a girl poet, and I—filed into one of the courtrooms on the third floor of the old Postoffice Building, which was used as a Federal Court, and took our places about a large table in the front enclosure. Ahead was a table at which sat three smiling men from the district attorney's office; up on the dais, behind a desk, sat a black-gowned judge, busy with some papers; to the right was a jury box with twelve empty chairs; and behind us, filling the room, was a venire of a hundred and fifty men, from whom a jury was presently to be selected, to try us on the charge of 'conspiring to promote insubordination and mutiny in the military and naval forces of the United States, and to obstruct recruiting and enlistment to the injury of the service.'

We rose to answer to our names, sat down, and the trial had begun. Our liberties to the extent of twenty years apiece, and our hypothetical fortunes to the extent of ten thousand dollars apiece, were now at stake. On the bench was Judge Augustus N. Hand, a rather slender and slightly grizzled man of reassuringly judicious and patient demeanor. In charge of the prosecution was Assistant District Attorney Earl B. Barnes, a thin and angular man with a perpetual sharp smile; it was apparent that he would send us to prison, if he could, in the most good-humored way possible, as a matter of duty, and with no personal grudge. He was assisted by two affable young men, Mr. Cobb and Mr. Rothwell. We were, after all, in New York City, where there were some elements of civilization left—not in the South, or in California. But ranged against us were the newspapers with their screaming headlines of Allied defeat, and the militant tunes of a Liberty Bond band in the park beneath the windows. On our side were certain constitutional rights of the press—which were being deliberately violated every day by the government. Our attorneys were Morris Hillquit, recently Socialist candidate for mayor of New York City, and Dudley Field Malone, who had resigned his position as Collector of the Port of New York as a protest against President Wilson's refusal to fulfill the Democratic party's pledge to give the vote to women.

The jury box filled up, and after questioning by defense and prosecution one man after another was excused. In the panel were real-estate agents, retired capitalists, bankers, managers, foremen and salesmen—never a wage-worker. It was composed almost entirely of old men. The prospective jurors frankly admitted extreme prejudice against Socialists, pacifists and conscientious objectors, though it was usually ready to assent cheerfully to the prosecuting attorney's suggestion that these prejudices were not such as would stand in the way of an impartial consideration of the evidence.

It is hard to tell what a man is like from a few brief answers to a few questions. It was a species of lightning guess-work to decide what kind of mind and heart and conscience a prospective juror had—what malevolent prejudices, what weak susceptibilities to popular emotions, what impenetrable stupidities might lurk behind those unrevealing, brief replies. "Are you prejudiced?" "Yes." "Can you set aside that prejudice?" "Yes." These might be the replies of a fool or a coward or a liar; or they might be the replies of an honest man, open to conviction of the truth, and steadfast as a rock in maintaining that truth against all opposition. We had to gamble on our impressions of character, and choose irrevocably.

The jury was finally selected in the course of two days. The judge quashed one count of the indictment, leaving us now charged only with conspiracy to obstruct recruiting or enlisting; but we could still be given twenty years in prison for that. And the girl-poet, Josephine Bell, was let go.

The case thereupon went to the jury, and somewhat to our surprise a great deal of time was taken up in establishing beyond the peradventure of a doubt, by the testimony of office boys and printers, that such a magazine as ours really existed. Then, much more interesting, there was presented to the jury the evidence against us, in the form of editorials, jokes, pictures, and poems which we had printed. It took a long time to read everything we had written—a whole day. I felt a certain pride as an author in having my own writings, among others, thus treated as matters of social and political importance; and I reflected that even if during the rest of my literary career my work should receive no other public testimonial, I should never complain that it had been permitted to languish neglected. There are different ways in which the State may encourage its young writers; if this present ceremonial was open to criticism from some points of view, yet it could not be said that it was lacking in impressiveness. And if this were not exactly a wreath of laurel that had been handed me, yet I wore it as proudly.

Among my writings, one particular paragraph had been cited in the indictment as an 'overt act' in violation of the Espionage law. This passage, constituting an introduction to a brief account of the tortures inflicted on British conscientious objectors, was read to the jury: "There are some laws that the individual feels he cannot obey, and he will suffer any punishment, even that of death, rather than recognize them as having authority over him. This fundamental stubbornness of the free soul, against which all the powers of the State are helpless, constitutes a conscientious objection, whatever its sources may be in political or social opinion."

So it was, I reflected, a tribute to courage which had brought me into court! I had not ceased, at the proper moment, to admire a certain 'stubbornness of the free soul'. Or, admiring it if I must, I had not duly reflected that the time was inopportune for utterance of the disturbing truth that against such heroic stubbornness all the powers of the State are helpless! A fault of taste, perhaps; but I had observed that all times are inopportune for the utterance of truth. Truth is always in bad taste. . . . Meanwhile, our legal defenders addressed the jury, pointing out that these 'overt acts' constituted simply a lawful exercise of the constitutional right of free expression of opinion.

In turn, then, we the defendants took the stand and explained our views. And I felt that the jurors, who looked and listened so intently hour after hour while we were testifying, were having a spiritual adventure as gratifying as it was doubtless unique in their experience. Busy men all their lives, too tired perhaps at the end of the day's getting and spending ever to explore for themselves the realms of economic and social thought, they were now given by an odd chance an opportunity to view some fascinating landscapes of thought. And though they might in the end, reminded of their duty by a tune outside the window, decide that we were dangerous men and send us off to prison, still this would be a thing to remember. . . .

I did not fail to recognize why it was that we were thus permitted to entertain the jury with reasoned and eloquent discourse. I had observed in certain other war-time trials that the defendants were not treated with such courteous consideration. No, for in these war-time trials the defendants were often both poor and of foreign origin—and as such not entitled by American custom to the civilities which we reserve for our peers. These 'foreigners' were here to do our dirty work and take our orders, with no right to criticize. But we, as it appeared, were American-born and bred, obviously well-educated, belonging by prescriptive right among those who give rather than among those who take orders; and if we were found on the 'wrong' side of such a controversy, along with discontented foreign-born workers, it would naturally be inquired how the devil we came to be there, and our reply would meet with a respectful, if puzzled, hearing. In our case, the mention of constitutional rights could not be met with the judicial sneer which is accorded to those who mention such rights with a foreign accent; it was 'our' constitution, and we had a right to talk about it. We did not wave our hands when we started to explain ourselves, nor were we shabby; and so we were not interrupted by an impatient judge.

Art Young had been busy all through the trial drawing humorous pictures of the judge, the jury, the witnesses, the court attendants. But once he fell asleep. "For heaven's sake, wake him up and give him a pencil," whispered one of our attorneys. For there is an etiquette of the court-room. It is discourteous to show weariness or boredom while being tried. One may not smoke, or read, or whisper much, or laugh at all. And this, to such as have not yet got used to it, is one of the serious hardships of being on trial.

I was told to take the stand, and I did so with pleasure. It was not only an agreeable break in the routine, but a chance to speak after an enforced silence that had lasted for days. Moreover, here was a perfect audience. The government does not do things by halves: it had provided a carefully selected group of men for me to talk to; others might tire and go away, but they had to sit there and listen to me. Under such circumstances, it was easy to explain what I thought about war, militarism, conscientious objectors, and other related subjects.

Also, I found in cross-examination the distinct excitement of a primitive sort of game of wits. The method of conducting a discussion in a court-room is faintly suggestive of a Socratic dialogue. And though your questioner stands twenty feet away, and you are speaking up so the jury can hear, you lose all sense of any presence save that of your interlocutor. You are surprised when, at some interruption from outside that magic circle of question and answer, you discover yourself in a court-room full of people. It is a strange, stimulating, and—or so I found it—an agreeable experience.

All this discussion of our various opinions on almost every conceivable political topic had extended the trial into its second week. On the ninth day, the attorneys for both sides summed up. The district attorney most surprisingly paid us all compliments in asking the jury to convict us. "These men," he said, "are men of extraordinary intelligence." And me in particular he characterized thus: "Dell, a trained journalist, a writer of exquisite English, keenly ironical, bitingly sarcastic." Thank you, Mr. Barnes! "And so, gentlemen of the jury," he concluded, "I confidently expect you to bring in a verdict of guilty against each and every one of the defendants."

The jury, being duly charged, retired late that afternoon. And we awaited the verdict. We thought a good deal about those jurors as we walked up and down the corridors, smoking and talking with our friends, through the long hours that passed so slowly thereafter. A defendant cannot sit for days in the same room with twelve jurymen without getting to some extent acquainted with them, and feeling that they are for or against him. . . .

But that, after all, was mere guessing. How could we be sure that the man we thought most hostile might not turn out to be our best friend?—perhaps our only friend! And of those who were for us, how could we be certain that they had the courage to hold out? Some friend experienced in the ways of juries would take our arm and whisper: "Expect anything." From behind the heavy door of the jury-room came sounds of excited argument. . . .

Art Young took me aside and asked me quietly: "Floyd, when you were a little boy did you ever read any books about the Nihilists?" "Yes," I said. "And did you think that maybe some day you might have to go to prison for something you believed?" "Yes," I said. "Then it's all right," said Art Young, "no matter what happens." And I was glad to know that Art Young was spiritually ready to go to prison.

I realized that I had never been more serene and at ease in my whole life than during the nine days of this trial. I had been curiously happy. It might be unreasonable, but it was so. And one who is being psychoanalyzed is not surprised to find his emotions unreasonable.

While we waited, I began to ponder for myself the question which the jury had retired to decide. Were we innocent or guilty? We certainly hadn't 'conspired' to do anything. But what had we tried to do? Defiantly tell the truth. For what purpose? To keep some truth alive in a world full of lies. And what was the good of that? I didn't know. But I was glad I had taken part in that act of defiant truth-telling.

The jury could be heard noisily arguing about us—or about something.

After dinner we returned, with a few friends, and bivouacked in the dim corridor, waiting. Late that night the judge was sent for, and we went eagerly into the court-room. The jury filed in. Had they brought in a verdict? No; they desired further instructions.

The judge then repeated a definition of 'conspiracy' which no one but a lawyer would pretend to understand, and the jury went back. And already the inevitable rumors began to percolate. "Six to six."

Six to six! The struggle of contending views of life had ceased in the court-room, and been taken up by the jury. Other protagonists and antagonists, whose exact identity was unknown to us, were fighting the thing out in that little room. The debate had not ended, it had merely changed its place and personnel. . . . And then we remembered that our fate was involved in that debate; and we felt a warm rush of emotion, of gratitude toward these unknown defenders who had made our cause their own.

Next morning the debate in the jury-room grew fiercer, noisier. At noon the jury came in, hot, weary, angry, limp, and exhausted. They had fought the case amongst themselves for eleven vehement hours. And they could not agree upon a verdict.

But the judge refused to discharge them; and they went back, after further instructions, with grim determination on their faces.

And again we wandered about the corridors—all day; and returned in the evening to camp outside the court-room. . . . Then, in the unlighted windows of the skyscraper opposite, we discovered a dim and ghostly reflection of the interior of the jury-room. Men were standing up and sitting down, four and five at a time. A vote? Someone raised his arm. Someone strode across the room. Someone took off his coat. I stood at our window and watched . . . and then went away. I had waited for twenty-nine hours. I could wonder no more. The whole thing seemed as dim and unreal as that ghostly reflection in the window. I thought about stars and flowers and ideas and my sweetheart. . . .

At eleven o'clock the jurors reported continued disagreement, but were sent back.

The next noon, hopelessly deadlocked, the jury was discharged, with all our thanks. And so we were free.

CHAPTER XXXI

ALARUMS AND CONFUSIONS

1

IN THE spring of 1918, Germany had been invading Soviet Russia, and there were rumors, afterward confirmed, that Trotsky, through Raymond Robins, had been proposing non-ratification of the Brest-Litovsk treaty, on condition that the Allies and the United States aid Russia against Germany. President Wilson had prevented the Japanese from invading Siberia, had sent a friendly message to Soviet Russia, and it was believed in many quarters that American recognition of Soviet Russia was imminent. In the light of this situation, Germany seemed to many of us the special enemy of revolutionary progress. It was charged by H. G. Wells that the Tory Pacifists in England were anxious to effect a negotiated peace in order to keep the Kaiser on the throne and prevent a German revolution. And in America, President Wilson had by executive order freed from long terms of imprisonment several hundred conscientious objectors, and established the rights of such conscientious objectors: "Persons ordered to report for military service under the above act who . . . object to participation in war because of conscientious scruples, but have failed to receive certificates as members of a religious sect or organization from their local board will be assigned to non-combatant services as designed in paragraph 1 to the extent that such persons are able to accept service as aforesaid without violation of the religious or other conscientious scruples by them in good faith entertained . . ." (March 20, 1918).

In July, 1917, the Masses, in an article written by me, had demanded exactly this recognition of the rights of conscientious objectors. War is a confused time. I had been indicted for publicly defending the rights of conscientious objectors; those rights had already been granted when I was put on trial; and I defended those rights in court, although I no longer expected to be a conscientious objector. When after The Masses trial, I was called up as a conscript, I offered no conscientious objections to a war which, as I felt, had now become a war against the chief enemy of Soviet Russia, and I was sent to the training camp at Spartanburg, South Carolina.

The evening before I went to camp I had dinner with a girl in a New York back garden. When the dusk deepened into darkness, she put some candles into what had once been a living tree, now a trunk with some short amputated limbs; and the sight of those blossoms of fire in that dead tree was curiously beautiful in its strangeness—and even more eerily beautiful when, in the wind, the blossoms of fire seemed to drip with icy stalactites. It was like a symbol of something—I scarcely knew what.

But my being sent to camp was a confused blunder on the part of everybody; I, still being under indictment under the Espionage Act, had no right to be in the army, and after ten days, when the mistake was discovered, I was sent home with an honorable discharge. Perhaps it was supposed that I had got into the army with the idea of trying to stir up the mutinies and insurrections with which I had at first been charged in The Masses indictment. That suspicion would have been an undeserved compliment; for, the government having spent millions of dollars and having hired the most expert liars in the country to convert me and other radicals to the war, I had refused to believe any of this expensive propaganda, only to find reasons of my own for believing in the war. I went very amiably to camp; and I enjoyed my ten days there. It was a relief to be taking orders from other people instead of having to decide things for myself. I liked the grub, the company of my tent-mates, kitchen police, and even the drill. Remembering my childhood lessons from my father in drill, I was rather good at it; and I think if the war had lasted long enough, and I had survived long enough, I should inevitably have risen to be a corporal. It is curious to reflect that all the gruesome horrors of war, to which I as a Pacifist had been giving publicity, did not in the least affect my willingness to be a soldier in a war which I had come to believe was going to help Soviet Russia and the cause of Revolution. I was not, however, bigoted about my new views. I did not, having changed my mind, reproach the conscientious objectors who had not changed theirs. I might even, I realized, be mistaken; but it was only my own skin I was risking.

In camp, the night before I was sent back home, I had a curious dream. I had taken an elementary trigonometry book with me, and some squared paper, as well as a volume of Browning's poems; and 'sines' and 'cosines' haunted my mind. In my dream—and, as one who was being psychoanalyzed, I was very much interested in dreams, and deeply impressed by them—I was engaged in measuring by trigonometry the angles of a coffin; and then the dream changed into a literally sexual dream, the solemn naked embrace of a girl; but into this erotic dream the trigonometry nevertheless persisted, for it was as though now I was triumphantly working out the baffling problem of my own human destiny in terms of the gracious, suave, tender angles (for so I thought of them) of a girl's body. It was a starkly sexual dream, but something more, too—a solemn procreative mystery, in which I was finding the trigonometrical solution of the problem of death; and that solution—it seemed, in my dream, a new and dazzling mathematical discovery—was the creation of new life: the promise of its emergence, in defiance of death, out of the gracious and tender loveliness of a girl's body—life that I had created, life that was my own. And then, in my dream, a gray, hooded, Norn-like figure appeared, and recited this rune:

> Find the cosine of the womb
> Ere the cosine of the tomb.

And the next morning I was handed my papers, and sent home.

2

Back in New York, I found that life had adjusted itself remarkably well to my absence. Nobody expected me back so soon. Somebody else had my job on the Liberator; my girl seemed to have fallen in love with somebody else; I had no place to live, and no money—I had sent all I had in the bank to my family when I went into the army.

I wrote something and sold it to Frank Harris—that curious, loud, gentle, bombastic old pirate who was running Pearson's Magazine. He told fascinating stories of his friendships with Wilde, Shaw and other great men; but he told them over and over; and how he boomed! He loved poetry, and recited it well. He had a beautiful young wife, and he set an excellent table and served a wine that could be drunk with pleasure. He liked me, and I had a curious almost filial affection for him, though he bored me with his bragging. He said he would print anything I wrote for him, and what was more, he would make an exception in my favor and pay me for what I wrote. And he did, too.

I found a curious place to live—a whole floor in a little wooden house with a tin roof, at 11 Christopher Street: a large room with a fireplace, and two small rooms, for ten dollars a month. I fixed it up, and put on my dresser a box of Dorin's blonde and a box of Dorin's brunette rouge, as a token of hospitality, and settled down to write on my novel. Presently I was back at my desk in the Liberator office; and I started a series of articles on modern education, under the title of 'Were You Ever a Child?', which ran through four issues.

In Frank Harris's magazine I published this sonnet:

> The sunny magic of a tree in flower
> Some day perhaps shall allure me as of old;
> But now the blossoms of your garden bower,
> That never drew their sustenance from the mould,
> So haunt me that I cannot even lift
> My eyes to look, walking the orchard through:
> Cherry-bloom, apple-bloom, all the season's gift
> Is worthless now in my eyes because of you—
>
> Who lit three candles on a windy night
> And hung them like three blossoms in a tree:
> Three frost-flowers, each with icy stalactite
> Drip-dripping into the darkness. Foolish me,
> That in my petal-dripping orchard close
> Must shut my eyes and think of flowers like those!

And in the Liberator I published two other sonnets:

> Can you not let me sleep? Why for your sake
> That neither wake nor weep, must I still lift
> Wet eyelids over waking eyes, awake
> And watching the wrecked fantasies that drift
> Down the slow dark? Will you not let me be?
> I have kept watch through a long night of years,
> And still keep watch. Why do you ask of me
> This vigil and this foolish gift of tears?

You sleep, I know, soft-smiling, bedded deep
In a kind darkness. Why torment me so?
You that are free, that neither wake nor weep,
Give me back sleep. Let me go.
    Let me shut eyes against the poisoned gleam
    Of drifting sticks that were brave ships of dream.

    One thing I may not give you, two I must—
And these you have, and that you'll not be wanting,
So bright this beauty moulded from the dust,
So careless-trampled in the high God's hunting—
Trampled so cruelly back into the sod,
Broken at last as beauty must be, yet
So bright that even the careless-trampling God
Shall lift and cherish, having broken it.

    Two things I give you, one I dare not. Why,
In this sweet terrible interlude that is
Between what was and shall be, why should I
Proffer a third thing you will never miss,
Two being pity and wonder: these I'm granting,
And these you have, and that you'll not be wanting.

One day I wrote:

    I dreamed last night I had come back to you,
    Laying my head upon your knees and weeping;
    And you said nothing, only gently drew
    My hands into your hands for rest and keeping. . . .

It had been a real dream that I was writing about; and, having written these lines, I recalled the dream, seeking to finish the poem. I saw myself on my knees, with my head in a girl's lap; and in memory I looked more clearly at her as she was in the dream, and saw—my mother! That, to a man who was being psychoanalyzed, was a very illuminating thing. I did not finish the poem.

3

Greenwich Village had become commercialized during the war. The little basement and garret restaurants, decorated according to our own taste, proved a lure to up-towners, who came into the Village with their pockets full of money and their hearts full of a pathetic eagerness to participate in the celebrated joys of Bohemian life. The restaurants responded by laying on Village quaintness in thick daubs, to tickle the fancy of the visiting bourgeoisie; and every month new restaurants sprang up underfoot and overhead to meet the demands of this new clientele. As for the Villagers, they left these restaurants as fast as they were invaded by the up-town crowds; they found new eating-places, as yet unknown to the invaders, only to be forced to flee from these in turn. It was partly a question of money; the Villagers wanted good food at cheap prices, while the up-towners were willing to pay dear for 'atmosphere'. But also these up-towners frequently had abominable manners; they stared, giggled, and made loud re- marks; and, half anxiously and half contemptuously, they tried to buy their way into Village companionship—they thought nothing of intruding themselves upon a private party, introducing themselves, and asking to be shown about. There began to be places especially designed for the up-town trade, with waiters in quaint costumes. In one of these depressing places I had never been until one late evening when I went in for a cup of coffee. A small cup of bad coffee was served for twenty-five cents; and a 'typical' up-towner arose from his party at a neighboring table, came over to me, and asked in an ingratiating tone: "Are you a merry Villager?" I did not commit homicide upon him, nor even assault and battery, though it required all the self-control I had; I merely told him to go to hell, and walked out. But I was pleased when, a few weeks later, some young gangsters broke all the furniture in that restaurant and set fire to it.

I loathed what the Village had now become. It was a show-place, where there was no longer any privacy from the vulgar stares of an up-town rabble. The Village fancy-dress balls had now degenerated into mere money-making enterprises. The earlier of these balls were all that the credulous up-towner could have dreamed; they were spontaneously joyous and deliberately beautiful, focusing in a mood of playfulness the passion for loveliness which was one of the things that had brought us to the Village; but the later balls were almost all dreadful. The Village had advertised too well its freedom and hap- piness; and canny Villagers were now providing cheap substitutes to up-towners who wouldn't know the difference.

The Villagers were beginning to leave the Village; and those that still remained were hard to find, so closely did they secrete them- selves. To fill the gap left by their disappearance from their old haunts, there now appeared a kind of professional 'Villager', playing his antics in public for pay. It was doubtless an honest way of making a living; but it was shocking to one who had been a Villager. It was a bitter thing to have to look at these professionals, and realize that this was the sort of person oneself was supposed to be.

4

The United States joined with the Allies in sending troops to make war on Soviet Russia. The forged 'Sisson documents' were published, and fourteen, as I remember, American historians patriotically threw their scholars' honor on the dungheap by guaranteeing the authenticity of these forgeries. John Reed came back from Russia, spoke at a public meeting against intervention in Russia, and was arrested and indicted. Fantastically enough, we had private advices from people who talked with President Wilson that he was grimly determined to have The Masses editors sent to prison. A new trial was called, and again we went into court, before Judge Martin Manton, with Seymour Stedman as our attorney. Jack Reed held the court-room spellbound with stories of what he had seen as a war correspondent in Europe. Of this trial, Jack Reed wrote: "The attitude of the defendants was different from what it had been in the first [Masses trial]. Last spring Germany was invading Russia; this fall the United States was invading Russia; and Socialists were in a different frame of mind. Moreover, the persecution of Socialists had grown more bitter, and it had become more and more clearly a class issue.

"I think we all felt tranquil, and ready to go to prison if need be. At any rate we were not going to dissemble what be believed. This had its effect on the jury, and on the Judge. When Max Eastman defended the St. Louis declaration of the Socialist Party, when Floyd Dell defended the conscientious objectors, when Art Young made it clear that he disapproved of this war and all wars on social and economic grounds,* . . . a new but perfectly logical and consistent point of view was presented. . . . The one great factor in our victory was Max Eastman's summing up. . . . Max boldly took up the Russian question, and made it part of our defence. The jury was held tense by his eloquence; the Judge listened with all his energy. In the

---

*Footnote in The Liberator: 'And when Jack Reed defended the class-war.—Editor.'

court-room there was utter silence." The jury disagreed—eight for acquittal, four against. "The second trial was over," wrote Jack Reed. "We await the third with equanimity." Jack Reed had just resigned as an editor of The Liberator, not wishing to be responsible for a magazine which was cautious enough or non-revolutionary enough to get through the U. S. mails at that time; but he continued to be a writer for the magazine.

5

Jack Reed I began to know for the first time; he had been away much of the four years I had been in New York. He was a great, husky, untamed youth of immense energies and infantine countenance, who had helped Elizabeth Gurley Flynn and Arturo Giovannitti organize the Paterson strike, had been arrested and jailed there, and then had organized the magnificent Paterson Strike Pageant in Madison Square Garden; he had been a war-correspondent with Villa in Mexico, and then in Europe reporting the World War, and then in Russia. Along the way he tossed off beautiful poems, and poetic plays, and stories full of a profound zest for life. He was adventurer and artist, playboy and propagandist. He wrote casually like this, reporting the I. W. W. trial in Chicago: "Small on a huge bench sits a wasted man with untidy white hair, an emaciated face in which two burning eyes are set like jewels, parchment skin split by a crack for a mouth; the face of Andrew Jackson three years dead. This is Judge Kenesaw Mountain Landis." He had been in Russia during the Bolshevik Revolution, and was now completing a history of it, soon to be published under the title of 'Ten Days That Shook the World'. He was also starting a new magazine, of which Frank Harris, Jack Reed and I were to be the editors. It was to be called 'These States', and it was to be full of the finest modernist literature now being produced in America. Jack collected together most of the contents of the first issue, but at that point Frank Harris, who had been very enthusiastic about it, read some of the contents of this modernist magazine of which he was to be one of the editors, and suddenly and furiously revolted. What he disliked most, it seemed, was Carl Sandburg's poetry—which we had been printing with pride in The Masses and The Liberator. "No, no—good God!" he repeated violently, "no, no—good God!" And so the whole project was abruptly abandoned.

Jack read me a very beautiful poem that he had written while in Russia, about New York, of which only a fragment was printed, the rest being lost.

He told me that he was going to organize a Communist Party in America—which he subsequently did, though it turned out to be one of several, which later coalesced. It would be a disciplined party of professional revolutionists, he said. "Then I shan't join it," I told him; "I am a professional writer." Jack wanted to be everything, artist, revolutionist, adventurer.

He had secret news, of a conclusive character, of the negotiations to end the war, a month before the Armistice was officially declared. The slaughter was going to end! He and Edna Millay and I celebrated the event by riding back and forth half the night on the Staten Island ferry, in a dense fog. He was telling her his most thrilling adventures as a war correspondent and Communist conspirator, and she said, like Desdemona, "I love you for the dangers you have passed!" She was writing 'Aria da Capo' then.

It was true—the 'false' Armistice day came, and New York went mad with joy. Then the 'real' Armistice day, celebrated more decorously. And now that the war was over, and human life counted for something again, one could think of the soldiers uselessly killed in the last days, after it was really all over—a final touch of horrible meaninglessness in all that meaningless horror.

CHAPTER XXXII

MARRIAGE

1

THAT summer I had become friends with a man named Alex Gumberg, who had been born in Russia, had come to America as a boy, and had gone back to Russia after the March Revolution; he was in Moscow during the Bolshevik Revolution, and he had acted as interpreter for Raymond Robins in the Red Cross Mission's negotiations with Lenin and Trotsky; he had a vast fund of fascinating knowledge about Soviet Russia, and we became boon companions.

Alex Gumberg was an extraordinary man, combining an intuitive understanding of men and their motives, with a childish and malicious sense of humor. He was shrewd to the point of genius, with immense executive capacity and great energy; his most remarkable quality was his ability to talk to men of the most diverse opinions with convincing effect. Men in business and politics who disagreed with all of Gumberg's views and aims, and whose interests were directly opposed to his, would meet him; Gumberg would talk and would win their complete confidence and trust. A man of the highest integrity, extravagant in his generosity, and with a warm and sensitive kindness which he tried vainly to conceal beneath a gruff and bearlike manner, he had a capacity for friendships with people of all kinds and classes.

In those days, before everybody had been to Russia, I used to review all the books on Russia for the Liberator, with the help of the information Gumberg furnished me.

That fall Albert Rhys Williams, a war-correspondent with an incredibly romantic history, who, his other clothes having been stolen, had gone through the Bolshevik Revolution in a dress-suit, came back with more fascinating tales of Soviet Russia.

One evening I was taken by Alex Gumberg to call on two young women who had just moved into Greenwich Village. Both girls were recently from California, and were friends of Albert Rhys Williams. The dark-haired one, in whom my friend Alex was interested, was Miss Frances Adams, who was running a free-speech forum in connection with the church of Dr. Percy Stickney Grant. The other, golden-haired and blue-eyed, seemed to have stepped out of that novel of Frank Norris's which had so impressed me in my boyhood. She had been born in Minnesota, and looked like a Scandinavian girl, though she was really of mixed Scotch, Irish, English and Dutch ancestry. Her name was B. Marie Gage; she didn't like her first name and had shortened it to an initial. She was a Socialist; she had gone to the University of Wisconsin in the earlier days of the war, and had led in the organization of the free-speech forum there. Going back to her home in Pasadena, California, she had been active in organizing a very extensive league of Pacifist groups throughout the West, and had been indicted for selling a Pacifist book then under Government ban. Put on trial under the Espionage Act, her youth and courage and candor—and without doubt her good looks, too, her blue eyes, golden hair and peaches-and-cream complexion—were much in her favor, and she heard with astonishment the Prosecutor plead her case for her; her lawyer was John Beardsley, who afterwards won before the U. S. Supreme Court a decision declaring unconstitutional one of the most hideously reactionary of the California 'anti-Red' laws; and she was given a nominal fine at a time when other Pacifists were being given twenty years in prison—a discrimination, with which, in her earnestness, she was not altogether pleased. She was a friend of Upton Sinclair, and of Mrs. Kate Crane Gartz, who had been one of the backers of the Liberator. As two who had been through war-time trials, we had much in common; I fell in love with B. Marie at once, recognizing her as the most splendid young woman I had ever seen; and we were everywhere together from that moment. Though one is poor, there are always bus-tops to ride on to nowhere and back under the stars, there are the ferries that slide out into a night of mystery, there are woods to walk in and secluded beaches to lie upon in the darkness, there are picnic fires beside whose embers poetry may be remembered and said;

and there are little florists' shops where yellow daffodils may be bought for one's sweetheart, and delicatessen stores whence slices of all sorts of meat, and rye bread and butter and pickles, can be brought in a bag for her dinner. And my Christopher Street place was hers, as Alex and I made the girls' Eleventh Street place ours. And there was always talk—each other's lives to explore. Politics we were agreed upon, but we argued about whether she was going to marry me. I think it was at our third meeting that I told her that she must. She was alarmed at the idea of marriage with me, and thought of ending the argument by going back to California. Doubtless I did not seem a very marriageable young man; others had taken pains to tell her how inconstant I was in love, but I had told her the worst about myself, so it perhaps produced the less impression. The chapters of my unfinished novel wooed her for me; she saw in those pages a boy that she liked. But till the last moment she was hesitant and uncertain about so decisive a step as marriage, particularly as I was so serious about it. Once we quarreled, and separated for three miserable days, during which I wrote a sonnet:

> I dreamed of us as eagles in the air,
> Adventurers through lightning-riven space,
> Children of danger—for you seemed to wear
> Her careless colors in your laughing face;
> I thought of us met high above the press
> Of common hopes and fears, too swiftly daring
> To forfeit our own storm-bright happiness,
> And what our doom might be, too little caring.
>
> Will nothing less content me? No, not me—
> Who too familiar am with wind and star
> To have much patience with mortality.
> Will you put off your human guise, unbar
> Your strong-winged spirit to the realms of sky?
> You will not, Sweet? Forgive me!—and good-bye.

Then we were brought together again by Alex and Frances, who were going through the same dramatics themselves; and our reconciliation gave the poem a happy meaning contrariwise. And one Saturday morning early in February, 1919, ten weeks after we had first met, we set out, accompanied by Alex and Frances, to get married. This turned out to be more difficult than we had anticipated. At the City Hall, I found a regulation requiring divorced persons to produce their divorce papers in getting a license. I asked to see a copy of the law establishing this requirement, and was referred to the City Clerk, who admitted that there was no such law and that he had made the regulation upon his own authority; I was annoyed at this smug bureaucratic impertinence, and I vehemently told the city clerk that I regarded his regulation as an illegal usurpation of authority, and so saying tore up my application for a license and threw it on the floor, and walked out with B. Marie, who regarded me with some surprise, having heretofore thought me a mild-mannered person. So we all took the ferry to Jersey City, where, as we approached the City Hall, we were met by a man who asked if we were going to be married. He went on to explain that in New Jersey, in order to get a license, one must be accompanied by a friend who was a resident of the locality and had known the applicant for a certain number of years; this 'friend' would be furnished us from a cheap lodging house; that was the way it was done, he said. For twenty-five dollars a bum would swear that he had known me for the requisite length of time; and when I whistled at the mention of twenty-five dollars, he said, "You needn't think the bum gets it all—it's split several ways—the captain of the district has to get his cut"; however, he was willing to furnish the service for ten dollars. Then we found that twenty-four hours must elapse before the marriage could be performed, and that no marriages were performed on Sundays, which meant waiting till Monday; and we were sick of the whole disgusting business, so we left the state of New Jersey and came back to New York. I had a better idea.

Jane Burr, a writer with a very forceful personality, had an inn at Croton-on-Hudson, New York, an hour north of New York City—the Drowsy Saint Inn, she called it—a place with pleasant rooms furnished in the colonial style, where writers roomed in summer, and with a restaurant decorated in the Greenwich Village fashion with gay colors. It was not open in the winter, but Jane Burr lived there, and asked occasional guests out to visit her; and a few weeks before this, seeing me somewhere, she had asked me to come up for a winter week-end; "and have you a girl?" Yes, I had; "then bring her, of course." The invitation was for this particular week-end; so B. Marie and I now took the train for Croton, and when we were welcomed by Jane, we exclaimed: "We want to get married—and we want you to help us!" Jane was shocked; she protested that she did not believe in marriage; then she said that I would make a very good first husband for B. Marie; and then she entered whole-heartedly and enthusiastically into the wedding preparations. The Town Clerk's office was closed by this time, but there was to be a meeting of the Town Board at Peekskill that evening, and he would be there; and Jane arranged with him by telephone to issue our license. At eight o'clock, then, in Peekskill, we got our license, and came back to Croton, and waited at Judge Decker's residence for him to come and marry us; I begged B. Marie not to make any feminist objections to anything she was asked to promise, but to say yes to whatever he asked; but we told the judge that we wished the simplest possible ceremony, and he found a very simple and honest one in his little book, according to which we took each other as husband and wife; the good Judge asked B. Marie if she wanted a marriage certificate, and she shook her head negatively in a determined way. "Lots of people don't, nowadays," he remarked. Going back to the Drowsy Saint Inn, we found that Jane had got a cake from one of the neighbors, one which had been intended for a Sunday dinner, but was gladly surrendered for its glorification and apotheosis as a wedding-cake. And so, at ten o'clock, with Jane seeming very happy about it all in spite of her theoretical objections to marriage, we sat down to our wedding supper. After all the day's mad scurrying, here was friendly peace. B. Marie, who had started out on the day's adventure rather scared, looked flushed and radiant now; her blue eyes sparkled, her golden hair glinted in the candlelight, and I, looking at her, was happy to feel the proud conviction that her youth and courage and wisdom and beauty, given to me in marriage, were not going to be wasted upon a coward or a fool. I had learned something in ten years.

> 'Ah, Conchobar, had you seen her,
> With that high, laughing, turbulent head of hers' . . .

In New York, some of our surprised and cynical friends gave our marriage six months. I knew it was forever. Some of my feelings were put into a 'Birthday Sonnet' that I gave B. Marie the next April:

Not only that I love you—that in you
I find old dreams incredibly come true,
And you in every dream, world without end,
Goddess and girl-child, lover and guest and friend:
Not only that I love you, seeking still
To bend and break the guarding of your will,
And find, behind your stubbornness, the splendor
Of body and soul in triumph of surrender:
But that, deep under deep, in you I find
Something to my caresses deaf and blind—
Something not mine to take nor yours to give,
But only by whose light our love may live.
Lovelier in you than all your laughing youth
Is that which holds love lightly beside truth.

2

It was on her birthday that we went for a week-end visit to some
friends in Croton-on-Hudson, and, as we walked up Mt. Airy Road,
we were met by Jack Reed and some others walking down. Jack
embraced us, and said: "This is the Mount Airy Soviet, and we
have decided that you two are to live here in Croton. And this is
the house you are to live in!" We were led into a little house
wedged in a tiny yard; the artist and his wife who owned it were
going away, and it was for sale; the price, three thousand dollars,
seemed to me perfectly enormous; half the sum was covered by a
mortgage that could be taken over, but they wanted the rest in
cash. Yet this, I felt, was our home. I had a ten-dollar bill in my
pocket. I said, "We will buy the house." B. Marie looked frightened—a home of our own seemed like 'settling down.' But I paid
the ten dollars to bind the bargain, and then tried to think where
I could raise all that cash. Somehow or other, perhaps because the
world smiled on two young people who wanted a home of their
own, we succeeded in raising the money that month.

We came out to our new home the first of May, and I knocked
the scroll-work off the porch with a hammer, and we tore the
ancient paper off the walls, and began kalsomining and painting. I
had fixed over enough rooms and apartments to know about such
things, and how to use gay colors and bring the sunlight into a
house and keep it there. Albert Rhys Williams, Jack Reed and
Max Eastman dropped in. Rose Wilder Lane came up from Jane

Burr's Drowsy Saint Inn and sat and watched us paint, and took a brush and helped us; she was writing Freddy O'Brien's 'White Shadows in the South Seas' for him that summer; and when the day's work was over, there were long hours of beautiful talk and story-telling, and a friendship begun that was to continue over the years.

That summer our friends Alex Gumberg and Frances Adams were married, after going through courtship storms similar to ours; and Raymond Robins made a little speech at their wedding supper. He said that there had been three separate times when the Allies planned to invade Russia and destroy the Soviet Government; at the two earlier times, President Wilson had blocked these plans by refusing American participation; upon each of these two occasions, the President's refusal had been determined by the strong representations made to him by Americans in Moscow; these anti-interventionist sentiments had been created by the friendly relations established in Moscow between the Americans and Lenin and Trotsky, in which work Alex Gumberg's activities as interpreter for the Red Cross Mission had been of decisive importance—and in Raymond Robin's belief it was due to Alex Gumberg more than to any other individual that the Soviet Republic had not been crushed by Allied military force at a time when it was too weak to make effective resistance.

The year of 1919 was to be for us one of great hopes and terrible disillusionments, as revolutionary uprisings in one middle-European country after another were crushed, betrayed and overwhelmed in the bloody massacres of the White Terror. Soviet Russia itself was fighting the Allies; the counter-revolutionary adventurers Yudenitch, Denikin, Kolchak, Wrangel, were pressing against the young Republic from every side. Petrograd was reported fallen again and again. And American troops were mutinying in Siberia; this was to be denied and glossed over, raising the question: when is a mutiny not a mutiny? The answer evidently was: when it is embarrassing to admit that a mutiny has occurred; the time would come when mutinies on British battleships would be glossed over in the same way, to save the decaying prestige of British imperialism. Upton Sinclair, who had been an ardent pro-war patriot, awoke from his trance, and changed the patriotic novel he was writing, 'Jimmie Higgins,' into an attack upon imperialist war, by sending his Socialist soldier-hero to Siberia to participate in such a mutiny.

Jack Reed left his Croton home that year and went back to Soviet Russia, where he became a member of the executive committee of the Third International; he died in Moscow in October, 1920, of typhus, and was buried with honor under the walls of the Kremlin.

3

Our summer vacation over, B. Marie and I walked every morning the two and a half miles to the Harmon station, and after our day's work on our jobs was over, up the hill again in the late afternoon, laden with bundles of food. At first I had been the cook, but presently B. Marie revealed that she could cook marvelously. And that summer I added some chapters to my serial on education, 'Were You Ever a Child?' and it was brought out in the fall as a book by a publisher who had been so kind as to ask me to give him something of mine to publish. I had begun again to be an author. And people who were interested in modern education liked my little book. It was thrilling to hold it in my hand, and see my name on the title page; and most thrilling of all to hear that it was being translated for publication in Soviet Russia. (It was indeed translated, but never published there, though others of my books were.)

That fall, B. Marie and I took a week's walking trip through Vermont, carrying packs on our backs, with blankets and simple cooking utensils, cooking our meals at a fire built by the roadside, and sleeping usually in the woods or fields. We were enchanted with the little white-painted New England houses with their fan-lighted and side-lighted doorways, and their connecting summer kitchens and woodsheds; we saw abandoned farms, for sale for a few hundred dollars—making our narrow half-acre at Croton seem very tiny indeed. Nevertheless, we envied nobody. The people in Vermont were very kind to us, taking me for a painter on account of my paint-spattered corduroys. Before our walking trip was quite over, after I had fed my eyes and mind upon the beauty of the autumn, always to me the most magical of the four seasons, I began to compose a book in my mind, showing the relations between literature and the historical periods in which it was written, a kind of Marxian essay in literary criticism. And when we got home I wrote this essay, which I called 'Literature and the Machine Age,' and which was later published serially in the Liberator under Robert Minor's editorship. It was, though slight in size, ambitious in quality—the first attempt in America to apply a particular principle of historical criticism to any wide range of literary productions. It was later published in book form, with additions, under another title, 'Intellectual Vagabondage: An Apology for the Intelligentsia'.

Prohibition came, and I was glad of it, for I thought the saloon a bore. I indulged in some predictions as to the social results of the abolition of the saloon. Men and women, I wrote, would spend more of their play-time together, with benefits to American civilization. My prediction came true, though I had no prevision of the speakeasy as a coeducational institution. I very naïvely believed that Prohibition would work. I had no notion of the incredible ingenuity that would go into home-brewing, nor of the pride that respectable citizens would take in safe, popular and petty lawbreaking (for which I, a law-breaker in the grand style, only despised them), and least of all did I foresee the devastating tiresomeness of the conversations about booze that were to afflict American social life for years. No one, I think, could have imagined beforehand the appalling taste of the cocktails that were to be served at most parties under Prohibition. But I was right in predicting a popular romanticization of the pre-Prohibition era.

4

In the winter B. Marie and I lived at 11 Christopher Street, but came out every week-end to Croton, laden with food. At the Christopher Street place we had moved from the ground floor to the top floor, where there were two great rooms and a little hall bedroom. In the front room we had a Franklin stove—a little iron stove that is built like an open fireplace—where we broiled our steaks and chops. There were paintings by Nordfeldt, and Japanese prints—presents from Arthur Ficke, and a few things picked up at auction sales—on the walls; orange-yellow curtains at the windows, which overlooked an alley and a stable; brass candlesticks and candles to light our dinner table; a big couch; and in the large kitchen, gaily painted shelves, with an array of Chinese cups and saucers and plates, orange-red and yellow, like a bed of tulips.

I have spoken of a curious dream I had had intermittently ever since I was twelve years old—a dream of an empty room in the top of a barn, and of a dream-companionship there with a girl who always slipped out of sight as I awoke, so that I never could remember what she looked like. I had that dream again for the last time, with some differences, and with a decisive finality. It was very clearly B. Marie who was now my companion in the barn-attic; and it caught fire—I saw the smoke pouring up through the cracks in the floor, and knew the place was doomed; I felt no regret, but took B. Marie safely out of danger, and let it go up in flames. An amusing dream!—and I knew what it meant. It was a good omen for our happiness.

February 1920 came; we had been married a year; the cynics and sober-minded people who thought they knew me had apparently known, rather, a more or less mythical Village figure who went by my name.

And now I was going to take a three-months leave of absence from my job, and finish my novel, 'Moon-Calf'. The leave of absence was to have begun the first of February; but Max Eastman wheedled me into consenting to postpone it till the next issue of the magazine was out. Suddenly I began having blinding headaches, which incapacitated me for editorial work; the doctor and the X-ray showed a slight sinus inflammation; and after a week or so it occurred to me that the cause might be psychic. I 'associated' to the subject for an hour, and the headaches disappeared completely. I knew why I had them; the fact was that I was homesick for work on my novel, and unwilling to postpone it. I quit work on the magazine that day and went to work on my novel.

CHAPTER XXXIII

'Felix Fay'

1

I HAD ALREADY written about thirty thousand words of my novel. In years of revision, these chapters had become somewhat too polished, too much like a prose poem. I rewrote them in a simpler and more flexible narrative style, expanding that portion of my book to about fifty thousand words. I had hit upon a curiously effective way of conveying the impression of growth, in the childhood part: the scene broadened, chapter by chapter, from the home to the yard and then to the school and the outside world, as the boy grew older; the passage of the years was stated partly in terms of expanding geography.

In the later part, the task had been to find a clear emotional pattern in a bewildering variety of remembered experiences. What I had learned from psychoanalysis helped me to select the emotionally important incidents and people in my youthful life, and to emphasize certain aspects of these. When nobody would be hurt, I merely changed people's names, and described them exactly as they were; but my sweetheart at the end of the book I disguised thoroughly, giving her the appearance of B. Marie, whom it was an added pleasure to describe. Some few characters I invented, such as 'Wheels', instead of putting in my friend Gibson, or Dr. Lindley, or others; every town, I assumed, has its lovable eccentrics, who generously give their friendship to a young idealist. I left out of the story, or 'played down', my hero's energies; I was actually unaware of, or completely forgetful of, when writing the story, his social capacities, thinking of him as being always a shy, lonely, sensitive youth, and not as a bumptious, aggressive fellow, which he was at times; and I emphasized and, to my present view, somewhat sentimentalized him as a dreamer, easily hurt by the world. It was a much more appealing character, the 'Felix Fay' of that novel, than the one I have drawn here of myself; perhaps, in attempting to redress the balance in the interests of truth, I have in these present pages overemphasized the aggressiveness and have not said enough about the shyness and sensitiveness to hurt which were set forth in 'Moon-Calf'. Some very early childhood memories, those included in the first chapter of the present book, were not then at my command, being still buried in oblivion. My family was the hardest part of the story to deal with; and, having described it, I broke up the family, in the story, so as not to have to keep on talking about it. The only touch of real falsity in the account of Felix's character was in making him dream in childhood of future literary success, whereas my actual childhood ambitions were political, military and oratorical—Napoleonic, in fact; but I did not realize that when I wrote the book.

My intention was, when I began that three months' work, to carry it on through my actual life, ending it with the dreamer's purposeful adaptation of himself to reality in marriage; but I saw that it would be too much for one volume, and decided to stop it at the time when Felix, thrown over by his first sweetheart, planned to go to Chicago.

Aside, however, from any conscious intentions of mine, the novel had an identity of its own; I would write passages that were true and, it seemed to me, beautiful—but I would have to throw them away, for they were like alien strains of music in a tune—they rang false, not to fact, but to an artistic conception never consciously formulated. I had been actually at work upon this novel for six years; in peace and war, in love and out, through a chaotic variety of personal fortunes, I had worked, very slowly and intermittently, but without the slightest change of intention or mood, upon a novel which reflected none of this outward confusion; it had been incredibly painful to write certain things, but the writing itself was serene; that novel had been the one unity in my disordered life. It could scarcely have been written as the result of any conscious intellectual purpose; it proceeded from unconscious motives about which I might theorize, but which I might perhaps never really understand. And the swiftness and ease with which I finished it now were, apparently, the results of a psychoanalytic experience through which my conscious mind had gained easier access to the sources of literary creation in my unconscious mind.

I had no idea that any considerable number of people would be interested in what seemed to me the very special life of Felix Fay; but I wrote the story as simply as possible, so that anybody who might be interested should find no difficulty in reading it. I had come to detest tricks of style, and I wished to write a prose that was clear as air, through which life itself could be seen without the distortion of the writer's temperament, which had sufficiently exercised its prerogative in the selection of the facts to be viewed. These things I did for my own satisfaction, without any expectation of their pleasing more than two or three thousand readers, which was the largest audience for which a first novel by an unknown writer could reasonably hope. And I knew that my novel would not please those serious-minded 'radical' readers who thought it the duty of an editor of The Masses to write about strikes, lynchings and working-class misery; fiction, I knew, is like poetry, in not being written from a sense of duty, but from some inward impulse which seeks to make beauty out of pain, and heeds not at all the consideration of social usefulness.

2

President Wilson came to New York City, in March, to make a speech at the Metropolitan Opera House on behalf of his abysmal and ignoble failure in world-reconstruction; and the militant suffragists made this the occasion of a demonstration, demanding votes for women. B. Marie was to take part in this demonstration; since she expected to spend the night in jail, she prepared herself with a ten-cent-store comb and tooth-brush put into her hand-bag. She went off to demonstrate and get arrested, and I sat at home finishing a chapter of my novel. Having finished it, late in the evening, I went uptown to find her, and succeeded in doing so in the midst of a swirling crowd of soldiers, sailors, by-standers and policemen. The demonstrators had battled for several hours with the police; they had been stopped in a final charge toward the Metropolitan Opera House as Wilson was leaving it; they had been carted in patrol-wagons to the police station, and then let go; and they were now marching back to the suffrage headquarters. I walked alongside B. Marie, hearing about it. She held the only suffrage banner yet uncaptured by the jeering crowd of young soldiers and sailors. As we walked along, there were many attempts to seize her banner, but she held it safely out of reach. We had nearly got to the headquarters when a sailor made a flying leap, seized the banner and ran. And I, like a fool, was after him. There was a yell of joy from the crowd, a fist hit my mouth, and in another instant I was at the bottom of a huge pile of soldiers and sailors. Then an officer came along and dispersed them. I had got off with no hurts but a bruised lip, and the loss of a brand-new velour hat, which one of the buddies carried off as a souvenir. Now B. Marie and I went back to Fifth Avenue, followed by a mob of soldiers and sailors, spoiling for a racket; they were sufficiently gallant not to attack me while I had a girl at my side, who was thus my protection; but when we got on a Fifth Avenue bus, they were enraged to see their legitimate prey escape, and they followed and stopped the bus. B. Marie and I were on top of the bus, and the conductor and motorman stood at the foot of the winding steps, fighting them off for fifteen minutes. Some of them climbed up the sides of the bus, and B. Marie took out her ten-cent-store comb, and combed their faces savagely as they appeared, until they dropped off. It was a curious sensation to be the prospective victim of a mob, and yet, preposterously, I enjoyed the danger, and so did B. Marie. Several policemen at last came along, and the bus started again, leaving the mob behind. B. Marie and I, made hungry by all this excitement, had supper at a hot-dog stand in the Village, and then went up to Fourteenth Street to buy the morning papers, which were now off the press. In the first paper we opened we saw one of the flashlight photographs of an earlier stage of these riotous proceedings, taken just after B. Marie had hit a policeman over the head with the staff of her banner. Startled by the flashes, everybody had stood still for a moment, and there was the scene, looking as if it had been posed for the camera, with B. Marie's sturdy blonde figure in the middle of everything, holding up her banner triumphantly.

3

The novel was duly finished in the three months, and handed

over to my publisher. Published in the fall, it was completely ignored for a month, and then a review by Heywood Broun, which told his readers to stop whatever they were doing and read 'Moon-Calf', exhausted the supply in the New York bookstores within twenty-four hours, and a new edition had to be published. The particular chapter which evoked his deepest enthusiasm was one which it had been terribly painful for me to write; a memory of having once made an awful fool of myself, writing my name on the side of Blair's Boarding-House, and getting bawled out for it by the principal of the school—something which I had blushed to remember, an uncomfortable childhood folly and humiliation; but apparently other people had had similar follies and humiliations in their memories, and felt grateful to have me confess these for them. Thus far the response to my novel seemed quite genuine. Some of its subsequent booming seemed to me accidental if not artificial, and I did not take too seriously the implications of wide popularity in the repeated printings of the book. Sinclair Lewis's 'Main Street' and Zona Gale's 'Miss Lulu Bett' were the best sellers of that year, marking a revulsion of feeling against the mob-hysteria of the war period; and my novel, which was usually referred to in all the reviews along with 'Main Street', was carried along with it to a considerable sale, and even during a few weeks in the following summer, when book sales were low, to a place in the list of 'best-sellers', which of course suggested to many people a sale of fabulous proportions, instead of—what was astonishing enough— a sale of between thirty and forty thousand copies in two years. My book achieved that success by the accident of its coming at the time it did; if I had finished it in any year earlier than 1920, it would have been as much neglected, I believe, as Sherwood Anderson's first novel was. It profited by a sudden and rather hysterical fury of popular resentment against business, regimentation and conventional life. It was often described in reviews as an exposé of the Middle West, which was ridiculously untrue; 'Main Street' and 'Miss Lulu Bett' were what people wanted, and they very generously misconstrued my novel as a third of the same sort. But, really, if it was an exposé of anything or anybody, it was an exposé of 'Felix Fay'. Indeed, I at first supposed that Sinclair Lewis's novel was intended as an exposé of Carol Kennicott, not of Main

Street; we had some correspondence on the subject, and he wrote me that *of course* I approved of 'Felix Fay'; not at all, I told him— I thought it would serve 'Felix Fay' and Carol Kennicott right if they had to marry one another and live on a desert island the rest of their lives. My book was doubtless tender to its hero, and said all that could be truly said in his behalf; but I knew better than to think of him as a model or ideal personage; he had a great deal to learn about life, and it had taken me ten years and much pain to learn it. What amazed me most was to discover that I had not told merely my own story in 'Moon-Calf', but that of many other people. They wrote and told me so in detail. And that discovery made me feel humble. It was, perhaps, unimportant what I had thought I was doing when I wrote it; and perhaps it had a meaning at which I had never guessed. If it interpreted people's lives for them, made them understand themselves better, then it justified its existence. It was not mine, now, it was other people's book, to make of what they would. And what some people chose to make of this study of a boy living between the years 1887 and 1908 was, to my surprise, a comment upon 'post-war' youth. I was said to have described what was going on among the young people of America as a result of their disillusionment by the war. And, oddly enough, there seemed to be some truth in that. Post-war youth wrote letters to me confirming that notion.

My friend Lucian Cary sat, one day early the next spring, figuring with a pencil and paper. He looked up and said: "You must have already made about six thousand dollars." "What!" I exclaimed. It seemed impossible. But it figured out that way on paper. I had not thought of asking for any advance on my novel; and, according to my contract, the royalties accrued by January first were to be paid the next May first, and the further royalties accrued by July first would be paid the next November first. Thus we would have over a thousand dollars on May first, and the rest next November. Why, then we could afford to have a baby!

4

I took three months off, that spring, and wrote 'The Briary-Bush'. My ten years of struggle to achieve happiness and stability in love and marriage were condensed into an imaginary story of 'Felix

Fay's' marriage in Chicago to 'Rose-Ann'. The South-Side studios which had been the scene of the break-up of my actual marriage in Chicago, were made the scene of the trials of 'Felix' and 'Rose-Ann', ending with their reconciliation and decision to have a baby. It was what one wishes one's life had been like. In fiction it can all come true with less pain and waste. 'Felix' learned in a couple of years what it had taken me ten years to learn. But fiction has that privilege of condensation—it owes no allegiance to specific facts of time and place. And I did enrich the book with the pain and beauty of my experience in those ten years; it was, from that point of view, a very true book, since every page, every paragraph, every sentence, was a transcript from life. At the end of the book, where my hero 'Felix' gave up being a poetic infant and accepted his adult responsibilities, I wrote: "His mind, as by a shadowy wing, was touched by a faint regret . . . for what? . . . for an old dream, beautiful in its way, the dream of freedom; but a dream only—and worthy only the farewell tribute of a faint and shadowy regret." It *was* a beautiful dream, to which I was paying now the farewell tribute of a novel filled with more than a faint and shadowy regret: I had made the dream so beautiful that people who had found in 'Felix's' and 'Rose-Ann's' freedom the story of their own hearts' wildest wishes, would be saddened at that dream's turning into a mere marriage, and would feel that I had betrayed them.

I did not realize that the publication of a novel, and the achievement of some reputation and a little money, would cause me to be hated by some former friends and acquaintances, who thought me unworthy of such 'success', who hugely exaggerated its extent, and who would feel at liberty to think ill of me in every respect from that time forth. At this moment, though I did not know about it till years later, there was a man, of sensitive and brooding nature, who thought I had deliberately not spoken to him at some public gathering—thought that I had 'cut' him, as he explained to me afterward: "I supposed that you were too proud to speak to your old friends, now that you were successful," he told me. So he put me into a novel, which he later showed me; and I would never have recognized myself, if he had not told me who it was supposed to be—this smug commercialized author, living upon a vast estate in Westchester County (my narrow half-acre on Mt. Airy Road!), speeding about in high-powered motor-cars (I owned no car), and so on, all that any struggling author might wish, made to come true in me and then bitterly hated in me. Unknown to myself, I had become in some minds a myth, to be shaped into whatever ugly form those minds wished, without any regard for truth, and with no curiosity as to what the actual truth might be. It was to become, though I did not know that, a test of friendship. I did not even realize that one who has made a little money by publishing a novel is supposed necessarily to repudiate any 'radical' beliefs he formerly had. My first novel had been a psychological study, not a social satire, and all that followed would be of the same character; but these would be supposed by some people to illustrate my gradual turning away from 'radicalism'. But of all these natural psychological phenomena I was happily ignorant in 1921. It did not occur to me that anyone could hate me because I had been lucky, and had money enough coming in so that my wife could have a baby.

The thousand dollars, or a little more than that, came in on May first, and—in anticipation of the baby that was coming—we put in a bathroom and running water, and electric lights; and we planned for a furnace in the fall. There was still some money left; and so we decided to go West that summer, and visit my parents, who were getting old, and B. Marie's family, before her baby came.

In 1921 there was an economic slump—the post-war panic; and I wondered if the banks would break before November first. I was worried about my royalties. But I was terribly happy about our having a baby.

And now, whatever else might fail, the star of Soviet Russia burned bright. Yudenich and Wrangel and Denikin had been defeated, Kolchak was killed by his own soldiers, the gigantic White offensive had collapsed, and the Soviet Republic was free from sea to sea, a portent of the new world that was to be created amidst the ruins of the old.

As a citizen, I would always be passionately interested in the political destinies of mankind; and as an artist, I would always find in my political hopes a stimulus to creative effort. But, as an artist, I felt the wish to detach myself from the immediate and daily anxieties of the political situation, and to renew my contacts with the ageless and timeless aspects of nature, which afford a deep refreshment to the restless mind. On the first anniversary of the Armistice, I was at the printer's, reading final proofs on the magazine, and I happened to look out of the window and see a flock of pigeons; they reminded me first of war-planes, and then of the fluttering snow of torn paper on Armistice Day a year ago— and I wrote:

> White against the housetops, and black against the sky,
> Wheeling in squadrons, the pigeons fly—
>
> Like deadly planes that hover over towns aflame—
> Like confetti flung from windows when the peace-news came!
>
> War and peace—peace and war—that is all I know:
> Shall I never see birds as I saw them long ago?

CHAPTER XXXIV

HOMECOMING

1

No MAN who is normally superstitious would boast of his happiness, lest he lose it; and I, being normally superstitious, took pains not to do that—I did not wish to attract the attention of the jealous gods to my felicity. But I did write and debate on the subject of marriage. It perhaps scarcely behooved one who had signally failed in marriage to discuss that theme at all so early in his new venture; but these considerations, if they occurred to me, were overruled by the public interest that existed in my small 'radical' world in my views of marriage.

It was not at all unusual for a 'radical' to get married; but it was rather unusual for a 'radical' to approve of marriage theoretically. Even Anarchists got married, as a rule. But they regarded their being married as a compromise with convention, and they were rather ashamed of it. They might live on rent, interest and profit, but such defections from the Ideal lay lightly on their Anarchist consciences; it was being legally married that they were ashamed of. So I had observed among my Anarchist friends. And many Socialists were nearly as absurd. As for the Communists, who were still very few, they had usually been left-wing Socialists the year before, and their attitude on this matter was indistinguishable from the current Socialist attitude—that is, some held conventional and others unconventional and vaguely Anarchist views of marriage— 'radical' views, as these latter were usually called. They had—the ones whose views were not merely conventional—a notion that there was something reactionary and 'bourgeois' about marriage: not about religious ceremonials or divorce laws—there would have been much sense in that attitude—but about 'Marriage'. What they meant by 'Marriage' was hard to find out. And in the same way they tended to regard 'the Family' as a bourgeois and reactionary institution. They had an idea that there would be no private marriage under Socialism or Communism in its perfect form—though they didn't know exactly what there would be. They sometimes had an idea that babies would be taken care of by the State. Insofar as these ideas had any definition, they were Platonic-Anarchist ideas; but they didn't know that. All they knew, or thought they knew, was that 'marriage was a bourgeois institution'.

Now I did know something about the subject historically, from ten years of reading and thinking about it in the light of the Marxian idea. I knew what exactly was the rôle which the patriarchal family had played in the conservation of private landed property, through loveless arranged marriages bulwarked by the dowry system, and operating through the principle of 'legitimacy'—which meant the denial of all social rights to 'illegitimate' children; I knew that prostitution and aristocratic adultery were necessary parts of this system, and that sex-segregation and military-educational homosexuality and the degredation of women had been a part of it in every country. It was this system which Plato had hated and proposed to replace with sexual communism in his Utopia. It was the vestiges of this aristocratic system, taken over by the bourgeoisie, that Engels had said would be abolished by Socialism. But there was a non-aristocratic kind of marriage, of plebeian origin, having nothing to do with the conservation of property, a love-marriage, which was instinctively human, and which arose whenever and wherever property considerations were removed; it was the instinctive arrangement by which in our species the nurture of children was ensured—and this natural marriage and natural family, which had already begun to exist in a modern form under capitalism, was, with certain legal reforms, what would exist in the Socialist state: not irresponsible 'freedom' and not Platonic public nurseries. This may seem obvious now, but it was not obvious in 1921 to many people who considered themselves Socialists, Communists, or 'radicals'. Russia was in the throes of a post-war famine, and had no time to spare to the discussion or decision of a question of intellectual attitude toward marriage which was later to be discussed and decided along these lines precisely. During the civil war in

Russia, the sexual code had been what it always and everywhere is in war-time, the snatching of such happiness as the moment can give. But this, to some observers, seemed like a revolutionary model.

So that in New York in 1921—though marriage itself was sufficiently commonplace among 'radicals'—it was like a daring heresy for one of the younger 'radicals' to say that he believed in marriage. And when he went on to say that Marriage and the Family in their modern form should be part and parcel of our revolutionary ideals —why, people would pay money and crowd into a public hall just to hear him say it. We had debates to help support the Liberator, and the most popular and crowded debates were those in which I defended Marriage and the Family upon these grounds. I once debated with Michael Gold on Freedom vs. Marriage; and Michael Gold upheld what he fondly believed to be the true revolutionary position of Freedom. I afterward debated with V. F. Calverton, who upheld the same vague Anarchist ideal of Freedom in the belief that it was revolutionary. No young 'radical' was surprised at their views; but mine seemed strange and fantastic. I don't think I made my views quite clear, or was quite clear about some of them myself; and public speaking at that time was something which I did only with a painful effort. It is difficult to co-ordinate the Marxian social-economic and the Freudian psychoanalytic points of view, which was what I was heroically attempting; and to listening minds, unaccustomed to any but the vague 'radical' pattern of thought on this subject, much of what I said must have sounded merely paradoxical. The young women seemed to understand it better than the young men; at least, they were pleased that I did not regard their desire to have babies, and to have the babies' father around the place, as counter-revolutionary.

It was not, then, that I insisted on talking about this subject; young people wanted to hear about it. And when I went away with B. Marie on our trip West to see our families, I was importuned to write a series of articles on 'Freedom and Marriage' for the magazine; and I did write it, on trains and in hotels—a gay and whimsical piece, but packed as full as I could pack it with sound history, economics and psychology.

Outside of this audience, in and out of the Village, there was a fringe of general public which had been aware of my existence in a way, though it was a way of which I was uninformed till now, and not especially pleased to learn about—for it seemed that they had chosen to regard me as an apostle of Freedom in Love. Somebody ought to be an apostle of Freedom in Love, no doubt, just to make this an interesting world. It was doubtless a compliment to suppose I was that, instead of merely a poor wretch who had fallen dazedly in and out of love in a commonplace neurotic fashion, until he had sense enough to go and get psychoanalyzed. Still, the fact was—ridiculous and uninteresting as it might seem— that I had believed in marriage all along, and had hoped always for permanency, like practically everybody else. But to these people, my defection from the glorious ideal of Freedom was felt as a loss, for which I was naturally blamed. Their world was the poorer for the absence of a picturesque though totally imaginary figure. Lots of people believed in Marriage and the Family—President Harding, and Bishop Manning, and John S. Sumner, among others; it was a disappointment to learn that I did, too. And nobody wished particularly to know in what respects, if any, my belief in Marriage and the Family differed from that of these other respectable personages. It would be assumed that my views would necessarily be stupid, reactionary, hypocritical and sanctimonious.

Under these circumstances, when other people were quite sure that they knew what my views were without troubling to inquire, I could only resolve to write a book, at my first opportunity, which would make my views clear, and—more important than that—let in a little light into a realm of thought in which there was perhaps more silliness and muddlement in the minds of intelligent people than any other. It would have to be a serious historical, social-economic and psychological study of childhood, adolescence, love, courtship, marriage and parenthood. A big book! And I must prepare to write it. I must study more history, more social-economics, more psychology. It was not until several years later that I gained the leisure for that work, and wrote 'Love in the Machine Age'.

2

Just before B. Marie and I started upon our Westward trip there came a letter from my mother which cast over my prospective visit to her the atmosphere of a fairy-tale. The circumstances were these: my mother was one of three sisters, of whom the other two, my 'Aunt Becky' and my 'Aunt Lyde', had remained unmarried. My mother, now seventy-five years old, had been taking care of her sister Becky during her last feeble years, and now Becky had died; the little house and tiny farm where she had lived, and where my mother and father hoped to spend their own declining years, was to have been given to my mother; but Aunt Becky had neglected to make a will, and the other sister, my Aunt Lyde, threatened to sell the farm at public auction unless her third—which she valued at fifteen hundred dollars—was paid her at once in cash. My Aunt Lyde was like that. Of course my mother and father had no money to buy off Aunt Lyde with. But—just as in a fairy-tale —her foolish youngest son had killed the Giant and stolen the singing harp and the hen that laid the golden eggs. My success with my first novel had come just in time for me to save the little farm for my mother and father. Her letter did not ask me to do this, it only stated the facts of the situation; but I could see my mother's happy confidence in me shining in her eyes as she wrote. The people of Pike County might doubt that she had a son like that: but they would see! And I was happy to be able to give my mother this fairy-tale ending to her life, a life in which so many hopes had been centered in a son who must have seemed, to all the world but herself, unworthy of such faith. To be sure, I hadn't fifteen hundred dollars in cash, and hadn't the least idea that I could get it from my publisher; but I wired my friend Arthur Ficke in Davenport, and the money was waiting for me when I reached Pike County. It was paid over, the farm was saved, and my mother was triumphantly happy.

That little house I had once visited as a child; I could remember the grassy front yard, the flower-bordered path, the moss-roses on each side of the door, the thick syringa bushes beside the house, the tall dark jungle of greenery through which I had gone back to see the bee-hives, and the peacock that screamed so raucously. Now the yard was hard-packed clay without a blade of grass, there was not a bush or flower on the place, it was naked and bare; the gray little weatherbeaten house seemed not to have been painted in the thirty years since I was there as a child; only the trees remained, thirty years taller than they had been before, giving some shady refuge from the blazing summer sun. When I shut my eyes, I could see it all as it had been—the memory seemed more real than this bare neglected place before my eyes; and perhaps it was still as it had been, to my mother's mind.

I had not seen my parents in eight years; and it seemed like fifty, for I had been remembering them as they had been in my earlier years, and now suddenly they were very old people, not far from death—strangely little and withered; but, for aged people, amazingly full of energy, spry and active. My mother fell in love with B. Marie, accepted her as a daughter, and was very happy about our having a baby. My father, exploding like a firework of belligerent wrath as he chased my mother's chickens off the back porch, would as instantly lapse into mildness—just like me, B. Marie said. My father told me again his stories of the Civil War. One of these stories was about an incident in a Southern state. "We'd just ridden into town as the enemy left, and we followed them out, chased 'em till dark"—it began in some such way, but I am not sure about the introduction. "Then we stopped at a big plantation, and went in to look for grub. The rebels who lived there had all gone. They hadn't expected us, for everything was just as they dropped it. There was a supper in the oven they hadn't stopped to eat. And after we'd e't, we went into the big front room, and there was a piano." One of the cavalrymen "set down and played on the piano. I guess he must have played for an hour, and we all set absolutely quiet listening to him, and some of the boys was crying. And then, when he finished, he got up and swung the piano stool over his head, and smashed the piano all to pieces." That story shocked and troubled me, as it always had done; my father told it quietly, without comment. Another of his stories was about the death of Colonel Mudd of the Second Illinois cavalry. The Colonel carried a toilet case, which sometimes got lost in battle; and when it was found by the enemy, the gallant Southern officers would always send it back, under a flag of truce, with their compliments. When Colonel Mudd was killed during a surprise attack, his body was found by the enemy; and, as they themselves were now retreating in turn, they put his body safely up on the roof of a pig-sty, so that it would not be eaten by the pigs that roamed about; and there it was found by Company K the next day when they reoccupied the place. I liked that story better.

B. Marie and I went over and visited my Aunt Lyde for a day or two. She too was old, but full of pride. She must have been a very beautiful, independent, wilful, stubborn girl; she was reputed a miser, and she respected me greatly for having the money to buy out her share of Becky's farm; but she said: "I suppose there's no use my willing you my land, you'd only give it away." The Pike County farmers believed that land was gold; they could not imagine that in a few years it might be as worthless as those abandoned New England farms we had seen on our walking trip, sweated over generation after generation, only to be sold for taxes. Nor could Aunt Lyde dream that her precious hoard of savings, investments, mortgages, the achievement of her lifetime, would before she died be only a hatful of dry autumn leaves.

We lingered at the little farm with my father and mother for a while; it would be the last time we would ever see each other. My father was happy in being a farmer again, and in being independent; his pension made him a man of means now. My mother was happy in running the house, cooking the meals; happy in her little boy's success; happy in having a beautiful, strong, good daughter in B. Marie; happy in the prospect of there being children to carry on the Dell name. Their lives, which had always seemed to me tragic examples of unsuccessful struggle, were to them successful and triumphant. At last we said good-bye, and went on our way. My mother died the next year, at the age of seventy-six; and my father the year afterward, at the age of eighty-four.

We had some other relatives in the county; Pike County people are taciturn, and it wasn't until after I went away that I realized the existence there of a certain situation. My father had quarreled with one of his brothers, and wouldn't speak to him; I had forgotten all about that, but afterward it occurred to me that one of my cousins, whom I had casually met, was a son of that brother of my father's; he had remarked quite casually that he had a little boy named Floyd. When I had time to take it in, it seemed to me that this was a gracious gesture of friendliness, a way of making up a family quarrel. I hadn't thought about the quarrel at all; now I was touched, and I wished I had realized the situation, and said or done something appropriate; I hoped they didn't think I was keeping up the old grudge. I felt that I had been clumsy in my ignorance. But, after a Greenwich Village world in which everything is talked out freely, Pike County with its few words, so like New England, is a strange land, and a stranger in it is an awkward ignoramus.

3

In the Middle-West and in California we visited B. Marie's relations. Then we went to San Francisco, that magical city of my youthful dreams, and I found it as enchanting a place as I had ever dreamed it was. San Francisco—the place which had nourished the youth and genius of Frank Norris and Jack London—was a shrine to me, the only literary shrine my heart had ever had. We went, B. Marie and I, with Lydia Gibson and her handsome Spanish husband, Pat Mestre, to spend a week or so at Lloyd and Ethel Osbourne's ranch, Vanumanatonga, which is Samoan for 'the Valley of Singing Birds'. Lloyd Osbourne read us a beautiful little piece he had just written about his step-father, Robert Louis Stevenson, which was to be the preface to the reprint of 'Moral Emblems', some playful verses which Stevenson had written in mockery of Victorian morality. At the ranch there was a large swimming pool, where I actually learned to swim with my legs, holding my arms straight in front of me, and with my arms, holding my legs straight back, but I never did get the arm and leg strokes co-ordinated. We swam without clothes, and lay on the edge of the pool in Samoan pareus or nothing at all, as in our Greenwich Village bathing parties; we talked, sunbathed, lunched, siesta'd, swam again, dined on steaks or chops thrown on the coals of an outdoor fireplace with pungent-smelling bay-leaves, and then, in the moonlight, played charades, each syllable being a one-act play, with fanciful costumes, much imagination and hilarious humor, the swimming pool always being a lovely part of each scene, from which shipwrecked mariners clinging to a plank were rescued by lovely Samoan maidens with flowers in their hair, or into which a Sultan was thrown by his rebellious wives—an idyllic time of play. But for me the memorable moment was the one when we had climbed the neighboring mountain and there, on the Norris place, I saw, in a little flat clearing among the trees, the big packing-box which had been Frank Norris's outdoor desk. Like a pilgrim approaching a sacred relic, I touched with my own hands the surface which the writing hand of Frank Norris had touched. There was no chair or box to sit on, but I stooped at the desk, as if, by putting my body in the place where Frank Norris's had been, some slight portion of the 'mana' of that wonderful writer might be magically communicated to me. I am afraid that it wasn't; but it was a spiritually invigorating experience.

4

On our way West, we had stopped in a number of cities to visit friends; I was everywhere treated with respect and friendliness by people who knew merely that I was an author whose name they had seen in the papers. It appeared that I was in some way a possession of the general public—not, as is natural enough, in some sense a possession of the small public that read my books, but quite astonishingly the possession of a larger public, which was being very friendly to its possessee. There was a queer and very disconcerting feeling about this; and the friendlier people were, the queerer it was; it seemed as though I had ceased to belong to myself—and I did not like it. My friends supposed it to be very jolly and thrilling and wonderful to be a person of public interest as a new author; and if I told them it was extremely painful, they only thought that a stupid pose. There was no use telling the truth about my emotions when the truth was greeted with a burst of hearty laughter, and the rejoinder, "Oh, come now, you know you like it!" The truth, however, was that the public friendliness to me during that trip threw me into a state of emotional wretchedness. When I am unhappy, I only grow more outwardly polite, so as not to inflict my miseries on others; but this misery was so extreme that I tried hard to explain it to myself. I had no just grudge against the people who were trying to be nice to me; but why were they behaving like that? Three years before, the respectable people of America had been trying to put me into prison. Now they seemed to think well of me. But I had not changed. When I was interviewed by newspaper reporters, I always told of my two trials under the Espionage Act for anti-war opinions; but no reference to such matters ever appeared in any paper. My past was evidently to be forgiven and forgotten; and I did not like that. I was exactly what I was, and not somebody's notion of what a 'successful author' is. Could I not even keep my identity?

Apparently not. I found that I was supposed to be rich. I had, indeed, thought myself rich, with enough money coming in to save my mother's home, fix up our house, and have a baby; but that wasn't what other people meant by 'rich'. A successful author's rewards, in popular estimation, run up to a hundred thousand dollars or more a year, what with serials in the women's magazines and the oodles of money he gets from Hollywood. By that standard I was an unsuccessful writer, and a mere masquerader. But any statement from me as to the facts was treated as mere modesty. People wish to believe that a writer whose books are talked about is fabulously successful in a financial way. There were, truly enough, some things to object to in the situation; anyone who is fond of the truth does not wish to seem other than what he is. But that was no reason for my being so miserable. When I was in San Francisco I re-read Jack London's 'Martin Eden', and was struck by his description of the frightful gloom into which his hero's literary success had plunged him—a gloom which ended in suicide in the story. Up to that point, the account must have been fairly autobiographical. Jack London, then, had been depressed by his literary success, so hard fought for; but he had explained it on rational grounds, as a bitter realization of the hollowness of achievement in bourgeois society. There was something to that, but not enough to commit suicide about—or even enough to afflict one with the kind of inward misery which I was concealing under a cheerfully polite exterior. I was inclined to think it was because I was used to meeting the bourgeois world on fighting terms, and hardly knew how to act when it wished to be friendly to me. I remembered that when I was on trial, with twenty years of my freedom at stake, I had been serene and happy—happier than I had ever been in my whole life before; and now, when I was supposed to be successful, I was more unhappy than I had ever been in my life. B. Marie was the only one whom I told about my feelings, and she comforted me as if I were a sick child. She thought, and perhaps rightly, that going back to my birthplace, and seeing my parents again, had put me into an especially sensitive state. At all events, no one but she knew how miserable I was. And these feelings of misery lifted and vanished when I got back home, where I was among people who knew me as I was.

CHAPTER XXXV

PATERNITY

1

B. Marie was driven to a New York hospital on New Year's Eve, and for three days I camped at the hospital, and slept not at all, awaiting the culmination of that strangely archaic and uncivilized process by which new life is brought into our human world. B. Marie endured all this with the dignity and serenity of a creator, but I was full of anxieties and terrors. On the third of January I saw my son, on his way from the delivery room, just born; his forehead was cut and bruised by the doctor's forceps, and he was very angry; he looked exactly like my father. A beautiful, proud, wilful boy—and I knew that we would be friends, and understand each other, and that he would forgive me my blunders as a father. Then I saw B. Marie— utterly exhausted, but with a triumphant look. I kissed her forehead, and she summoned up the last of her strength, and whispered: "Shall we name him Anthony?" That was my father's name. "Yes," I said, and she fell asleep.

There is, I read in books on anthropology, a quaint custom in various parts of the world, called in Brittany the 'couvade', according to which it is the father who goes to bed after a child is born; something like that happened to me, for by the time B. Marie could leave the hospital and go to the Hotel Brevoort, I had spent so many sleepless nights, keeping my friends up in talk till dawn, that I was sick and apparently in danger of pneumonia; B. Marie's nurse put me to bed, gave me an opiate, and I slept for two days. B. Marie was a little annoyed with me; this was her show, not mine; but a father seems bound to make himself ridiculous upon such occasions, out of sheer helpless anxiety; and we agreed that there might be some wisdom in what had seemed the offensive old custom of the father's going off and getting drunk with his friends at such a time.

During one of those sleepless nights of talk I had made the acquaintance of Joseph Freeman, a young poet, who was subsequently to go to Russia and write about it, and be one of the editors of the Liberator and the New Masses; one of the most interesting talkers in the world, and a friend of whom I was very fond from that first meeting. Upon another of those evenings I had been one of the Liberator crowd who met with H. G. Wells; he started in to tell us how wrong we were in our Marxian ideas; there were no 'classes' in America, he said, only 'phases' through which an individual might pass, up or down; his notion of 'classes' was apparently fixed castes; and he pronounced 'capitalist' in a funny British way, with the accent on the 'pit'. There is something disillusioning in seeing a writer, into whose magnificent fabrics of imagination so much of one's own youth has been built—that mind which has ranged the world of time and space, from the primeval slime to the glories of the Future—suddenly introduced in the guise of a small, plump, argumentative Britisher. My natural piety and respect for greatness would have demanded a demigod as the author of the works of H. G. Wells; I was confronted with the amazing paradox of artistic and intellectual creation—that, somehow, it is mere human beings, far less impressive to look at than any member of the Pennsylvania constabulary, who produce all that gives us imaginative freedom and joy. How the devil do they do it? H. G. Wells was just a man, with, apparently, less sense than any of us, about everything he talked about so confidently—and yet it was he who had written 'The Time Machine', 'The History of Mr. Polly', 'Tono-Bungay', 'When the Sleeper Wakes', 'The Country of the Blind'—an incredible number of purely magical things to which my mind would always respond with a thrill—and now the author of a short history of the world which was the beginning of a new era in public historical education—a man for many of whose ideas I had only amused scorn or vast contempt, a man whom I would have liked to be schoolmaster to, pounding some sense into his silly head—and yet one of the world's great prophets, for whose poetic vision I had the most profound reverence— a literary artist who in the field of the novel towered above all the writers of his time—and apparently a very jolly, companionable fellow, if one got to know him. Strange!

2

My novel, 'The Briary-Bush', extravagantly praised by some critics and more judiciously by others, was disappointing to many readers because—as they told me in their letters—'Felix' and 'Rose-Ann' were going to 'settle down' at the end of the book. It was 'Felix' as a symbol of unfettered freedom that they adored; it would be all right, I was told in one letter, for 'Felix' to end as a mere married man, provided that the author recognized this as a tragedy; but my failure to so recognize this, ruined the book!

For some years I had observed the manners and morals of Greenwich Village conquering bourgeois America; its color-schemes, its bobbed hair, were even now sweeping across the continent; its tastes in art, literature and music were beginning to be widely popular; what Greenwich Village had liked yesterday was evidently what the suburbs would like tomorrow. The American middle class had come to the end of its Puritan phase; it had its war-profits to spend, and it was turning to Bohemia to learn how to spend them. This was very interesting to a student of history. I had amused myself by making predictions in the fields of custom and dress: that army life would popularize the cheaper brands of cigarettes and sweep the more expensive Turkish and Egyptian brands into oblivion; that the corset would go; that short skirts would come, and so on. I thought I could predict post-war literary tastes just as correctly. It would be a taste for chaos, romantic disillusionment and despair; James Joyce and James Branch Cabell and Eugene O'Neill were portents. Sinclair Lewis was said to have cut out from his 'Main Street', on the advice of Cabell, the one sensible character in the book, through whom his own constructive views were to have been expressed. Middle-class morale had been shattered by the war; people knew they had been lied to, fooled, betrayed; they would not want to believe anything, or think hard about anything. It would be a period of cynicism—already it was, under President Harding, a period of tolerance for the grossest corruption. The era was unfavorable for me as a novelist, I felt; this accidental popularity of mine would not endure. Nevertheless, if I were to write novels, I needed time in which to write them. So I quit my editorial job. If I could not make a living writing novels, I could go back and get a job as editor, for I was a good editor. In the meantime I would write the kind of novels I wanted to write, and the public could take them or leave them; that it would go on taking them in such numbers seemed much too good to be true.

Earlier in the year my friend George Cook had come to a crisis in his life; he was spiritually centered in the plays of Eugene O'Neill, and now the young playwright had decided to deal directly with Broadway, refusing to allow the Provincetown Players to put on his plays before they went uptown. This was an entirely reasonable decision on his part, but it broke George Cook's heart. In February, the Provincetown Theatre suspended operations, and a month later, George Cook and Susan Glaspell sailed for Greece. I saw George shortly before he left—the day before, I think it was. I was having lunch with a friend in the basement of the Brevoort, when George came in. He was drunk; he said he had been drunk for eight days. He talked about Greece, and Greek dances, with an intense earnestness; and, picking up my plate, he did some kind of solemn Phyrric dance with it all over the floor of the restaurant; and I felt embarrassed, and ashamed of him. Then he said to me: "Floyd, let's gather the old Davenport crowd together, and go back there, and make it a new Athens!" And I was touched, and ashamed of myself for being ashamed of him. It was, at least, a beautiful dream that was driving him into exile. That was the last time I ever saw him.

3

So I began work on my third novel, 'Janet March'—an attempt to present a characteristic modern girl truly against her social-historical background.

This would be my first book of imaginative fiction, as distinguished from novels which were the imaginative interpretation of memories; it would take me two years to write it; it would be misunderstood and attacked by my friends, to say nothing of the sharp-nosed Mr. Sumner; but then, I had never supposed that the path of novel-writing was strewn with rose-petals. I felt that I understood my literary rôle; it would never be a popular one, except through some accident, but it was a career into which I could put all the energy, knowledge and skill that I had—I would write in fictional terms the true story of the break-up of the old patriarchal family institution in contemporary America.

In the meantime I was enjoying as a private person the deep satisfactions of good fortune in marriage and in fatherhood.

A few years later Frank Adams ('F. P. A.') took me into the nursery and showed me his firstborn infant son, and said solemnly: "Mr. Dell, you will never know what it is like to be a father for the first time at the age of forty-five." True enough; but I knew what it was like to be a father for the first time in my thirty-fifth year.

Postscript

I sit at my desk, wondering if I have told the story I wished to tell—the story of a child that grew up. To look back upon one's own life is to contemplate a mysterious and fascinating dramatic pageant. One might ponder it forever, and not know how it came about that the boy one was ever became the man one is. To some people, growing up seems a spiritual tragedy—we lose, they say, so much that is fine and beautiful. I have lost much, but I dare to believe that I have gained something more beautiful than all I have lost. I can face the boy of eighteen that I once was, without shame. I have gained the courage to love.

NOTES

1

Page 379. 'The section of Burton's book on Love-Melancholy fascinated me, as it had fascinated so many others, my favorite poet Keats among them. In 1927, in collaborating with my friend Paul Jordan-Smith upon an all-English edition of Burton's 'Anatomy of Melancholy', I made a Keats discovery.

For a century it has been suspected by critics that Keats may have got the inspiration for his 'Ode on Melancholy' from Burton's 'Anatomy of Melancholy', from which he did get the story of 'Lamia'. The 'Ode on Melancholy', however, had never been traced directly to Burton's pages. And I found its central idea there in plain prose in Burton. Amy Lowell—in denying dogmatically the possibility that Keats could have got the idea for his great ode from Burton—stated quite truly that its core was in these lines:

> 'Ay, in the very temple of Delight
> Veil'd Melancholy has her sovran shrine'.

And it is this that is to be found in Burton's prose. This discovery had never been made, apparently because Burton called the Goddess of Melancholy by the name of 'Angerona'. It is in another part of his voluminous work that he defines *Angerona Dea* as *"this our goddess of Melancholy"*. And *"Angerona had her holy day, to whom in the Temple of Volupia, or Goddess of Pleasure, their Augurs and Bishops did yearly sacrifice."** Ay, in the very temple of Delight,* echoed Keats, *Veil'd Melancholy has her sovran shrine!*

To him it was a profoundly fascinating psychological truth, and not a mere quaint historical fact, as it was to Burton. But the passage in Burton awoke the mind of Keats to that truth, and brought forth the great Ode.

2

Page 420. 'I found a curious place to live—a whole floor in a little wooden house with a tin roof, at 11 Christopher Street.'

In 1925, at Antibes, where I was severely ill with gastritis and was very home-sick, I heard from some fellow-American that the little house at 11 Christopher Street had been torn down. The red-painted door of my upstairs apartment,

---

*These two passages are in partition 2, section 1, member 3, first paragraph, and partition 1, section 2, member 3, subsection 5, first paragraph, of Burton's 'Anatomy of Melancholy'. In both passages, Burton quotes or paraphrases Macrobius.

I was told, had been piously rescued by Frank Shay, and was being kept in his book-shop across the street; he was using it as an autograph-'album', on which all the authors who came into his place were asked to write their names. . . . So 11 Christopher Street was gone! And being gone, it lived again more vividly in my memory. That day I wrote a poem about it. Since poems write themselves, it was not by any conscious intention that I put into 11 Christopher Street, instead of any actual remembered love-affair, one which summed up all the love affairs of my youth. Nor was I aware as I wrote it that I was altering the facts when I told of moving into it amid the snows of winter, instead of in the sweltering heat of July. It was not, indeed, in any literal sense a true story that I told in the poem; its truth was a poetic truth. It was entitled

THE BALLAD OF CHRISTOPHER STREET

"Is it still there, I wonder, down in Christopher Street,
That little rickety house of ours where life was young and sweet?"
No, my dear, they've torn it down, a year and a day ago;
There's nothing there but an empty lot where the purple burdocks grow.
The wreckers came, and spat on their hands, and gave it a final thrust,
And the roof fell into the cellar, and the walls went up in dust!
The boys have carried away the boards to kindle their mothers' fires,
And over the moldering fragments creep burdocks and briers.
So it will stay for a year and a day; and then some morning soon,
Builders will come, with riveters, and rivet loud till noon,
And call it a day, and go away, leaving against the sky
A great brand-new apartment-building fourteen stories high.
And women with dogs, and men with cars, will quarrel and sleep and eat,
After the fashion of their kind, at Eleven Christopher Street.

In that big apartment-building up against the sky
There'll be lovers, lovers, lovers—never you and I!
It will not matter to them in the least, if out of the dust and grime
Impossible beauty flamed and flowered, once upon a time!
If a boy and a girl for a year and a day laughed bravely at despair,
No one will know in Christopher Street, and certainly none will care.
But you and I, shall we ever forget, till our hearts forget to beat,
The year and a day of life in flower that we had in Christopher Street?

Wakened by the jingling-harnessed, trampling teams from next-door's stable,
Lingering late in happy laughter over the bright breakfast table,
Sharing every secret fancy, finding courage and delight
In each other's jests and kisses, sitting up all hours of night
In deep talk before the fireplace—happy that we could remember
One more lovely story always to outlast the final ember!
Kisses in the darkness, laughter in the night,

And a white moon rising over the roofs to look on our delight!
All that was ever good in life, all that was ever sweet,
Kept house with us for a year and a day in Eleven Christopher Street.
A painted cupboard on the wall, colored cups and dishes—
Tulip-garden crockery to match our happiest wishes!—
A Japanese print, and a candlestick, with candles burning bright,
Curtain-folds of sunny gold at windows left and right,
A couch with tattered tapestry, a cigarette-scarred table,
A view from either window of an alley and a stable,
Ash-trays scattered round about in all the likely nooks,
And everywhere, on shelf and chair—books, books, books!

I remember the way we found it, when our love was fire-new,
And we were troubled, and bold, and shy, wondering what to do;
Night after night we had walked the streets, through blasts of wind and snow,
Wanting a place to call our own, a roof to sleep below—
And some folks thought it funny, and laughed aloud to spy
Huddling close in doorways, two lovers, you and I!
Pooling our desperate fortunes, all we could scrape together,
We sought to find our love four walls against the bitter weather;
We only hoped for an eyrie high over the street's abyss,
A room for two, where we'd have the right to laugh and talk and kiss;
Ah! happy the chance that led us, at last, with tired feet,
Across the snowy door-sill of Eleven Christopher Street.
We stood by the little fireplace, and in each other's eyes
We watched the bright tears welling up in wonder and surprise.
Here we knew was a home for us, and not for us too narrow—
We furnished the place from a junk-shop quick and moved in a big wheel-
    barrow!
And I tacked up my Japanese print, while you, with your candles lit,
Sat on the tattered-tapestried couch and laughed for the joy of it.
Soon you knelt to tend the fire, and I glimpsed through a half-shut door
Your dresses flung across a chair, your slippers on the floor.
And so may all dear lovers who are starved for love's delight
Find rest and peace, and food and fire, and a kind bed at night!

In that big apartment-building underneath the moon,
Something of our love may linger, like a ghostly tune;
Troubled wives will wake at midnight, hearing from the rafter
Thin and faint, the silver echoes of delicious laughter.
At these glimmering hints and shadowings of our lost delight
They will frown and they will wonder, in the haunted night;
Tossing on their pillows while the midnight minutes creep,
They will think about love, a little—and then go back to sleep.
And over their lawful slumbers, in silvery disdain,
Your airy mocking laughter will chime through the night again.

It stands no more in the sight of men, in the traffic's roar and beat,
That little rickety house of ours where life was young and sweet;
There's nothing left but an empty lot, and a stray board, and a brick,
And—you've the Japanese print, my dear, and I've the candlestick;
The world is wide, with many a path that's pleasant to the feet,
But none that will ever turn back again to Eleven Christopher Street;
Time has triumphed and earth's deep dust has claimed its ancient right
To be enriched with our memories of laughter and delight;
There's nothing to do, there's nothing to say—except that life was sweet
To a boy and a girl for a year and a day in Eleven Christopher Street.

3

Page 474. 'George Cook and Susan Glaspell sailed for Greece.'

My friend George Cram Cook died in Greece in 1926. I had seen pictures of him in his shepherd's costume, and with a great black and grey-streaked beard; I had heard that he got drunk with the shepherds, and was adored by them. Susan Glaspell has told the story of those days with great sympathy in 'The Road to the Temple'. His love of Greece meant something to the Greeks. A stone from the ruins of Delphi was given for his gravestone. I was glad that he had found a people to honor him.

But it seemed strange to me, his turning away from the present—and from the future—to the past. My sympathies could not follow him there. And I knew that the adoration of drunken shepherds was not what he wanted back in Davenport. He had wanted to be one of the creators of the world's future. And he had failed. It was a poetic way of dealing with failure, but it was not a magnificent way, in my eyes.

To fail in one's part in so heroic an undertaking as the remaking of this sorry scheme of things entire, seems to me a wholly honorable fate; it must inevitably be the fate of most of us who dream so grandly. And yet, when the world, however slowly and painfully, yet actually, *is* being remade before our eyes, a personal failure to contribute significantly to that great work should not matter so much.

It does not matter now to George.

> 'He has outsoared the shadow of our night,
> Envy and calumny and hate and pain.'

His death restored to my mind the gentle and prophetic dreamer that I knew back in Davenport. He saw, then, in the Russian Revolution of 1905 that failed, a Revolution that was to succeed. Susan Glaspell has said in her book that she has sometimes thought I would write a book about George. He was too close to me for me to be just to him. I loved him, and I would have had his life and death other than they were. I would have had him die for Russia and the future, rather than for Greece and the past. And if I wrote a book about George, that is what I should wish him to do.

71
72
74
75
76
77
79
83
85
89